PRINCIPLES
OF
ARTIFICIAL INTELLIGENCE

Principles
of
Artificial Intelligence

NILS J. NILSSON
SRI International

tioga
publishing
company
palo alto,
california

Library of Congress Cataloging in Publication Data
Nilsson, Nils J   1933-

   Principles of artificial intelligence.
   Bibliography: p.
   Includes indexes.
   1. Artificial intelligence.   I. Title.
   Q335.N515   001.53'5   79-67584
   ISBN 0-935382-01-1

Copyright © 1980 by Tioga Publishing Co.
P.O. Box 98, Palo Alto, CA 94302

   The figures listed below are from "Problem-Solving Methods in Artificial Intelligence" by Nils J. Nilsson, copyright © 1971 McGraw-Hill
Book Company. Used with permission of McGraw-Hill Book Company.
Figures 1.4, 1.5, 1.6, 1.13, 2.6, 2.7, 2.8, 2.9, 2.12, 2.13, 3.8, 3.9, 3.10,
3.11, 3.12, 5.8, 5.9, 5.10, 5.11, 5.12, 5.13, and 5.14.

ISBN 0-935382-01-1

   ABCDEFG-DO-432109

for Kristen and Lars

TABLE OF CONTENTS

PREFACE

Previous treatments of Artificial Intelligence (AI) divide the subject into its major areas of application, namely, natural language processing, automatic programming, robotics, machine vision, automatic theorem proving, intelligent data retrieval systems, etc. The major difficulty with this approach is that these application areas are now so extensive, that each could, at best, be only superficially treated in a book of this length. Instead, I have attempted here to describe fundamental AI ideas that underly many of these applications. My organization of these ideas is not, then, based on the subject matter of their application, but is, instead, based on general computational concepts involving the kinds of data structures used, the types of operations performed on these data structures, and the properties of control strategies used by AI systems. I stress, in particular, the important roles played in AI by generalized production systems and the predicate calculus.

The notes on which the book is based evolved in courses and seminars at Stanford University and at the University of Massachusetts at Amherst. Although certain topics treated in my previous book, *Problem-solving Methods in Artificial Intelligence,* are covered here as well, this book contains many additional topics such as rule-based systems, robot problem-solving systems, and structured-object representations.

One of the goals of this book is to fill a gap between theory and practice. AI theoreticians have little difficulty in communicating with each other; this book is not intended to contribute to that communication. Neither is the book a handbook of current AI programming technology; other sources are available for that purpose. As it stands, the book could be supplemented either by more theoretical treatments of certain subjects, for AI theory courses, or by project and laboratory sessions, for more practically oriented courses.

The book is designed as a text for a senior or first-year graduate course in AI. It is assumed that the reader has a good background in the fundamentals of computer science; knowledge of a list-processing language, such as LISP, would be helpful. A course organized around this book could comfortably occupy a full semester. If separate practical or theoretical material is added, the time required might be an entire year. A one-quarter course would be somewhat hurried unless some material (perhaps parts of chapter 6 and chapter 8) is omitted.

The exercises at the end of each chapter are designed to be thought-provoking. Some expand on subjects briefly mentioned in the text. Instructors may find it useful to use selected exercises as a basis for class discussion. Pertinent references are briefly discussed at the end of every chapter. These citations should provide the interested student with adequate entry points to much of the most important literature in the field.

I look forward someday to revising this book—to correct its inevitable errors, and to add new results and points of view. Toward that end, I solicit correspondence from readers.

Nils J. Nilsson

ACKNOWLEDGEMENTS

Several organizations supported and encouraged the research, teaching, and discussions that led to this book. The Information Systems Program, Marvin Denicoff, Director, of the Office of Naval Research, provided research support under contract no. N00014-77-C-0222 with SRI International. During the academic year 1976-77, I was a part-time visiting professor in the Computer Science Department at Stanford University. From September 1977 to January 1978, I spent the Winter Semester at the Computer and Information Sciences Department of the University of Massachusetts at Amherst. The students and faculty of these departments were immensely helpful in the development of this book.

I want to give special thanks to my home organization, SRI International, for the use of its facilities and for its liberal attitude toward book-writing. I also want to thank all my friends and colleagues in the Artificial Intelligence Center at SRI. One could not find a more dynamic, intellectually stimulating, and constructively critical setting in which to work and write.

Though this book carries the name of a single author, it has been influenced by several people. It is a pleasure to thank here everyone who helped guide me toward a better presentation. Some of those who provided particularly detailed and extensive suggestions are: Doug Appelt, Michael Arbib, Wolfgang Bibel, Woody Bledsoe, John Brown, Lew Creary, Randy Davis, Jon Doyle, Ed Feigenbaum, Richard Fikes, Northrup Fowler, Peter Friedland, Anne Gardner, David Gelperin, Peter Hart, Pat Hayes, Gary Hendrix, Doug Lenat, Vic Lesser, John Lowrance, Jack Minker, Tom Mitchell, Bob Moore, Allen Newell, Earl Sacerdoti, Len Schubert, Herb Simon, Reid Smith, Elliot Soloway, Mark Stefik, Mabry Tyson, and Richard Waldinger.

I also want to thank Robin Roy, Judy Fetler, and Georgia Navarro, for patient and accurate typing; Sally Seitz for heroic insertion of typesetting instructions into the manuscript; and Helen Tognetti for creative copy-editing.

Most importantly, my efforts would not have been equal to this task had they not been generously supported, encouraged, and understood by my wife, Karen.

CREDITS

The manuscript for this book was prepared on a Digital Equipment Corporation KL-10 computer at SRI International. The computer manuscript file was processed for automatic photo-typesetting by W. A. Barrett's TYPET system on a Hewlett-Packard 3000 computer. The main typeface is Times Roman.

Book design: Ian Bastelier
Cover design: Andrea Hendrick
Illustrations: Marla Masterson
Typesetting: Typothetae, Palo Alto, CA
Page makeup: Vera Allen Composition, Castro Valley, CA
Printing and binding: R. R. Donnelley and Sons Company

PROLOGUE

Many human mental activities such as writing computer programs, doing mathematics, engaging in commonsense reasoning, understanding language, and even driving an automobile are said to demand "intelligence." Over the past few decades, several computer systems have been built that can perform tasks such as these. Specifically, there are computer systems that can diagnose diseases, plan the synthesis of complex organic chemical compounds, solve differential equations in symbolic form, analyze electronic circuits, understand limited amounts of human speech and natural language text, or write small computer programs to meet formal specifications. We might say that such systems possess some degree of *artificial intelligence.*

Most of the work on building these kinds of systems has taken place in the field called *Artificial Intelligence (AI)*. This work has had largely an empirical and engineering orientation. Drawing from a loosely structured but growing body of computational techniques, AI systems are developed, undergo experimentation, and are improved. This process has produced and refined several general AI principles of wide applicability.

This book is about some of the more important, core AI ideas. We concentrate on those that find application in several different problem areas. In order to emphasize their generality, we explain these principles abstractly rather than discuss them in the context of specific applications, such as automatic programming or natural language processing. We illustrate their use with several small examples but omit detailed case studies of large-scale applications. (To treat these applications in detail would each certainly require a separate book.) An abstract understanding of the basic ideas should facilitate understanding specific AI systems (including strengths and weaknesses) and should also prove a sound basis for designing new systems.

1

AI has also embraced the larger scientific goal of constructing an information-processing theory of intelligence. If such a *science of intelligence* could be developed, it could guide the design of intelligent machines as well as explicate intelligent behavior as it occurs in humans and other animals. Since the development of such a general theory is still very much a goal, rather than an accomplishment of AI, we limit our attention here to those principles that are relevant to the engineering goal of building intelligent machines. Even with this more limited outlook, our discussion of AI ideas might well be of interest to cognitive psychologists and others attempting to understand natural intelligence.

As we have already mentioned, AI methods and techniques have been applied in several different problem areas. To help motivate our subsequent discussions, we next describe some of these applications.

0.1. SOME APPLICATIONS OF ARTIFICIAL INTELLIGENCE

0.1.1. NATURAL LANGUAGE PROCESSING

When humans communicate with each other using language, they employ, almost effortlessly, extremely complex and still little understood processes. It has been very difficult to develop computer systems capable of generating and "understanding" even fragments of a natural language, such as English. One source of the difficulty is that language has evolved as a communication medium between *intelligent* beings. Its primary use is for transmitting a bit of "mental structure" from one brain to another under circumstances in which each brain possesses large, highly similar, surrounding mental structures that serve as a common context. Furthermore, part of these similar, contextual mental structures allows each participant to know that the other also possesses this common structure and that the other can and will perform certain processes using it during communication "acts." The evolution of language use has apparently exploited the opportunity for participants to use their considerable computational resources and shared knowledge to generate and understand highly condensed and streamlined messages: A word to the wise from the wise is sufficient. Thus generating and understanding language is an encoding and decoding problem of fantastic complexity.

2

A computer system capable of understanding a message in natural language would seem, then, to require (no less than would a human) both the contextual knowledge and the processes for making the inferences (from this contextual knowledge and from the message) assumed by the message generator. Some progress has been made toward computer systems of this sort, for understanding spoken and written fragments of language. Fundamental to the development of such systems are certain AI ideas about structures for representing contextual knowledge and certain techniques for making inferences from that knowledge. Although we do not treat the language-processing problem as such in this book, we do describe some important methods for knowledge representation and processing that do find application in language-processing systems.

0.1.2. INTELLIGENT RETRIEVAL FROM DATABASES

Database systems are computer systems that store a large body of facts about some subject in such a way that they can be used to answer users' questions about that subject. To take a specific example, suppose the facts are the personnel records of a large corporation. Example items in such a database might be representations for such facts as "Joe Smith works in the Purchasing Department," "Joe Smith was hired on October 8, 1976," "The Purchasing Department has 17 employees," "John Jones is the manager of the Purchasing Department," etc.

The design of database systems is an active subspecialty of computer science, and many techniques have been developed to enable the efficient representation, storage, and retrieval of large numbers of facts. From our point of view, the subject becomes interesting when we want to retrieve answers that require deductive reasoning with the facts in the database.

There are several problems that confront the designer of such an *intelligent* information retrieval system. First, there is the immense problem of building a system that can understand queries stated in a natural language like English. Second, even if the language-understanding problem is dodged by specifying some formal, machine-understandable query language, the problem remains of how to deduce answers from stored facts. Third, understanding the query and deducing an answer may require knowledge beyond that explicitly represented in the subject domain database. Common knowledge (typically omitted in the subject domain database) is often required. For example, from the personnel facts mentioned above, an intelligent system ought to be able

3

to deduce the answer "John Jones" to the query "Who is Joe Smith's boss?" Such a system would have to know somehow that the manager of a department is the *boss* of the people who work in that department. How common knowledge should be represented and used is one of the system design problems that invites the methods of Artificial Intelligence.

0.1.3. EXPERT CONSULTING SYSTEMS

AI methods have also been employed in the development of automatic consulting systems. These systems provide human users with expert conclusions about specialized subject areas. Automatic consulting systems have been built that can diagnose diseases, evaluate potential ore deposits, suggest structures for complex organic chemicals, and even provide advice about how to use other computer systems.

A key problem in the development of expert consulting systems is how to represent and use the knowledge that human experts in these subjects obviously possess and use. This problem is made more difficult by the fact that the expert knowledge in many important fields is often imprecise, uncertain, or anecdotal (though human experts use such knowledge to arrive at useful conclusions).

Many expert consulting systems employ the AI technique of *rule-based deduction*. In such systems, expert knowledge is represented as a large set of simple rules, and these rules are used to guide the dialogue between the system and the user and to deduce conclusions. Rule-based deduction is one of the major topics of this book.

0.1.4. THEOREM PROVING

Finding a proof (or disproof) for a conjectured theorem in mathematics can certainly be regarded as an intellectual task. Not only does it require the ability to make deductions from hypotheses but demands intuitive skills such as guessing about which lemmas should be proved first in order to help prove the main theorem. A skilled mathematician uses what he might call judgment (based on a large amount of specialized knowledge) to guess accurately about which previously proven theorems in a subject area will be useful in the present proof and to break his main

4

problem down into subproblems to work on independently. Several automatic theorem proving programs have been developed that possess some of these same skills to a limited degree.

The study of theorem proving has been significant in the development of AI methods. The formalization of the deductive process using the language of predicate logic, for example, helps us to understand more clearly some of the components of reasoning. Many informal tasks, including medical diagnosis and information retrieval, can be formalized as theorem-proving problems. For these reasons, theorem proving is an extremely important topic in the study of AI methods.

0.1.5. ROBOTICS

The problem of controlling the physical actions of a mobile robot might not seem to require much intelligence. Even small children are able to navigate successfully through their environment and to manipulate items, such as light switches, toy blocks, eating utensils, etc. However these same tasks, performed almost unconsciously by humans, performed by a machine require many of the same abilities used in solving more intellectually demanding problems.

Research on robots or robotics has helped to develop many AI ideas. It has led to several techniques for modeling *states of the world* and for describing the process of change from one world state to another. It has led to a better understanding of how to generate *plans* for action sequences and how to monitor the execution of these plans. Complex robot control problems have forced us to develop methods for planning at high levels of abstraction, ignoring details, and then planning at lower and lower levels, where details become important. We have frequent occasion in this book to use examples of robot problem solving to illustrate important ideas.

0.1.6. AUTOMATIC PROGRAMMING

The task of writing a computer program is related both to theorem proving and to robotics. Much of the basic research in automatic programming, theorem proving, and robot problem solving overlaps. In a sense, existing compilers already do "automatic programming." They take in a complete source code specification of what a program is to accomplish, and they write an object code program to do it. What we mean here by automatic programming might be described as a "super-compiler," or a program that could take in a very high-level description of what the program is to accomplish and produce a program. The high-level description might be a precise statement in a formal language, such as the predicate calculus, or it might be a loose description, say, in English, that would require further dialogue between the system and the user in order to resolve ambiguities.

The task of automatically writing a program to achieve a stated result is closely related to the task of proving that a given program achieves a stated result. The latter is called *program verification*. Many automatic programming systems produce a verification of the output program as an added benefit.

One of the important contributions of research in automatic programming has been the notion of *debugging* as a problem-solving strategy. It has been found that it is often much more efficient to produce an inexpensive, errorful solution to a programming or robot control problem and then modify it (to make it work correctly), than to insist on a first solution completely free of defects.

0.1.7. COMBINATORIAL AND SCHEDULING PROBLEMS

An interesting class of problems is concerned with specifying optimal schedules or combinations. Many of these problems can be attacked by the methods discussed in this book. A classical example is the *traveling salesman's problem*, where the problem is to find a minimum distance tour, starting at one of several cities, visiting each city precisely once, and returning to the starting city. The problem generalizes to one of finding a minimum cost path over the edges of a graph containing n nodes such that the path visits each of the n nodes precisely once.

Many puzzles have this same general character. Another example is the *8-queens problem*, where the problem is to place eight queens on a standard chessboard in such a way that no queen can capture any of the others; that is, there can be no more than one queen in any row, column or diagonal. In most problems of this type, the domain of possible combinations or sequences from which to choose an answer is very large. Routine attempts at solving these types of problems soon generate a *combinatorial explosion* of possibilities that exhaust even the capacities of large computers.

Several of these problems (including the traveling salesman problem) are members of a class that computational theorists call *NP-complete*. Computational theorists rank the difficulty of various problems on how the worst case for the time taken (or number of *steps* taken) using the theoretically best method grows with some measure of the problem size. (For example, the number of cities would be a measure of the size of a traveling salesman problem.) Thus, problem difficulty may grow linearly, polynomially, or exponentially, for example, with problem size.

The time taken by the best methods currently known for solving NP-complete problems grows exponentially with problem size. It is not yet known whether faster methods (involving only polynomial time, say) exist, but it has been proven that if a faster method exists for one of the NP-complete problems, then this method can be converted to similarly faster methods for all the rest of the NP-complete problems. In the meantime, we must make do with exponential-time methods.

AI researchers have worked on methods for solving several types of combinatorial problems. Their efforts have been directed at making the time-versus-problem-size curve grow as slowly as possible, even when it must grow exponentially. Several methods have been developed for delaying and moderating the inevitable combinatorial explosion. Again, knowledge about the problem domain is the key to more efficient solution methods. Many of the methods developed to deal with combinatorial problems are also useful on other, less combinatorially severe problems.

0.1.8. PERCEPTION PROBLEMS

Attempts have been made to fit computer systems with television inputs to enable them to "see" their surroundings or to fit them with microphone inputs to enable them to "hear" speaking voices. From these experiments, it has been learned that useful processing of complex input data requires "understanding" and that understanding requires a large base of knowledge about the things being perceived.

The process of perception studied in Artificial Intelligence usually involves a set of operations. A visual scene, say, is encoded by sensors and represented as a matrix of intensity values. These are processed by detectors that search for primitive picture components such as line segments, simple curves, corners, etc. These, in turn, are processed to infer information about the three-dimensional character of the scene in terms of its surfaces and shapes. The ultimate goal is to represent the scene by some appropriate model. This model might consist of a high-level description such as "A hill with a tree on top with cattle grazing."

The point of the whole perception process is to produce a condensed representation to substitute for the unmanageably immense, raw input data. Obviously, the nature and quality of the final representation depend on the goals of the perceiving system. If colors are important, they must be noticed; if spatial relationships and measurements are important, they must be judged accurately. Different systems have different goals, but all must reduce the tremendous amount of sensory data at the input to a manageable and meaningful description.

The main difficulty in perceiving a scene is the enormous number of possible candidate descriptions in which the system might be interested. If it were not for this fact, one could conceivably build a number of detectors to decide the *category* of a scene. The scene's category could then serve as its description. For example, perhaps a detector could be built that could test a scene to see if it belonged to the category "A hill with a tree on top with cattle grazing." But why should this detector be selected instead of the countless others that might have been used?

The strategy of making hypotheses about various levels of description and then testing these hypotheses seems to offer an approach to this problem. Systems have been constructed that process suitable representations of a scene to develop hypotheses about the components of a description. These hypotheses are then tested by detectors that are specialized to the component descriptions. The outcomes of these tests, in turn, are used to develop better hypotheses, etc.

This *hypothesize-and-test* paradigm is applied at many levels of the perception process. Several aligned segments suggest a straight line; a line detector can be employed to test it. Adjacent rectangles suggest the faces of a solid prismatic object; an object detector can be employed to test it.

The process of hypothesis formation requires a large amount of knowledge about the expected scenes. Some AI researchers have suggested that this knowledge be organized in special structures called *frames* or *schemas*. For example, when a robot enters a room through a doorway, it activates a *room schema*, which loads into working memory a number of expectations about what might be seen next. Suppose the robot perceives a rectangular form. This form, in the context of a room schema, might suggest a window. The *window schema* might contain the knowledge that windows typically do not touch the floor. A special detector, applied to the scene, confirms this expectation, thus raising confidence in the window hypothesis. We discuss some of the fundamental ideas underlying frame-structured representations and inference processes later in the book.

0.2. OVERVIEW

The book is divided into nine chapters and a prospectus. In chapter 1, we introduce a generalized production system and emphasize its importance as a basic building block of AI systems. Several distinctions among production systems and their control strategies are introduced. These distinctions are used throughout the book to help classify different AI systems.

The major emphasis in chapters 2 and 3 is on the search strategies that are useful in the control of AI systems. Chapter 2 concerns itself with heuristic methods for searching the graphs that are implicitly defined by many AI systems. Chapter 3 generalizes these search techniques to extended versions of these graphs, called AND/OR graphs, and to the graphs that arise in analyzing certain games.

In chapter 4, we introduce the predicate calculus and describe the important role that it plays in AI systems. Various rules of inference, including *resolution*, are described. Systems for proving theorems using resolution are discussed in chapter 5. We indicate how several different kinds of problems can be posed as theorem-proving problems.

Chapter 6 examines some of the inadequacies of simple resolution systems and describes some alternatives, called rule-based deduction systems, that are more suitable for many AI applications. To illustrate how these deduction systems might be used, several small examples, ranging from information retrieval to automatic programming, are presented.

In chapters 7 and 8, we present methods for synthesizing sequences of actions that achieve prescribed goals. These methods are illustrated by considering simple problems in robot planning and automatic programming. Chapter 7 introduces some of the more basic ideas, and chapter 8 elaborates on the subjects of complex goal interactions and hierarchical planning.

Chapter 9 discusses some representational formalisms in which the structure of the representation itself is used to aid retrieval processes and to make certain common deductions more immediate. Two examples are semantic networks and the so-called frame-based representations. Our point of view toward such representations is that they can best be understood as a form of predicate calculus.

Last, in the prospectus, we review some outstanding AI problems that are not yet sufficiently well understood to be included in the main part of a textbook. It is hoped that a discussion of these problems will provide perspective about the current status of the field and useful directions for future research.

0.3. BIBLIOGRAPHICAL AND HISTORICAL REMARKS

In this section, and in similar sections at the end of each chapter, we discuss very briefly some of the relevant literature. The material cited is listed alphabetically by first author in the bibliography at the end of the book. Many of these citations will be useful to readers who wish to probe more deeply into either theoretical or applications topics. For completeness, we have occasionally referenced unpublished memoranda and reports. Authors (or their home institutions) will sometimes provide copies of such material upon request.

Several books have been written about AI and its applications. The book by Slagle (1971) describes many early AI systems. Nilsson's (1971) book on problem solving in AI concentrates on search methods and applications of resolution theorem proving. An introductory book by Jackson (1974) treats these problem-solving ideas and also describes applications to natural language processing and image analysis. The book by Hunt (1975) treats pattern recognition, as well as other AI topics.

Introductory articles about AI topics appear in a book edited by Barr and Feigenbaum (1980). Nilsson's (1974) survey describes the field in the early 1970s and contains many references. Michie's (1974) book contains several of his articles on AI.

Raphael's (1975) book and Winston's (1977) book are easy-to-read and elementary treatments of AI ideas. The latter contains an excellent introduction to AI programming methods. A book edited by Bundy (1978) contains material used in an introductory AI course given at the University of Edinburgh. A general discussion of AI and its connection with human intelligence is contained in Boden (1977). McCorduck (1979) has written an interesting book about the history of artificial intelligence. Marr's (1977) essay and Simon's (1969) book discuss AI research as a scientific endeavor. Cohen (1979) discusses the relationships between artistic imagery and visual cognition.

The most authoritative and complete account of mechanisms of human problem solving from an AI perspective is the book by Newell and Simon (1972). The book edited by Norman and Rumelhart (1975) contains articles describing computer models of human memory, and a psychology text by Lindsay and Norman (1972) is written from an information-processing viewpoint. A multidisciplinary journal, *Cognitive Science*, contains articles on information-processing aspects of human cognition, perception, and language.

0.3.1. NATURAL LANGUAGE PROCESSING

Grosz (1979) presents a good survey of current techniques and problems in natural language processing. A collection of important papers on this topic is contained in a book edited by Rustin (1973). One of the first successful AI systems for understanding limited fragments of natural language is described in a book by Winograd (1972).

The book by Newell et al. (1973) describes the five-year goals of a research project to develop a speech understanding system; the major results of this research are described in papers by Medress et al. (1977), and Klatt (1977); reports by Reddy et al. (1977), Woods, et al (1976), and Bernstein (1976); and a book edited by Walker (1978).

A forthcoming book by Winograd (1980a) will present the foundations of computational mechanisms in natural language processing. Some interface systems for subsets of natural language are described in an article edited by Waltz (1977).

Proceedings of biannual conferences on *Theoretical Issues in Natural Language Processing* (*TINLAP*) contain several important papers. Work in language processing draws on several disciplines besides AI— most notably, computational linguistics, philosophy, and cognitive psychology.

0.3.2. INTELLIGENT RETRIEVAL FROM DATABASES

Two excellent books on database systems are those of Date (1977) and Wiederhold (1977). An important paper by Codd (1970) formalizes a relational model for database management. Papers describing various applications of AI and logic to database organization and retrieval are contained in a book edited by Gallaire and Minker (1978). The article edited by Waltz (1977) contains several descriptions of systems for querying databases using simplified natural language.

0.3.3. EXPERT CONSULTING SYSTEMS

Expert consulting systems have been developed for a variety of domains. The most prominent applications of AI ideas to medical consulting are those of Pople (1977), for internal medicine; Weiss et al. (1978), for the glaucomas; and Shortliffe (1976) and Davis (1976), for bacterial infection diagnosis and therapy.

A consulting system to aid a geologist in evaluating potential mineral deposits is described by Duda et al. (1978a, 1978b, 1979). Several expert systems developed at Stanford University are summarized by Feigenbaum (1977). The most highly developed of these, DENDRAL, computes structural descriptions of complex organic chemicals from their mass spectrograms and related data [Buchanan and Feigenbaum (1978)].

Other important expert systems are those of Sussman and Stallman (1975) [see also Stallman and Sussman (1977)] for analyzing the performance of electronic circuits; and Genesereth (1978, 1979), for helping casual users of the MACSYMA mathematical formula manipulation system [Martin and Fateman (1971)].

12

0.3.4. THEOREM PROVING

Early applications of AI ideas to proving theorems were made by Gelernter (1959) to plane geometry; and by Newell, Shaw, and Simon (1957) to propositional logic. The resolution principle of Robinson (1965) greatly accelerated work on automatic theorem proving. Resolution theorem proving is thoroughly explained in books by Chang and Lee (1973), Loveland (1978), and Robinson (1979).

Bledsoe and his co-workers have developed impressive theorem-proving systems for analysis [Ballantyne and Bledsoe (1977)], for topology [Bledsoe and Bruell (1974)], and for set theory [Bledsoe (1971)]. Wos and his co-workers have achieved excellent results with resolution-based systems [McCharen et al. (1976); Winker and Wos (1978); Winker (1979)]. Boyer and Moore (1979) have developed a theorem-proving system that proves theorems about recursive functions and makes strong use of induction.

Regular workshops are held on automatic deduction. An informal proceedings was issued for the Fourth Workshop [see *WAD* in the Bibliography].

0.3.5. ROBOTICS

Much of the theoretical research in robotics was conducted through robot projects at MIT, Stanford University, Stanford Research Institute and the University of Edinburgh in the late 1960s and early 1970s. This work has been described in several papers and reports. Good accounts are available for the MIT work by Winston (1972); for the Stanford Research Institute work by Raphael et al. (1971) and Raphael (1976, chapter 8); for the Stanford University work by McCarthy et al. (1969); and for the Edinburgh work by Ambler, et al. (1975).

Practical applications of robotics in industrial automation are becoming commonplace. A paper by Abraham (1977) describes a prototype robot system for assembling small electric motors. Automatic visual sensing with a solid-state TV camera is used to guide manipulators in the system. Rosen and Nitzan (1977) discuss the use of vision and other sensors in industrial automation. For a sample of advanced work in robotics applications see Nitzan (1979), Binford et al. (1978), Nevins and

13

Whitney (1977), Will and Grossman (1975), Takeyasu et al. (1977), Okhotsimski et al. (1979), and Cassinis (1979). International symposia on industrial robots are held regularly.

0.3.6. AUTOMATIC PROGRAMMING

One of the earliest attempts to use AI ideas for automatically synthesizing computer programs was by Simon (1963, 1972b). Pioneering papers by Waldinger and Lee (1969) and by Green (1969a) showed how small programs could be synthesized using theorem-proving techniques.

Surveys by Biermann (1976) and by Hammer and Ruth (1979) discuss several approaches to automatic programming. The PSI project of Green (1976) includes several components, one of which is a rule-based system for synthesizing programs from descriptions of abstract algorithms [Barstow (1979)]. Rich and Shrobe (1979) describe a *programmer's apprentice system* for assisting a human programmer.

The related topic of program verification is surveyed by London (1979). [See also the discussion by Constable (1979) in the same volume.] The formal verification of properties of programs was discussed early in the history of computing by Goldstine and von Neumann (1947) and by Turing (1950). Program verification was mentioned by McCarthy (1962) as one of the applications of a proposed mathematical science of computation. Work by Floyd (1967) and Naur (1966) explicitly introduced the idea of invariant assertions. A collection of papers in a book by Manna and Waldinger (1977) describe logic-based methods for program verification, synthesis, and debugging.

0.3.7. COMBINATORIAL AND SCHEDULING PROBLEMS

Scheduling problems are usually studied in operations research. Good general references are the books by Wagner (1975) and by Hillier and Lieberman (1974). For a discussion of NP-complete problems and other topics in the mathematical analysis of algorithms, see the book by Aho, Hopcroft, and Ullman (1974). Lauriere (1978) presents a computer language and a system for solving combinatorial problems using AI methods.

0.3.8. PERCEPTION PROBLEMS

Many good papers on the problems of visual perception by machine are contained in volumes edited by Hansen and Riseman (1978) and by Winston (1975). Representative systems for processing visual images include those of Barrow and Tenenbaum (1976) and Shirai (1978). An important paper by Marr (1976) theorizes about the computational and representational mechanisms of human vision. Kanade (1977) reviews some of the important general aspects of vision systems, and Agin (1977) surveys some of the uses of vision systems in industrial automation.

A book by Duda and Hart (1973) describes some of the fundamentals of computer vision. International Joint Conferences on Pattern Recognition are regularly held and proceedings are published by the IEEE. The Information Processing Techniques Office of the U. S. Defense Advanced Research Projects Agency sponsors *Image Understanding Workshops;* proceedings of these workshops are available.

0.3.9. OTHER APPLICATIONS

Applications of AI ideas have been made in other areas as well. Latombe (1977) and Sussman (1977) describe systems for automatic design; Brown (1977) discusses applications in education; and Gelernter et al. (1977) and Wipke, Ouchi, and Krishnan (1978) have developed systems for organic chemical synthesis.

0.3.10. IMPORTANT SOURCE MATERIALS

In addition to the books already mentioned, several volumes of collected papers are cited at the beginning of the bibliography. These include a series of nine volumes called *Machine Intelligence* (*MI*) and a volume entitled *Computers and Thought* (*CT*) of important early papers edited by Feigenbaum and Feldman (1963).

The international journal *Artificial Intelligence* is a primary publication medium for papers in the field. AI papers are also published in the *Journal of the Association for Computing Machinery* (*JACM*), the *Communications of the Association for Computing Machinery* (*CACM*), and in various publications of the Institute of Electrical and Electronic Engineers (IEEE).

15

International Joint Conferences on Artificial Intelligence (IJCAI) have been held biannually since 1969. The Association for Computing Machinery (ACM) publishes a newsletter devoted to AI called the *SIGART Newsletter*. In Britain, the Society for the Study of Artificial Intelligence and Simulation of Behavior publishes the *AISB Quarterly* and holds biannual summer conferences. The Canadian Society for Computational Studies of Intelligence (CSCSI/SCEIO) publishes an occasional newsletter.

Some of the topics treated in this book assume some familiarity with the programming language LISP. For a readable introduction, see the book by Weissman (1967). Friedman (1974) is an entertaining programmed instruction manual. For a more technical treatment, see the book by Allen (1978).

CHAPTER 1

PRODUCTION SYSTEMS AND AI

Most AI systems display a more or less rigid separation between the standard computational components of *data, operations,* and *control.* That is, if these systems are described at an appropriate level, one can often identify a central entity that might be called a *global database* that is manipulated by certain well-defined *operations,* all under the control of some global *control strategy.* We stress the importance of identifying an appropriate *level* of description; near the machine-code level, any neat separation into distinct components can disappear; at the top level, the complete AI system can consist of several database/operations/control modules interacting in a complex fashion. Our point is that a system consisting of separate database, operations, and control components represents an appropriate metaphorical building block for constructing lucid descriptions of AI systems.

1.1. PRODUCTION SYSTEMS

Various generalizations of the computational formalism known as a *production system* involve a clean separation of these computational components and thus seem to capture the essence of operation of many AI systems. The major elements of an AI production system are a *global database,* a set of *production rules,* and a *control system.*

The global database is the central data structure used by an AI production system. Depending on the application, this database may be as simple as a small matrix of numbers or as complex as a large, relational, indexed file structure. (The reader should not confuse the phrase "global database," as it is used in this book, with the databases of database systems.)

The production rules operate on the global database. Each rule has a *precondition* that is either satisfied or not by the global database. If the precondition is satisfied, the rule can be *applied*. Application of the rule changes the database. The control system chooses which applicable rule should be applied and ceases computation when a *termination condition* on the global database is satisfied.

There are several differences between this production system structure and conventional computational systems that use hierarchically organized programs. The global database can be accessed by all of the rules; no part of it is local to any of them in particular. Rules do not "call" other rules; communication between rules occurs only through the global database. These features of production systems are compatible with the evolutionary development of large AI systems requiring extensive knowledge. One difficulty with using conventional systems of hierarchically organized programs in AI applications is that additions or changes to the knowledge base might require extensive changes to the various existing programs, data structures, and subroutine organization. The production system design is much more modular, and changes to the database, to the control system, or to the rules can be made relatively independently.

We shall distinguish several varieties of production systems. These differ in the kinds of control systems they use, in properties of their rules and databases, and in the ways in which they are applied to specific problems.

As a short example of what we mean by an AI production system, we shall illustrate how one is used to solve a simple puzzle.

1.1.1. THE 8-PUZZLE

Many AI applications involve composing a sequence of operations. Controlling the actions of a robot and automatic programming are two examples. A simple and perhaps familiar problem of this sort, useful for illustrating basic ideas, is the *8-puzzle*. The 8-puzzle consists of eight numbered, movable tiles set in a 3×3 frame. One cell of the frame is always empty thus making it possible to move an adjacent numbered tile into the empty cell—or, we could say, to move the empty cell. Such a puzzle is illustrated in Figure 1.1. Two configurations of tiles are given. Consider the problem of changing the initial configuration into the goal

18

configuration. A solution to the problem is an appropriate sequence of moves, such as "move tile 6 down, move tile 8 down, . . ., etc."

[To solve a problem using a production system, we must specify the global database, the rules, and the control strategy.] Transforming a problem statement into these three components of a production system is often called *the representation problem* in AI. Usually there are several ways to so represent a problem. Selecting a good representation is one of the important arts involved in applying AI techniques to practical problems.

For the 8-puzzle and certain other problems, we can easily identify elements of the problem that correspond to these three components. These elements are the problem *states*, *moves*, and *goal*. In the 8-puzzle, each tile configuration is a problem state. The set of all possible configurations is the *space* of problem states or the *problem space*. Many of the problems in which we are interested have very large problem spaces. The 8-puzzle has a relatively small space; there are only 362,880 (that is, 9!) different configurations of the 8 tiles and the blank space. (This space happens to be partitioned into two disjoint subspaces of 181,440 states each.)

Once the problem states have been conceptually identified, we must construct a computer representation, or description, of them. This description is then used as the global database of a production system. For the 8-puzzle, a straightforward description is a 3 × 3 array or matrix of numbers. [The initial global database is this description of the initial problem state.] Virtually any kind of data structure can be used to describe states. These include symbol strings, vectors, sets, arrays, trees, and lists. Sometimes, as in the 8-puzzle, the form of the data structure bears a close resemblance to some physical property of the problem being solved.

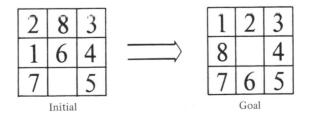

Fig. 1.1 Initial and goal configurations for the 8-puzzle.

A move transforms one problem state into another state. The 8-puzzle is conveniently interpreted as having the following four moves: Move empty space (blank) to the left, move blank up, move blank to the right, and move blank down. These moves are modeled by production rules that operate on the state descriptions in the appropriate manner. The rules each have preconditions that must be satisfied by a state description in order for them to be applicable to that state description. Thus, the precondition for the rule associated with "move blank up" is derived from the requirement that the blank space must not already be in the top row.

In the 8-puzzle, we are asked to produce a particular problem state, namely, the goal state shown in Figure 1.1. We can also deal with problems for which the goal is to achieve any one of an explicit list of problem states. A further generalization is to specify some true/false condition on states to serve as a *goal condition*. Then the goal would be to achieve any state satisfying this condition. Such a condition implicitly defines some set of goal states. For example, in the 8-puzzle, we might want to achieve any tile configuration for which the sum of the numbers labeling the tiles in the first row is 6. (In our language of states, moves, and goals, a solution to a problem is a sequence of moves that transforms an initial state into a goal state.)

The problem goal condition forms the basis for the termination condition of the production system. The control strategy repeatedly applies rules to state descriptions until a description of a goal state is produced. It also keeps track of the rules that have been applied so that it can compose them into the sequence representing the problem solution.

In certain problems, we want the solution to be subject to certain additional constraints. For example, we may want the solution to our 8-puzzle problem having the smallest number of moves. In general we ascribe a *cost* to each move and then attempt to find a solution having minimal cost. These elaborations can easily be handled by methods we describe later on.

1.1.2. THE BASIC PROCEDURE

The basic production system algorithm for solving a problem like the 8-puzzle can be written in nondeterministic form as follows:

20

Procedure **PRODUCTION**

1   *DATA* ← initial database

2   **until** *DATA* satisfies the termination condition, **do:**

3   **begin**

4   **select** some rule, *R*, in the set of rules
            that can be applied to *DATA*

5   *DATA* ← result of applying *R* to *DATA*

6   **end**

1.1.3. CONTROL

The above procedure is nondeterministic because we have not yet specified precisely how we are going to *select* an applicable rule in statement 4. Selecting rules and keeping track of those sequences of rules already tried and the databases they produced constitute what we call the *control strategy* for production systems. In most AI applications, the information available to the control strategy is not sufficient to permit selection of the most appropriate rule on every pass through step 4. The operation of AI production systems can thus be characterized as a *search process* in which rules are tried until some sequence of them is found that produces a database satisfying the termination condition. Efficient control strategies require enough knowledge about the problem being solved so that the rule selected in step 4 has a good chance of being the most appropriate one.

We distinguish two major kinds of control strategies: *irrevocable* and *tentative*. In an *irrevocable* control regime, an applicable rule is selected and applied irrevocably without provision for reconsideration later. In a *tentative* control regime, an applicable rule is selected (either arbitrarily or perhaps with some good reason), the rule is applied, but provision is made to return later to this point in the computation to apply some other rule.

We further distinguish two different types of tentative control regimes. In one, which we call *backtracking*, a *backtracking point* is established when a rule is selected. Should subsequent computation encounter difficulty in producing a solution, the state of the computation reverts to the previous backtracking point, where another rule is applied instead, and the process continues.

In the second type of tentative control regime, which we call *graph-search control*, provision is made for keeping track of the effects of several sequences of rules simultaneously. Various kinds of graph structures and graph searching procedures are used in this type of control.

1.1.4. EXAMPLES OF CONTROL REGIMES

1.1.4.1. Irrevocable. At first thought, it might seem that an irrevocable control regime would never be appropriate for production systems expected to solve problems requiring search. Trial-and-error methods seem to be inherent in solving puzzles, for example. One might argue that if a control strategy of a production system possessed sufficient knowledge about a puzzle to select irrevocably an appropriate rule to apply to each state description, then it would have the puzzle's solution built into it and, if so, can hardly be said to have "solved" the puzzle, for it already knew the solution. Such an argument fails to acknowledge the distinction between the explicit *local knowledge*, about how to proceed toward a goal from any state, and the implicit *global knowledge*, of the complete solution. When infallible local knowledge is available, an irrevocable production system can use it to construct the explicit global knowledge of a solution (without having the explicit global knowledge originally).

Outside of AI, one of the most common examples of the use of local knowledge to construct a global solution is in the "hill-climbing" process of finding the maximum of a function. At any point, we proceed in the direction of the steepest gradient (the local knowledge) to find eventually a maximum of the function (the global knowledge). For certain kinds of functions (those with a single maximum and certain other properties), knowledge of the direction of the steepest gradient is sufficient to find a solution.

We can use the hill-climbing process directly in an irrevocable production system. We need only some real-valued function on the global databases. The control strategy uses this function to select a rule. It selects (irrevocably) the applicable rule that produces a database giving the largest increase in the value of the function. Our hill-climbing function must be such that it attains its highest value for a database satisfying the termination condition.

Applying hill-climbing to the 8-puzzle we might use, as a function of the state description, the negative of the number of tiles "out of place," as compared to the goal state description. For example, the value of this function for the initial state in Figure 1.1 is −4, and the value for the goal state is 0. We can easily compute the value of this function for any state description.

From the initial state, we achieve maximum increase in the value of this function by moving the blank up, so our production system selects the corresponding rule. In Figure 1.2 we show the sequence of states traversed by such a production system in solving this puzzle. The value of our hill-climbing function for each state description is circled. The figure shows that one of the rule applications along the path did not increase the value of our function. If none of the applicable rules permits an increase in the value of our function, a rule is selected (arbitrarily) that does not diminish the value. If there are no such rules, the process halts.

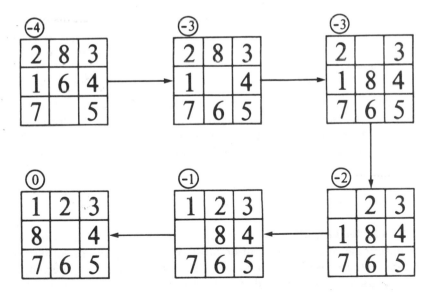

Fig. 1.2 Hill-climbing values for states of the 8-puzzle.

For the instance of the 8-puzzle in Figure 1.2, the hill-climbing strategy allowed us to find a path to a goal state. In general, however, hill-climbing functions can have multiple local maxima, which frustrates hill-climbing methods. For example, suppose the goal state is

```
1 2 3
  7 4
8 6 5
```

and the initial state is

```
1 2 5
  7 4
8 6 3
```

Any applicable rule applied to the initial state description lowers the value of our hill-climbing function. In this case the initial state description is at a local (but not a global) maximum of the function.

Other types of hill-climbing frustrations also occur: The process may get stuck on "plateaus" and "ridges." Of course, these difficulties could be solved if we could devise a better behaved hill-climbing function—one that had just one global maximum and no plateaus, for example. Easily computable functions for problems of interest in AI typically have some of the difficulties we have mentioned. Thus, the use of hill-climbing methods to guide rule selection in irrevocable production systems is quite limited.

Even though the control strategy cannot always select the best rule to apply at any stage, there are times where an irrevocable regime is appropriate. For example, if the application of what might turn out to be an inappropriate rule does not foreclose a subsequent application of an appropriate rule, nothing (other than making superfluous rule applications) is risked by applying rules irrevocably. We shall see some examples of this possibility later.

1.1.4.2. Backtracking. In many problems of interest, applying an inappropriate rule may prevent or substantially delay successful termination. In these cases, we want a control strategy that can *try* a rule and, if it later discovers that this rule was inappropriate, can go back and try another one instead.

The *backtracking* process is one way in which the control strategy can be tentative. A rule is selected, and if it doesn't lead to a solution, the intervening steps are "forgotten," and another rule is selected instead. Formally, the backtracking strategy can be used regardless of how much or how little knowledge is available to bear on rule selection. If no knowledge is available, rules can be selected according to some arbitrary scheme. Ultimately, control will backtrack to select the appropriate rule. Obviously, if good rule-selection knowledge can be used, backing up to consider alternative rules will occur less often, and the whole process will be more efficient.

As an example, let us apply the backtracking strategy to our 8-puzzle example of Figure 1.1 where rules are selected according to the arbitrary scheme of first attempting to move the blank square left, then up, then right, then down. Backing up will occur (a) whenever we generate a state description that already occurs on the path back to the initial state description, (b) whenever we have applied an arbitrarily set number of rules without having generated a goal state description, or (c) whenever there are no (more) applicable rules. In (b) above, the number chosen is the *depth bound* of this backtracking process. In Figure 1.3 we show a sequence of tentative rule applications and backups to illustrate how backtracking might be applied to the 8-puzzle. In Figure 1.3, each state description is labeled by a (circled) number to indicate its order in the sequence of state descriptions produced by the production system. We cannot depict the entire search for a solution in the figure; it is too extensive. Eventually though, a solution path will be found, because all possible paths (of length less than 6) will be explored. Note that if the depth bound is set too low, the process may not find a solution.

The backtracking process is more efficient if rule selection is not arbitrary but is instead guided by information about what might be the best move. If this information is reasonably reliable, then the appropriate rule will usually be selected and there will be little need for backing up. In the 8-puzzle, for example, we might use a hill-climbing function as the means for selecting a rule. Whereas hill-climbing with an irrevocable control regime might get stuck on local maxima, backtracking allows alternative paths to be pursued.

1.1.4.3. Graph Search. Graphs (or more specially, trees) are extremely useful structures for keeping track of the effects of several sequences of rules. We will be discussing these structures in much more detail in chapters 2 and 3, giving only a short example here of their use.

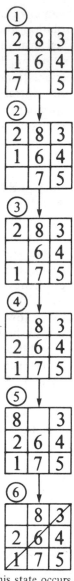

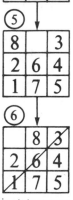

This state occurs on the path back to the initial state, so we retract the last move and apply "move blank right" to state ⑤ instead. Continuation is in the next column.

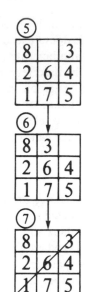

Again, this repeats one on the path, so we retract the last move and apply "move blank down" to state ⑥ instead. Continuation is in the next column.

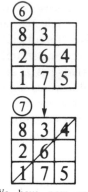

We have now applied six rules without reaching the goal, so we retract the last move. There are no more untried rules to apply to the previous state (number ⑥), so we retract the next-to-the-last move also and apply "move blank down" to state ⑤. Continuation is in the next column.

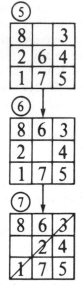

Again, we have applied six rules without reaching a goal, so, etc.

Fig. 1.3 A backtracking control strategy applied to the 8-puzzle.

Suppose we decide to use a graph-search control regime in solving the 8-puzzle problem posed in Figure 1.1. We can keep track of the various rules applied and the databases produced by a structure called a *search tree*. An example of such a tree is in Figure 1.4. At the top or *root* of the tree is a description of the initial configuration. The various rules that can be applied correspond to links or *directed arcs* to *descendant* nodes, representing those states that can be reached by just one move from the initial state. A graph-search control strategy grows such a tree until a database is produced that satisfies the termination condition.

In Figure 1.4, we show *all* applicable rules being applied to every state description. This sort of indecision on the part of the control system is usually grossly inefficient because the resulting tree grows too rapidly. An intelligent control strategy would grow a much narrower tree, using its special knowledge to focus the growth more directly toward the goal. We shall be discussing several methods for achieving such focusing in chapter 2.

Even though we use graphs of this sort only with graph-search control regimes, it is useful to notice that an irrevocable control regime corresponds to following just a single path down through the search tree. (We have already seen that such a simple strategy can sometimes be usefully employed.) A backtracking regime does not maintain the entire search tree structure; it merely keeps track of the path that it is working on currently, modifying it when necessary.

1.1.5. PROBLEMS OF REPRESENTATION

Efficient problem solution requires more than an efficient control strategy. It requires selecting good representations for problem states, moves, and goal conditions. The representation of a problem has a great influence on the effort needed to solve it. Obviously one prefers representations with small state spaces. There are many examples of seemingly difficult puzzles that, when represented appropriately, have trivially small state spaces. Sometimes a given state space can be collapsed by recognizing that certain rules can be discarded or that rules can be combined to make more powerful ones. Even when such simple transformations cannot be achieved, it is possible that a complete reformulation of the problem (changing the very notion of what a state is, for example) will result in a smaller space.

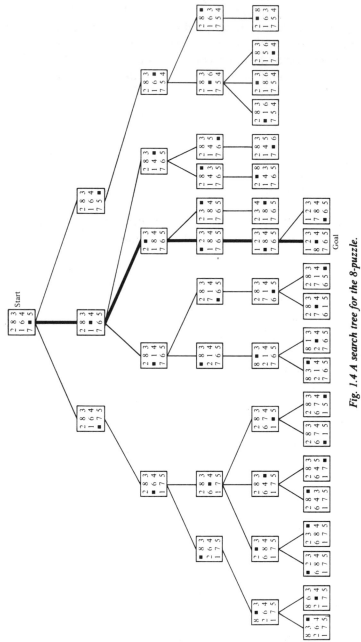

Fig. 1.4 A search tree for the 8-puzzle.

The processes required to represent problems initially and to improve given representations are still poorly understood. It seems that desirable shifts in a problem's representation depend on experience gained in attempts to solve it in a given representation. This experience allows us to recognize the occurrence of simplifying notions, such as symmetries, or useful sequences of rules that ought to be combined into macro-rules. For example, an initial representation of the 8-puzzle might specify the 32 rules corresponding to: move tile 1 left, move tile 1 right, move tile 1 up, move tile 1 down, move tile 2 left, etc. Of course, most of these rules are never applicable to any given state description. After this fact becomes apparent to a problem solver, he would perhaps hit upon the better representation involving moving just the blank space.

We shall next examine two more example problems to illustrate how they might be represented for solution by a production system.

1.1.6. SOME EXAMPLE PROBLEM REPRESENTATIONS

A wide variety of problems can be set up for solution by our production system approach. The formulations that we use in the following examples do not necessarily represent the only ways in which these problems can be solved. The reader may be able to think of good alternatives.

1.1.6.1. A Traveling Salesman Problem. A salesman must visit each of the 5 cities shown in the map of Figure 1.5. There is a road between every pair of cities, and the distance is given next to the road. Starting at city A, the problem is to find a route of minimal distance that visits each of the cities only once and returns to A.

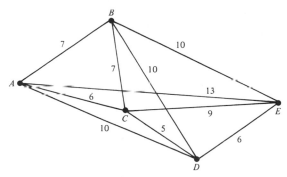

Fig. 1.5 A map for the traveling salesman problem.

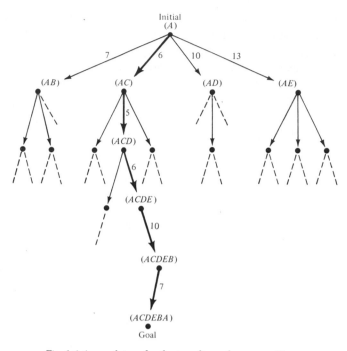

Fig. 1.6 A search tree for the traveling salesman problem.

To set up this problem we specify the following:

> The global database shall be a list of the cities visited so far. Thus the initial database is described by the list (A). We do not allow lists that name any city more than once, except that after all of the other cities have been named, A can be named again.

> The rules correspond to the decisions (a) go to city A next, (b) go to city B next, . . ., and (e) go to city E next. A rule is not applicable to a database unless it transforms it into some legal one. Thus the rule corresponding to "go to city A next" is not applicable to any list not already naming all of the cities.

> Any global database beginning and ending with A and naming all of the other cities

satisfies the termination condition. Notice that
we can use the distance chart of Figure 1.5 to
compute the total distance for any trip. Any
trip proposed as a solution must be of
minimal distance.

Figure 1.6 shows part of the search tree that might be generated by a graph-search control strategy in solving this problem. The numbers next to the edges of the tree are the increments of distance added to the trip by applying the corresponding rule.

1.1.6.2. A Syntax Analysis Problem. Another problem we might want to solve using a production system approach is whether an arbitrary sequence of symbols is a *sentence* in a language; that is, could it have been generated by a grammar. Deciding whether a symbol string is a sentence is called the *parsing problem*, and production systems can be used to do parsing.

Suppose we are given a simple context-free grammar that defines a language. As an example, let the grammar contain the following *terminal symbols*,

of approves new president company sale the

and the following *non-terminal symbols*,

S NP VP PP P V DNP DET A N

The grammar is defined by the following rewrite rules:

$$DNP \quad VP \quad \rightarrow \quad S$$
$$V \quad DNP \quad \rightarrow \quad VP$$
$$P \quad DNP \quad \rightarrow \quad PP$$
$$\textbf{of} \quad \rightarrow \quad P$$
$$\textbf{approves} \quad \rightarrow \quad V$$
$$DET \quad NP \quad \rightarrow \quad DNP$$
$$DNP \quad PP \quad \rightarrow \quad DNP$$
$$A \quad NP \quad \rightarrow \quad NP$$
$$N \quad \rightarrow \quad NP$$
$$\textbf{new} \quad \rightarrow \quad A$$
$$\textbf{president} \quad \rightarrow \quad N$$
$$\textbf{company} \quad \rightarrow \quad N$$
$$\textbf{sale} \quad \rightarrow \quad N$$
$$\textbf{the} \quad \rightarrow \quad DET$$

31

This grammar is too simple to be useful in analyzing most English sentences, but it could be expanded to make it a bit more realistic.

Suppose we wanted to determine whether or not the following string of symbols is a sentence in the language:

The president of the new company approves the sale

To set up this problem, we specify the following:

> The global database shall consist of a string of symbols. The initial database is the given string of symbols that we want to test.

> The production rules are derived from the rewrite rules of the grammar. The right-hand side of a grammar rule can replace any occurrence of the left-hand side in a database. For example, the grammar rule $DNP \quad VP \rightarrow S$ is used to change any database containing the subsequence $DNP \quad VP$ to one in which this subsequence is replaced by S. A rule is not applicable if the database does not contain the left-hand side of the corresponding grammar rule. Also, a rule may be applicable to a database in different ways, corresponding to different occurrences of the left-hand side of the grammar rule in the database.

> Only that database consisting of the single symbol S satisfies the termination condition.

Part of a search tree for this problem is shown in Figure 1.7. In this simple example, aside from different possible orderings of rule applications, there is very little branching in the tree.

1.1.7. BACKWARD AND BIDIRECTIONAL PRODUCTION SYSTEMS

We might say that our production system for solving the 8-puzzle worked *forward* from the initial state to a goal state. Thus, we could call it a *forward production system*. We could also have solved the problem in a backward direction, by starting at the goal state, applying *inverse moves*, and working toward the initial state. Each inverse move would produce a *subgoal* state from which the immediately superordinate goal state could be reached by one forward move. A production system for solving the 8-puzzle in this manner would merely reverse the roles of states and goals and would use rules that correspond to inverse moves.

Setting up a backward-directed production system in the case of the 8-puzzle is simple because the goal is described by an explicit state. We can also set up backward-directed production systems when the goal is described by a condition. We discuss this situation later, after introducing an appropriate language (predicate logic) for talking about goals described by conditions.

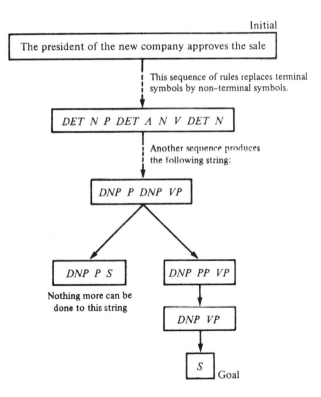

Fig. 1.7 A search tree for the syntax analysis problem.

33

Although there is no formal difference between a production system that works on a problem in a forward direction and one that works in a backward direction, it is often convenient to make this distinction explicit. When a problem has intuitively clear *states* and *goals* and when we choose to employ descriptions of these states as the global database of a production system, we say that the system is a *forward production system*. Rules are applied to the state descriptions to produce new state descriptions, and these rules are called *F-rules*. If, instead, we choose to employ problem goal descriptions as the global database, we shall say that the system is a *backward production system*. Then, rules are applied to goal descriptions to produce subgoal descriptions, and these rules will be called *B-rules*.

In the 8-puzzle, with a single initial state and a single goal state, it makes no difference whether the problem is solved in the forward or the backward direction. The computational effort is the same for both directions. There are occasions, however, when it is more efficient to solve a problem in one direction rather than the other. Suppose, for example, that there were a large number of explicit goal states and one initial state. It would not be very efficient to try to solve such a problem in the backward direction; we do not know a priori which goal state is "closest" to the initial state, and we would have to begin a search from all of them. The most efficient solution direction, in general, depends on the structure of the state space.

It is often a good idea to attempt a solution to a problem searching bidirectionally (that is, both forward and backward simultaneously). We can achieve this effect with production systems also. To do so, we must incorporate both state descriptions and goal descriptions into the global database. F-rules are applied to the state description part, while B-rules are applied to the goal description part. In this type of search, the termination condition to be used by the control system (to decide when the problem is solved) must be stated as some type of matching condition between the state description part and the goal description part of the global database. The control system must also decide at every stage whether to apply an applicable F-rule or an applicable B-rule.

1.2. SPECIALIZED PRODUCTION SYSTEMS

1.2.1. COMMUTATIVE PRODUCTION SYSTEMS

Under certain conditions, the order in which a set of applicable rules is applied to a database is unimportant. When these conditions are satisfied, a production system improves its efficiency by avoiding needless exploration of redundant solution paths that are all equivalent except for rule ordering.

In Figure 1.8 we have three rules, $R1$, $R2$, and $R3$, that are applicable to the database denoted by SO. After applying any one of these rules, all three rules are still applicable to the resulting databases; after applying any pair in sequence, the three are still applicable. Furthermore, Figure 1.8 demonstrates that the same database, namely SG, is achieved regardless of the sequence of rules applied in the set { $R1$, $R2$, $R3$ }.

We say that a production system is _commutative_ if it has the following properties with respect to any database D :

(a) Each member of the set of rules applicable to D
    is also applicable to any database produced by
    applying an applicable rule to D.

(b) If the goal condition is satisfied by D, then it is also
    satisfied by any database produced by applying any
    applicable rule to D.

(c) The database that results by applying to D any
    sequence composed of rules that are applicable to
    D is invariant under permutations of the sequence.

The rule applications in Figure 1.8 possess this commutative property. In producing the database denoted by SG in Figure 1.8, we clearly need consider only _one_ of the many paths shown. Methods for avoiding exploration of redundant paths are obviously of great importance for commutative systems.

Note that commutativity of a system does _not_ mean that the entire sequence of rules used to transform a given database into one satisfying a certain condition can be reordered. After a rule is applied to a database, additional rules might become applicable. Only those rules that are initially applicable to a database can be organized into an arbitrary sequence and applied to that database to produce a result independent of order. This distinction is important.

35

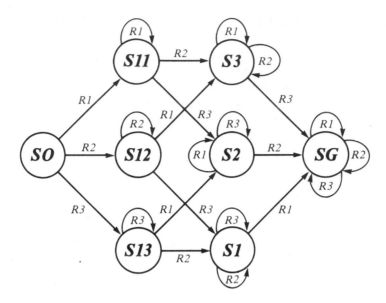

Fig. 1.8 Equivalent paths in a graph.

Commutative production systems are an important subclass enjoying special properties. For example, an irrevocable control regime can always be used in a commutative system because the application of a rule never needs to be taken back or undone. Any rule that was applicable to an earlier database is still applicable to the current one. There is no need to provide a mechanism for applying alternative sequences of rules. Applying an inappropriate rule delays, but never prevents, termination; after termination, extraneous rules can be removed from the solution sequence. We have occasion later to investigate commutative systems in more detail.

It is interesting to note that there is a simple way to transform *any* production system into a commutative one. Suppose we have already represented a problem for solution by a production system. Imagine that this production system has a global database, rules that can modify it, and a graph-search control strategy that generates a search tree of global databases. Now consider another production system whose global database is the entire search tree of the first. The rules of the new production system represent the various ways in which a search tree can be modified by the action of the control strategy of the first production system. Clearly, any rules of the second system that are applicable at any

36

stage remain applicable thereafter. The second system explicitly embodies in its commutative properties the nondeterministic tentativeness that we conferred upon the control strategy of the first system. Employing this conversion results in a more complex global database and rule set and in a simpler sort of control regime (irrevocable). This change in representation simply shifts the system description to a lower level.

1.2.2. DECOMPOSABLE PRODUCTION SYSTEMS

Commutativity is not the only condition whose fulfillment permits a certain freedom in the order in which rules are applied.

Consider, for example, a system whose initial database is (C, B, Z), whose production rules are based on the following rewrite rules,

$$R1: \quad C \rightarrow (D, L)$$
$$R2: \quad C \rightarrow (B, M)$$
$$R3: \quad B \rightarrow (M, M)$$
$$R4: \quad Z \rightarrow (B, B, M)$$

and whose termination condition is that the database contain only Ms.

A graph-search control regime might explore many equivalent paths in producing a database containing only Ms. Two of these are shown in Figure 1.9. Redundant paths can lead to inefficiencies because the control strategy might attempt to explore all of them, but worse than this, in exploring paths that do not terminate successfully, the system may nevertheless do much useful work that ultimately is wasted. (Many of the rule applications in the right-hand branch of the tree in Figure 1.9 are ones needed in a solution.)

One way to avoid the exploration of these redundant paths is to recognize that the initial database can be decomposed or split into separate components that can be processed independently. In our example, the initial database can be split into the components C, B, and Z. Production rules can be applied to each of these components independently (possibly in parallel); the results of these applications can also be split, and so on, until each component database contains only Ms.

AI production systems often have global databases that are decomposable in this manner. Metaphorically, we might imagine that such a global database is a "molecule" consisting of individual "atoms" bound together in some way. If the applicability conditions of the rules involve tests on individual atoms only, and if the effects of the rules are to substitute a qualifying atom by some new molecule (that, in turn, is composed of atoms), then we might as well split the molecule into its atomic components and work on each part separately and independently. Each rule application affects only that component of the global database used to establish the precondition of the rule. Since some of the rules are being applied essentially in parallel, their order is unimportant.

In order to decompose a database, we must also be able to decompose the termination condition. That is, if we are to work on each component separately, we must be able to express the global termination condition using the termination conditions of each of the components. The most important case occurs when the global termination condition can be expressed as the _conjunction_ of the same termination condition for each component database. Unless otherwise stated, we shall always assume this case.

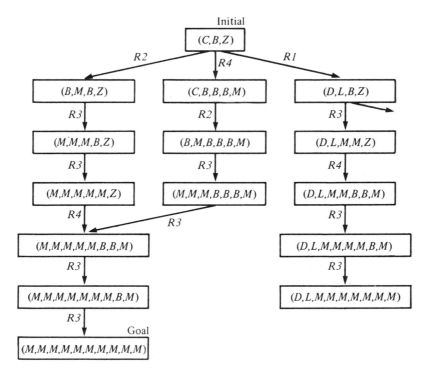

Fig. 1.9 Solution sequences for a rewriting problem.

Production systems that are able to decompose their global databases and termination conditions are called *decomposable*. The basic procedure for a decomposable production system might look something like the following:

Procedure **SPLIT**

1   $DATA \leftarrow$ initial database

2   $\{Di\} \leftarrow$ decomposition of $DATA$; the individual Di are now regarded as separate databases

3   **until** all $\{Di\}$ satisfy the termination condition, **do:**

4   **begin**

5   **select** D^* from among those $\{Di\}$ that do not satisfy the termination condition

6   remove D^* from $\{Di\}$

7   **select** some rule R in the set of rules that can be applied to D^*

8     $D \leftarrow$ result of applying R to D^*

9     $\{di\} \leftarrow$ decomposition of D

10   append $\{di\}$ to $\{Di\}$

11   **end**

The control strategy for **SPLIT** must select a component database, D^*, in Step 5 and must select a rule, R, to apply in Step 7. Whatever the form of this strategy, in order to satisfy Step 3, it must ultimately select *all* the elements in $\{Di\}$. For any D^* selected, though, it need only select *one* applicable rule.

Even though processing component databases in parallel is possible, we are typically interested in control strategies that process them in some serial order. There are two major ways to order the components: (a) the components can either be arranged in some fixed order at the time they are generated, or (b) they can be dynamically reordered during processing. In the former mode, each component is processed to completion before processing begins on the next. Of course, when a production rule is applied to a component, a database may result that can itself be split. The components of this database are processed in order also. Typically, a backtracking strategy for making rule selections is used in conjunction with this fixed-order strategy for processing components.

More flexible control strategies for decomposable production systems allow the component databases to be reordered dynamically as the processing unfolds. Structures called *AND/OR graphs* are useful for depicting the activity of production systems under this control regime. We show an example AND/OR tree for our rewrite problem in Figure 1.10. Just as with ordinary graphs, an AND/OR graph consists of nodes labeled by global databases. Nodes labeled by compound databases have sets of successor nodes each labeled by one of the components. These successor nodes are called *AND nodes* because in order to process the compound database to termination, *all* of the component databases must be processed to termination. Sets of AND nodes are so indicated in our illustrations by a circular mark linking their incoming arcs.

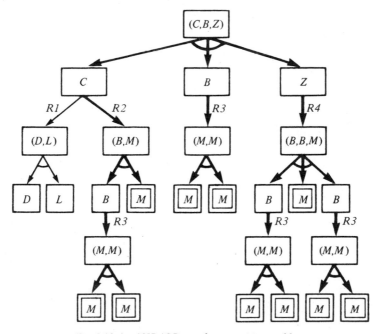

Fig. 1.10 An AND/OR tree for a rewriting problem.

Rules can be applied to component databases. Nodes labeled by these component databases have successor nodes labeled by the results of rule applications. These successor nodes are called *OR nodes* because in order to process a component database to termination, the database resulting from just *one* of the rule applications must be processed to termination.

In Figure 1.10, any node corresponding to a component database satisfying the termination condition (in this case consisting of the symbol *M*) is enclosed in a double box. Such nodes are called *terminal nodes*. (We could also have drawn the tree of Figure 1.10 as a graph. For example, the database (*M*, *M*) occurs as four nodes in Figure 1.10, and these could have been collapsed into one.)

A solution to this rewriting problem can be illustrated by a subgraph of the AND/OR graph. Such a solution subgraph is shown by darkened branches in Figure 1.10. It is a graph whose "tip nodes" correspond to databases that each satisfy the termination condition. We shall discuss strategies for searching AND/OR graphs to find solution graphs in chapter 3.

We next discuss how decomposable production systems can be used on some example problems.

1.2.2.1. Chemical Structure Generation. An important problem in organic chemistry involves determining the structure of a complex organic compound, given certain experimental data such as a mass spectrogram of a sample of the compound. A large AI system called DENDRAL can propose plausible structures for rather complex compounds. [An important part of the DENDRAL system involves the generation of candidate structures, given the chemical formula of the compound.] A full explanation of how these candidate structures are generated is beyond the scope of our present discussion, but we can give a brief description of how the process works for a simple hydrocarbon.

The system for generating candidate structures can be viewed as a production system. The global database is a "partially structured" compound. The production system operates on this database to increase its degree of structure: Initially, the database describes no chemical structure and contains merely the chemical formula; at intermediate stages, the database describes some of the structure of the compound; at the end of the process, the database contains a representation of the entire structure of the compound.

We can use a decomposable production system for this problem because the databases are decomposable into segments, some of which are unstructured chemical formulas of part of the original compound. The production rules are "structure-proposing" rules that convert databases representing unstructured chemical formulas into databases representing partial structures. Any database that contains no unstructured formulas satisifies the termination condition.

Briefly, we can illustrate how the structure-proposing rules work by a simple example. Let us suppose that we are given the chemical formula C_5H_{12}. Our production system proposes some candidate structures for this compound. (Not all of the proposed structures will be chemically possible. At this stage of the process we are merely describing how we could generate structures that are plausible, given only simple valence bond considerations. The actual **DENDRAL** system drastically prunes the candidates by using other chemical knowledge as well as features of the mass spectrogram.)

The initial database is simply the formula C_5H_{12}. In this case, the rules propose the following partial structures:

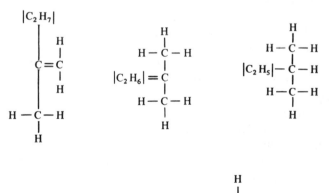

In the partial structures above, the formulas within vertical bars (| |) are unstructured. These can be split from the structured part of the database, and relevant structure-proposing rules can be applied to each of them independently. For example, the rules propose the following structure for the formula $—|C_2H_5|$:

A partial AND/OR tree for our C_5H_{12} problem is shown in Figure 1.11. Each solution tree corresponds to a candidate structure. The one indicated by dark lines corresponds to the following structure:

$$H-C-C-C-C-C-H \quad \text{(pentane)}$$

1.2.2.2. Symbolic Integration. In the problem of symbolic integration we want an automatic process that will accept any indefinite integral as input, say, $\int x \sin 3x \, dx$ and deliver the answer $1/9 \sin 3x - 1/3\, x \cos 3x$ as output. We allow a table containing such simple integral forms as:

$$\int u \, du = \frac{u^2}{2}$$

$$\int \sin u \, du = -\cos u$$

$$\int a^u \, du = a^u \log_a e$$

etc.

Solutions to symbolic integration problems can then be attempted by a production system that converts the given integral into expressions involving only instances of those integral forms given in the table.

The production rules can be based on the integration by parts rule, the decomposition of an integral of a sum rule, and other transformation rules such as those involving algebraic and trigonometric substitutions. A production rule based on integration by parts would transform the expression $\int u\, dv$ into the expression $u\int dv - \int v\, du$. If there is an option about which part of the original integrand is to be u and which is to be dv, then a separate rule instantiation covers each alternative.

The decomposition rule states that the integral of a sum can be replaced by the sum of the integrands. Another rule, called the factoring rule, allows us to replace the expression $\int k\, f(x)\, dx$ by the expression $k\int f(x)\, dx$. Other rules are based on the processes shown in Figure 1.12.

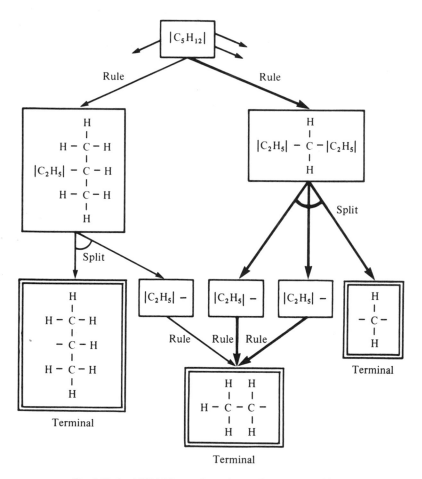

Fig. 1.11 An AND/OR tree for a chemical structure problem.

Any expression involving the sum of integrals can be split into the separate integrals. Each of these can be processed separately, so we see that our production system is decomposable.

The utility of these various rules depends strongly on the form of the integrand. In a symbolic integration system called SAINT (Slagle, 1963), the integrands were classified according to various features that they possessed. For each class of integrand, the various rules were selected according to their heuristic applicability.

In Figure 1.13 we show an AND/OR tree that illustrates a possible search performed by a decomposable production system. The problem is to integrate

$$\int \frac{x^4}{(1 - x^2)^{5/2}} dx$$

Algebraic substitutions

Example

$$\int \frac{x^2 dx}{(2 + 3x)^{2/3}} \rightarrow \int \frac{1}{9} (z^6 - 4z^3 + 4) \, dz \qquad \text{using } z^2 = (2 + 3x)^{2/3}$$

Trigonometric substitutions

Example

$$\int \frac{dx}{x^2 \sqrt{25x^2 + 16}} \rightarrow \int \frac{5}{16} \cot \theta \csc \theta \, d\theta \qquad \text{using } x = \frac{4}{5} \tan \theta$$

Division of numerator by denominator

Example

$$\int \frac{z^4 dz}{z^2 + 1} \rightarrow \int \left(z^2 - 1 + \frac{1}{1 + z^2} \right) dz$$

Completing the square

Example

$$\int \frac{dx}{(x^2 - 4x + 13)^2} \rightarrow \int \frac{dx}{[(x - 2)^2 + 9]^2}$$

Fig. 1.12 Examples of integration rules.

45

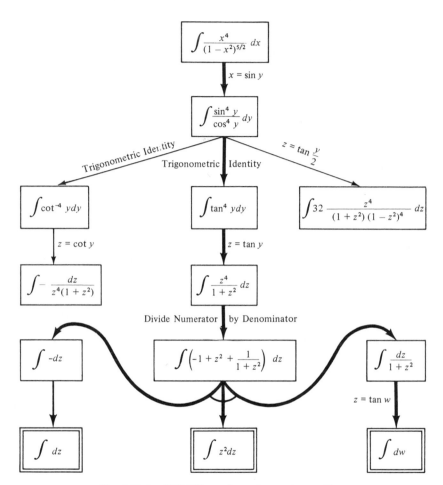

Fig. 1.13 An AND/OR tree for an integration problem.

The nodes of the tree represent expressions to be integrated. Expressions corresponding to basic integrals in an integral table satisfy the termination condition and are enclosed in double boxes. The darkened arcs indicate a solution tree for this problem. From this solution tree and from the integrals obtained from the integral table, we compute the answer:

$$\arcsin x + \frac{1}{3} \tan^3 (\arcsin x) - \tan (\arcsin x)$$

1.3. COMMENTS ON THE DIFFERENT TYPES OF PRODUCTION SYSTEMS

In summary, we shall be discussing two major types of AI production systems in this book, namely, the ordinary type, described by procedure **PRODUCTION,** and the decomposable type, described by procedure **SPLIT**. Depending on the way a problem is represented for solution by a production system, either of these types might be used in a forward or backward direction. They might be controlled by irrevocable or tentative control regimes. The taxonomy of production systems based on these distinctions will help greatly in organizing various AI systems and concepts into a coherent framework.

It is important to note that we are drawing distinctions only between different kinds of AI *systems;* we are not making *any* distinctions between different kinds of *problems*. We shall see instances later in which the same problem can be represented and solved by entirely different kinds of systems.

We will present many more examples of problem representation. Setting up global databases, rules, and termination conditions for any given problem is still a bit of an art and can best be taught by example. Since most of the examples used so far have been elementary puzzles and problems, the reader might well wonder whether production systems are really powerful enough to form the basis of intelligent systems. Later we shall consider some more realistic and difficult problems to show the broad utility of these organizations.

[Efficient AI systems require knowledge of the problem domain.]We can naturally subdivide this knowledge into three broad categories corresponding to the global database, the rules, and the control subdivisions of production systems. The knowledge about a problem that is represented in the global database is sometimes called *declarative knowledge*. In an intelligent information retrieval system, for example, the declarative knowledge would include the main database of specific facts. The knowledge about a problem that is represented in the rules is often called *procedural knowledge*. In intelligent information retrieval, the procedural knowledge would include general information that allows us to manipulate the declarative knowledge. The knowledge about a problem that is represented by the control strategy is often called the *control knowledge*. Control knowledge includes knowledge about a variety of processes, strategies, and structures used to coordinate the entire problem-solving process. The central problem considered in this book is how best to organize problem knowledge into its declarative, procedural, and control components for use by AI production systems. Our first concern, to be treated in some detail in the next two chapters, is with control—especially graph-searching control regimes. Then we move on to consider the uses of the predicate calculus in Artificial Intelligence.

1.4. BIBLIOGRAPHICAL AND HISTORICAL REMARKS

1.4.1. PRODUCTION SYSTEMS

The term *production system* has been used rather loosely in AI, although it usually refers to more specialized types of computational systems than those discussed in this book. Production systems derive from a computational formalism proposed by Post (1943) that was based on string replacement rules. The closely related idea of a *Markov algorithm* [Markov (1954), Galler and Perlis (1970)] involves imposing an order on the replacement rules and using this order to decide which applicable rule to apply next. Newell and Simon (1972) use string-modifying production rules, with a simple control strategy, to model certain types of human problem-solving behavior [see also Newell (1973)]. Rychener (1976) proposes an AI programming language based on string-modifying production rules.

Generalizations of these production system formalisms have been used in AI and called, variously, *production systems, rule-based systems, blackboard systems*, and *pattern-directed inference systems*. The volume edited by Waterman and Hayes-Roth (1978) provides many examples of these sorts of systems [see also Hayes-Roth and Waterman (1977)]. A paper by Davis and King (1977) thoroughly discusses production systems in AI.

Our notion of a production system involves no restrictions on the form of the global database, the rules, or the control strategy. We introduce the idea of *tentative* control regimes to allow a form of controlled nondeterminism in rule application. Thus generalized, production systems can be used to describe the operation of many important AI systems.

Our observation that rule application order can be unimportant in *commutative* and *decomposable* production systems is related to *Church-Rosser* theorems of abstract algebra. [See, for example, Rosen (1973), and Ehrig and Rosen (1977,1980).]

The notion of a *decomposable production system* encompasses a technique often called *problem reduction* in AI. [See Nilsson (1971).] The problem reduction idea usually involves replacing a problem *goal* by a set of subgoals such that if the subgoals are solved, the main goal is also solved. Explaining problem reduction in terms of decomposable production systems allows us to be indefinite about whether we are decomposing problem *goals* or problem *states*. Slagle (1963) used structures that he called *AND/OR goal trees* to deal with problem decomposition; Amarel (1967) proposed similar structures. Since then, AND/OR trees and graphs have been used frequently in AI. Additional references for AND/OR graph methods are given in chapter 3.

The problem of finding good representations for problems has been treated by only a few researchers. Amarel (1968) has written a classic paper on the subject; it takes the reader through a series of progressively better representations for the missionaries-and-cannibals problem. [See Exercise 1.1.] Simon (1977) described a system called UNDERSTAND for converting natural language (English) descriptions of problems into representations suitable for problem solution.

1.4.2. CONTROL STRATEGIES

Hill-climbing is used in control theory and systems analysis as one method for finding the maximum (*steepest ascent*) or minimum (*steepest descent*) of a function. See Athans et al. (1974, pp. 126ff) for a discussion.

49

In computer science, Golomb and Baumert (1965) suggested *backtracking* as a selection mechanism. Various AI programming languages use backtracking as a built-in search strategy [Bobrow and Raphael (1974)]. The literature on heuristic graph searching is extensive; several references are cited in the next two chapters.

1.4.3. EXAMPLE PROBLEMS

Problem-solving programs have sharpened their techniques on a variety of puzzles and games. Some good general books of puzzles are those of Gardner (1959, 1961), who edits a puzzle column in *Scientific American*. Also see the books of puzzles by Dudeney (1958, 1967), a famous British puzzle inventor, a book of logical puzzles by Smullyan (1978), and a book on how to solve problems by Wickelgren (1974). The 8-puzzle is a small version of the 15-puzzle, which is discussed by Gardner (1964, 1965a,b,c) and by Ball (1931, pp. 224-228).

The traveling-salesman problem arises in operations research [see Wagner (1975), and Hillier and Lieberman (1974)]. A method for finding optimal tours has been proposed by Held and Karp (1970, 1971), and a method for finding "approximately" optimum tours has been proposed by Lin (1965).

A good general reference on formal languages, grammars, and syntax analysis is Hopcroft and Ullman (1969).

The technique for proposing chemical structures is based on the DENDRAL system of Feigenbaum et al. (1971). The symbolic integration example is based on the SAINT system of Slagle (1963). A more powerful symbolic integration system, SIN, was developed later by Moses (1967). Moses (1971) discusses the history of techniques for symbolic integration.

EXERCISES

1.1 Specify a global database, rules, and a termination condition for a production system to solve the missionaries and cannibals problem:

> Three missionaries and three cannibals come
> to a river. There is a boat on their side of the
> river that can be used by either one or two
> persons. How should they use this boat to
> cross the river in such a way that cannibals
> never outnumber missionaries on either side
> of the river?

Specify a hill-climbing function over the global databases. Illustrate how an irrevocable control strategy and a backtracking control strategy would use this function in attempting to solve this problem.

1.2 Specify a global database, rules, and a termination condition for a production system to solve the following water-jug problem:

> Given a 5-liter jug filled with water and an
> empty 2-liter jug, how can one obtain
> precisely 1 liter in the 2-liter jug? Water may
> either be discarded or poured from one jug
> into another; however, no more than the
> initial 5 liters is available.

1.3 Describe how the rewrite rules of section 1.1.6. can be used in a production system that *generates* sentences. What is the global database and the termination condition for such a system? Use the system to generate five grammatical (even if not meaningful) sentences.

1.4 My friend, Tom, claims to be a descendant of Paul Revere. Which would be the easier way to verify Tom's claim: By showing that Revere is one of Tom's ancestors or by showing that Tom is one of Revere's descendants? Why?

1.5 Suppose a rule R of a commutative production system is applied to a database D to produce D'. Show that if R has an inverse, the set of rules applicable to D' is identical to the set of rules applicable to D.

1.6 A certain production system has as its global database a set of integers. A database can be transformed by adding to the set the product of any pair of its elements. Show that this production system is commutative.

1.7 Describe how a production system can be used to convert a decimal number into a binary one. Illustrate its operation by converting 141.

1.8 Critically discuss the following thesis: Backtracking (or depth-first graph-search) control strategies should be used when there are multiple paths between problem states because these strategies tend to avoid exploring all of the paths.

1.9 In using a backtracking strategy with procedure **SPLIT**, should the selection made in step 5 be a backtracking point? Discuss. If step 5 is not a backtracking point, are there any differences between procedure **SPLIT** under backtracking and procedure **PRODUCTION** under backtracking?

CHAPTER 2

SEARCH STRATEGIES FOR AI PRODUCTION SYSTEMS

In this chapter we examine some control strategies for AI production systems. Referring to the basic procedure for production systems given on page 21, the fundamental control problem is to select an applicable rule to apply in step 4. For decomposable production systems (page 39), the control problem is to select a component database in step 6 and an applicable rule to apply in step 8. Other subsidiary but important tasks of the control system include checking rule applicability conditions, testing for termination, and keeping track of the rules that have been applied.

An important characteristic of computations for selecting rules is the amount of information, or "knowledge," about the problem at hand that these computations use. At the uninformed extreme, the selection is made completely arbitrarily, without regard to any information about the problem at hand. For example, an applicable rule could be selected completely at random. At the informed extreme, the control strategy is guided by problem knowledge great enough for it to select a "correct" rule every time.

The overall computational efficiency of an AI production system depends upon where along the informed/uninformed spectrum the control strategy falls. We can separate the computational costs of a production system into two major categories: rule application costs and control costs. A completely uninformed control system incurs only a small control strategy cost because merely arbitrary rule selection need not depend on costly computations. However, such a strategy results in high rule application costs because it generally needs to try a large number of rules to find a solution. To inform a control system completely about the problem domains of interest in AI typically involves a high-cost control strategy, in terms of the storage and computations required.

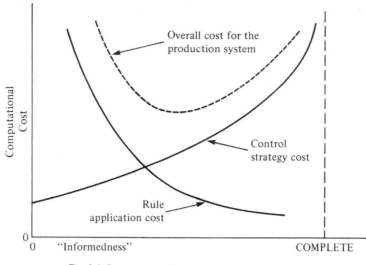

Fig. 2.1 Computational costs of AI production systems.

Completely informed control strategies, however, result in minimal rule application costs; they guide the production system directly to a solution. These tendencies are shown informally in Figure 2.1.

The overall computational cost of an AI production system is the combined rule application cost and control strategy cost. Part of the art of designing efficient AI systems is deciding how to balance these two costs. In any given problem, optimum production system efficiency might be obtained from less than completely informed control strategies. (The cost of a completely informed strategy may simply be too high.)

Another important aspect of AI system design involves the use of techniques that allow the control strategy to use a large amount of problem information without incurring excessive control costs. Such techniques help to decrease the slope of the control strategy cost curve of Figure 2.1, lowering the overall cost of the production system.

The behavior of the control system as it makes rule selections can be regarded as a *search* process. Some examples of the ways in which the control system might search for a solution were given in chapter 1. There, we discussed the *hill-climbing* method of irrevocable rule selection, exploring a surface for a maximum, and the *backtracking* and *graph-search* regimes, search processes that permitted tentative rule selection.

54

Our main concern in the present chapter is tentative control regimes, even though the irrevocable ones have important applications, especially with commutative production systems. Some of the search methods that we develop for tentative control regimes can be adapted for use with certain types of commutative production systems using irrevocable control regimes. We begin our discussion of tentative control by describing backtracking methods.

2.1. BACKTRACKING STRATEGIES

In chapter 1 we presented a general description of the backtracking control strategy and illustrated its use on the 8-puzzle. For problems requiring only a small amount of search, backtracking control strategies are often perfectly adequate and efficient. Compared with graph-search control regimes, backtracking strategies are typically simpler to implement and require less storage.

A simple recursive procedure captures the essence of the operation of a production system under backtracking control. This procedure, which we call **BACKTRACK**, takes a single argument, *DATA*, initially set equal to the global database of the production system. Upon successful termination, the procedure returns a list of rules, that, if applied in sequence to the initial database, produces a database satisfying the termination condition. If the procedure halts without finding such a list of rules, it returns *FAIL*. The **BACKTRACK** procedure is defined as follows:

Recursive procedure **BACKTRACK(** *DATA* **)**

1 **if TERM(** *DATA* **), return** *NIL*; **TERM** is a
        predicate true for arguments that satisfy
        the termination condition of the production
        system. Upon successful termination, *NIL*,
        the empty list, is returned.

2 **if DEADEND(** *DATA* **), return** *FAIL*; **DEADEND**
        is a predicate true for arguments that are
        known not to be on a path to a solution. In
        this case, the procedure returns the symbol
        FAIL.

55

3 *RULES* ← **APPRULES**(*DATA*); **APPRULES** is a
function that computes the rules applicable to
its argument and orders them (either arbitrarily
or according to heuristic merit).

4 LOOP: **if NULL(** *RULES* **), return** *FAIL*;
if there are no (more) rules to apply, the
procedure fails.

5 *R* ← **FIRST**(*RULES*); the best of the applicable
rules is selected.

6 *RULES* ← **TAIL**(*RULES*); the list of applicable
rules is diminished by removing the one just
selected.

7 *RDATA* ← **R**(*DATA*); rule *R* is applied to
produce a new database.

8 *PATH* ← **BACKTRACK**(*RDATA*); **BACKTRACK** is
called recursively on the new database.

9 **if** *PATH* = *FAIL*, **go** LOOP; if the
recursive call fails, try another rule.

10 **return CONS(** *R*, *PATH* **)**; otherwise, pass the
successful list of rules up, by adding *R*
to the front of the list.

We can make several comments about this procedure. First, it
terminates successfully (in step 1) only if it produces a database satisfying
the termination condition. The list of rules used in producing this
database is built up in step 10. Unsuccessful terminations can occur in
steps 2 and 4. When an unsuccessful termination occurs within a
recursive call, the procedure *backtracks* to a higher level. Step 2 performs
a test to check whether or not a solution is even possible from the
database in question. In step 4, the procedure fails if it has already tried
all applicable rules.

Procedure **BACKTRACK** may never terminate; it may generate new
nonterminal databases indefinitely or it may cycle. Both of these cases
can be arbitrarily prevented by imposing a *depth bound* on the recursion.

56

Any recursive call fails when its depth exceeds this bound. Cycling can be more straightforwardly prevented by maintaining a list of the databases produced so far and by checking new ones to see that they do not match any on the list. Later we present a slightly more complicated procedure that makes these tests.

In step 3, the procedure orders the rules that are applicable to the database in question. Here, any available heuristic information about the problem domain is used. Those rules that are "guessed," using the heuristic information, most appropriate for that database occur early in the ordering. The applicable rules can be ordered arbitrarily if no ordering information is available, although, in that case, extensive backtracking may cause the procedure to be prohibitively inefficient. By definition, if a "correct" rule is always first in the ordering, no backtracking will occur at all.

We have used a specific procedure, **BACKTRACK**, to explain how backtracking control strategies operate. Several practical concerns—such as the need to avoid recopying large, complex global databases—would dictate implementations of the backtracking strategy that are more efficient than the procedure given here.

Another illustrative example of how the backtracking strategy is applied to a simple problem is perhaps useful. Suppose we are given the problem of placing 4 queens on a 4×4 chess board so that none can capture any other. For our global database, we use a 4×4 array with marked cells corresponding to squares occupied by queens. The termination condition, expressed by the predicate **TERM**, is satisfied for a database if and only if it has precisely 4 queen marks and the marks correspond to queens located so that they cannot capture each other.

There are many alternative formulations possible for the production rules. A useful one for our purposes involves the following rule schema, for $1 \leq i, j \leq 4$:

R_{ij}

      Precondition:
            $i = 1$: There are no queen marks in the array.
            $1 < i \leq 4$: There is a queen mark in row $i - 1$
                        of the array.

Effect:
Puts a queen mark in row i, column j of the array.

Thus, the first queen mark added to the array must be in row 1, the second must be in row 2, etc.

To use the **BACKTRACK** procedure to solve the 4-queens problem, we have still to specify both the predicate **DEADEND** and an ordering relation for applicable rules. Suppose we arbitrarily say that R_{ij} is ahead of R_{ik} in the ordering only when $j < k$. The predicate **DEADEND** might be defined so that it is satisfied for databases where it is obvious that no solution is possible; for example, certainly no solution is possible for any database containing a pair of queen marks in mutually capturing positions. (The reader is encouraged to try working through **BACK-TRACK** by hand using this simple test for **DEADEND**.) Altogether, the algorithm backtracks 22 times before finding a solution; even the very first rule applied must ultimately be taken back.

A more efficient algorithm (with less backtracking) can be obtained if we use a more informed rule ordering. One simple, but useful ordering for this problem involves using the function $diag(i,j)$, defined to be the length of the longest diagonal passing through cell (i,j). Let R_{ij} be ahead of R_{mn} in the ordering if $diag(i,j) < diag(m,n)$. (For equal values of $diag$, use the same order as before.) Using this ordering relation, the rules that are applicable to the initial database would be ordered as follows: $(R_{12}, R_{13}, R_{11}, R_{14})$. The reader might verify that this ordering scheme solves the 4-queens problem with only 2 backtracks.

As previously mentioned, we need a slightly more complex algorithm to avoid cycles. All databases on a path back to the initial one must be 'checked to insure that none are revisited. In order to implement this backtracking strategy as a recursive procedure, the entire chain of databases must be an argument of the procedure. Again, practical implementations of AI backtracking production systems use various techniques to avoid the need for explicitly listing all of these databases in their entirety.

Let us call our cycle-avoiding algorithm **BACKTRACK1**. It takes a list of databases as its argument; when first called, this list contains the initial database as its single element. Upon successful termination, **BACK-TRACK1** returns a sequence of rules that can be applied to the initial database to produce one that satisfies the termination condition. The **BACKTRACK1** algorithm is defined as follows:

Recursive procedure **BACKTRACK1**(*DATALIST*)

1 *DATA* ← **FIRST**(*DATALIST*); *DATALIST*
    is a list of all databases on a path back
    to the initial one. *DATA* is the most
    recent one produced.

2 **if MEMBER**(*DATA*, **TAIL**(*DATALIST*)), **return**
    FAIL; the procedure fails if it revisits
    an earlier database.

3 **if TERM**(*DATA*), **return** *NIL*

4 **if DEADEND**(*DATA*), **return** *FAIL*

5 **if LENGTH**(*DATALIST*) > *BOUND*, **return**
    FAIL; the procedure fails if too many
    rules have been applied. *BOUND* is a global
    variable specified before the procedure is
    first called.

6 *RULES* ← **APPRULES**(*DATA*)

7 LOOP: **if NULL**(*RULES*), **return** *FAIL*

8 *R* ← **FIRST**(*RULES*)

9 *RULES* ← **TAIL**(*RULES*)

10 *RDATA* ← **R**(*DATA*)

11 *RDATALIST* ← **CONS**(*RDATA*, *DATALIST*); the
     list of databases visited so far is extended
     by adding *RDATA*.

12 *PATH* ← **BACKTRACK1**(*RDATALIST*)

13 **if** *PATH* = *FAIL*, **go** LOOP

14 **return CONS**(*R*, *PATH*)

The 8-puzzle example of backtracking in chapter 1 used $BOUND = 7$ and also checked to see if a tile configuration had been visited previously. Note that the recursive algorithm does not remember *all* databases that it visited previously. Backtracking involves "forgetting" all databases whose paths lead to failures. The algorithm remembers only those databases on the *current* path back to the initial one.

The backtracking strategies just described "fail back" one level at a time. If a level n recursive call of **BACKTRACK** fails, control returns to level $n - 1$ where another rule is tried. But sometimes the reason, or *blame*, for the failure at level n can be traced to rule choices made many levels above. In these cases it would be obviously futile to try another rule choice at level $n - 1$; predictably, any such choice there would again lead to a failure. What is needed, then, is a way to jump several levels at a time, all the way back to one where a different rule choice will make a useful difference.

To see an example of this multilevel backtracking phenomenon, consider using **BACKTRACK** to solve the 8-queens problem. In this problem, we must place 8 queens on an 8×8 board so that none of them can capture any others.

Suppose we are at a stage of the algorithm in which the database just produced is illustrated by the array in Figure 2.2. (In fact, the **BACK-TRACK** algorithm would produce precisely this array using the arbitrary rule ordering that we originally discussed.) The algorithm must now attempt to place a queen in row 6. Note that no cell in row 6 is satisfactory; each attempt to place a queen in that row would fail. In such a circumstance, **BACKTRACK** would attempt to relocate the queen in row 5, moving it eventually to column 8. But a more detailed analysis of the reasons for the row-6 failures would reveal that all of them would have still occurred *regardless of the position of the queen in row 5*. The row-6 failures were predestined by the positions of the first 4 queens. Therefore, since there is no point in relocating queen 5, we can jump over one recursive level, back to the point where we were selecting row-4 locations. Some AI systems have used backtracking strategies that are able to analyze failures in this manner and to back up to the appropriate point.

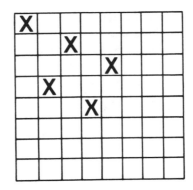

Fig. 2.2 Queen positions during a stage of **BACKTRACK**.

2.2. GRAPH-SEARCH STRATEGIES

In backtracking strategies, the control system effectively forgets any trial paths that result in failures. Only the path currently being extended is stored explicitly. A more flexible procedure would involve the explicit storage of all trial paths so that any of them could be candidates for further extension.

For example, in Figure 2.3 we show an initial database, *DB1*, to which rules *R1* and *R2*, say, are applicable; suppose the control system selects and applies *R1* producing database *DB2*; then suppose the control system selects applicable rule *R3* and applies it to *DB2*, to produce *DB3*; and at this point, suppose the control system decides that this path is not promising and backs up to apply rule *R2* to *DB1*, to produce database *DB4*. As stated, a backtracking strategy would erase the records of *DB2* and *DB3*. But if the control system were to maintain this record, then, should a path through *DB4* ultimately prove futile, it could resume work immediately from either *DB2* or *DB3*. In order to achieve this sort of flexibility, a control system must keep an explicit record of a graph of databases linked by rule applications. We say that control systems that operate in this manner use *graph-search* strategies.

61

In our discussions of graph-search strategies, we speak as if the various databases produced by rule applications are actually represented, each in its entirety, as nodes in a graph or tree. Because these databases are usually very large structures, it would be impractical to store each of them explicitly. Fortunately, there are ways in which the effect of explicit storage of all of the databases can be achieved, by explicitly storing just the initial database and records of incremental changes from which any of the other databases can rapidly be computed.

2.2.1. GRAPH NOTATION

We can think of a graph-search control strategy as a means of finding a path in a graph from a node representing the initial database to one representing a database that satisfies the termination condition of the production system. Graph-searching algorithms are thus of special interest to us. Before describing these algorithms, we first review some graph-theory terminology.

A *graph* consists of a (not necessarily finite) set of *nodes*. Certain pairs of nodes are connected by *arcs*, and these arcs are *directed* from one member of the pair to the other. Such a graph is called a *directed graph*. For our purposes, the nodes are labeled by databases, and the arcs are labeled by rules. If an arc is directed from node n_i to node n_j, then node n_j is said to be a *successor* of node n_i, and node n_i is said to be a *parent* of node n_j. In the graphs that are of interest to us, a node can have only a finite number of successors. (Our production systems have only a finite number of applicable rules.) A pair of nodes may be successors of each other; in this case the pair of directed arcs is sometimes replaced by an *edge*.

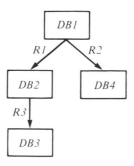

Fig. 2.3 A tree of databases.

A *tree* is a special case of a graph in which each node has at most one parent. A node in the tree having no parent is called a *root node*. A node in the tree having no successors is called a *tip node*. We say that the root node is of *depth* zero. The depth of any other node in the tree is defined to be the depth of its parent plus 1.

A sequence of nodes $(n_{i1}, n_{i2}, \ldots, n_{ik})$, with each n_{ij} a successor of $n_{i,j-1}$ for $j = 2, \ldots, k$, is called a *path* of *length* k from node n_{i1} to node n_{ik}. If a path exists from node n_i to node n_j, then node n_j is said to be *accessible* from node n_i. Node n_j is then a *descendant* of node n_i, and node n_i is an *ancestor* of node n_j. We see that the problem of finding a sequence of rules transforming one database into another is equivalent to the problem of finding a path in a graph.

Often it is convenient to assign positive *costs* to arcs, to represent the cost of applying the corresponding rule. We use the notation $c(n_i, n_j)$ to denote the cost of an arc directed from node n_i to node n_j. It will be important in some of our later arguments to assume that these costs are all greater than some arbitrarily small positive number, e. The cost of a path between two nodes is then the sum of the costs of all of the arcs connecting the nodes on the path. In some problems, we want to find that path having *minimal* cost between two nodes.

In the simplest type of problem, we desire to find a path (perhaps having minimal cost) between a given node s, representing the initial database and another given node t, representing some other database. The more usual situation, though, involves finding a path between a node s and *any* member of a set of nodes $\{ t_i \}$ that represent databases satisfying the termination condition. We call the set $\{ t_i \}$ the *goal set*, and each node t in $\{ t_i \}$ is a *goal node*.

A graph may be specified either explicitly or implicitly. In an explicit specification, the nodes and arcs (with associated costs) are explicitly given by a table. The table might list every node in the graph, its successors, and the costs of the associated arcs. Obviously, an explicit specification is impractical for large graphs and impossible for those having an infinite set of nodes.

In our applications, the control strategy generates (makes explicit) part of an implicitly specified graph. This implicit specification is given by the *start* node, s, representing the initial database, and the rules that alter databases. It will be convenient to introduce the notion of a *successor operator* that is applied to a node to give *all* of the successors of that node (and the costs of the associated arcs). We call this process of applying the successor operator to a node, *expanding* the node. The successor operator depends in an obvious way on the rules. Expanding *s*, the successors of *s*, ad infinitum, makes explicit the graph that is implicitly defined by *s* and the successor operator. A graph-search control strategy, then, can be viewed as a process of making explicit a portion of an implicit graph sufficient to include a goal node.

2.2.2. A GENERAL GRAPH-SEARCHING PROCEDURE

The process of explicitly generating part of an implicitly defined graph can be informally defined as follows.

Procedure GRAPHSEARCH

1 Create a *search graph*, *G*, consisting solely of the start node, *s*. Put *s* on a list called *OPEN*.

2 Create a list called *CLOSED* that is initially empty.

3 LOOP: if *OPEN* is empty, exit with failure.

4 Select the first node on *OPEN*, remove it from *OPEN*, and put it on *CLOSED*. Call this node *n*.

5 If *n* is a goal node, exit successfully with the solution obtained by tracing a path along the pointers from *n* to *s* in *G*. (Pointers are established in step 7.)

6 Expand node *n*, generating the set, *M*, of its successors that are not ancestors of *n*. Install these members of *M* as successors of *n* in *G*.

7 Establish a pointer to *n* from those members of *M* that were not already in *G* (i.e., not already on either *OPEN* or *CLOSED*). Add these members of *M* to *OPEN*. For each member of *M* that was already on *OPEN* or *CLOSED*, decide whether or not to redirect its pointer to *n*. (See text.) For each member of

> *M* already on *CLOSED*, decide for each of its
> descendants in *G* whether or not to redirect its
> pointer. (See text.)

8   Reorder the list *OPEN*, either according to some
    arbitrary scheme or according to heuristic merit.

9   Go LOOP

This procedure is sufficiently general to encompass a wide variety of special graph-searching algorithms. The procedure generates an explicit graph, *G*, called the *search graph* and a subset, *T*, of *G* called the *search tree*. Each node in *G* is also in *T*. The search tree is defined by the pointers that are set up in step 7. Each node (except *s*) in *G* has a pointer directed to just one of its parents in *G*, which defines its unique parent in *T*. The search graph forms a partial ordering because no node in *G* is one of its own ancestors (Step 6). Each possible path to a node discovered by the algorithm is preserved explicitly in *G*; a single distinguished path to any node is defined by *T*. Roughly speaking, the nodes on *OPEN* are the tip nodes of the search tree, and the nodes on *CLOSED* are the nontip nodes. More precisely, at step 3 of the procedure, the nodes on *OPEN* are those (tip) nodes of the search tree that have not yet been selected for expansion. The nodes on *CLOSED* are either tip nodes selected for expansion that generated no successors in the search graph or nontip nodes of the search tree.

The procedure orders the nodes on *OPEN* in step 8 so that the "best" of these is selected for expansion in step 4. This ordering can be based on a variety of heuristic ideas (discussed below) or on various arbitrary criteria. Whenever the node selected for expansion is a goal node, the process terminates successfully. The successful path from start node to goal node can then be recovered (in reverse) by tracing the pointers back from the goal node to *s*. The process terminates unsuccessfully whenever the search tree has no remaining tip nodes that have not yet been selected for expansion. (Some nodes may have no successors at all, so it is possible for the list *OPEN*, ultimately, to become empty.) In the case of unsuccessful termination, the goal node(s) must have been inaccessible from the start node.

Step 7 of the procedure requires some additional explanation. If the implicit graph being searched was a tree, we could be sure that none of the successors generated in step 6 had been generated previously: Every node (except the root node) of a tree is the successor of only one node and thus is generated once only when its unique parent is expanded. Thus, in this special case, the members of M in steps 6 and 7 are not already on either $OPEN$ or $CLOSED$. In this case, each member of M is added to $OPEN$ and is installed in the search tree as a successor of n. The search graph is the search tree throughout the execution of the algorithm, and there is no need to change parents of the nodes in T.

If the implicit graph being searched is not a tree, it is possible that some of the members of M have already been generated, that is, they may already be on $OPEN$ or $CLOSED$. The problem of determining whether a newly generated database is identical to one generated before can be computationally expensive. For this reason, some search processes avoid making this test, with the result that the search tree may contain several nodes labeled by the same database. Node repetitions, of course, lead to redundant successor computations. Hence, there is a tradeoff between the computational cost of testing for matching databases and the computational cost of generating a larger search tree (containing multiple nodes labeled by identical databases). In steps 6 and 7 of procedure **GRAPHSEARCH**, we are assuming that it is worthwhile to test for node identities.

When the search process generates a node that it had generated before, it finds a (perhaps better) path to it other than the one already recorded in the search tree. We desire that the search tree preserve the least costly path found so far from s to any of its nodes. (The cost of a path from s to n in the search tree can be computed by summing the arc costs encountered in the tree while tracing back from n to s. In problems for which no arc costs are given, we assume that the arcs have unit cost.) When a newly found path is less costly than an older one, the search tree is adjusted by changing the parentage of the regenerated node to its more recent parent.

If a node n on $CLOSED$ has its parentage in T changed, a less costly path has been found to n. The less costly path may be part of less costly paths to some of the successors of n in the search graph, G; in this case, a change might be in order to the parentage in T of the successors of n in G. Because G is finite and is a partial order on its nodes, the process of propagating the costs of the new paths downward to the successors of n in G is straightforward and finite. After this computation, the search tree is adjusted to record these paths, if appropriate.

A simple example will serve to show how such search tree adjustments are accomplished. Suppose a search process has generated the search graph and search tree shown in Figure 2.4. The dark arrows along certain arcs in this search graph are the pointers that define parents of nodes in the search tree. The solid nodes are on *CLOSED*, and the other nodes are on *OPEN* at the time the algorithm selects node 1 for expansion. (We assume unit arc costs.) When node 1 is expanded, its single successor, node 2, is generated. But node 2, with parent node 3 in the search tree, had previously been generated, and node 2 is also on *CLOSED* with successor nodes 4 and 5. Note, however, that node 4's parent in the search tree is node 6, because the shortest (least costly) path from *s* to node 4 in the search graph is through node 6. Since the algorithm now discovers a path to node 2 through node 1 that is less costly than the previous path through node 3, the parent of node 2 in the search tree is changed from node 3 to node 1. The costs of the paths to the descendants of node 2 in the search graph (namely, the paths to nodes 4 and 5) are recomputed. These costs are now also lower than before, with the result that the parent of node 4 is changed from node 6 to node 2. The adjusted search tree is defined by the pointers on the arcs of the search graph of Figure 2.5.

As described, the **GRAPHSEARCH** algorithm generates *all* of the successors of a node at once. It is possible to modify the algorithm so that a node is selected for expansion and successors are generated one at a time [sec, for example, Michie and Ross (1970)]. The modified algorithm does not put a node on *CLOSED* until all of its successors have been generated. Since the process of applying rules to a database to produce new databases is typically computationally expensive, the modified algorithm is often preferable even though it is slightly more difficult to describe. To facilitate explaining some general properties of graph-searching procedures, we continue to use that version of the algorithm in which all successors are generated simultaneously.

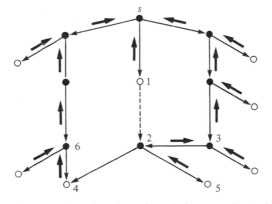

Fig. 2.4 A search graph and search tree before expanding node 1.

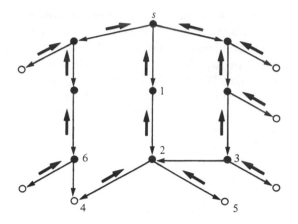

Fig. 2.5 A search graph and search tree after expanding node 1.

2.3. UNINFORMED GRAPH-SEARCH PROCEDURES

If no heuristic information from the problem domain is used in ordering the nodes on *OPEN*, some arbitrary scheme must be used in step 8 of the algorithm. The resulting search procedure is called *uninformed*. In AI, we are typically not interested in uninformed procedures, but we describe two types here for purposes of comparison: depth-first search and breadth-first search.

The first type of uninformed search orders the nodes on *OPEN* in descending order of their depth in the search tree. The deepest nodes are put first in the list. Nodes of equal depth are ordered arbitrarily. The search that results from such an ordering is called *depth-first* search because the deepest node in the search tree is always selected for expansion. To prevent the search process from running away along some fruitless path forever, a depth bound is provided. No node whose depth in the search tree exceeds this bound is ever generated. (The process can be made to terminate virtually as soon as a goal node is generated by putting goal nodes at the very beginning of *OPEN*; but, of course, this procedure would involve a goal test during step 8 of **GRAPHSEARCH**. If the result is saved, then the goal test in step 5 need only look up the result instead of repeating a possibly costly computation.)

The depth-first procedure generates new databases in an order similar to that generated by an uninformed backtracking control strategy. The correspondence would be exact if the graph-search process generated only one successor at a time. Usually, the backtracking implementation is preferred to the depth-first version of **GRAPHSEARCH** because backtracking is simpler to implement and involves less storage. (Backtracking strategies save only one path to a goal node; they do not save the entire record of the search as do depth-first graph-search strategies.)

The search tree generated by a depth-first search process in an 8-puzzle problem is illustrated in Figure 2.6. The nodes are labeled with their corresponding databases and are numbered in the order in which they are selected for expansion. We assume a depth bound of five. The dark path shows a solution involving five rule applications. We see that a depth-first search process progresses along one path until it reaches the depth bound, then it begins to consider alternative paths of the same depth, or less, that differ only in the last step; then those that differ in the last two steps; etc.

The second type of uninformed search procedure orders the nodes on *OPEN* in increasing order of their depth in the search tree. (Again, to promote earlier termination, goal nodes should be put immediately at the very beginning of *OPEN*.) The search that results from such an ordering is called *breadth-first* because expansion of nodes in the search tree proceeds along "contours" of equal depth. In Figure 2.7, we show the search tree generated by a breadth-first search in the 8-puzzle problem. The numbers next to each node indicate the order in which nodes are selected for expansion. Note that the goal node is selected immediately after it is generated.

Later we show that breadth-first search is guaranteed to find a shortest-length path to a goal node, providing a path exists at all. (If no path exists, the method will exit with failure for finite graphs or will never terminate for infinite graphs.)

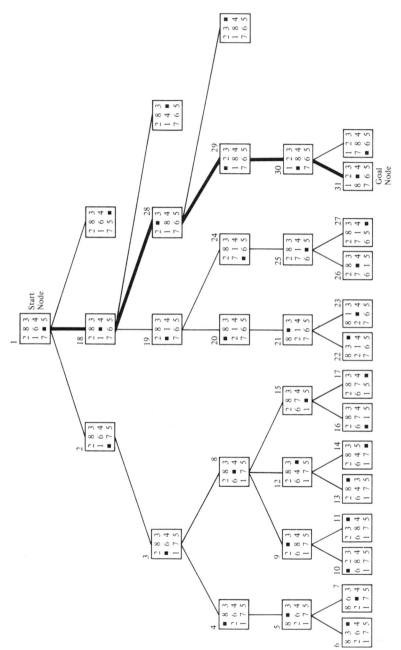

Fig. 2.6 A search tree produced by a depth-first search.

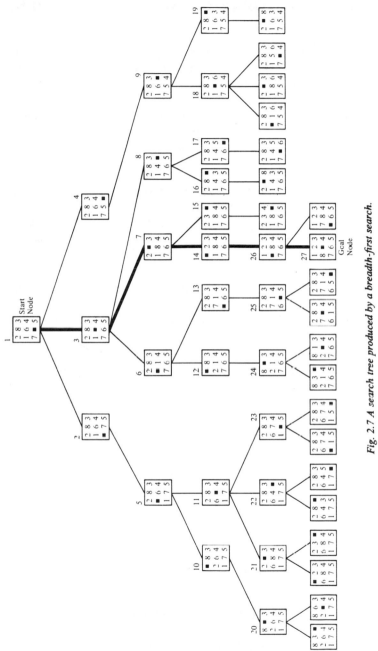

Fig. 2.7 A search tree produced by a breadth-first search.

2.4. HEURISTIC GRAPH-SEARCH PROCEDURES

The uninformed search methods, whether breadth-first or depth-first, are exhaustive methods for finding paths to a goal node. In principle, these methods provide a solution to the path-finding problem, but they are often infeasible to use to control AI production systems because the search expands too many nodes before a path is found. Since there are always practical limits on the amount of time and storage available to expend on the search, more efficient alternatives to uninformed search must be found.

For many tasks it is possible to use task-dependent information to help reduce search. Information of this sort is usually called *heuristic information*, and search procedures using it are called *heuristic search methods*. It is often possible to specify heuristics that reduce search effort (below that expended by, say, breadth-first search) without sacrificing the guarantee of finding a minimal length path. Some heuristics greatly reduce search effort but do not guarantee finding minimal cost paths. In most practical problems, we are interested in minimizing some *combination* of the cost of the path and the cost of the search required to obtain the path. Furthermore, we are usually interested in search methods that minimize this combination *averaged* over all problems likely to be encountered. If the averaged combination cost of search method 1 is lower than the averaged combination cost of search method 2, then search method 1 is said to have more *heuristic power* than search method 2. Note that according to our definition, it is not necessary (though it is a common misconception) that a search method with more heuristic power give up any guarantee for finding a minimal cost path.

Averaged combination costs are never actually computed, both because it is difficult to decide on the way to combine path cost and search effort cost and because it would be difficult to define a probability distribution over the set of problems to be encountered. Therefore, the matter of deciding whether one search method has more heuristic power than another is usually left to informed intuition, gained from actual experience with the methods.

2.4.1. USE OF EVALUATION FUNCTIONS

Heuristic information can be used to order the nodes on *OPEN* in step 8 of **GRAPHSEARCH** so that search expands along those sectors of the frontier thought to be most promising. In order to apply such an ordering procedure, we need a method for computing the "promise" of a node. One important method uses a real-valued function over the nodes called an *evaluation function*. Evaluation functions have been based on a variety of ideas: Attempts have been made to define the probability that a node is on the best path; distance or difference metrics between an arbitrary node and the goal set have been suggested; or in board games or puzzles, a configuration is often scored points on the basis of those features that it possesses that are thought to be related to its promise as a step toward the goal.

Suppose we denote the evaluation function by the symbol f. Then $f(n)$ gives the value of the function at node n. For the moment we let f be any arbitrary function; later, we propose that it be an estimate of the cost of a minimal cost path from the start node to a goal node constrained to go through node n.

We use the function f to order the nodes on *OPEN* in step 8 of **GRAPHSEARCH**. By convention, the nodes on *OPEN* are ordered in increasing order of their f values. Ties among f values are ordered arbitrarily, but always in favor of goal nodes. Supposedly, a node having a low evaluation is more likely to be on an optimal path.

The way in which **GRAPHSEARCH** uses an evaluation function to order nodes can be illustrated by considering again our 8-puzzle example. We use the simple evaluation function:

$$f(n) = d(n) + W(n)$$

where $d(n)$ is the depth of node n in the search tree and $W(n)$ counts the number of misplaced tiles in that database associated with node n. Thus the start node configuration

```
2 8 3
1 6 4
7   5
```

has an f value equal to $0 + 4 = 4$.

The results of applying **GRAPHSEARCH** to the 8-puzzle using this evaluation function are summarized in Figure 2.8. The value of f for each node is circled; the uncircled numbers show the order in which nodes are

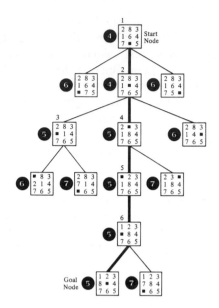

Fig. 2.8 A search tree using an evaluation function.

expanded. We see that the same solution path is found here as was found by the other search methods, although the use of the evaluation function has resulted in substantially fewer nodes being expanded. (If we simply use the evaluation function $f(n) = d(n)$, we get the breadth-first search process.)

The choice of evaluation function critically determines search results. The use of an evaluation function that fails to recognize the true promise of some nodes can result in nonminimal cost paths; whereas, the use of an evaluation function that overestimates the promise of all nodes (such as the evaluation function yielding breadth-first search) results in expansion of too many nodes. In the next few sections, we develop some theoretical results about the performance of **GRAPHSEARCH** when it uses a particular kind of evaluation function.

2.4.2. ALGORITHM A

Let us define the evaluation function f so that its value, $f(n)$, at any node n estimates the sum of the cost of the minimal cost path from the start node s to node n plus the cost of a minimal cost path from node n to a goal node. That is, $f(n)$ is an estimate of the cost of a minimal cost path *constrained to go through node n*. That node on *OPEN* having the smallest value of f is then the node estimated to impose the least severe constraint; hence it is appropriate that it be expanded next.

Before demonstrating some of the properties of this evaluation function, we first introduce some helpful notation. Let the function $k(n_i, n_j)$ give the *actual* cost of a minimal cost path between two arbitrary nodes n_i and n_j. (The function k is undefined for nodes having no path between them.) The cost of a minimal cost path from node n to some particular goal node, t_i, is then given by $k(n, t_i)$. We let $h*(n)$ be the minimum of all of the $k(n, t_i)$ over the entire set of goal nodes $\{t_i\}$. Thus, $h*(n)$ is the cost of the minimal cost path from n to a goal node, and any path from node n to a goal node that achieves $h*(n)$ is an *optimal* path from n to a goal. (The function $h*$ is undefined for any node n that has no accessible goal node.)

Often we are interested in knowing the cost $k(s,n)$ of an optimal path from a given start node, s, to some arbitrary node n. It will simplify our notation somewhat to introduce a new function $g*$ for this purpose. The function $g*$ is defined as

$$g*(n) = k(s,n),$$

for all n accessible from s.

We next define the function $f*$ so that its value $f*(n)$ at any node n is the actual cost of an optimal path from node s to node n plus the cost of an optimal path from node n to a goal node, that is,

$$f*(n) = g*(n) + h*(n).$$

The value of $f*(n)$ is then the cost of an optimal path from s constrained to go through node n. (Note that $f*(s) = h*(s)$ is the actual cost of an unconstrained optimal path from s to a goal.)

We desire our evaluation function f to be an estimate of $f*$. Our estimate can be given by

$$f(n) = g(n) + h(n),$$

where g is an estimate of $g*$ and h is an estimate of $h*$. An obvious choice for $g(n)$ is the cost of the path in the search tree from s to n given by summing the arc costs encountered while tracing the pointers from n to s. (This path is the lowest cost path from s to n found so far by the search algorithm. The value of $g(n)$ for certain nodes may decrease if the search tree is altered in step 7.) Notice that this definition implies $g(n) \geq g^*(n)$. For the estimate $h(n)$, of $h^*(n)$, we rely on heuristic information from the problem domain. Such information might be similar to that used in the function $W(n)$ in the 8-puzzle example. We call h the *heuristic function* and will discuss it in more detail later.

Suppose we now use as an evaluation function

$$f(n) = g(n) + h(n).$$

We call the **GRAPHSEARCH** algorithm using this evaluation function for ordering nodes, *algorithm* **A**. Note that when $h \equiv 0$ and $g \equiv d$ (the depth of a node in the search tree), algorithm **A** is identical to breadth-first search. We claimed earlier that the breadth-first algorithm is guaranteed to find a minimal length path to a goal. We now show that if h is a lower bound on h^* (that is, if $h(n) \leq h^*(n)$ for all nodes n), then algorithm **A** will find an optimal path to a goal. When algorithm **A** uses an h function that is a lower bound on h^*, we call it *algorithm* **A*** (read "A-star"). Since $h \equiv 0$ is certainly a lower bound on h^*, the fact that the breadth-first algorithm finds minimal length paths follows directly as a special case of this more general result for algorithm **A***.

2.4.3. THE ADMISSIBILITY OF A*.

Let us say that a search algorithm is *admissible* if, for any graph, it always terminates in an optimal path from s to a goal node whenever a path from s to a goal node exists. In this section we show informally that **A*** is admissible.

To show that an algorithm is admissible, it is necessary to show, at least, that it terminates whenever a goal node is accessible. The **GRAPH-SEARCH** algorithm terminates (if at all) either in step 3 or in step 5. Notice that in every cycle through the loop of the algorithm, a node is removed from *OPEN* and that only a finite number of new successors are added to *OPEN*. For finite graphs, we ultimately run out of new successors, and thus, unless the algorithm terminates successfully in step 5 by finding a goal node, it will terminate in step 3 after eventually depleting *OPEN*. Therefore,

RESULT 1: **GRAPHSEARCH** always terminates for finite graphs.

Next we would like to show that if a path from s to a goal node exists, **A*** will terminate even for infinite graphs. To do so, let us suppose the opposite, that **A*** does not terminate. Termination is prevented only if new nodes are forever added to *OPEN*. But in this case we can show that even the smallest of the f values of the nodes on *OPEN* will grow impossibly large.

Let $d^*(n)$ be the length of the shortest path in the implicit graph being searched from s to any node n in the search tree produced by **A***. Then since the cost of each arc in the graph is at least some small positive number e, $g^*(n) \geq d^*(n)e$. (Recall that $g^*(n)$ is the cost of the optimal path from s to n, and that $g(n)$ is the cost of the path in the search tree from s to node n.) Clearly, $g(n) \geq g^*(n)$, and thus $g(n) \geq d^*(n)e$. If $h(n) \geq 0$ (which we henceforth assume), $f(n) \geq g(n)$, and thus $f(n) \geq d^*(n)e$. In particular, for every node n on *OPEN*, the value of $f(n)$ is at least as large as $d^*(n)e$. Even though **A*** selects for expansion that node on *OPEN* whose f value is smallest, the node selected will ultimately have an arbitrarily large value of d^* and therefore also of f if **A*** does not terminate.

Now, to show that **A*** must eventually terminate, we show that before termination of **A***, there is always a node n on *OPEN* such that $f(n) \leq f^*(s)$. Let the ordered sequence $(s = n_0, n_1, \ldots, n_k)$, where n_k is a goal node, be an optimal path from s to a goal node. Then, for any time before **A*** terminates, let n' be the first node in this sequence that is on *OPEN*. (There must be at least one such node, because s is on *OPEN* at the beginning and if n_k is on *CLOSED*, **A*** has terminated.) By the definition of f for **A***, we have

$$f(n') = g(n') + h(n') .$$

We know that **A*** has already found an optimal path to n' since n' is on an optimal path to a goal and all of the ancestors on this path are on *CLOSED*. Therefore, $g(n') = g^*(n')$ and

$$f(n') = g^*(n') + h(n') .$$

Since we are assuming $h(n') \leq h^*(n')$, we can write

$$f(n') \leq g^*(n') + h^*(n') = f^*(n') .$$

But the $f*$ value of any node on an optimal path is equal to $f*(s)$, the minimal cost, and therefore $f(n') \leq f*(s)$. Thus, we have:

RESULT 2: At any time before **A*** terminates, there exists on *OPEN* a node n' that is on an optimal path from s to a goal node, with $f(n') \leq f*(s)$.

Combining this result with our previous argument, that even the smallest f values of the nodes on *OPEN* of a nonterminating **A*** become unbounded, shows that **A*** must terminate even for infinite graphs. Thus,

RESULT 3: If there is a path from s to a goal node, **A*** terminates.

RESULT 3 has an interesting corollary, namely, that any node, n, on *OPEN* with $f(n) < f*(s)$ will eventually be selected for expansion by **A***. We leave the proof as an exercise for the reader.

Now it is a simple matter to show that **A*** is admissible. First, we note again that **A*** can either terminate by finding a goal node in step 5 or, after depleting *OPEN*, in step 3. But *OPEN* can never become empty before termination if there is a path from s to a goal node because, by RESULT 2, there will always be a node on *OPEN* (and on an optimal path). Therefore, **A*** must terminate by finding a goal node.

Next we would like to show that **A*** only terminates by finding an optimal path to a goal node. Suppose **A*** were to terminate at some goal node, t, without finding an optimal path, that is, $f(t) = g(t) > f*(s)$. But, by RESULT 2, there existed just before termination a node, n', on *OPEN* and on an optimal path with $f(n') \leq f*(s) < f(t)$. Thus, at this stage, **A*** would have selected n' for expansion rather than t, contradicting our supposition that **A*** terminated. Therefore, we finally have

RESULT 4: Algorithm **A*** is admissible. (That is, if there is a path from s to a goal node, **A*** terminates by finding an optimal path.)

Each node selected for expansion by **A*** has an interesting property that follows directly from RESULT 2: Its f value is never greater than the cost, $f*(s)$, of an optimal path. This result will be important to us later. To show that it is true, let n be any node selected for expansion by **A***. If n

is a goal node, we have $f(n) = f^*(s)$ by RESULT 4; so suppose n is not a goal node. Now **A*** selected n before termination, so at this time (by RESULT 2) we know that there existed on *OPEN* some node n' on an optimal path from s to a goal with $f(n') \leq f^*(s)$. If $n = n'$, our result is established. Otherwise, we know that **A*** chose to expand n rather than n'; therefore it must have been the case that

$$f(n) \leq f(n') \leq f^*(s).$$

Therefore, we have

> **RESULT 5:** For any node n selected for expansion by **A***, $f(n) \leq f^*(s)$.

2.4.4. COMPARISON OF A* ALGORITHMS

The precision of our heuristic function h depends on the amount of heuristic knowledge it possesses about the problem domain. Clearly, using $h(n) \equiv 0$ reflects complete absence of any heuristic information about the problem, even though such an estimate is a lower bound on $h^*(n)$ and therefore leads to an admissible algorithm.

Let us compare two versions of **A***, namely, **A₁** and **A₂** using the following evaluation functions:

$$f_1(n) = g_1(n) + h_1(n)$$

and

$$f_2(n) = g_2(n) + h_2(n)$$

where h_1 and h_2 are both lower bounds on h^*. We say that algorithm **A₂** is *more informed* than algorithm **A₁** if for all nongoal nodes, n, $h_2(n) > h_1(n)$. This definition seems intuitively reasonable, since with h bounded from above by h^* for admissibility, one suspects that using larger values of h (and thus values closer to h^*) requires more accurate heuristic information.

As an example, consider the 8-puzzle solved in Figure 2.8. There we used the evaluation function $f(n) = d(n) + W(n)$. We can interpret the search process of that example as an application of **A*** with

$h(n) = W(n)$ and unit arc costs. (Note that $W(n)$ is a lower bound on the number of steps remaining to the goal.) It is reasonable to say that **A*** with $h(n) = W(n)$ is more informed than breadth-first search, which uses $h(n) \equiv 0$.

We would expect intuitively that the more informed algorithm typically would need to expand fewer nodes to find a minimal cost path. In the case of the 8-puzzle, this observation is supported by comparing Figure 2.7 with Figure 2.8. Of course, merely because one algorithm expands fewer nodes than another does not imply that it is more efficient. The more informed algorithm may indeed have to make more costly computations, which would destroy efficiency. Nevertheless, the number of nodes expanded by an algorithm is one of the factors that determines efficiency, and it is a factor that permits simple comparisons.

Suppose that $\mathbf{A_2}$ is more informed than $\mathbf{A_1}$ and that both $\mathbf{A_1}$ and $\mathbf{A_2}$ are versions of **A***. Suppose that $\mathbf{A_1}$ and $\mathbf{A_2}$ are used to search an implicit graph having a path from a given node s to a goal node. Both, of course, will terminate in an optimal path. We will show that, at termination, if node n in G was expanded by $\mathbf{A_2}$, it was also expanded by $\mathbf{A_1}$. Thus, $\mathbf{A_1}$ always expands at least as many nodes as does the more informed $\mathbf{A_2}$.

We prove this result using induction on the depth of a node in the $\mathbf{A_2}$ search tree at termination. First, we prove that if $\mathbf{A_2}$ expands a node n having zero depth in its search tree, then so will $\mathbf{A_1}$. But, in this case, $n = s$. If s is a goal node, neither algorithm expands any nodes. If s is not a goal node, both algorithms expand node s. Continuing the inductive argument, we assume (the induction hypothesis) that $\mathbf{A_1}$ expands all the nodes expanded by $\mathbf{A_2}$ having depth k, or less, in the $\mathbf{A_2}$ search tree. We must now prove that any node n expanded by $\mathbf{A_2}$ and of depth $k + 1$ in the $\mathbf{A_2}$ search tree is also expanded by $\mathbf{A_1}$. By the induction hypothesis, any ancestor of n in the $\mathbf{A_2}$ search tree is also expanded by $\mathbf{A_1}$. Thus, node n is in the $\mathbf{A_1}$ search tree and there is a path from s to n in the $\mathbf{A_1}$ search tree that is no more costly than the cost of the path from s to n in the $\mathbf{A_2}$ search tree; that is,

$$g_1(n) \le g_2(n).$$

Let us suppose the opposite of what we are trying to prove, namely, that $\mathbf{A_1}$ did not expand node n expanded by $\mathbf{A_2}$. Certainly, at termination of $\mathbf{A_1}$, node n must be on *OPEN* for $\mathbf{A_1}$, because $\mathbf{A_1}$ expanded a parent of node n. Since $\mathbf{A_1}$ terminated in a minimal cost path without expanding node n, we know that

$$f_1(n) \geq f^*(s),$$

thus,

$$g_1(n) + h_1(n) \geq f^*(s).$$

Since we have already shown that $g_1(n) \leq g_2(n)$, we have

$$h_1(n) \geq f^*(s) - g_2(n).$$

But, by RESULT 5, since A_2 expanded node n, we have

$$f_2(n) \leq f^*(s)$$

or

$$g_2(n) + h_2(n) \leq f^*(s)$$

or

$$h_2(n) \leq f^*(s) - g_2(n).$$

Comparing this inequality for $h_2(n)$ with the earlier one for $h_1(n)$ (i.e., $h_1(n) \geq f^*(s) - g_2(n)$) reveals that, at least at node n, h_1 must be as large as h_2, which violates the assumption that A_2 is more informed than A_1. Thus, we have

> **RESULT 6**: If A_1 and A_2 are two versions of **A*** such that A_2 is more informed than A_1, then at the termination of their searches on any graph having a path from s to a goal node, every node expanded by A_2 is also expanded by A_1. It follows that A_1 expands at least as many nodes as does A_2.

2.4.5. THE MONOTONE RESTRICTION

Describing the **GRAPHSEARCH** procedure, we noted that when a node n is expanded, some of its successors may already be on *OPEN* or *CLOSED*. The search tree may then need to be adjusted so that it defines the least costly paths in G from node s to the descendants of node n. In addition to the burden of adjusting the search tree, it is often computationally quite expensive to test whether a node has been generated before. We now show that given a rather mild and reasonable restriction on h, when **A*** selects a node for expansion it has already found an optimal path to that node. Thus, with this restriction, there is no need for **A*** to test to see if a newly generated node is already on *CLOSED*, and there is no need to change the parentage in the search tree of any successors of this node in the search graph.

A heuristic function, h, is said to satisfy the *monotone restriction* if for all nodes n_i and n_j, such that n_j is a successor of n_i,

$$h(n_i) - h(n_j) \le c(n_i, n_j)$$

with

$$h(t) = 0 .$$

If we write the monotone restriction in the form

$$h(n_i) \le h(n_j) + c(n_i, n_j),$$

it is seen to be similar to a triangle inequality. It specifies that the estimate of the optimal cost to a goal from node n_i not be more than the cost of the arc from n_i to n_j plus the estimate of the optimal cost from n_j to a goal. We might say that the monotone restriction imposes the rather reasonable condition that the heuristic function be locally consistent with the arc costs.

In the 8-puzzle, it is easily verified that $h(n) = W(n)$ satisfies the monotone restriction. If the function h is changed in any manner *during* the search process, then the monotone restriction might not be satisfied.

We now show that, given the monotone restriction, when **A*** expands a node, it has found an optimal path to that node. Let n be any node selected for expansion by **A***. If $n = s$, **A*** has trivially found an optimal path to s; so let us suppose that n is not s. Let the sequence $P = (s = n_0, n_1, n_2, \ldots, n_k = n)$ be an optimal path from s to n. Let node n_l be the last node in this sequence that is on *CLOSED* at the time **A*** selects n for expansion. (Node s is on *CLOSED*, but node n_k is not, because it is just now being selected for expansion.) Thus, node n_{l+1} in the sequence P is on *OPEN* at the time **A*** selects node n.

Using the monotone restriction, we have that

$$g*(n_i) + h(n_i) \leq g*(n_i) + c(n_i, n_{i+1}) + h(n_{i+1}).$$

Since n_i and n_{i+1} are on an optimal path

$$g*(n_{i+1}) = g*(n_i) + c(n_i, n_{i+1}),$$

therefore

$$[g*(n_i) + h(n_i)] \leq [g*(n_{i+1}) + h(n_{i+1})].$$

By transitivity, we then have

$$g*(n_{l+1}) + h(n_{l+1}) \leq g*(n_k) + h(n_k)$$

or

$$f(n_{l+1}) \leq g*(n) + h(n).$$

Therefore, at the time **A*** selected node n, in preference to node n_{l+1}, it must have been the case that $g(n) \leq g*(n)$; otherwise, $f(n)$ would have been greater than $f(n_{l+1})$. Since $g(m) \geq g*(m)$ for all nodes m in the search tree, we have

> **RESULT 7:** If the monotone restriction is satisfied, then **A*** has already found an optimal path to any node it selects for expansion. That is, if **A*** selects n for expansion, and if the monotone restriction is satisfied, $g(n) = g*(n)$.

The monotone restriction also implies another interesting result, namely, that the f values of the sequence of nodes expanded by **A*** are nondecreasing. Suppose node n_2 is expanded immediately after node n_1. If n_2 was on *OPEN* at the time n_1 was expanded, we have (trivially) that $f(n_1) \leq f(n_2)$. Suppose n_2 is not on *OPEN* at the time n_1 is expanded. (Node n_2 is not on *CLOSED* either, because we are assuming that it has not been expanded yet.) Then, if n_2 is expanded immediately after n_1, it must have been added to *OPEN* by the process of expanding n_1. Therefore, n_2 is a successor of n_1. Under these conditions, when n_2 is selected for expansion we have

$$f(n_2) = g(n_2) + h(n_2)$$

$$= g^*(n_2) + h(n_2) \quad \text{(RESULT 7)}$$

$$= g^*(n_1) + c(n_1,n_2) + h(n_2)$$

$$= g(n_1) + c(n_1,n_2) + h(n_2)$$
(RESULT 7)

Since the monotone restriction implies

$$c(n_1,n_2) + h(n_2) \geq + h(n_1),$$

we have

$$f(n_2) \geq g(n_1) + h(n_1) = f(n_1).$$

Since this fact is true for any adjacent pair of nodes in the sequence of nodes expanded by **A***, we have

> **RESULT 8**: If the monotone restriction is satisfied, the f values of the sequence of nodes expanded by **A*** is nondecreasing.

When the monotone restriction is not satisfied, it is possible that some node has a smaller f value at expansion than that of a previously expanded node. We can exploit this observation to improve the efficiency of **A*** under this condition. By RESULT 5, when node n is expanded, $f(n) \leq f^*(s)$. Suppose, during the execution of **A***, we maintain a global variable, F, as the maximum of the f values of all nodes so far expanded. Certainly $F \leq f^*(s)$ at all times. If ever a node, n, on *OPEN* has $f(n) < F$, we know by the corollary to RESULT 3 that it will eventually be expanded. In fact, there may be several nodes on *OPEN* whose f values are strictly less than F. Rather than choose, from these, that node with the smallest f value, we might rather choose that node with the smallest g value. (All of them must eventually be expanded anyway.)

The effect of this altered node selection rule is to enhance the chances that the first path discovered to a node will be an optimal path. Thus, even when the monotone restriction is not satisfied, this alteration will diminish the need for pointer redirection in step 7 of the algorithm. (Note that when the monotone restriction is satisfied, RESULT 8 implies that there will never be a node on *OPEN* whose f value is less than F.)

84

2.4.6. THE HEURISTIC POWER OF EVALUATION FUNCTIONS

The selection of the heuristic function is crucial in determining the heuristic power of search algorithm **A**. Using $h \equiv 0$ assures admissibility but results in a breadth-first search and is thus usually inefficient. Setting h equal to the highest possible lower bound on h^* expands the fewest nodes consistent with maintaining admissibility.

Often, heuristic power can be gained at the expense of admissibility by using some function for h that is not a lower bound on h^*. This added heuristic power then allows us to solve much harder problems. In the 8-puzzle, the function $h(n) = W(n)$ (where $W(n)$ is the number of tiles in the wrong place) is a lower bound on $h^*(n)$, but it does not provide a very good estimate of the difficulty (in terms of number of steps to the goal) of a tile configuration. A better estimate is the function $h(n) = P(n)$, where $P(n)$ is the sum of the distances that each tile is from "home" (ignoring intervening pieces). Even this estimate is too coarse, however, in that it does not accurately appraise the difficulty of exchanging the positions of two adjacent tiles.

An estimate that works quite well for the 8-puzzle is

$$h(n) = P(n) + 3S(n).$$

The quantity $S(n)$ is a *sequence score* obtained by checking around the noncentral squares in turn, allotting 2 for every tile not followed by its proper successor and allotting 0 for every other tile; a piece in the center scores one. We note that this h function does not provide a lower bound for h^*. With this heuristic function used in the evaluation function $f(n) = g(n) + h(n)$, we can easily solve much more difficult 8-puzzles than the one we solved earlier. In Figure 2.9 we show the search tree resulting from applying **GRAPHSEARCH** with this evaluation function to the problem of transforming

```
2 1 6
4   8
7 5 3
```

into

```
1 2 3
8   4
7 6 5
```

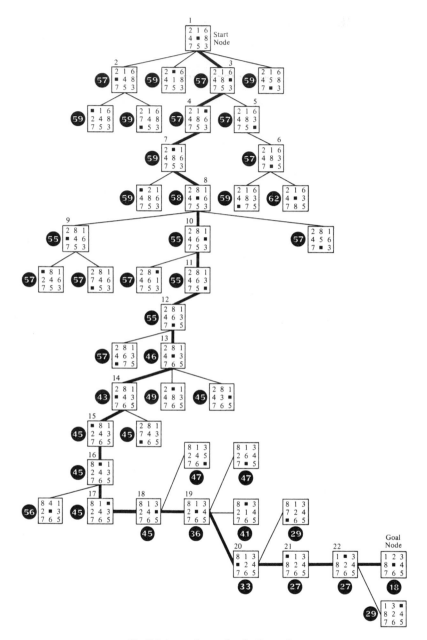

Fig. 2.9 A search tree for the 8-puzzle.

Again, the f values of each node are circled in the figure, and the uncircled numbers show the order in which nodes are expanded. (In the search depicted in Figure 2.9, ties among minimal f values are resolved by selecting the deepest node in the search tree.)

The solution path found happens to be of minimal length (18 steps); although, since the h function is not a lower bound for $h*$, we were not guaranteed of finding an optimal path. Note that this h function results in a focused search, directed toward the goal; only a very limited spread occurred, near the start.

Another factor that determines the heuristic power of search algorithms is the amount of effort involved in calculating the heuristic function. The best function would be one identically equal to $h*$, resulting in an absolute minimum number of node expansions. (Such an h could, for example, be determined as a result of a separate complete search at every node; but this obviously would not reduce the total computational effort.) Sometimes an h function that is not a lower bound on $h*$ is easier to compute than one that is a lower bound. In these cases, the heuristic power might be doubly improved—because the total number of nodes expanded can be reduced (at the expense of admissibility) and because the computational effort is reduced.

In certain cases the heuristic power of a given heuristic function can be increased simply by multiplying it by some positive constant greater than one. If this constant is very large, the situation is as if $g(n) \equiv 0$. In many problems we merely desire to find *some* path to a goal node and are unconcerned about the cost of the resulting path. (We are, of course, concerned about the amount of search effort required to find a path.) In such situations, we might think that g could be ignored completely since, at any stage during the search, we don't care about the costs of the paths developed thus far. We care only about the remaining seach effort required to find a goal node. This search effort, while possibly dependent on the h values of the nodes on *OPEN*, would seem to be independent of the g values of these nodes. Therefore, for such problems, we might be led to use $f \equiv h$ as the evaluation function.

To ensure that *some* path to a goal will eventually be found, g should be included in f even when it is not essential to find a path of minimal cost. Such insurance is necessary whenever h is not a perfect estimator; if the node with minimum h were always expanded, the search process might expand deceptive nodes forever without ever reaching a goal node.

Including g tends to add a breadth-first component to the search and thus ensures that no part of the implicit graph will go permanently unsearched.

The relative weights of g and h in the evaluation function can be controlled by using $f = g + wh$, where w is a positive number. Very large values of w overemphasize the heuristic component, while very small values of w give the search a predominantly breadth-first character. Experimental evidence suggests that search efficiency is often enhanced by allowing the value of w to vary inversely with the depth of a node in the search tree. At shallow depths, the search relies mainly on the heuristic component, while at greater depths, the search becomes increasingly breadth-first, to ensure that some path to a goal will eventually be found.

To summarize, there are three important factors influencing the heuristic power of Algorithm **A**:

(a)   the cost of the path,

(b)   the number of nodes expanded in finding the path, and

(c)   the computational effort required to compute h.

The selection of a suitable heuristic function permits one to balance these factors to maximize heuristic power.

2.5.   RELATED ALGORITHMS

2.5.1.   BIDIRECTIONAL SEARCH

Some problems can be solved using production systems whose rules can be used in either a forward or a backward direction. An interesting possibility is to search in both directions simultaneously. The graph-searching process that models such a bidirectional production system can be viewed as one in which search proceeds outward simultaneously from both the start node and from a set of goal nodes. The process terminates when (and if) the two search frontiers meet in some appropriate fashion.

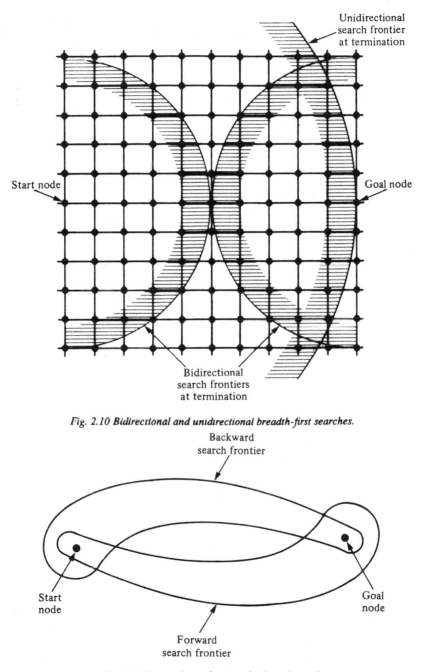

Unidirectional
search frontier
at termination

Start node

Goal node

Bidirectional
search frontiers
at termination

Fig. 2.10 Bidirectional and unidirectional breadth-first searches.

Backward
search frontier

Start
node

Goal
node

Forward
search frontier

Fig. 2.11 Forward search misses backward search.

Breadth-first versions of bidirectional graph-searching processes compare favorably with breadth-first unidirectional search. In Figure 2.10 we compare two searches over a two-dimensional grid of nodes. We see that the bidirectional process expands many fewer nodes than does the unidirectional one.

The situation is more complex, however, when comparing bidirectional and unidirectional *heuristic* searches. If the heuristic functions used by the bidirectional process are even slightly inaccurate, the search frontiers may pass each other without intersecting. In such a case, the bidirectional search process may expand twice as many nodes as would the unidirectional one. This situation is illustrated in Figure 2.11.

2.5.2. STAGED SEARCH

The use of heuristic information as discussed so far can substantially reduce the amount of search effort required to find acceptable paths. Its use, therefore, also allows much larger graphs to be searched than would be the case otherwise. Even so, occasions may arise when available storage is exhausted before a satisfactory path is found. Rather than abandon the search process completely, in such cases, it may be desirable to prune the search graph, to free needed storage space to press the search deeper.

The search process can then continue in stages, punctuated by pruning operations obtaining storage space. At the end of each stage, some subset of the nodes on *OPEN*, for example those having the smallest values of f, are marked for retention. The best paths to these nodes are remembered, and the rest of the search graph is thrown away. Search then resumes with these best nodes. This process continues until either a goal node is found or until resources are exhausted. Of course, even if **A*** is used in each stage and if the whole process does terminate in a path, there is now no guarantee that it is an optimal path.

2.5.3. LIMITATION OF SUCCESSORS

One technique that may save search effort is the disposal immediately after expansion of all successors except a few having the smallest values of f. Of course the nodes thrown away may be on the best (or the only!) paths to a goal, so the worth of any such pruning method for a particular problem can be determined only by experience.

90

Knowledge about the problem domain may sometimes be adequate to recognize that certain nodes cannot possibly be on a path to a goal node. (Such nodes satisfy a predicate like the **DEADEND** predicate used in the backtracking algorithm.) These nodes can be pruned from the search graph by modifying algorithm **A** to include this test. Alternatively, we could assign such nodes a very high h value so that they would never be selected for expansion.

There are also search problems for which the successors of a node can be enumerated and their h values computed before the corresponding databases themselves are explicitly calculated. Furthermore, it may be advantageous to delay calculating the database associated with a node until it itself is expanded; then the process never calculates any successors not expanded by the algorithm.

2.6. MEASURES OF PERFORMANCE

The heuristic power of a searching technique depends heavily on the particular factors specific to a given problem. Estimating heuristic power involves judgements, based on experience rather than calculation. Certain measures of performance can be calculated, however, and though they do not completely determine heuristic power, they are useful in comparing various search techniques.

One such measure is called *penetrance*. The penetrance, P, of a search is the extent to which the search has focused toward a goal, rather than wandered off in irrelevant directions. It is simply defined as

$$P = L/T,$$

where L is the length of the path found to the goal and T is the total number of nodes generated during the search (including the goal node but not including the start node). For example, if the successor operator is so precise that the only nodes generated are those on a path toward the goal, P will attain its maximum value of 1. Uninformed search is characterized by values of P much less than 1. Thus, penetrance measures the extent to which the tree generated by the search is "elongated" rather than "bushy."

The penetrance value of a search depends on the difficulty of the problem being searched as well as on the efficiency of the search method. A given search method might have a high penetrance value when the optimal solution path is short and a much lower one when it is long. (Increasing the length of the solution path L usually causes T to increase even faster.)

Another measure, the *effective branching factor, B,* is more nearly independent of the length of the optimal solution path. Its definition is based on a tree having (a) a depth equal to the path length and (b) a total number of nodes equal to the number generated during the search. The effective branching factor is the constant number of successors that would be possessed by each node in such a tree. Therefore, B is related to path length L and to the total number of nodes generated, T, by the expressions:

$$B + B^2 + \ldots + B^L = T$$

$$[B^L - 1]B/(B - 1) = T.$$

Although B cannot be written explicitly as a function of L and T, a plot of B versus T for various values of L is given in Figure 2.12. A value of B near unity corresponds to a search that is highly focused toward the goal, with very little branching in other directions. On the other hand, a "bushy" search graph would have a high B value. Penetrance can be related to B and path length by the expression $P = L(B - 1)/B[B^L - 1]$. In Figure 2.13 we illustrate how penetrance varies with path length for various values of B.

To the extent that the effective branching factor is reasonably independent of path length, it can be used to give a prediction of how many nodes might be generated in searches of various lengths. For example, we can use Figure 2.12 to calculate that the use of the evaluation function $f = g + P + 3S$ results in a B value equal to 1.08 for the 8-puzzle problem illustrated in Figure 2.9. Suppose we wanted to estimate how many nodes would be generated using this same evaluation function in solving a more difficult 8-puzzle problem, say, one requiring 30 steps. From Figure 2.12, we note that the 30-step puzzle would involve the generation of about 120 nodes, assuming that the branching factor remained constant. This estimate, incidentally, is not inconsistent with the experimental results of Doran and Michie (1966) on a wide variety of 8-puzzle problems.

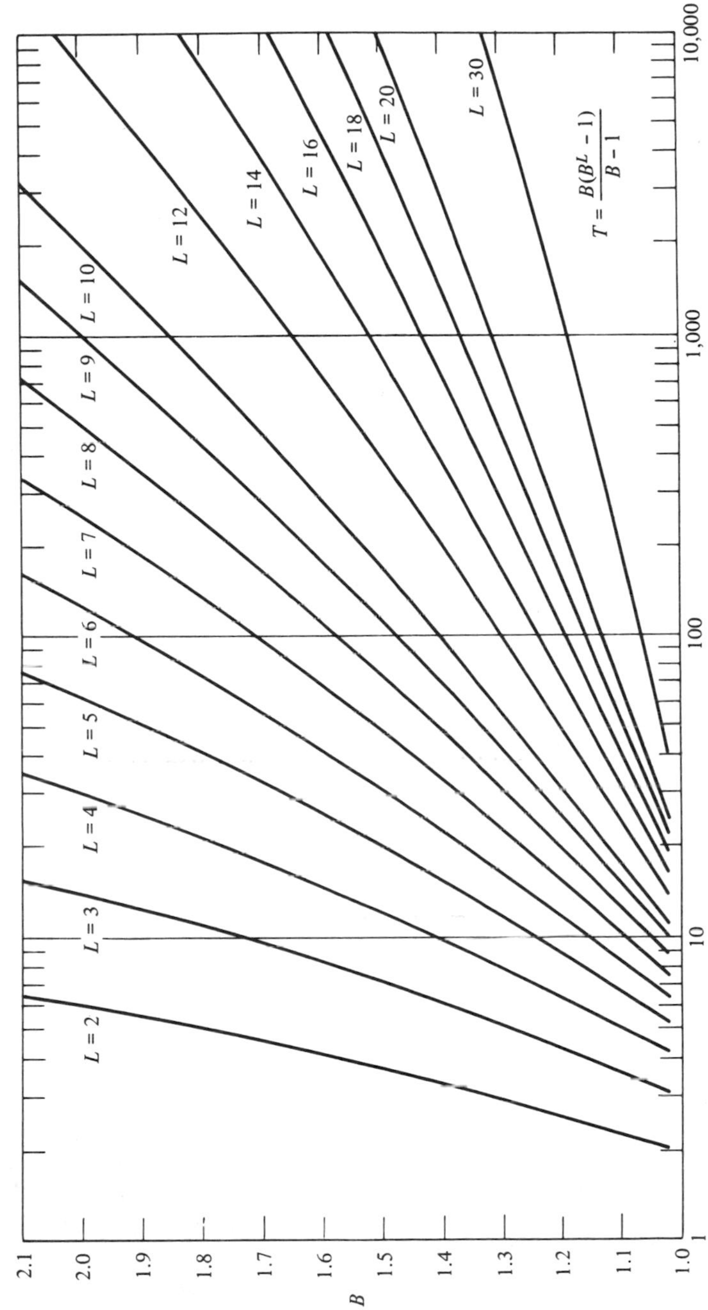

Fig. 2.12 B versus T for various values of L.

The figure shows lines labeled:
$L = 2$, $L = 3$, $L = 4$, $L = 5$, $L = 6$, $L = 7$, $L = 8$, $L = 9$, $L = 10$, $L = 12$, $L = 14$, $L = 16$, $L = 18$, $L = 20$, $L = 30$

$$T = \frac{B(B^L - 1)}{B - 1}$$

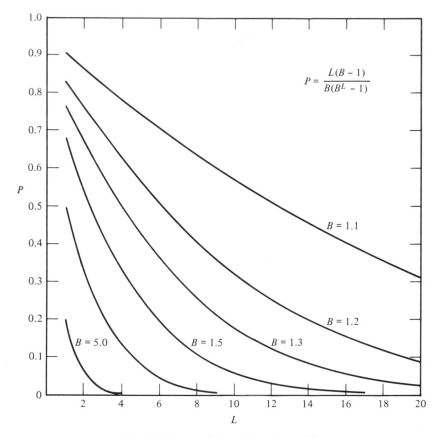

Fig. 2.13 P versus L for various values of B.

2.7. BIBLIOGRAPHICAL AND HISTORICAL REMARKS

The book by Horowitz and Sahni (1978) contains a thorough discussion of backtracking and other search methods. Gaschnig (1979) presents experimental efficiency comparisons of backtracking and related algorithms. In some problems involving constraint satisfaction, relaxation techniques can be employed to reduce search effort; these methods are discussed by Waltz (1975), Montanari (1974), and Mackworth (1977).

Graph-search procedures of the sort that we termed *uninformed* have arisen in a variety of contexts. Dijkstra (1959) and Moore (1959) both proposed essentially breadth-first procedures. Dynamic programming [Bellman and Dreyfus (1962)] is a type of breadth-first search process. Our **GRAPHSEARCH** procedure differs from many previous ones in that we do not transfer nodes from *CLOSED* back to *OPEN* when they are revisited. [We redirect pointers in the search tree instead.]

The use of heuristic information to increase search efficiency has been studied both in AI and in operations research. In AI, heuristic search was a main theme of the work of Newell, Shaw, and Simon (1957, 1960). The use of evaluation functions to direct search in graphs was proposed by Doran and Michie (1966), from whom we take our 8-puzzle examples.

A general theory of the use of evaluation functions to guide search was presented in a paper by Hart, Nilsson, and Raphael (1968). Our description of A* and its properties is based on that paper. [The fact that A* expands no more nodes than other algorithms that are no more informed than A* was originally mistakenly thought to depend on a restriction similar to the monotone restriction. This error, originally pointed out by R. Coleman, was corrected in Hart, Nilsson, and Raphael (1972). Corrections and refinements were also proposed by Gelperin (1977).] VanderBrug (1976) presents an interesting geometric interpretation of heuristic search processes.

Pohl has proposed several generalizations of A*, including a scheme for bidirectional search [Pohl (1971)], and a method that changes the relative weighting of h and g as search proceeds [Pohl (1973)]. Our use of the *monotone restriction* is based on Pohl (1977). (The earlier *consistency restriction*, of Hart, Nilsson, and Raphael, is stronger than needed and harder to establish than the monotone restriction.) Pohl (1970,1977) and Harris (1974) analyze some of the effects of errors in the heuristic function on search, and Martelli (1977) analyzes the complexity of heuristic search algorithms. [The node selection rule described on page 84 is based on Martelli's paper.] Simon and Kadane (1975) describe search methods designed to find *any* solution rather than insisting on optimal solutions. Michie and Ross (1970) describe a heuristic search process that generates just one successor at a time.

The *staged search* variant was investigated by Doran and Michie (1966) and by Doran (1967). A process involving staged search has been used rather effectively in systems for speech understanding [Lowerre (1976)] and visual scene interpretation [Rubin (1978)]. Jackson (1974, pp. 104) discusses an application to the 15-puzzle (by A. K. Chandra) of an interesting search process that uses "mileposts."

Doran and Michie (1966) proposed the penetrance measure for judging the efficiency of a given search. Slagle and Dixon (1969) proposed another measure that they called the "depth ratio." Our "effective branching factor" was motivated by these earlier measures.

Heuristic search finds many applications, sometimes outside of the context of conventional AI systems. Montanari (1970) makes use of heuristic search in chromosome matching, and Kanal (1979) discusses an application in pattern classification.

EXERCISES

2.1 Consider a sliding block puzzle with the following initial configuration:

B	B	B	W	W	W	E

there are three black tiles (B), three white tiles (W), and an empty cell (E). The puzzle has the following moves:

> (a) A tile may move into an adjacent empty cell with unit cost.

> (b) A tile may hop over at most two other tiles into an empty cell with a cost equal to the number of tiles hopped over.

The goal of the puzzle is to have all of the white tiles to the left of all of the black tiles (without regard for the position of the blank cell).

Specify a heuristic function, h, for this problem and show the search tree produced by algorithm **A** using this heuristic function. Can you tell whether or not your h function satisfies the monotone restriction? Does it satisfy the monotone restriction for the nodes in your search tree?

2.2 Propose two (non-zero) h functions for the traveling salesman problem of section 1.1.6. Is either of these h functions a lower bound on h^*? In your opinion, which of them would result in more efficient search? Apply algorithm **A** with these h functions to the five-city problem shown in Figure 1.5.

2.3 Assume unit costs for each rule application in the formulation of the 4-queens problem of section 2.1. Describe the general characteristics of the h^* function for this problem. Can you think of any h functions that would be useful for guiding search?

2.4 Describe how to modify procedure **GRAPHSEARCH** so that only one successor of a node (at a time) is generated in step 6. The modified procedure must make two selections: which node to expand and which successor to generate. (In controlling a production system, the modified procedure must select a database and an applicable rule.)

2.5 Prove, as a corollary to RESULT 3, that any node, n, on $OPEN$ with $f(n) < f^*(s)$, will eventually be selected for expansion by **A***.

2.6 Explain why algorithm **A*** remains admissible if it removes from $OPEN$ any node n for which $f(n) > F$, where F is an upper bound on $f^*(s)$.

2.7 Use the evaluation function $f(n) = d(n) + W(n)$ (defined in section 2.4.2.) with algorithm **A** to search backward from the goal node of Figure 2.8 to the start node. Where would the backward search meet the forward search?

2.8 Discuss ways in which an h function might be improved *during* a search.

CHAPTER 3

SEARCH STRATEGIES FOR DECOMPOSABLE PRODUCTION SYSTEMS

In chapter 1, we introduced decomposable production systems and structures called AND/OR trees, for controlling their operation. In this chapter we describe some heuristic strategies for searching AND/OR trees and graphs. We also describe some search techniques for graphs used in game-playing systems.

3.1. SEARCHING AND/OR GRAPHS

Recall that the *AND* or the *OR* label given to a node in an AND/OR tree depends upon that node's relation to its parent. In one case, a parent node labeled by a compound database has a set of AND successor nodes, each labeling one of the component databases. In the other case, a parent node labeled by a component database has a set of OR successor nodes, each labeling the database resulting from the application of alternative rules to the component database.

We are generally concerned with AND/OR graphs rather than with the special case of trees, because different sequences of rule applications may generate identical databases. For example, a node could be labeled by a component database resulting both from having split a compound one and from having applied a rule to another one. In this case, it would be called an OR node with respect to one parent and an AND node with respect to the other parent. For this reason, we do not generally refer to the nodes of an AND/OR graph as being AND nodes or OR nodes;

instead, we introduce some more general notation, appropriate for graphs. We continue to call these structures AND/OR graphs, however, and use the terms AND nodes and OR nodes when discussing AND/OR trees.

We define AND/OR graphs here as *hypergraphs*. Instead of arcs connecting *pairs* of nodes, there are *hyperarcs* connecting a parent node with a *set* of successor nodes. These hyperarcs are called *connectors*. Each *k-connector* is directed from a *parent* node to a set of *k successor* nodes. (If all of the connectors are 1-connectors, we have the special case of an ordinary graph.)

In Figure 3.1, we show an example of an AND/OR graph. Note that node n_0 has a 1-connector directed to successor n_1 and a 2-connector directed to the set of successors $\{n_4, n_5\}$. For $k > 1$, k-connectors are denoted in our illustrations by a curved line joining the arcs from parent to elements of the successor set. (Using our earlier terminology, we could have regarded nodes n_4 and n_5 as a set of AND nodes, and we could have regarded node n_1 as an OR node, relative to their common parent n_0; but note that node n_8, for example, belongs to a set of AND nodes relative to its parent n_5 but is an OR node relative to its parent n_4.)

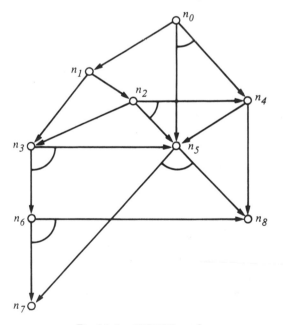

Fig. 3.1 An AND/OR graph.

In an AND/OR tree, each node has at most one parent. In trees and graphs we call a node without any parent a *root* node. In graphs, we call a node having no successors a *leaf node* (a *tip* node for trees).

A decomposable production system defines an implicit AND/OR graph. The initial database corresponds to a distinguished node in the graph called the *start node*. The start node has an outgoing connector to a set of successor nodes corresponding to the components of the initial database (if it can be decomposed). Each production rule corresponds to a connector in the implicit graph. The nodes to which such a connector is directed correspond to component databases resulting after rule application and decomposition into components. There is a set of *terminal* nodes in the implicit graph corresponding to databases satisfying the termination condition of the production system. The task of the production system can be regarded as finding a *solution graph* from the start node to the terminal nodes.

Roughly speaking, a solution graph from node n to node set N of an AND/OR graph is analogous to a path in an ordinary graph. It can be obtained by starting with node n and selecting exactly one outgoing connector. From each successor node to which this connector is directed, we continue to select one outgoing connector, and so on, until eventually every successor thus produced is an element of the set N. In Figure 3.2, we show two different solution graphs from node n_0 to $\{n_7, n_8\}$ in the graph of Figure 3.1.

We can give a precise recursive definition of a solution graph. The definition assumes that our AND/OR graphs contain no cycles, that is, it assumes that there is no node in the graph having a successor that is also its ancestor. The nodes thus form a partial order which guarantees termination of the recursive procedures we use. We henceforth make this assumption of acyclicity.

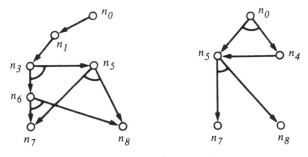

Fig. 3.2 Two solution graphs.

101

Let G' denote a solution graph from node n to a set N of nodes of an AND/OR graph G. G' is a subgraph of G.

If n is an element of N, G' consists of the single node n;

otherwise, if n has an outgoing connector, K, directed to nodes $\{n_1,\ldots,n_k\}$ such that there is a solution graph to N from each of n_i, where $i = 1,\ldots,k$, then G' consists of node n, the connector, K, the nodes $\{n_1,\ldots,n_k\}$, and the solution graphs to N from each of the nodes in $\{n_1,\ldots,n_k\}$;

otherwise, there is no solution graph from n to N.

Analogous to the use of arc costs in ordinary graphs, it is often useful to assign costs to connectors in AND/OR graphs. (These costs model the costs of rule applications; again we need to assume that each cost is greater than some small positive number, e.) The connector costs can then be used to calculate the cost of a solution graph. Let the cost of a solution graph from any node n to N be denoted by $k(n,N)$. The cost $k(n,N)$ can be recursively calculated as follows:

If n is an element of N, $k(n,N) = 0$.

Otherwise, n has an outgoing connector to a set of successor nodes $\{n_1,\ldots,n_i\}$ in the solution graph. Let the cost of this connector be c_n. Then,

$$k(n,N) = c_n + k(n_1,N) + \ldots + k(n_i,N).$$

We see that the cost of a solution graph, G', from n to N is the cost of the outgoing connector from n (in G') plus the sum of the costs of the solution graphs from the successors of n (in G') to N. This recursive definition is satisfactory because we are assuming acyclic graphs.

Note that our definition of the cost of a solution graph might count the costs of some connectors in the solution graph more than once. In general, the cost of an outgoing connector from some node m is counted in the cost of a solution graph from n to N just as many times as there are paths from n to m in the solution graph. Thus, the costs of the two solution graphs in Figure 3.2 are 8 and 7 if the cost of each k-connector is k.

Beyond merely finding *any* solution graph from the start node to a set of terminal nodes, we may want to find one having minimal cost. We call such a solution graph an *optimal* solution graph. Let the cost of an optimal solution graph from n to a set of terminal nodes be denoted by the function $h^*(n)$.

3.2. AO*: A HEURISTIC SEARCH PROCEDURE FOR AND/OR GRAPHS

As with ordinary graphs, we define the process of *expanding* a node as the application of a successor operator that generates *all* of the successors of a node (through all outgoing connectors). We might now define a breadth-first search algorithm for searching implicit AND/OR graphs to find solution graphs. Again, since breadth-first procedures are uninformed about the problem domain, they are typically not sufficiently efficient for AI applications. We are naturally led to ask whether some search procedure using an evaluation function with a heuristic component can be devised for AND/OR graphs.

We now describe a search procedure that uses a heuristic function $h(n)$ that is an estimate of $h^*(n)$, the cost of an optimal solution graph from node n to a set of terminal nodes. Just as with **GRAPHSEARCH**, simplifications in the statement of the procedure are possible if h satisfies certain restrictions.

Let us impose a monotone restriction on h, that is, for every connector in the implicit graph directed from node n to successors $n_1, \ldots, n_k$, we assume:

$$h(n) \leq c + h(n_1) + \ldots + h(n_k),$$

where c is the cost of the connector. This restriction is analogous to the monotone restriction on heuristic functions for ordinary graphs. If $h(n) = 0$ for n in the set of terminal nodes, then the monotone restriction implies that h is a lower bound on h^*, that is, $h(n) \leq h^*(n)$ for all nodes n.

Our heuristic search procedure for AND/OR graphs can now be stated as follows:

Procedure **AO***

1   Create a search graph, G, consisting solely of the start node, s. Associate with node s a cost $q(s) = h(s)$.
If s is a terminal node, label s *SOLVED*.

2 **until** s is labeled *SOLVED*, **do:**

3 **begin**

4   Compute a *partial* solution graph, G', in G by tracing down the *marked* connectors in G from s. (Connectors of G will be marked in a subsequent step.)

5 **select** any nonterminal leaf node, n, of G'. (We discuss later how this selection might be made.)

6   Expand node n generating all of its successors and install these in G as successors of n. For each successor, n_j, not already occurring in G, associate the cost $q(n_j) = h(n_j)$.
Label *SOLVED* any of these successors that are terminal nodes. (See text for discussion of what to do in case node n has no successors.)

7   Create a singleton set of nodes, S, containing just node n.

8 **until** S is empty, **do:**

9   **begin**

10   Remove from S a node m such that m has no descendants in G occurring in S.

11   Revise the cost $q(m)$ for m, as follows:
for each connector directed from m to a
set of nodes $\{n_{1i}, \ldots, n_{ki}\}$
compute $q_i(m) = c_i + q(n_{1i}) + \ldots$
$+ q(n_{ki})$. [The $q(n_{ji})$ have
either just been computed in a
previous pass through this inner loop
or (if this is the first pass) they were
computed in step 6.]
Set $q(m)$ to the minimum over all
outgoing connectors of $q_i(m)$ and
mark the connector through which this
minimum is achieved, erasing the previous
marking if different. If all of the
successor nodes through this connector
are labeled *SOLVED*, then label node m
SOLVED.

12   If m has been marked *SOLVED* or if the
revised cost of m is different than its
just previous cost, then add to S all
those parents of m such that m is one
of their successors through a marked
connector.

13   **end**

14   **end**

Algorithm **AO*** can best be understood as a repetition of the following two major operations. First, a top-down, graph-growing operation (steps 4-6) finds the best partial solution graph by tracing down through the marked connectors. These (previously computed) marks indicate the current best partial solution graph from each node in the search graph. (Before the algorithm terminates, the best partial solution graph does not yet have all of its leaf nodes terminal, which is why it is called *partial*.) One of the nonterminal leaf nodes of this best partial solution graph is expanded, and a cost is assigned to its successors.

The second major operation in **AO*** is a bottom-up, cost-revising, connector-marking, *SOLVE*-labeling procedure (steps 7-12). Starting with the node just expanded, the procedure revises its cost (using the newly computed costs of its successors) and marks the outgoing connector on the estimated best "path" to terminal nodes. This revised cost estimate is propagated upward in the graph. (Acyclicity of our graphs guarantees no loops in this upward propagation.) The revised cost, $q(n)$, is an updated estimate of the cost of an optimal solution graph from n to a set of terminal nodes. Only the ancestors of nodes having their costs revised can possibly have their costs revised, so only these need be considered. Because we are assuming the monotone restriction on h, cost revisions can only be cost increases. Therefore, not all ancestors need have cost revisions, but only those ancestors having best partial solution graphs containing descendants with revised costs (hence step 12).

When the AND/OR graph is an AND/OR tree, the bottom-up operation can be simplified somewhat (because then each node has only one parent).

To avoid making algorithm **AO*** appear more complex than it already does, we ignored the possibility (in step 6) that the node selected for expansion might not have any successors. This case is easily handled in step 11 by associating a very high q value cost with any node, m, having no successors (or, more generally, any node recognized as not belonging to any solution graph). The bottom-up operation will then propagate this high cost upward, which eliminates any chance that a graph containing this node might be selected as an estimated best solution graph.

Suppose some node n has a finite number of descendants in the implicit AND/OR graph and that these do not comprise a solution graph from n to a set of terminal nodes. Then, eventually, the revised cost, $q(n)$, for node n will have a very high value. The assignment of a very high value, $q(s)$, to the start node can therefore be taken to signal that there is no solution graph from the start node.

It is possible to prove that if there is a solution graph from a given node to a set of terminal nodes, and if $h(n) \le h^*(n)$ for all nodes, and if h satisfies the monotone restriction, then algorithm **AO*** will terminate in an optimal solution graph. (This optimal solution graph can be obtained by tracing down from s through the marked connectors at termination. The cost of this optimal solution graph is equal to the q value of s at termination.) Thus, we can say that algorithm **AO*** with these restrictions is admissible. We omit the proof of this result here; the interested reader is referred to Martelli and Montanari (1973).

A breadth-first algorithm can be obtained from **AO*** by using $h = 0$. Because such an h function satisfies the monotone restriction (and is a lower bound on $h*$), the breadth-first algorithm using it is admissible.

As an example of the use of **AO***, let us consider again the graph of Figure 3.1. Suppose that the following estimates are available:

$$h(n_0) = 0, h(n_1) = 2, h(n_2) = 4, h(n_3) = 4,$$

$$h(n_4) = 1, h(n_5) = 1, h(n_6) = 2, h(n_7) = 0,$$

$$h(n_8) = 0.$$

Let nodes n_7 and n_8 be terminal nodes, and let the cost of each k-connector be k. Note that our h function provides a lower bound on $h*$ and satisfies the monotone restriction.

The search graphs obtained after various cycles through the outer loop of **AO*** are shown in Figure 3.3. In each graph, the revised q values are shown next to each node; heavy arrows are used to mark connectors, and nodes labeled *SOLVED* are indicated by solid circles. During the first cycle, we expand node n_0; next we expand node n_1, then node n_5, and then node n_4. After node n_4 is expanded, node n_0 is labeled *SOLVED*. The solution graph (with minimal cost equal to 5) is obtained by tracing down through the marked connectors.

We have not yet discussed how **AO*** selects (in step 5) a nonterminal leaf node of the estimated best partial solution graph to expand. Perhaps it would be efficient to select that leaf node most likely to change the estimate of the best partial solution graph. If the estimate of the best partial solution graph never changes, **AO*** must eventually expand all of the nonterminal leaf nodes of this graph anyway. However, if the estimate is eventually going to change to some more nearly optimal graph, the sooner **AO*** makes this change, the better. Possibly the expansion of that leaf node having the *highest* h value would most likely result in a changed estimate.

As with algorithms **A** and **A*** for ordinary graphs, **AO*** may be modified in a variety of ways to render it more practical in special situations. First, rather than recompute a new estimated best partial solution graph after every node expansion, one might instead expand one

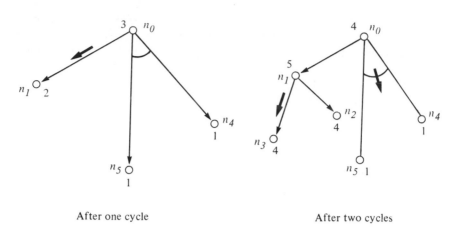

After one cycle

After two cycles

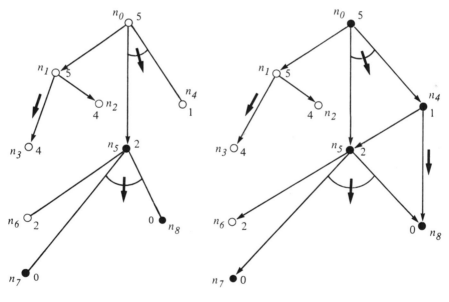

After three cycles

After four cycles

Fig. 3.3 Search graphs after various cycles of **AO***.

or more leaf nodes and some number of their descendants all at once, and then recompute an estimated best partial solution graph. This strategy reduces the overhead expense of frequent bottom-up operations but incurs the risk that some node expansions may not be on the best solution graph.

A staged-search strategy may also be used for AND/OR graphs. To employ it, one periodically reclaims needed storage space by discarding some of the AND/OR search graph. One might, for example, determine a few of those partial solution graphs within the entire search graph having the *largest* estimated costs. These can then be discarded periodically (with the risk, of course, of discarding one that might turn out to be the top of an optimal solution graph.)

3.3. SOME RELATIONSHIPS BETWEEN DECOMPOSABLE AND COMMUTATIVE SYSTEMS

In chapter 1 we mentioned that several problems could be solved by production systems working in either forward or backward directions. (Whether one chooses to call a given direction forward, or backward, is often arbitrary.) Here we illustrate that certain types of commutative forward systems are dual to decomposable backward ones.

Suppose that we have a production system based on the following rewrite rules:

$$R1: \quad T \to A, B$$

$$R2: \quad T \to B, C$$

$$R3: \quad A \to D$$

$$R4: \quad B \to E, F$$

$$R5: \quad B \to G$$

$$R6: \quad C \to G$$

These rules are to be applied to a global database consisting of a string of symbols. A rule is applicable if the global database contains a symbol matching its left-hand side. The effect of applying the rule is to substitute an occurrence of the left-hand side of the rule in the global database by its right-hand side.

Production systems using such context-free rewrite rules with singleton left-hand sides are decomposable. An AND/OR search graph that results from applying the rewrite rules to an initial global database consisting of the single symbol, T, is shown in Figure 3.4.

There is an interesting manner in which the rewrite rules of our example can be used in the reverse direction. We say that such a reverse rule is applicable if the global database contains symbols matching all the symbols of the right-hand side. The effect of the rule is to *add* (not replace by) the symbol occurring on the left-hand side. In Figure 3.5 we show an example in which some (reverse direction) rules are applied to an initial global database consisting of the set $\{ D, E, F, G \}$. (We indicate a reverse direction application of rule R by R'.) We note that the production system that results from using these rewrite rules in the reverse direction, in the manner we have indicated, is *commutative*. Thus, as we discussed in chapter 1, an irrevocable control regime can be used without the danger of foreclosing any possible rule applications.

If we continue to apply (irrevocably) the reverse rules $R1', \ldots, R6'$, to a database that is initially the set $\{ D, E, F, G \}$, and to its descendants, we eventually obtain the set $\{ D, E, F, G, A, B, C, T \}$. We can keep track of these rule applications and the resulting global databases by an interesting structure called a *derivation graph*. A derivation graph is a way of structuring the global database at any stage of the production system process so that it indicates something about the history of rule applications.

We show a derivation graph for our example in Figure 3.6. The global database consists of the derivation graph. The way in which each boxed expression in the graph is derived is indicated by an incoming set of arcs labeled by the reverse rule.

It is obvious, of course, that the two structures of Figure 3.4 and Figure 3.6 are identical except for arc directions. In many problems in which we are interested, if we reverse the direction of a commutative production system, we obtain a decomposable production system. Often we think of

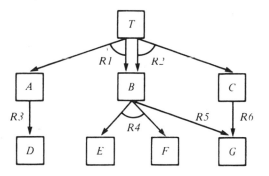

Fig. 3.4 A search graph.

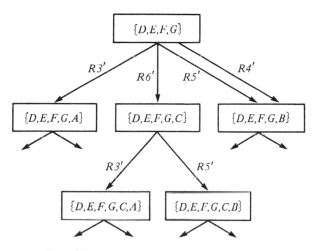

Fig. 3.5 Using rewrite rules in the reverse direction.

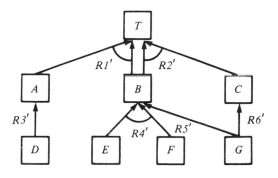

Fig. 3.6 A derivation graph.

111

the commutative system, using its rules, as the forward-directed system and the decomposable system, using reverse direction rules, as the backward-directed system.

We can use an evaluation function in connection with derivation graphs to control this type of commutative production system. Any rule applied to a derivation graph can be regarded as producing a new derivation graph. The rule application adds one new node to the structure. Thus, rule $R1'$ adds the node labeled T in Figure 3.6. We can define the cost of the derivation through this rule as the cost of both the rule itself plus the costs of the least costly derivation (sub)graphs associated with the nodes that are "inputs" to the rule. Such a cost definition is exactly analogous to the recursive definition of the cost of an AND/OR solution graph.

The cost of a derivation graph can be regarded as a way of computing a g function for a commutative production system. There are several alternative rules that can be applied to any derivation graph. Each has associated with it a g value computed as we have just described. We can also define a heuristic function, h, over derivation graphs. Such a function estimates the additional cost of all subsequent rule applications to that derivation graph and to its descendants along an optimal path to termination. When used to evaluate alternative rules, we let the h value of the rule application be the value obtained from this heuristic function for the derivation graph after the rule is applied. We can now add the g and h values of a rule application to obtain an f value for evaluating rules. That applicable rule with the smallest f value is selected for irrevocable application.

In this manner, a commutative production system with an irrevocable control strategy can be guided by a process very much like that used by algorithm A in graph searching. Given the assumption that h is a lower bound on h^*, we could show that such a strategy yields minimal cost derivations and that a more informed h uses fewer rule applications.

3.4. SEARCHING GAME TREES

Search techniques similar to those already discussed can be used to find playing strategies for certain kinds of games. The games that we consider are those called two-person, perfect-information games. These are played by two players who move in turn. They each know completely what both players have done and can do. Specifically, we are interested in those games where either one of the two players *wins* (and the other *loses*) or where the result is a *draw*. Example games from this class are checkers, tic-tac-toe, chess, go, and nim. We are not going to consider here any games whose results are determined even partially by chance; thus, dice games and most card games are ruled out. (Our treatment could be generalized to include certain chance games, however.)

We can use systems that are very much like production systems to analyze games. For example, in chess, the global database would contain a representation of the positions of all of the pieces on the board. The production rules model the legal moves of the game. The application of these rules to the initial database and to its successors, and so on, generates what is called a *game* graph or tree.

We can illustrate these ideas using a simple game called "Grundy's game." The rules of the game are as follows: Two players have in front of them a single pile of objects, say a stack of pennies. The first player divides the original stack into two stacks that *must* be unequal. Each player alternately thereafter does the same to *some* single stack when it is his turn to play. The game proceeds until every stack has either just one penny or two—at which point continuation becomes impossible. The player who first cannot play is the loser. Suppose we call our two players *MAX* and *MIN* and let *MIN* play first.

Let us start with seven pennies in the stack. A database for this game is an unordered sequence of numbers representing the number of pennies in the various stacks plus an indication of who is to move next. Thus $(7, MIN)$ is the starting configuration. From $(7, MIN)$, *MIN* has three alternative moves creating the configurations $(6,1,MAX)$, $(5,2,MAX)$, or $(4,3,MAX)$. The complete game graph for this game (produced by applying all applicable rules to all databases) is shown in Figure 3.7. All of the leaf nodes represent losing situations for the player next to move.

We can use the game graph to show that, no matter what *MIN* does, *MAX* can always win. A winning strategy for *MAX* is shown in Figure 3.7 by heavy lines. For every node representing a game situation in which it is *MIN*'s move next, we must show that *MAX* can win from every position to which *MIN* might move. For every node representing a situation for which it is *MAX*'s move next, we need only show that *MAX* can win from just one of the positions to which he might move.

113

Note the similarity between the winning strategy for *MAX* shown in Figure 3.7 and a solution graph of an AND/OR graph. Nodes corresponding to *MIN*'s next move have successors that are like AND nodes. From *MAX*'s point of view, a solution (that is, a win) must be obtainable from all of these successors. Nodes corresponding to *MAX*'s next move have successors that are like OR nodes. Again, from *MAX*'s point of view, a win must be obtainable from at least one of these successors. Terminal nodes are nodes corresponding to winning situations for *MAX*.

In our discussion of games, we adopt the convention that we are trying to find a winning strategy for *MAX*. Also, we assume that *MAX* moves first and that thereafter the moves alternate between the two players. With these conventions we can suppress any explicit mention of whose move is next in further illustrations of game graphs and trees. Nodes at even-numbered depths correspond to positions in which it is *MAX*'s move next; these will be called *MAX* nodes. Nodes at odd-numbered depths correspond to positions in which it is *MIN*'s move next; these are the *MIN* nodes. A terminal node is any node corresponding to a winning position for *MAX*. (The top node of a game graph is of depth zero, an even number.)

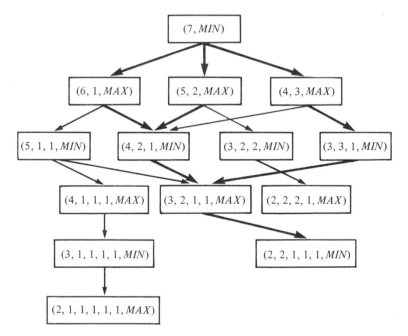

Fig. 3.7 A game graph for Grundy's game.

3.4.1. THE MINIMAX PROCEDURE

Many simple games (as well as some "ending" sequences of more complex games) can be handled by search techniques that are analogous to those used for finding AND/OR solution graphs. The solution graph, then, represents a complete playing strategy. Grundy's game, tic-tac-toe (naughts and crosses), various versions of nim, and some chess and checker end-games are examples of simple games in which AND/OR search to termination is feasible. A gross estimate of the size of the tic-tac-toe game tree, for example, can be obtained by noting that the start node has nine successors, these in turn have eight, etc., yielding 9! (or 362,880) nodes at the bottom of the tree. Many of the paths end in terminal nodes at shallower levels, however, and further reductions in the size of the tree result if symmetries are acknowledged.

For more complex games, such as complete chess and checker games, AND/OR search to termination is wholly out of the question. It has been estimated that the complete game tree for checkers has approximately 10^{40} nodes and the chess tree has approximately 10^{120} nodes. (It would take about 10^{21} centuries to generate the complete checker tree, even assuming that a successor could be generated in $1/3$ of a nanosecond.) Furthermore, heuristic search techniques do not reduce the effective branching factor sufficiently to be of much help. Therefore, for complex games, we must accept the fact that search to termination is impossible; that is, we must abandon the idea of using this method to prove that a win or draw can be obtained (except perhaps during the end-game).

● Our goal in searching a game tree might be, instead, merely to find a good first move. We could then make the indicated move, await the opponent's reply, and search again to find a good first move from this new position. We can use either breadth-first, depth-first, or heuristic methods, except that the termination conditions must now be modified. Several artificial termination conditions can be specified based on such factors as a time limit, a storage-space limit, and the depth of the deepest node in the search tree. It is also usual in chess, for example, not to terminate if any of the tip nodes represent "live" positions, that is, positions in which there is an immediate advantageous swap.

● After search terminates, we must extract from the search graph an estimate of the "best" first move. This estimate can be made by applying a *static* evaluation function to the leaf nodes of the search graph. The evaluation function measures the "worth" of a leaf node position. The

115

measurement is based on various features thought to influence this worth; for example, in checkers some useful features measure the relative piece advantage, control of the center, control of the center by kings, and so forth. It is customary in analyzing game trees to adopt the convention that game positions favorable to *MAX* cause the evaluation function to have a positive value, while positions favorable to *MIN* cause the evaluation function to have a negative value; values near zero correspond to game positions not particularly favorable to either *MAX* or *MIN*.

A good first move can be extracted by a procedure called the *minimax* procedure. (For simplicity we explain this procedure and others depending on it as if the game graph were really just a game tree.) We assume that were *MAX* to choose among tip nodes, he would choose that node having the largest evaluation. Therefore, the (*MAX* node) parent of *MIN* tip nodes is assigned a *backed-up* value equal to the maximum of the evaluations of the tip nodes. On the other hand, if *MIN* were to choose among tip nodes, he would presumably choose that node having the smallest evaluation (that is, the most negative). Therefore, the (*MIN* node) parent of *MAX* tip nodes is assigned a backed-up value equal to the minimum of the evaluations of the tip nodes. After the parents of all tip nodes have been assigned backed-up values, we back up values another level, assuming that *MAX* would choose that node with the largest backed-up value while *MIN* would choose that node with the smallest backed-up value.

We continue to back up values, level by level, until, finally, the successors of the start node are assigned backed-up values. We are assuming it is *MAX*'s turn to move at the start, so *MAX* should choose as his first move the one corresponding to the successor having the largest backed-up value.

The utility of this whole procedure rests on the assumption that the backed-up values of the start node's successors are more reliable measures of the ultimate relative worth of these positions than are the values that would be obtained by directly applying the static evaluation function to these positions. The backed-up values are, after all, based on "looking ahead" in the game tree and therefore depend on features occurring nearer the end of the game.

A simple example using the game of tic-tac-toe illustrates the minimaxing method. Let us suppose that *MAX* marks crosses (✗) and *MIN* marks circles (O) and that it is *MAX*'s turn to play first. We conduct a breadth-first search, until all of the nodes at level 2 are generated, and then we apply a static evaluation function to the positions at these nodes. Let our evaluation function $e(p)$ of a position p be given simply by:

If p is not a winning position for either player,

> $e(p)$ = (number of complete rows, columns, or diagonals that are still open for *MAX*) − (number of complete rows, columns, or diagonals that are still open for *MIN*).

If p is a win for *MAX*,

> $e(p) = \infty$ (∞ denotes a very large positive number).

If p is a win for *MIN*,

> $e(p) = -\infty$.

Thus, if p is

we have $e(p) = 6 \quad 4 = 2$.

We make use of symmetries in generating successor positions; thus the following game states

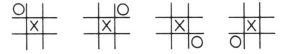

are all considered identical. (Early in the game, the branching factor of the tic-tac-toe tree is kept small by symmetries; late in the game, it is kept small by the number of open spaces available.)

In Figure 3.8 we show the tree generated by a search to depth 2. Static evaluations are shown below the tip nodes, and backed-up values are circled.

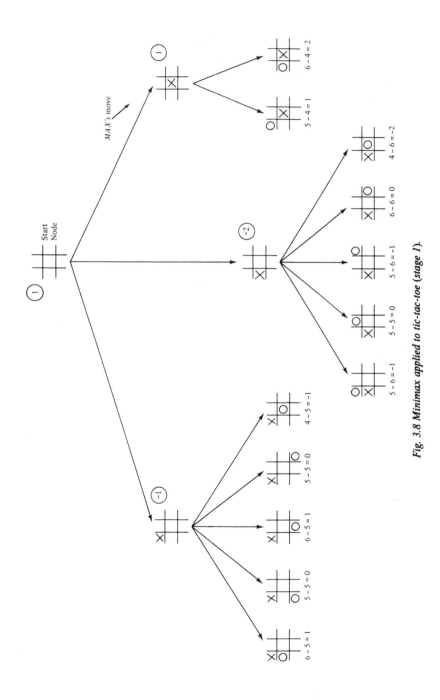

Fig. 3.8 Minimax applied to tic-tac-toe (stage 1).

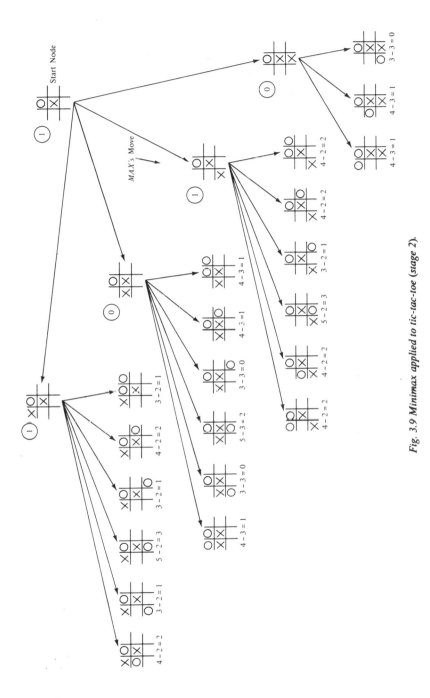

Fig. 3.9 Minimax applied to tic-tac-toe (stage 2).

119

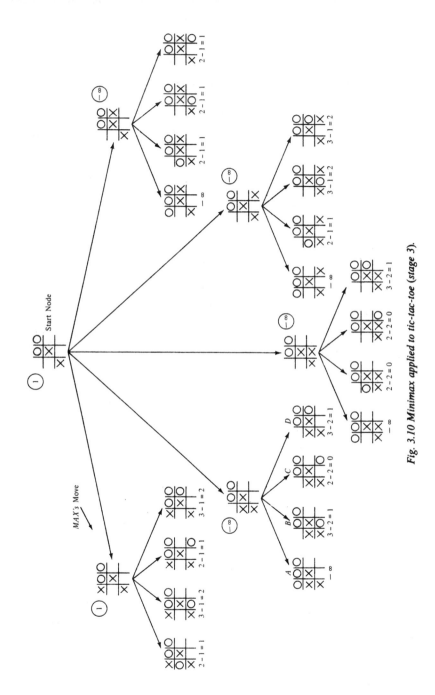

Fig. 3.10 Minimax applied to tic-tac-toe (stage 3).

Since

has the largest backed-up value, it is chosen as the first move. (Coincidentally, this is *MAX*'s best first move.)

Now let us suppose that *MAX* makes this move and *MIN* replies by putting a circle in the square directly above the × (a bad move for *MIN*, who must not be using a good search strategy). Next *MAX* searches to depth 2 below the resulting configuration, yielding the search tree shown in Figure 3.9. There are now two possible "best" moves; suppose *MAX* makes the one indicated. Now *MIN* makes the move that avoids his immediate defeat, yielding

MAX searches again, yielding the tree shown in Figure 3.10. Some of the tip nodes in this tree (for example, the one marked *A*) represent wins for *MIN* and thus have evaluations equal to $-\infty$. When these evaluations are backed up, we see that *MAX*'s best move is also the only one that avoids his immediate defeat. Now *MIN* can see that *MAX* must win on his next move, so *MIN* gracefully resigns.

3.4.2. THE ALPHA-BETA PROCEDURE

 The search procedure that we have just described separates completely the processes of search-tree generation and position evaluation. Only after tree generation is completed does position evaluation begin. It happens that this separation results in a grossly inefficient strategy. Remarkable reductions (amounting sometimes to many orders of magnitude) in the amount of search needed (to discover an equally good move) are possible if one performs tip-node evaluations and calculates backed-up values simultaneously with tree generation.

Consider the search tree of Figure 3.10 (the last stage of our tic-tac-toe search). Suppose that a tip node is evaluated as soon as it is generated. Then after the node marked *A* is generated and evaluated, there is no point in generating (and evaluating) nodes *B*, *C*, and *D*; that is, since *MIN* has *A* available and *MIN* could prefer nothing to *A*, we know immediately that *MIN* will choose *A*. We can then assign *A*'s parent the backed-up value of $-\infty$ and proceed with the search, having saved the search effort of generating and evaluating nodes *B*, *C*, and *D*. (Note that the savings in search effort would have been even greater if we were searching to greater depths; for then none of the descendants of nodes *B*, *C*, and *D* would have to be generated either.) It is important to observe that failing to generate nodes *B*, *C*, and *D* can in no way affect what will turn out to be *MAX*'s best first move.

In this example, the search savings depended on the fact that node *A* represented a win for *MIN*. The same kind of savings can be achieved, however, even when none of the positions in the search tree represents a win for either *MAX* or *MIN*.

Consider the first stage of the tic-tac-toe tree shown in Figure 3.8. We repeat part of this tree in Figure 3.11. Suppose that search had progressed in a depth-first manner and that whenever a tip node is generated, its static evaluation is computed. Also suppose that whenever a position can be given a backed-up value, this value is computed. Now consider the situation occurring at that stage of the depth-first search immediately after node *A* and all of its successors have been generated, but before node *B* is generated. Node *A* is now given the backed-up value of -1. At this point we know that the backed-up value of the start node is bounded from below by -1. Depending on the backed-up values of the other successors of the start node, the final backed-up value of the start node may be greater than -1, but it cannot be less. We call this lower bound an *alpha value* for the start node.

Now let depth-first search proceed until node *B* and its first successor node, *C*, are generated. Node *C* is then given the static value of -1. Now we know that the backed-up value of node *B* is bounded from above by -1. Depending on the static values of the rest of node *B*'s successors, the final backed-up value of node *B* can be less than -1 but it cannot be greater. We call this upper bound on node *B* a *beta value*. We note at this point, therefore, that the final backed-up value of node *B* can never exceed the alpha value of the start node, and therefore we can discontinue search below node *B*. We are guaranteed that node *B* will not turn out to be preferable to node *A*.

This reduction in search effort was achieved by keeping track of bounds on backed-up values. In general, as successors of a node are given backed-up values, the bounds on backed-up values can be revised. But we note that:

(a) The alpha values of *MAX* nodes (including the start node) can never decrease, and

(b) the beta values of *MIN* nodes can never increase.

⟨Because of these constraints we can state the following rules for discontinuing the search:⟩

(1) Search can be discontinued below any *MIN* node having a beta value less than or equal to the alpha value of any of its *MAX* node ancestors. The final backed-up value of this *MIN* node can then be set to its beta value. This value may not be the same as that obtained by full minimax search, but its use results in selecting the same best move.

(2) Search can be discontinued below any *MAX* node having an alpha value greater than or equal to the beta value of any of its *MIN* node ancestors. The final backed-up value of this *MAX* node can then be set to its alpha value.

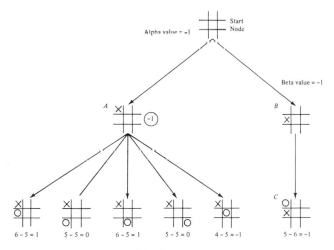

Fig. 3.11 Part of the first stage tic-tac-toe tree.

Fig. 3.12 An example illustrating the alpha-beta search procedure.

During search, alpha and beta values are computed as follows:

(a)   The alpha value of a *MAX* node is set equal to the current largest final backed-up value of its successors.

(b)   The beta value of a *MIN* node is set equal to the current smallest final backed-up value of its successors.

When search is discontinued under rule (1) above, we say that an alpha cutoff has occurred; when search is discontinued under rule (2), we say that a beta cutoff has occurred. The whole process of keeping track of alpha and beta values and making cutoffs when possible is usually called the alpha-beta procedure. The procedure terminates when all of the successors of the start node have been given final backed-up values, and the best first move is then the one creating that successor having the highest backed-up value. Employing this procedure always results in finding a move that is equally as good as the move that would have been found by the simple minimax method searching to the same depth. The only difference is that the alpha-beta procedure finds a best first move usually after much less search.

An application of the alpha-beta procedure is illustrated in Figure 3.12. We show a search tree generated to a depth of 6. (Our convention is to generate the left-most nodes first. *MAX* nodes are depicted by a square, and *MIN* nodes are depicted by a circle.) The tip nodes have the static values indicated. Now suppose we conduct a depth-first search employing the alpha-beta procedure. The subtree generated by the alpha-beta procedure is indicated by darkened branches. Those nodes cut off have ✗s drawn through them. Note that only 18 of the original 41 tip nodes had to be evaluated. (The reader can test his understanding of the procedure by attempting to duplicate the alpha-beta search on this example.)

3.4.3.   THE SEARCH EFFICIENCY OF THE ALPHA-BETA PROCEDURE

In order to perform alpha-beta cutoffs, at least some part of the search tree must be generated to maximum depth, because alpha and beta values must be based on the static values of tip nodes. Therefore some type of a depth-first search is usually employed in using the alpha-beta procedure. Furthermore, the number of cutoffs that can be made during a search depends on the degree to which the early alpha and beta values approximate the final backed-up values.

The final backed-up value of the start node is identical to the static value of one of the tip nodes. If this tip node could be reached first in a depth-first search, the number of cutoffs would be maximal. When the number of cutoffs is maximal, a minimal number of tip nodes need to be generated and evaluated.

Suppose a tree has depth D, and every node (except a tip node) has exactly B successors. Such a tree will have precisely B^D tip nodes. Suppose an alpha-beta procedure generated successors in the order of their true backed-up values—the lowest valued successors first for *MIN* nodes and the highest valued successors first for *MAX* nodes. (Of course, these backed-up values are not typically known at the time of successor generation, so this order could never really be achieved, except perhaps accidentally.)

It happens that this order maximizes the number of cutoffs that will occur and minimizes the number of tip nodes generated. Let us denote this minimal number of tip nodes by N_D. It can be shown that

$$N_D = 2B^{D/2} - 1 \text{ (for even } D)$$

and

$$N_D = B^{(D+1)/2} + B^{(D-1)/2} - 1 \text{ (for odd } D).$$

That is, the number of tip nodes of depth D that would be generated by optimal alpha-beta search is about the same as the number of tip nodes that would have been generated at depth $D/2$ without alpha-beta. Therefore, for the same storage requirements, the alpha-beta procedure with perfect successor ordering allows search depth to double. Even though perfect ordering cannot be achieved in search problems (if it could, we wouldn't need the search process at all!), the large potential payoff suggests the importance of using the best ordering function available.

3.5. BIBLIOGRAPHICAL AND HISTORICAL REMARKS

3.5.1. AND/OR GRAPHS

Decomposition and AND/OR graphs have been used in a variety of applications. Hinxman (1976) discusses applications to the "stock-cutting problem"; Martelli and Montanari (1975,1978) show how dynamic programming problems can be formulated as problems of AND/OR search and how such a formulation is used to optimize decision trees; Slagle (1963) uses AND/OR trees in symbolic integration; Stockman (1977) describes applications to the analysis of waveforms, and, as we shall see in chapter 6, AND/OR graphs can be used in theorem-proving systems.

Our algorithm **AO*** is essentially the same as the algorithm for searching AND/OR graphs of Martelli and Montanari (1973, 1978). We have taken some of our illustrative examples from Martelli and Montanari (1979). These AND/OR graph-searching algorithms are based on earlier work of Nilsson (1969, 1971). [See also Amarel (1967).] Hall (1973) has shown the equivalence between AND/OR graphs and context-free grammars. Levi and Sirovich (1976) generalize AND/OR graphs to represent interdependent subproblems and show that the generalized graphs are equivalent to type-0 grammars. Chang and Slagle (1971) also discuss AND/OR graphs, although their treatment seems to lose some of the advantages inherent in decomposition. Berliner (1979) presents a related search algorithm involving upper and lower bound values at each node.

Kowalski (1972) and vanderBrug and Minker (1975) discuss the relationships between what we term backward decomposable systems (using AND/OR graphs) and forward commutative ones (using derivation graphs). Michie and Sibert (1974) also describe heuristic search algorithms based on derivation graphs.

3.5.2. GAME TREES

Shannon (1950) proposed a minimax search procedure to be used with a static evaluation function in a proposal for a program to play chess. Newell, Shaw, and Simon (1958) used these ideas in constructing an early

127

chess-playing program. Samuel (1959, 1967) developed a checker (draughts) program that used polynomial evaluation functions, alpha-beta search methods, and learning strategies for improving play. Slagle (1970) has discussed the similarities between AND/OR trees and game trees.

The alpha-beta procedure was discovered independently by many of the early AI researchers. A version of it is first described by Newell, Shaw, and Simon (1958). Knuth and Moore (1975) present a thorough analysis of its properties and discuss its history. Newborn (1977) and Baudet (1978) present additional results. The results on search efficiency of alpha-beta were first stated by Edwards and Hart (1963) based on a theorem that they attribute to Michael Levin. Later, Slagle and Dixon (1969) give what they consider to be the first published proof of this theorem. Knuth and Moore (1975) contains the most complete account of these properties. Lindstrom (1979) reformulates the alpha-beta procedure for coroutine (rather than recursive) control. Harris (1974) proposes an alternative to minimax search for game trees.

Chess-playing programs are steadily improving in ability, and many AI experts continue to believe that a computer world chess champion is not far off. Good accounts of computer chess are given in an article by Berliner (1978) and in books by Newborn (1975) and by Levy (1976). A recent program by Wilkins (1979) incorporates knowledge about chess tactics, which greatly diminishes the amount of search needed. [See also Pitrat (1977).]

EXERCISES

3.1 The following rewrite rules can be used to replace the numeral on the left-hand side with the string of numerals on the right.

$$6 \rightarrow 3,3 \qquad 4 \rightarrow 3,1$$
$$6 \rightarrow 4,2 \qquad 3 \rightarrow 2,1$$
$$4 \rightarrow 2,2 \qquad 2 \rightarrow 1,1$$

Consider the problem of using these rules to transform the numeral 6 into a string of 1s. Illustrate how algorithm **AO*** works by using it to solve this problem. Assume that the cost of a k-connector is k units, and that the value of the h function at nodes labeled by the numeral 1 is zero and at nodes labeled by n ($n \neq 1$) is n.

3.2 The game *nim* is played as follows: Two players alternate in removing one, two, or three pennies from a stack initially containing five pennies. The player who picks up the last penny loses. Show, by drawing the game graph, that the player who has the second move can always win. Can you think of a simple characterization of the winning strategy?

3.3 Conduct on alpha-beta search of the game tree shown in Figure 3.12 by generating nodes in the order right-most node first. Indicate where cutoffs occur and compare with Figure 3.12, in which nodes were generated left-most node first.

3.4 Chapters 2 and 3 concentrated on search techniques for tentative control regimes (backtracking and graph-search). Discuss the search problem for an irrevocable control regime guiding a commutative production system. (You might base your discussion on Section 3.3., for example.) Specify (in detail) a search algorithm that uses an evaluation function with a heuristic component.

3.5 Represent the configuration of a tic-tac-toe board by a nine-dimensional vector, c, having components equal to $+1$, 0, or -1 according to whether the corresponding cells are marked with a $\times$, are empty, or are marked with a O, respectively. Specify a nine-dimensional vector w, such that the dot product $c \cdot w$ is a useful evaluation function for use by MAX (playing $\times$s) to evaluate nonterminal positions. Use this evaluation function to perform a few minimax searches making any adjustments to w that seem appropriate to improve the evaluation function. Can you find a vector w that appraises positions so accurately that search below these positions is not needed?

CHAPTER 4

THE PREDICATE CALCULUS IN AI

In many applications, the information to be encoded into the global database of a production system originates from descriptive statements that are difficult or unnatural to represent by simple structures like arrays or sets of numbers. Intelligent information retrieval, robot problem solving, and mathematical theorem proving, for example, require the capability for representing, retrieving and manipulating sets of statements.

The *first order predicate calculus* is a formal language in which a wide variety of statements can be expressed. Throughout the rest of the book, we use expressions in the predicate calculus language as components of the global databases of production systems. Before describing exactly how this language is used in AI systems, however, we must define the language, show how it is used to represent statements, explain how inferences can be made from sets of expressions in the language, and discuss how to deduce statements in the language from other statements in the language. These are fundamental concepts of formal logic and are also of great importance in AI. In this chapter we introduce the language and methods of logic and then show how they can be exploited in AI production systems.

4.1. INFORMAL INTRODUCTION TO THE PREDICATE CALCULUS

A language, such as the predicate calculus, is defined by its *syntax*. To specify a syntax we must specify the alphabet of symbols to be used in the language and how these symbols are to be put together to form legitimate expressions in the language. The legitimate expressions of the predicate calculus are called the _well-formed formulas_ (_wffs_). In the discussion that follows we give a brief, informal description of the syntax of the predicate calculus.

4.1.1. THE SYNTAX AND SEMANTICS OF ATOMIC FORMULAS

The elementary components of the predicate calculus language are _predicate symbols, variable symbols, function symbols_, and _constant symbols_ set off by parentheses, brackets, and commas, in a manner to be illustrated by examples. A predicate symbol is used to represent a relation in a domain of discourse. Suppose, for example, that we wanted to represent the fact that someone wrote something. We might use the predicate symbol _WRITE_ to denote a relationship between a person doing the writing and a thing written. We can compose a simple _atomic formula_ using _WRITE_ and two terms, denoting the writer and what is written. For example, to represent the sentence "Voltaire wrote _Candide_," we might use the simple atomic formula:

$$WRITE(VOLTAIRE, CANDIDE).$$

In this atomic formula, _VOLTAIRE_, and _CANDIDE_, are _constant symbols_. In general, atomic formulas are composed of predicate symbols and _terms_. A constant symbol is the simplest kind of term and is used to represent objects or entities in a domain of discourse. These objects or entities may be physical objects, people, concepts, or anything that we want to name.

Variable symbols, like x or y, are terms also, and they permit us to be indefinite about which entity is being referred to. Formulas using variable symbols, like $WRITE(x, y)$, are discussed later in the context of quantification.

We can also compose terms of _function symbols_. Function symbols denote functions in the domain of discourse. For example, the function symbol _father_ can be used to denote the mapping between an individual and his male parent. To express the sentence "John's mother is married to John's father," we might use the following atomic formula:

$$MARRIED[father(JOHN), mother(JOHN)].$$

Usually a mnemonic string of capital letters is used as a predicate

132

symbol. (Examples: *WRITE, MARRIED.*) In some abstract examples, short strings of upper-case letters and numerals (*P1, Q2*) are used as predicate symbols. A mnemonic string of capital letters or short strings of upper-case letters and numerals are also used as constant symbols; for example, *CANDIDE, A1,* or *B2.* Context prevents confusion between whether a string is a predicate symbol or a constant symbol.

Mnemonic strings of lower-case letters are used as function symbols. (Examples: *father, mother.*) Lower-case letters near the middle of the alphabet, like *f, g, h*, etc., are used in abstract examples.

To represent an English sentence by an atomic formula, we focus on the relations and entities that the sentence describes and represent them by predicates and terms. Often, the predicate is identified with the verb of the sentence, and the terms are identified with the subject or object of the verb. Usually we have several choices about how to represent a sentence. For example, we can represent the sentence "The house is yellow" either by a one-term predicate, as in *YELLOW(HOUSE-1)*, by a two-term predicate, as in *COLOR(HOUSE-1, YELLOW)*, or by a three-term predicate, as in *VALUE(COLOR, HOUSE-1, YELLOW)*, etc. The designer of a representation selects the alphabet of predicates and terms that he will use and defines what the elements of this alphabet will *mean.*

In the predicate calculus, a wff can be given an *interpretation* by assigning a correspondence between the elements of the language and the relations, entities, and functions in the domain of discourse. (To each predicate symbol, we must assign a corresponding relation in the domain; to each constant symbol, an entity in the domain; and to each function symbol, a function in the domain.) These assignments define the *semantics* of the predicate calculus language. In our applications, we are using the predicate calculus specifically to represent certain statements about a domain of discourse; thus we usually have a specific interpretation in mind for the wffs that we use. Once an interpretation for an atomic formula has been defined, we say that the formula has value *T* (true) just when the corresponding statement about the domain is true and that it has value *F* (false) just when the corresponding statement is false. Thus, using the obvious interpretation, the formula

WRITE(VOLTAIRE, CANDIDE)

has value *T*, and

WRITE(VOLTAIRE, COMPUTER-CHESS)

133

has value F. When an atomic formula contains variables, there may be some assignments to the variables (of entities in the domain) for which an atomic formula has value T and other assignments for which it has value F.

4.1.2. CONNECTIVES

Atomic formulas, like $WRITE(x,y)$, are merely the elementary building blocks of the predicate calculus language. We can combine atomic formulas to form more complex wffs by using *connectives* such as "$\wedge$" (and), "$\vee$" (or), and "$\Rightarrow$" (implies).

The connective "$\wedge$" has obvious use in representing compound sentences like "John likes Mary, and John likes Sue." Also, some simpler sentences can be written in a compound form. For example, "John lives in a yellow house" might be represented by the formula

$$LIVES(JOHN, HOUSE\text{-}1) \wedge COLOR(HOUSE\text{-}1, YELLOW),$$

where the predicate $LIVES$ represents a relation between a person and an object and where the predicate $COLOR$ represents a relation between an object and a color. Formulas built by connecting other formulas by $\wedge$s are called *conjunctions*, and each of the component formulas is called a *conjunct*. Any conjunction composed of wffs is also a wff.

The symbol "$\vee$" is used to represent inclusive "or." For example, the sentence "John plays centerfield or shortstop" might be represented by $[PLAYS(JOHN, CENTERFIELD) \vee PLAYS(JOHN, SHORT\text{-}STOP)]$. Formulas built by connecting other formulas by $\vee$s are called *disjunctions*, and each of the component formulas is called a *disjunct*. Any disjunction composed of wffs is also a wff.

The truth values of conjunctions and disjunctions are determined from the truth values of the components. A conjunction has value T if each of its conjuncts has value T; otherwise it has value F. A disjunction has value T if at least one of its disjuncts has value T; otherwise it has value F.

The other connective, "$\Rightarrow$," is used for representing "if-then" statements. For example, the sentence "If the car belongs to John, then it is green," might be represented by

$$OWNS(JOHN, CAR\text{-}1) \Rightarrow COLOR(CAR\text{-}1, GREEN).$$

A formula built by connecting two formulas with a $\Rightarrow$ is called an *implication*. The left-hand side of an implication is called the *antecedent*, and the right-hand side is called the *consequent*. If both the antecedent and the consequent are wffs, then the implication is a wff also. An implication has value T if either the consequent has value T (regardless of the value of the antecedent) or if the antecedent has value F (regardless of the value of the consequent); otherwise the implication has value F. This definition of implicational truth value is sometimes at odds with our intuitive notion of the meaning of "implies." For example, the predicate calculus representation of the sentence "If the moon is made of green cheese, then horses can fly" has value T.

The symbol "$\sim$" (not) is sometimes called a connective although it is really not used to connect two formulas. It is used to negate the truth value of a formula; that is, it changes the value of a wff from T to F, and vice versa. For example, the (true) sentence "Voltaire did not write *Computer Chess*" might be represented as

$\sim WRITE(VOLTAIRE, COMPUTER\text{-}CHESS)$.

A formula with a $\sim$ in front of it is called a *negation*. The negation of a wff is also a wff. An atomic formula and the negation of an atomic formula are both called *literals*.

It is easy to see that $\sim F1 \vee F2$ always has the same truth value as $F1 \Rightarrow F2$, so we really wouldn't ever need to use $\Rightarrow$. But our object here is not to propose a minimal representation but a useful one. There are occasions in which $F1 \Rightarrow F2$ is heuristically preferable to its equivalent $\sim F1 \vee F2$, and vice versa.

If we limited our sentences to those that could be represented by the constructs that we have introduced so far, and if we never used variables in terms, we would be using a subset of the predicate calculus called the *propositional calculus*. Indeed, the propositional calculus can be a useful representation for many simplified domains, but it lacks the ability to represent many statements (such as "All elephants are gray") in a useful manner. To extend its power, we need the capability to make statements with variables in the formulas.

4.1.3. QUANTIFICATION

Sometimes an atomic formula, like $P(x)$, has value T (with a given interpretation for P) no matter what assignment is given to the variable x. Or such an atomic formula may have value T for at least one value of x. In the predicate calculus these properties are used in establishing the truth values of formulas containing constructs called *quantifiers.* The formula consisting of the *universal quantifier* $(\forall x)$ in front of a formula $P(x)$ has value T for an interpretation just when the value of $P(x)$ under this interpretation is T for *all* assignments of x to entities in the domain. The formula consisting of the *existential quantifier* $(\exists x)$ in front of a formula $P(x)$ has value T for an interpretation just when the value of $P(x)$ under the interpretation is T for *at least one* assignment of x to an entity in the domain.

For example, the sentence "All elephants are gray" might be represented by

$$(\forall x)[ELEPHANT(x) \Rightarrow COLOR(x, GRAY)].$$

Here, the formula being quantified is an implication, and x is the quantified variable. We say that x is *quantified over*. The *scope* of a quantifier is just that part of the following string of formulas to which the quantifier applies. As another example, the sentence "There is a person who wrote *Computer Chess*" might be represented by

$$(\exists x) WRITE(x, COMPUTER\text{-}CHESS).$$

Any expression obtained by quantifying a wff over a variable is also a wff. If a variable in a wff is quantified over, it is said to be a *bound variable;* otherwise it is said to be a *free variable.* We are mainly interested in wffs having all of their variables bound. Such wffs are called *sentences.*

We note that if quantifiers occur in a wff, it is not always possible to use the rules for the semantics of quantifiers to compute the truth value of that wff. For example, consider the wff $(\forall x)P(x)$. Given an interpretation for P and an *infinite* domain of entities, we would have to check to see whether the relation corresponding to P held for every possible assignment of the value of x to a domain entity in order to establish that the wff had value T. Such a process would never terminate.

The version of the predicate calculus used in this book is called *first order* because it does not allow quantification over predicate symbols or function symbols. Thus, formulas like $(\forall P)P(A)$ are not wffs in first order predicate calculus.

4.1.4. EXAMPLES AND PROPERTIES OF WFFS

Using the syntactic rules that we have just informally discussed, we can build arbitrarily complex wffs, and we can compute whether or not an arbitrary expression is a wff. For example, the following expressions are wffs:

$$(\exists x)\{(\forall y)[(P(x,y) \land Q(y,x)) \Rightarrow R(x)]\}$$

$$\sim(\forall q)\{(\exists x)[P(x) \lor R(q)]\}$$

$$\sim P[A,g(A,B,A)]$$

$$\{\sim[P(A) \Rightarrow P(B)]\} \Rightarrow P(B)$$

In the above expressions, we have used parentheses, brackets, and braces as delimiters to group the component wffs. We use these delimiters to improve readability and to eliminate any ambiguity about how a wff is put together.

Some examples of expressions that are not wffs are:

$$\sim f(A)$$

$$f[P(A)]$$

$$Q\{f(A),[p(B) \Rightarrow Q(C)]\}$$

$$A \lor \sim \Rightarrow (\forall \sim)$$

Given an interpretation, the truth values of wffs (except for some containing quantifiers) can be computed given the rules we have informally described above. When truth values are computed in this manner, we are using what is called a *truth table method*. This method takes its name from a *truth table* that summarizes the rules we have already discussed. If *X1* and *X2* are any wffs, then the truth values of composite expressions made up of these wffs are given by the following truth table.

Table 4.1
Truth Table

$X1$	$X2$	$X1 \lor X2$	$X1 \land X2$	$X1 \Rightarrow X2$	$\sim X1$
T	T	T	T	T	F
F	T	T	F	T	T
T	F	T	F	F	F
F	F	F	F	T	T

If the truth values of two wffs are the same regardless of their interpretation, then we say that these wffs are *equivalent*. Using the truth table, we can easily establish the following equivalences:

$\sim(\sim X1)$ is equivalent to $X1$
$X1 \lor X2$ is equivalent to $\sim X1 \Rightarrow X2$

de Morgan's Laws:
$\sim(X1 \land X2)$ is equivalent to $\sim X1 \lor \sim X2$
$\sim(X1 \lor X2)$ is equivalent to $\sim X1 \land \sim X2$

Distributive Laws:
$X1 \land (X2 \lor X3)$ is equivalent to $(X1 \land X2) \lor (X1 \land X3)$
$X1 \lor (X2 \land X3)$ is equivalent to $(X1 \lor X2) \land (X1 \lor X3)$

Commutative Laws:
$X1 \land X2$ is equivalent to $X2 \land X1$
$X1 \lor X2$ is equivalent to $X2 \lor X1$

Associative Laws:
$(X1 \land X2) \land X3$ is equivalent to $X1 \land (X2 \land X3)$
$(X1 \lor X2) \lor X3$ is equivalent to $X1 \lor (X2 \lor X3)$

Contrapositive Law:
$X1 \Rightarrow X2$ is equivalent to $\sim X2 \Rightarrow \sim X1$

These laws justify the form in which we have written various of our example wffs in the discussion above. For example, the associative law allows us to write the conjunction $X1 \land X2 \land \ldots \land XN$ without any parentheses.

From the meanings of the quantifiers, we can also establish the following equivalences:

$$\sim(\exists x)P(x) \text{ is equivalent to } (\forall x)[\sim P(x)]$$

$$\sim(\forall x)P(x) \text{ is equivalent to } (\exists x)[\sim P(x)]$$

$$(\forall x)[P(x) \land Q(x)]\text{is equivalent to}$$
$$(\forall x)P(x) \land (\forall y)Q(y)$$

$$(\exists x)[P(x) \lor Q(x)] \text{ is equivalent to}$$
$$(\exists x)P(x) \lor (\exists y)Q(y)$$

$$(\forall x)P(x) \text{ is equivalent to } (\forall y)P(y)$$

$$(\exists x)P(x) \text{ is equivalent to } (\exists y)P(y)$$

In the last two equivalences, we see that the bound variable in a quantified expression is a kind of "dummy" variable. It can be arbitrarily replaced by any other variable symbol not already occurring in the expression.

To show the versatility of the predicate calculus as a language for expressing various assertions, we show below some example predicate calculus representations of some English sentences:

Every city has a dogcatcher who has been bitten by every dog in town.

$$(\forall x)\{ CITY(x) \Rightarrow (\exists y)\{ DOGCATCHER(x,y)$$
$$\land (\forall z)\{[DOG(z) \land LIVES\text{-}IN(x,z)] \Rightarrow BIT(y,z)\}\}\}$$

For every set x, there is a set y, such that the cardinality of y is greater than the cardinality of x.

$$(\forall x) \{ SET(x) \Rightarrow (\exists y)(\exists u)(\exists v)$$
$$[SET(y) \land CARD(x,u) \land CARD(y,v) \land G(u,v)]\}$$

139

All blocks on top of blocks that have been moved or that are attached to blocks that have been moved have also been moved.

$$(\forall x)(\forall y) \{\{ BLOCK(x) \wedge BLOCK(y)$$
$$\wedge [ONTOP(x,y) \vee ATTACHED(x,y)]$$
$$\wedge MOVED(y)\} \Rightarrow MOVED(x)\}$$

4.1.5. RULES OF INFERENCE, THEOREMS, AND PROOFS

In the predicate calculus, there are *rules of inference* that can be applied to certain wffs and sets of wffs to produce new wffs. One important inference rule is *modus ponens*. Modus ponens is the operation that produces the wff $W2$ from wffs of the form $W1$ and $W1 \Rightarrow W2$. Another rule of inference, *universal specialization*, produces the wff $W(A)$ from the wff $(\forall x) W(x)$, where A is any constant symbol. Using modus ponens and universal specialization together, for example, produces the wff $W2(A)$ from the wffs $(\forall x)[W1(x) \Rightarrow W2(x)]$ and $W1(A)$.

Inference rules, then, produce derived wffs from given ones. In the predicate calculus, such derived wffs are called *theorems*, and the sequence of inference rule applications used in the derivation constitutes a *proof* of the theorem. As we mentioned earlier, some problem-solving tasks can be regarded as the task of finding a proof for a theorem.

4.1.6. UNIFICATION

In proving theorems involving quantified formulas, it is often necessary to "match" certain subexpressions. For example, to apply the combination of modus ponens and universal specialization to produce $W2(A)$ from the wffs $(\forall x)[W1(x) \Rightarrow W2(x)]$ and $W1(A)$, it is necessary to find the substitution "A for x" that makes $W1(A)$ and $W1(x)$ identical. Finding substitutions of terms for variables to make expressions identical is an extremely important process in AI and is called *unification.* In order to describe this process, we must first discuss the topic of substitutions.

The terms of an expression can be variable symbols, constant symbols, or functional expressions, the latter consisting of function symbols and terms. A *substitution instance* of an expression is obtained by substituting terms for variables in that expression. Thus, four *instances* of $P[x, f(y), B]$ are:

$$P[z, f(w), B]$$
$$P[x, f(A), B]$$
$$P[g(z), f(A), B]$$
$$P[C, f(A), B]$$

The first instance is called an *alphabetic variant* of the original literal because we have merely substituted different variables for the variables appearing in $P[x, f(y), B]$. The last of the four instances shown above is called a *ground instance*, since none of the terms in the literal contains variables.

We can represent any substitution by a set of ordered pairs $s = \{t_1/v_1, t_2/v_2, \ldots, t_n/v_n\}$. The pair t_i/v_i means that term t_i is substituted for variable v_i throughout. We insist that a substitution be such that each occurrence of a variable have the same term substituted for it. Also, no variable can be replaced by a term containing that same variable. The substitutions used above in obtaining the four instances of $P[x, f(y), B]$ are:

$$s1 = \{z/x, w/y\}$$
$$s2 = \{A/y\}$$
$$s3 = \{g(z)/x, A/y\}$$
$$s4 = \{C/x, A/y\}$$

To denote a substitution instance of an expression, E, using a substitution, s, we write Es. Thus,

$$P[z, f(w), B] = P[x, f(y), B]s1 .$$

The composition of two substitutions $s1$ and $s2$ is denoted by $s1s2$, which is that substitution obtained by applying $s2$ to the terms of $s1$ and then adding any pairs of $s2$ having variables not occurring among the variables of $s1$. Thus,

$$\{g(x, y)/z\}\{A/x, B/y, C/w, D/z\} = \{g(A, B)/z, A/x, B/y, C/w\} .$$

It can be shown that applying $s1$ and $s2$ successively to an expression L is the same as applying $s1s2$ to L; that is, $(Ls1)s2 = L(s1s2)$. It can also be shown that the composition of substitutions is associative:

$$(s1s2)s3 = s1(s2s3) .$$

Substitutions are not, in general, commutative; that is, it is not generally the case that $s1s2 = s2s1$.

If a substitution s is applied to every member of a set $\{E_i\}$ of expressions, we denote the set of substitution instances by $\{E_i\}\,s$. We say that a set $\{E_i\}$ of expressions is *unifiable* if there exists a substitution s such that $E_1 s = E_2 s = E_3 s = \ldots$. In such a case, s is said to be a *unifier* of $\{E_i\}$ since its use collapses the set to a singleton. For example, $s = \{A/x, B/y\}$ unifies $\{P[x,f(y),B],\ P[x,f(B),B]\}$, to yield $\{P[A,f(B),B]\}$.

Although $s = \{A/x, B/y\}$ is a unifier of the set $\{P[x,f(y),B], P[x,f(B),B]\}$, in some sense it is not the simplest unifier. We note that we really did not have to substitute A for x to achieve unification. The most general (or simplest) unifier, *mgu*, g of $\{E_i\}$, has the property that if s is any unifier of $\{E_i\}$ yielding $\{E_i\}\,s$, then there exists a substitution s' such that $\{E_i\}\,s = \{E_i\}\,gs'$. Furthermore, the common instance produced by a most general unifier is unique except for alphabetic variants.

There are many algorithms that can be used to unify a finite set of unifiable expressions and which report failure when the set cannot be unified. The recursive procedure **UNIFY**, given informally below, is useful for establishing a general idea of how to unify a set of two *list-structured* expressions. [The literal $P(x,f(A,y))$ is written as $(P\ x\ (f\,A\ y))$ in list-structured form.]

Recursive Procedure **UNIFY**$(E1, E2)$

1   **if** either $E1$ or $E2$ is an atom (that is, a predicate symbol, a function symbol, a constant symbol, a negation symbol or a variable), interchange the arguments $E1$ and $E2$ (if necessary) so that $E1$ is an atom, and **do:**

2   **begin**

3   **if** $E1$ and $E2$ are identical, **return** NIL

4   **if** $E1$ is a variable, **do:**

5   **begin**

6   **if** *E1* occurs in *E2*, **return** *FAIL*

7   **return** { *E2/E1* }

8   **end**

9   **if** *E2* is a variable, **return** { *E1/E2* }

10   **return** *FAIL*

11   **end**

12   *F1* ← the first element of *E1*, *T1* ← the rest of *E1*

13   *F2* ← the first element of *E2*, *T2* ← the rest of *E2*

14   *Z1* ← **UNIFY**(*F1, F2*)

15   **if** *Z1* = *FAIL*, return *FAIL*

16   *G1* ← result of applying *Z1* to *T1*

17   *G2* ← result of applying *Z1* to *T2*

18   *Z2* ← **UNIFY**(*G1, G2*)

19   **if** *Z2* = *FAIL*, **return** *FAIL*

20   **return** the composition of *Z1* and *Z2*

It can be proven that **UNIFY** finds a most general unifier of a set of unifiable expressions or reports failure when the expressions are not unifiable.

As examples, we list the most general common substitution instances (those obtained by applying the mgu) for a few sets of literals.

Table 4.2
Unifiable Sets

Sets of Literals	Most General Common Substitution Instances
$\{P(x), P(A)\}$	$P(A)$
$\{P[f(x), y, g(y)], P[f(x), z, g(x)]\}$	$P[f(x), x, g(x)]$
$\{P[f(x, g(A, y)), g(A, y)], P[f(x, z), z]\}$	$P[f(x, g(A, y)), g(A, y)]$

Typically, we use unification to discover if one literal can match another one. There may be variables in both literals, and these variables may have terms substituted for them which would make the literals identical. The process of matching one expression to another template expression is sometimes called *pattern matching*. It plays a key role in AI systems. The unification process is more general than what is usually meant by pattern matching, however, because pattern matching processes typically do not allow variables to occur in both expressions.

4.1.7. VALIDITY AND SATISFIABILITY

If a wff has the value T for *all* possible interpretations, it is called *valid*. (Valid ground wffs are usually called *tautologies*.) Thus, by the truth table, the wff $P(A) \Rightarrow [P(A) \lor P(B)]$ has the value T regardless of the interpretation; therefore, it is valid. The truth table method can always be used to determine the validity of any wff that does not contain variables. One merely checks whether the wff has the value T for all possible valuations of the atomic formulas contained in the wff.

When quantifiers occur, one cannot always compute whether or not a wff is valid. It has been shown to be impossible to find a general method to decide the validity of quantified expressions, and, for this reason, the predicate calculus is said to be *undecidable*. However, the validity of certain kinds of formulas containing quantifiers can be decided; thus, one may speak of *decidable subclasses* of the predicate calculus. Furthermore, it has been shown that if a wff is, in fact, valid, then a procedure exists for verifying the validity of the wff. (This procedure applied to wffs that are not valid may never terminate.) Thus, the predicate calculus is said to be *semidecidable*.

If the *same* interpretation makes each wff in a set of wffs have the value T, then we say that this interpretation *satisfies* the set of wffs. A wff X *logically follows* from a set of wffs S if every interpretation satisfying S also satisfies X. Thus, it is easy to see that the wff $(\forall x)(\forall y)[P(x) \lor Q(y)]$ logically follows from the set

$$\{(\forall x)(\forall y)[P(x) \lor Q(y)], \ (\forall z)[R(z) \lor Q(A)]\} \ .$$

Also, the wff $P(A)$ logically follows from $(\forall x)P(x)$. It also happens that $(\forall x)Q(x)$ logically follows from the set $\{(\forall x)[\sim P(x) \lor Q(x)], (\forall x)P(x)\}$.

There is an important connection between the concept of a wff *logically following* from a set of wffs and the concept of a wff being a theorem *derived from* a set of wffs by applying inference rules. Suppose we are given a system of inference rules. We say that these rules are *sound* if any theorem derivable from any set of wffs also logically follows from that set of wffs. It can be shown, for example, that modus ponens is sound. We say that a system of inference rules is *complete* if all wffs that logically follow from any set are also theorems derivable from that set. We are always interested in sound inference rules, although sometimes we do not insist that the set of rules be complete.

4.2. RESOLUTION

4.2.1. CLAUSES

Resolution is an important rule of inference that can be applied to a certain class of wffs called *clauses.* A *clause* is defined as a wff consisting of a disjunction of literals. The resolution process, when it is applicable, is applied to a pair of *parent* clauses to produce a derived clause. Before explaining the resolution process itself, we first show that any predicate calculus wff can be converted to a set of clauses. We illustrate this conversion process by applying it to the following example wff:

$$(\forall x)\{\, P(x) \Rightarrow \{(\forall y)[\, P(y) \Rightarrow P(f(x,y))]$$
$$\wedge \sim(\forall y)[\, Q(x,y) \Rightarrow P(y)]\}\} \;.$$

The conversion process consists of the following steps:

(1) Eliminate implication symbols. All occurrences of the $\Rightarrow$ symbol in a wff are eliminated by making the substitution $\sim X1 \vee X2$ for $X1 \Rightarrow X2$ throughout the wff. In our example wff, this substitution yields:

$$(\forall x)\{\sim P(x) \vee \{(\forall y)[\sim P(y) \vee P(f(x,y))]$$
$$\wedge \sim(\forall y)[\sim Q(x,y) \vee P(y)]\}\} \;.$$

(2) Reduce scopes of negation symbols. We want each negation symbol, $\sim$, to apply to at most one atomic formula. By making repeated use of de Morgan's laws and other equivalences mentioned with them on pages 138–139, we change our example wff to:

$$(\forall x)\{\sim P(x) \vee \{(\forall y)[\sim P(y) \vee P(f(x,y))]$$
$$\wedge (\exists y)[\, Q(x,y) \wedge \sim P(y)]\}\} \;.$$

(3) Standardize variables. Within the scope of any quantifier, a variable bound by that quantifier is a dummy variable. It can be uniformly replaced by any other (non-occurring) variable throughout the scope of the quantifier without changing the truth value of the wff. Standardizing variables within a wff means to rename the dummy variables to ensure that each quantifier has its own unique dummy variable. Thus, instead of writing $(\forall x)[\, P(x) \Rightarrow (\exists x) Q(x)]$, we write $(\forall x)[\, P(x) \Rightarrow (\exists y) Q(y)]$. Standardizing our example wff yields:

$$(\forall x)\{\sim P(x) \vee \{(\forall y)[\sim P(y) \vee P(f(x,y))]$$
$$\wedge (\exists w)[\, Q(x,w) \wedge \sim P(w)]\}\} \;.$$

(4) Eliminate existential quantifiers. Consider the wff

$$(\forall y)[(\exists x) P(x,y)],$$

which might be read as "For all y, there exists an x (possibly depending on y) such that $P(x,y)$." Note that because the existential quantifier is within the scope of a universal quantifier, we allow the possibility that the x that exists might depend on the value of y. Let this dependence be explicitly defined by some function $g(y)$, which maps each value of y into the x that "exists." Such a function is called a *Skolem function*. If we use

146

the Skolem function in place of the x that exists, we can eliminate the existential quantifier altogether and write $(\forall y) P[g(y), y]$.

The general rule for eliminating an existential quantifier from a wff is to replace each occurrence of its existentially quantified variable by a Skolem function whose arguments are those universally quantified variables that are bound by universal quantifiers whose scopes include the scope of the existential quantifier being eliminated. Function symbols used in Skolem functions must be new in the sense that they cannot be ones that already occur in the wff. Thus, we can eliminate the $(\exists z)$ from

$$[(\forall w) Q(w)] \Rightarrow (\forall x)\{(\forall y)\{(\exists z)[P(x,y,z) \\ \Rightarrow (\forall u) R(x,y,u,z)]\}\},$$

to yield

$$[(\forall w) Q(w)] \Rightarrow (\forall x)\{(\forall y)[P(x,y,g(x,y)) \\ \Rightarrow (\forall u) R(x,y,u,g(x,y))] \quad .$$

If the existential quantifier being eliminated is not within the scope of any universal quantifiers, we use a Skolem function of no arguments, which is just a constant. Thus, $(\exists x) P(x)$ becomes $P(A)$, where the constant symbol A is used to refer to the entity that we know exists. It is important that A be a new constant symbol and not one used in other formulas to refer to known entities.

To eliminate all of the existentially quantified variables from a wff, we use the above procedure on each formula in turn. Eliminating the existential quantifiers (there is just one) in our example wff yields:

$$(\forall x)\{\sim P(x) \vee \{(\forall y)[\sim P(y) \vee P(f(x,y))] \\ \wedge [Q(x,g(x)) \wedge \sim P(g(x))]\}\},$$

where $g(x)$ is a Skolem function.

(5) Convert to prenex form. At this stage, there are no remaining existential quantifiers and each universal quantifier has its own variable. We may now move all of the universal quantifiers to the front of the wff and let the scope of each quantifier include the entirety of the wff following it. The resulting wff is said to be in *prenex form*. A wff in prenex

147

form consists of a string of quantifiers called a *prefix* followed by a quantifier-free formula called a *matrix*. The prenex form of our wff is:

$$(\forall x)(\forall y) \{\sim P(x) \lor \{[\sim P(y) \lor P(f(x,y))]$$
$$\land [Q(x,g(x)) \land \sim P(g(x))]\}\}.$$

(6) Put matrix in conjunctive normal form. Any matrix may be written as the conjunction of a finite set of disjunctions of literals. Such a matrix is said to be in *conjunctive normal form*. Examples of matrices in conjunctive normal form are:

$$[P(x) \lor Q(x,y)] \land [P(w) \lor \sim R(y)] \land Q(x,y)$$
$$P(x) \lor Q(x,y)$$
$$P(x) \land Q(x,y)$$
$$\sim R(y)$$

We may put any matrix into conjunctive normal form by repeatedly using one of the distributive rules, namely, by replacing expressions of the form $X1 \lor (X2 \land X3)$ by $(X1 \lor X2) \land (X1 \lor X3)$.

When the matrix of our example wff is put in conjunctive normal form, our wff becomes:

$$(\forall x)(\forall y)\{[\sim P(x) \lor \sim P(y) \lor P(f(x,y))]$$
$$\land [\sim P(x) \lor Q(x,g(x))] \land [\sim P(x) \lor \sim P(g(x))]\}.$$

(7) Eliminate universal quantifiers. Since all of the variables in the wffs we use must be bound, we are assured that all the variables remaining at this step are universally quantified. Furthermore, the order of universal quantification is unimportant, so we may eliminate the explicit occurrence of universal quantifiers and assume, by convention, that all variables in the matrix are universally quantified. We are left now with just a matrix in conjunctive normal form.

(8) Eliminate $\land$ symbols. We may now eliminate the explicit occurrence of $\land$ symbols by replacing expressions of the form $(X1 \land X2)$ with the set of wffs $\{X1, X2\}$. The result of repeated replacements is to obtain a finite set of wffs, each of which is a disjunction of literals. Any wff consisting solely of a disjunction of literals is called a *clause*. Our example wff is transformed into the following set of clauses:

$$\sim P(x) \vee \sim P(y) \vee P[f(x,y)]$$
$$\sim P(x) \vee Q[x,g(x)]$$
$$\sim P(x) \vee \sim P[g(x)]$$

(9) Rename variables. Variable symbols may be renamed so that no variable symbol appears in more than one clause. Recall that $(\forall x)[P(x) \wedge Q(x)]$ is equivalent to $[(\forall x)P(x) \wedge (\forall y)Q(y)]$. This process is sometimes called *standardizing the variables apart*. Our clauses are now:

$$\sim P(x1) \vee \sim P(y) \vee P[f(x1,y)]$$
$$\sim P(x2) \vee Q[x2,g(x2)]$$
$$\sim P(x3) \vee \sim P[g(x3)]$$

We note that the literals of a clause may contain variables but that these variables are always understood to be universally quantified. If terms not containing variables are substituted for the variables in an expression, we obtain what is called a *ground instance* of the literal. Thus, $Q(A,f(g(B)))$ is a ground instance of $Q(x,y)$.

When resolution is used as a rule of inference in a theorem-proving system, the set of wffs from which we wish to prove a theorem is first converted into clauses. It can be shown that if the wff X logically follows from a set of wffs, S, then it also logically follows from the set of clauses obtained by converting the wffs in S to clause form. Therefore, for our purposes, clauses are a completely general form in which to express wffs.

4.2.2. RESOLUTION FOR GROUND CLAUSES

The best way to obtain a general idea of the resolution inference rule is to understand how it applies to ground clauses. Suppose we have two ground clauses, $P1 \vee P2 \vee \ldots \vee PN$ and $\sim P1 \vee Q2 \vee \ldots QM$. We assume that all of the Pi and Qj are distinct. Note that one of these clauses contains a literal that is the exact negation of one of the literals in the other clause. From these two *parent* clauses we can infer a new clause, called the *resolvent* of the two. The resolvent is computed by taking the disjunction of the two clauses and then eliminating the complementary pair, $P1, \sim P1$. Some interesting special cases of resolution follow in Table 4.3.

Table 4.3
Clauses and Resolvents

Parent Clauses	Resolvent(s)	Comments
P and $\sim P \vee Q$ (i.e., $P \Rightarrow Q$)	Q	Modus Ponens
$P \vee Q$ and $\sim P \vee Q$	Q	The clause $Q \vee Q$ "collapses" to Q. This resolvent is called a *merge*.
$P \vee Q$ and $\sim P \vee \sim Q$	$Q \vee \sim Q$ and $P \vee \sim P$	Here, there are two possible resolvents; in this case, both are tautologies.
$\sim P$ and P	*NIL*	The *empty clause* is a sign of a contradiction.
$\sim P \vee Q$ (i.e, $P \Rightarrow Q$) and $\sim Q \vee R$ (i.e., $Q \Rightarrow R$)	$\sim P \vee R$ (i.e., $P \Rightarrow R$)	*Chaining*

From the table above, we see that resolution allows the incorporation of several operations into one simple inference rule. We next consider how this simple rule can be extended to deal with clauses containing variables.

4.2.3. GENERAL RESOLUTION

In order to apply resolution to clauses containing variables, we need to be able to find a substitution that can be applied to the parent clauses so that they contain complementary literals. In discussing this case, it is helpful to represent a clause by a set of literals (with the disjunction between the literals in the set understood). Let the prospective parent clauses be given by $\{L_i\}$ and $\{M_i\}$ and let us assume that the variables occurring in these two clauses have been standardized apart. Suppose that $\{l_i\}$ is a subset of $\{L_i\}$ and that $\{m_i\}$ is a subset of $\{M_i\}$ such that a most general unifier s exists for the union of the sets $\{l_i\}$ and $\{\sim m_i\}$. We say that the two clauses $\{L_i\}$ and $\{M_i\}$ *resolve* and that the new clause,

$$\{\{L_i\} - \{l_i\}\}s \cup \{\{M_i\} - \{m_i\}\}s,$$

is a *resolvent* of the two clauses.

If two clauses resolve, they may have more than one resolvent because there may be more than one way in which to choose $\{l_i\}$ and $\{m_i\}$. In any case, they can have at most a finite number of resolvents. As an example, consider the two clauses

$$P[x,f(A)] \vee P[x,f(y)] \vee Q(y)$$

and

$$\sim P[z,f(A)] \vee \sim Q(z).$$

With $\{l_i\} = \{P[x,f(A)]\}$ and $\{m_i\} = \{\sim P[z,f(A)]\}$, we obtain the resolvent

$$P[z,f(y)] \vee \sim Q(z) \vee Q(y).$$

With $\{l_i\} = [P(x,f(A)], P[x,f(y)]\}$ and $\{m_i\} = \{\sim P[z,f(A)]\}$, we obtain the resolvent

$$Q(A) \vee \sim Q(z).$$

Note that, in the latter case, two literals in the first clause were collapsed by the substitution into a single literal, complementary to an instance of one of the literals in the second clause.

There are, altogether, four different resolvents of these two clauses. Three of these are obtained by *resolving* on P and one by resolving on Q.

It is not difficult to show that resolution is a sound rule of inference; that is, that the resolvent of a pair of clauses also logically follows from that pair of clauses. When resolution is used in a special kind of theorem-proving system, described in the next chapter and called a refutation system, it is also complete. Every wff that logically follows from a set of wffs can be derived from that set of wffs using resolution refutation. For this reason and because of its simplicity, resolution systems are an important class of theorem-proving systems. Their very simplicity results, though, in certain inefficiencies that restrict their use in AI systems. Nevertheless. an understanding of resolution systems provides a basic foundation for understanding several other more efficient types of theorem-proving systems.

In the next two chapters, we examine a variety of these systems, beginning with ones using resolution.

4.3. THE USE OF THE PREDICATE CALCULUS IN AI

The situations, or states, and the goals of several types of problems can be described by predicate calculus wffs. In Figure 4.1, for example, we show a situation in which there are three blocks, A, B, and C, on a table. We can represent this situation by the conjunction of the following formulas:

$ON(C,A)$
$ONTABLE(A)$
$ONTABLE(B)$
$CLEAR(C)$
$CLEAR(B)$
$(\forall x)[CLEAR(x) \Rightarrow \sim(\exists y)ON(y,x)]$

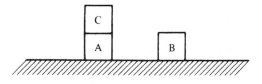

Fig. 4.1 A situation with three blocks on a table.

The formula $CLEAR(B)$ is intended to mean that block B has a clear top; that is, no other block is on it. The ON predicate is used to describe which blocks are (directly) on other blocks. (For this example, ON is not transitive; it is intended to mean *immediately* on top.) The formula $ONTABLE(B)$ is intended to mean that B is somewhere on the table. The last formula in the list gives information about how $CLEAR$ and ON are related.

A conjunction of several such formulas can serve as a description of a particular situation or "world state." We call it a *state description*. Actually, any finite conjunction of formulas really describes a *family* of different world states, each member of which might be regarded as an *interpretation* satisfying the formulas. Even assuming that we give the obvious "blocks-world" interpretation to constituents of the formulas, there is still an infinite family of states (perhaps involving additional blocks as well) whose members satisfy these formulas. We can always eliminate some of these interpretations by adding additional formulas to the state description; for example, the set listed above says nothing about the color of the blocks and, thus, describes the family of states in which the blocks can have various colors. If we added the formula $COLOR(B, YELLOW)$, some interpretations would obviously be eliminated. Even though a finite conjunction of formulas describes a family of states, we often loosely speak of *the* state described by the state description. We really mean, of course, the *set* of such states.

❧ We intend to use formulas, like those of our blocks-world example, as a global database in a production system. The way in which these formulas are used depends upon the problem and its representation.

Suppose the problem is to show that a certain property is true in a given state. For example, we might want to establish that there is nothing on block C in the state depicted in Figure 4.1. We can prove this fact by showing that the formula $\sim(\exists y)\,ON(y,C)$ logically follows from the state description for Figure 4.1. Equivalently, we could show that $\sim(\exists y)\,ON(y,C)$ is a theorem derived from the state description by the application of sound rules of inference.

We can use production systems to attempt to show that a given formula, called the *goal wff*, is a theorem derivable from a set of formulas (the state description). We call production systems of this sort *theorem-proving* systems or *deduction systems*. (In the next two chapters, we present various commutative production systems for theorem proving.)

153

In a forward production system, the global database is set to the initial state description, and (sound) production rules are applied until a state description is produced that either includes the goal formula or unifies with it in some appropriate fashion. In a backward production system, the global database is set to the goal formula and production rules are applied until a *subgoal* is produced that unifies with formulas in the state description. Combined, forward/backward, systems are also possible.

One obvious and direct use of theorem-proving systems is for proving theorems in mathematics and logic. A less obvious, but important, use of them is in intelligent information retrieval systems where deductions must be performed on a database of facts in order to derive an answer to a query. For example, from expressions like

$$MANAGER(PURCHASING\text{-}DEPT, JOHN\text{-}JONES),$$

$$WORKS\text{-}IN(PURCHASING\text{-}DEPT, JOE\text{-}SMITH),$$

and

$$\{[WORKS\text{-}IN(x,y) \wedge MANAGER(x,z)] \Rightarrow BOSS\text{-}OF(y,z)\},$$

an intelligent retrieval system might be expected to answer a query like "Who is Joe Smith's boss?" Such a query might be stated as the following theorem to be proved:

$$(\exists x) BOSS\text{-}OF(JOE\text{-}SMITH, x).$$

A constructive proof (that is, one that exhibited the "x" that exists) would provide an answer to the query.

Even many commonsense reasoning tasks that one would not ordinarily formalize can, in fact, be handled by predicate calculus theorem-proving systems. The general strategy is to represent specialized knowledge about the domain as predicate calculus expressions and to represent the problem or query as a theorem to be proved. The system then attempts to prove the theorem from the given expressions.

Other kinds of problems involve changing the state description to one that describes an entirely different state. Suppose, for example, that we have a "robot-type" problem in which the system must find a sequence of robot actions that change a configuration of blocks. We can specify the goal by a wff that describes the set of states acceptable as goal states. Referring to Figure 4.1, we might want to have block A on block B, and block B, in turn, on block C. Such a goal state (or rather set of states) could be expressed by the *goal formula* $[ON(A,B) \wedge ON(B,C)]$. Note that this goal formula certainly cannot be proved as a theorem from the state description for Figure 4.1. The robot must change the state to one that can be described by a set of formulas from which the goal wff can be proved.

Problems of this sort can be solved by production systems also. For a forward system, the global database is the state description. Each possible robot action is modeled by a production rule (an F-rule in forward systems). For example, if the robot can pick up a block, our production system would have a corresponding F-rule. The action of picking up a block changes the state of the world; application of the F-rule that models the action of picking up a block should make a corresponding change to the state description. A sequence of actions for achieving a goal can be computed by a forward production system that applies these F-rules to state descriptions until a terminal state description is produced, from which the goal wff can be proved. The solution sequence of F-rules constitutes a specification of a *plan* of actions for achieving the goal state.

Backward production systems for state-changing problems are also possible. They would use B-rules that are "inverse" models of the robot's actions. The formula describing the goal state would be used as the global database. B-rules would be applied until a subgoal formula was produced that could be proved from the initial state description.

Production systems that use F-rules and B-rules in this way, to model state-changing actions, are typically not commutative. An F-rule for picking up a block, for example, might have as a precondition that the block have a clear top. In Figure 4.1, this precondition is satisfied for block B, but it would not be true for block B after block C is placed on it. Thus, applying one F-rule to a certain state description might render other F-rules suddenly inapplicable. Production systems for solving state-changing problems are explored in detail in chapters 7 and 8. They find application especially in robot problem solving and in automatic programming.

4.4. BIBLIOGRAPHICAL AND HISTORICAL REMARKS

A book by Pospesel (1976) is a good elementary introduction to predicate calculus with many examples of English sentences represented as wffs. Two excellent textbooks on logic are those of Mendelson (1964) and Robbin (1969). Books by Chang and Lee (1973), Loveland (1978), and Robinson (1979) describe resolution methods.

A unification algorithm and a proof of correctness is presented in Robinson (1965). Several variations have appeared since. Raulefs et al. (1978) survey unification and matching. Paterson and Wegman (1976) present a linear-time (and space) unification algorithm.

The resolution rule was introduced by Robinson (1965) based on earlier work by Prawitz (1960) and others. The soundness and completeness of resolution was originally proved by Robinson (1965); proofs of these properties due to Kowalski and Hayes (1969) are presented in Nilsson (1971). The steps that we have outlined for converting any wff into clause form are based on the procedure of Davis and Putnam (1960). Clause form is also called *quantifier-free, conjunctive-normal form*. Manna and Waldinger (1979) have proposed a generalization of resolution that is applicable to wffs in nonclausal form. Maslov (1971 and other earlier papers in Russian) proposed a dual form of resolution, working with "goal clauses" that are disjunctions of conjunctions of literals. [See also Kuehner (1971).]

EXERCISES

$$\forall (x) \; [AM(B,x) \;=> \\ [F(B,x)]\lor \; M(B,x), \lor \\ \exists (z)[F(B,z) \lor M(B,z)]\land AM(z,x)]]$$

4.1 Suppose that we represent "Sam is Bill's father" by *FA-THER(BILL, SAM)* and "Harry is one of Bill's ancestors" by *ANCESTOR(BILL, HARRY)*. Write a wff to represent "Every ancestor of Bill is either his father, his mother, or one of their ancestors."

4.2 The connective $\otimes$ (exclusive or) is defined by the following truth table:

X1	X2	X1 ⊗ X2
T	T	F
F	T	T
T	F	T
F	F	F

What wff containing only $\sim$, $\vee$, and $\wedge$ connectives is equivalent to $(X1 \otimes X2)$?

4.3 Represent the following sentences by predicate calculus wffs. (Lean toward extravagance rather than economy in the number of different predicates and terms used. Do not, for example, use a single predicate letter to represent each sentence.)

(a) A computer system is intelligent if it can perform a task which, if performed by a human, requires intelligence.

(b) A formula whose main connective is a $\Rightarrow$ is equivalent to some formula whose main connective is a $\vee$.

(c) If the input to the unification algorithm is a set of unifiable expressions, the output is the mgu; if the input is a set of non-unifiable expressions, the output is *FAIL*.

(d) If a program cannot be told a fact, then it cannot learn that fact.

(e) If a production system is commutative, then, for any database, D, each member of the set of rules applicable to D is also applicable to any database produced by applying an applicable rule to D.

4.4 Show that modus ponens in the propositional calculus is sound.

157

4.5 Show that $(\exists z)(\forall x)[P(x) \Rightarrow Q(z)]$ and $(\exists z)[(\exists x)P(x) \Rightarrow Q(z)]$ are equivalent.

4.6 Convert the following wffs to clause form:

(a) $(\forall x)[P(x) \Rightarrow P(x)]$
(b) $\{\sim\{(\forall x)P(x)\}\} \Rightarrow (\exists x)[\sim P(x)]$
(c) $\sim(\forall x)\{P(x) \Rightarrow \{(\forall y)[P(y) \Rightarrow P(f(x,y))]$
$\qquad \wedge \sim(\forall y)[Q(x,y) \Rightarrow P(y)]\}\}\}$
(d) $(\forall x)(\exists y)$
$\qquad \{[P(x,y) \Rightarrow Q(y,x)] \wedge [Q(y,x) \Rightarrow S(x,y)]\}$
$\qquad \Rightarrow (\exists x)(\forall y)[P(x,y) \Rightarrow S(x,y)]$

4.7 Show by an example that the composition of substitutions is not commutative.

4.8 Show that resolution is sound; that is, show that the resolvent of two clauses logically follows from the two clauses.

4.9 Find the mgu of the set $\{P(x,z,y), P(w,u,w), P(A,u,u)\}$.

4.10 Explain why the following sets of literals do not unify:

(a) $\{P(f(x,x),A), P(f(y,f(y,A)),A)\}$
(b) $\{\sim P(A), P(x)\}$
(c) $\{P(f(A),x), P(x,A)\}$

4.11 The following wffs were given a "blocks-world" interpretation in this chapter:

$ON(C,A)$
$ONTABLE(A)$
$ONTABLE(B)$
$CLEAR(C)$
$CLEAR(B)$
$(\forall x)[CLEAR(x) \Rightarrow \sim(\exists y)ON(y,x)]$

Invent two different (non-blocks-world) interpretations that satisfy the conjunction of these wffs.

4.12 In our examples representing English sentences by wffs, we have not been concerned about tense. Can you express the following sentences as wffs:

Shakespeare writes "Hamlet." $\forall (t)\ PRESENT\ (t) = 7\ (WRITE(H,S))$
Shakespeare wrote "Hamlet."
Shakespeare will write "Hamlet." $\exists (x)\ Future\ (x) = 7($ $)$
Shakespeare will have written "Hamlet."
Shakespeare had written "Hamlet."

we invent a Now

WRITES (S, H, Now) for present

past $(\exists (t))\ [WRITES(S,H,t)) \wedge LT(t, Now)]$

future $(\exists (t)\ [WRITES(S,H,t)) \wedge GT(t, Now)]$

CHAPTER 5

RESOLUTION REFUTATION SYSTEMS

In this chapter and chapter 6, we are primarily concerned with systems that prove theorems in the predicate calculus. Our interest in theorem proving is not limited to applications in mathematics; we also investigate applications in information retrieval, commonsense reasoning, and automatic programming. Two main types of theorem-proving systems will be discussed: here, systems based on resolution, and in chapter 6, systems that use various forms of implications as production rules.

In the prototypical theorem-proving problem, we have a set, S, of wffs from which we wish to prove some goal wff, W. Resolution-based systems are designed to produce proofs by contradiction or *refutations*. In a resolution refutation, we first negate the goal wff and then add the negation to the set, S. This expanded set is then converted to a set of clauses, and we use resolution in an attempt to derive a contradiction, represented by the empty clause, NIL.

A simple argument can be given to justify the process of proof by refutation. Suppose a wff, W, logically follows from a set, S, of wffs; then, by definition, every interpretation satisfying S also satisfies W. None of the interpretations satisifying S can satisfy $\sim W$, and, therefore, no interpretation can satisfy the union of S and $\{\sim W\}$. A set of wffs that cannot be satisfied by any interpretation is called *unsatisfiable;* thus, if W logically follows from S, the set $S \cup \{\sim W\}$ is unsatisfiable.

It can be shown that if resolution is applied repeatedly to a set of unsatisfiable clauses, eventually the empty clause, NIL, will be produced. Thus, if W logically follows from S, then resolution will eventually produce the empty clause from the clause representation of $S \cup \{\sim W\}$. Conversely, it can be shown that if the empty clause is produced from the clause representation of $S \cup \{\sim W\}$, then W logically follows from S.

161

Let us consider a simple example of this process. Suppose the following statements are asserted:

(1) Whoever can read is literate.
$(\forall x)[R(x) \Rightarrow L(x)]$

(2) Dolphins are not literate.
$(\forall x)[D(x) \Rightarrow \sim L(x)]$

(3) Some dolphins are intelligent.
$(\exists x)[D(x) \wedge I(x)]$

From these, we want to prove the statement:

(4) Some who are intelligent cannot read.
$(\exists x)[I(x) \wedge \sim R(x)]$

The set of clauses corresponding to statements 1 through 3 is:

(1)　$\sim R(x) \vee L(x)$

(2)　$\sim D(y) \vee \sim L(y)$

(3a)　$D(A)$

(3b)　$I(A)$

where the variables have been standardized apart and where A is a Skolem constant. The negation of the theorem to be proved, converted to clause form, is

(4′)　$\sim I(z) \vee R(z)$.

To prove our theorem by resolution refutation involves generating resolvents from the set of clauses 1-3 and 4′, adding these resolvents to the set, and continuing until the empty clause is produced. One possible proof (there are more than one) produces the following sequence of resolvents:

(5)　$R(A)$　　resolvent of 3b and 4′

(6)　$L(A)$　　resolvent of 5 and 1

(7) $\sim D(A)$ resolvent of 6 and 2

(8) *NIL* resolvent of 7 and 3a

5.1. PRODUCTION SYSTEMS FOR RESOLUTION REFUTATIONS

We can think of a system for producing resolution refutations as a production system. The global database is a set of clauses, and the rule schema is resolution. Instances of this schema are applied to pairs of clauses in the database to produce a derived clause. The new database is then the old set of clauses augmented by the derived clause. The termination condition for this production system is a test to see if the database contains the empty clause.

It is straightforward to show that such a production system is commutative. Because it is commutative, we can use an irrevocable control regime. That is, after performing a resolution, we never need to provide for backtracking or for consideration of alternative resolutions instead. We must emphasize that using an irrevocable control regime does not necessarily mean that every resolution performed is "on the path" to producing the empty clause; usually there will be several irrelevant resolutions applied. But, because the system is commutative, we are never prevented from applying an appropriate resolution later, even after having applied some irrelevant ones.

Suppose we start with a set, S, of clauses called the *base set*. The basic algorithm for a resolution refutation production system can then be written as follows:

Procedure **RESOLUTION**

1 $CLAUSES \leftarrow S$

2 **until** *NIL* is a member of *CLAUSES*, **do:**

3   **begin**

163

4   **select** two distinct, resolvable clauses
c_i and c_j in *CLAUSES*

5   compute a resolvent, r_{ij} of c_i
and c_j

6   *CLAUSES* ← The set produced by adding r_{ij}
to *CLAUSES*

7   **end**

5.2. CONTROL STRATEGIES FOR RESOLUTION METHODS

The decisions about which two clauses in *CLAUSES* to resolve (statement 4) and which resolution of these clauses to perform (statement 5) are made irrevocably by the control strategy. Several strategies for selecting clauses have been developed for resolution; we give some examples shortly.

In order to keep track of which resolutions have been selected and to avoid duplicated effort, it is helpful for the control strategy to use a structure called a *derivation graph*. The nodes in such a graph are labeled by clauses; initially, there is a node for every clause in the base set. When two clauses, c_i and c_j, produce a resolvent, r_{ij}, we create a new node, labeled r_{ij}, with edges linking it to both the c_i and c_j nodes. Here we deviate from the usual tree terminology and say that c_i and c_j are the *parents* of r_{ij} and that r_{ij} is a *descendant* of c_i and c_j. (Recall that we introduced the concept of a derivation graph in chapter 3.)

A resolution refutation can be represented as a *refutation tree* (within the derivation graph) having a root node labeled by *NIL*. In Figure 5.1 we show a refutation tree for the example discussed in the last section.

The control strategy searches for a refutation by growing a derivation *graph* until a *tree* is produced with a root node labeled by the empty

164

clause, *NIL*. A control strategy for a refutation system is said to be *complete* if its use results in a procedure that will find a contradiction (eventually) whenever one exists. (The completeness of a *strategy* should not be confused with the *logical completeness* of an inference rule discussed in chapter 4.) In AI applications, complete strategies are not so important as ones that find refutations efficiently.

5.2.1. THE BREADTH-FIRST STRATEGY

In the breadth-first strategy, all of the first-level resolvents are computed first, then the second-level resolvents, and so on. (A *first-level resolvent* is one between two clauses in the base set; an *i-th level resolvent* is one whose deepest parent is an $(i - 1)$-th level resolvent.) The breadth-first strategy is complete, but it is grossly inefficient.

In Figure 5.2 we show the refutation graph produced by a breadth-first strategy for the example problem of the last section. All of the first- and second-level resolvents are shown, and we indicate that *NIL* is among the third-level resolvents. (Note that our refutation shown in Figure 5.1 did not produce the empty clause until the fourth level.)

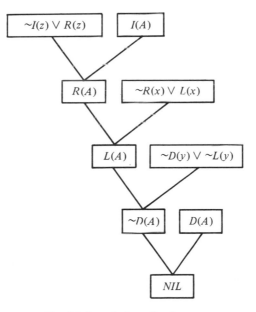

Fig. 5.1 A resolution refutation tree.

165

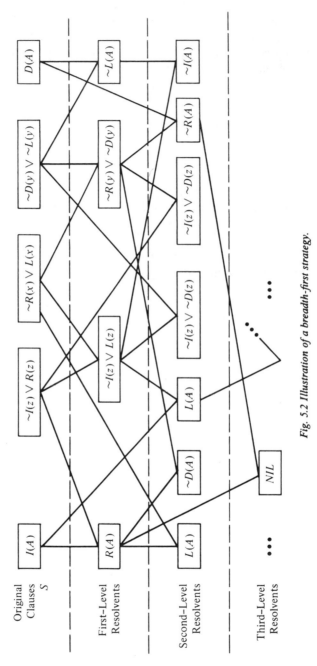

Fig. 5.2 Illustration of a breadth-first strategy.

5.2.2. THE SET-OF-SUPPORT STRATEGY

A set-of-support refutation is one in which at least one parent of each resolvent is selected from among the clauses resulting from the negation of the goal wff or from their descendants (the *set of support*). It can be shown that a set-of-support refutation exists whenever any refutation exists and, therefore, that the set of support can be made the basis of a complete strategy. The strategy need only guarantee to search for all possible set-of-support refutations (in breadth-first manner, say). Set-of-support strategies are usually more efficient than unconstrained breadth-first ones.

In a set-of-support refutation, each resolution has the flavor of a backward reasoning step because it uses a clause originating from the goal wff, or one of its descendants. Each of the resolvents in a set-of-support refutation might then correspond to a subgoal in a backward production system. One advantage of a refutation system is that it permits what are essentially backward and forward reasoning steps to occur in a simple fashion in the same production system. (Forward reasoning steps correspond to resolutions between clauses that do not descend from the theorem to be proved.)

In Figure 5.3 we show a refutation graph produced by the set-of-support strategy for our example problem. Notice that, in this case, set of support does not permit finding the empty clause at the third level. A third-level refutation for this problem necessarily involves resolving two clauses outside the set of support. Comparing Figure 5.2 with Figure 5.3, we see that set of support produces fewer clauses at each level than does unconstrained breadth-first resolution. Typically, the set-of-support strategy results in slower growth of the clause set and thus helps to moderate the usual combinatorial explosion. Usually this containment of clause-set growth more than compensates for the fact that a restrictive strategy, like set of support, often increases the depth at which the empty clause is first produced.

The refutation tree in Figure 5.1 is one that could have been produced by a set-of-support strategy. We show the top part of this tree by darkening some of the branches in Figure 5.3.

5.2.3. THE UNIT-PREFERENCE STRATEGY

The unit-preference strategy is a modification of the set-of-support strategy in which, instead of filling out each level in breadth-first fashion,

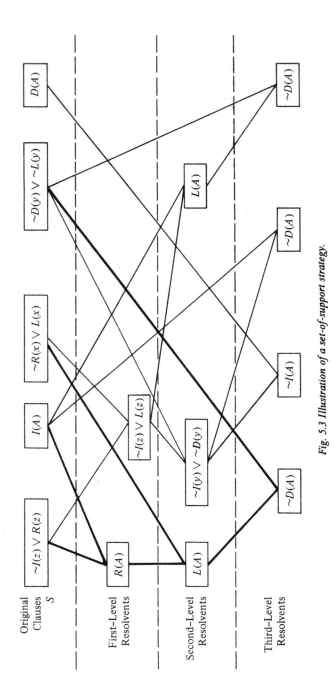

Fig. 5.3 Illustration of a set-of-support strategy.

we try to select a single-literal clause (called a *unit*) to be a parent in a resolution. Every time units are used in resolution, the resolvents have fewer literals than do their other parents. This process helps to focus the search toward producing the empty clause and, thus, typically increases efficiency.

The refutation tree of Figure 5.1 is one that might have been produced by a unit-preference strategy.

5.2.4. THE LINEAR-INPUT FORM STRATEGY

A linear-input form refutation is one in which each resolvent has at least one parent belonging to the base set. In Figure 5.4 we show how a refutation graph would be generated using this strategy on our example problem. Note that the first level of Figure 5.4 is the same as the first level of Figure 5.2. At subsequent levels, the linear-input form strategy does reduce the number of clauses produced. Again, the use of this strategy on our example problem does not permit us to find a third-level empty clause. Note that the refutation tree of Figure 5.1 qualifies as a linear-input form refutation. We indicate part of this tree by darkening some of the branches in Figure 5.4.

There are cases in which a refutation exists but a linear-input form refutation does not; therefore, linear-input form strategies are not complete. To see that linear-input form refutations do not always exist for unsatisfiable sets, consider the following example set of clauses:

$$Q(u) \lor P(A)$$
$$\sim Q(w) \lor P(w)$$
$$\sim Q(x) \lor \sim P(x)$$
$$Q(y) \lor \sim P(y)$$

The set is clearly unsatisfiable, as evidenced by the refutation tree of Figure 5.5. A linear-input form refutation must (in particular) have one of the parents of *NIL* be a member of the base set. But to produce the empty clause in this case, one must either resolve two single-literal clauses or two clauses that collapse in resolution to single-literal clauses. None of the members of the base set meets either of these criteria, so there cannot be a linear-input form refutation for this set.

Notwithstanding their lack of completeness, linear-input form strategies are often used because of their simplicity and efficiency.

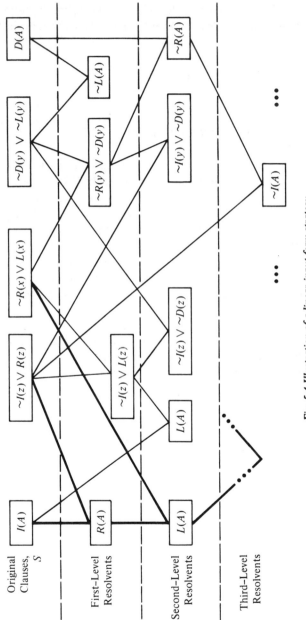

Fig. 5.4 Illustration of a linear-input form strategy.

5.2.5. THE ANCESTRY-FILTERED FORM STRATEGY

An ancestry-filtered form refutation is one in which each resolvent has a parent that is either in the base set or that is an ancestor of the other parent. Thus, ancestry-filtered form is very much like linear form. It can be shown that a control strategy guaranteed to produce all ancestry-filtered form proofs is complete.

As an example, the refutation tree of Figure 5.5 is one that could have been produced by an ancestry-filtered form strategy. The clause marked with an asterisk is used as an "ancestor" in this case. It can also be shown that completeness of the strategy is preserved if the ancestors that are used are limited to *merges*. (Recall from chapter 4 that a *merge* is a resolvent that inherits a literal from each parent such that this literal is collapsed to a singleton by the mgu.) We note in Figure 5.5 that the clause marked by an asterisk is a merge.

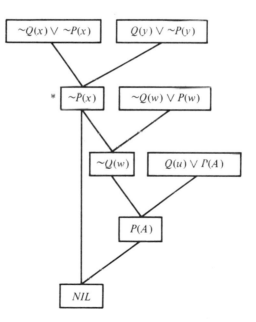

Fig. 5.5 A refutation tree.

5.2.6. COMBINATIONS OF STRATEGIES

It is also possible to combine control strategies. A combination of set of support with either linear-input form or ancestry-filtered form is common. Let us consider the set-of-support/linear-input form strategy, as an example. This strategy can be viewed as a simple type of reasoning backward from a goal to subgoal to sub-subgoal and so on. It happens that the first three levels in Figure 5.3 contain only clauses that are permitted by this combination strategy, so that the combination for those levels does not further restrict the set-of-support strategy used in that figure. Occasionally, however, the combination strategy leads to a slower growth of the clause set than would either strategy alone.

The set-of-support, linear-input form, and ancestry-filtered form strategies restrict resolutions. Of all the resolutions that these strategies allow, the strategies say nothing about the *order* in which these resolutions are performed. We have already mentioned that an inappropriate order does not *prevent* us from finding a refutation. This fact does not mean, however, that resolution order has no effect on the efficiency of the process. On the contrary, an appropriate order of performing resolutions can prevent the generation of large numbers of unneeded clauses. The unit-preference strategy is one example of an *ordering strategy*. Other ordering strategies based on the number of literals in a clause and the complexity of the terms in a clause can also be devised. The order in which resolutions are performed is crucial to the efficiency of resolution systems. Since we do not concentrate on applications of resolution refutation systems in this book, the interested reader is referred to the citations at the end of this chapter for references to papers and books dealing with ordering strategies for resolution systems.

5.3. SIMPLIFICATION STRATEGIES

Sometimes a set of clauses can be simplified by elimination of certain clauses or by elimination of certain literals in the clauses. These simplifications are such that the simplified set of clauses is unsatisfiable if and only if the original set is unsatisfiable. Thus, employing these simplification strategies helps to reduce the rate of growth of new clauses.

5.3.1. ELIMINATION OF TAUTOLOGIES

Any clause containing a literal and its negation (we call such a clause a *tautology*) may be eliminated, since any unsatisfiable set containing a tautology is still unsatisfiable after removing it, and conversely. Thus, clauses like $P(x) \vee B(y) \vee \sim B(y)$ and $P(f(A)) \vee \sim P(f(A))$ may be eliminated.

5.3.2. PROCEDURAL ATTACHMENT

Sometimes it is possible and more convenient to *evaluate* the truth values of literals than it would be to include these literals, or their negations, in the base set. Typically, evaluations are performed for ground instances. For example, if the predicate symbol "E" stands for the equality relation between numbers, it is a simple matter to evaluate ground instances such as $E(7,3)$ when they occur; whereas we would probably not want to include in the base set a table containing a large number of ground instances of $E(x,y)$ and $\sim E(x,y)$.

It is instructive to look more closely at what is meant by "evaluating" an expression like $E(7,3)$. Predicate calculus expressions are linguistic constructs that denote truth values, elements, functions, or relations in a domain. Such expressions can be interpreted with reference to a model which associates linguistic entities with appropriate domain entities. The end result is that the values T or F become associated with sentences in the language.

Given a model, we could use any finite processes for interpretation with respect to it as a way of deciding truth values of sentences. Unfortunately, models and interpretation processes are not, in general, finite. Often, we can use partial models, however. In our equality example, we can associate with the predicate symbol, E, a computer program that tests the equality of two numbers within the finite domain of the program. Let us call this program **EQUALS**. We say that the program **EQUALS** is *attached* to the predicate symbol E. We can associate the linguistic symbols 7 and 3 (i.e., *numerals*) with the computer data items **7** and **3** (i.e., *numbers*), respectively. We say that **7** is *attached* to 7, and that **3** is *attached* to 3, and that the computer program and arguments represented by **EQUALS(7,3)** are *attached* to the linguistic expression $E(7,3)$. Now we can run the program to obtain the value **F** (false) which in turn induces the value F for $E(7,3)$.

173

We can also attach procedures to function symbols. For example, an addition program can be attached to the function symbol *plus*. In this manner, we can establish a connection or *procedural attachment* between executable computer code and some of the linguistic expressions in our predicate calculus language. Evaluation of attached procedures can be thought of as a process of interpretation with respect to a *partial* model. When it can be used, procedural attachment reduces the search effort that would otherwise be required to prove theorems.

A literal is *evaluated* when it is interpreted by running attached procedures. Typically, not all of the literals in a set of clauses can be evaluated, but the clause set can nevertheless be simplified by such evaluations. If a literal in a clause evaluates to T, the entire clause can be eliminated without affecting the unsatisfiability of the rest of the set. If a literal evaluates to F, then the occurrence of just that literal in the clause can be eliminated. Thus the clause $P(x) \vee Q(A) \vee E(7,3)$ can be replaced by $P(x) \vee Q(A)$, since $E(7,3)$ evaluates to F.

5.3.3. ELIMINATION BY SUBSUMPTION

By definition, a clause $\{L_i\}$ *subsumes* a clause $\{M_i\}$ if there exists a substitution s such that $\{L_i\}s$ is a subset of $\{M_i\}$. As examples:

$P(x)$ subsumes $P(y) \vee Q(z)$

$P(x)$ subsumes $P(A)$

$P(x)$ subsumes $P(A) \vee Q(z)$

$P(x) \vee Q(A)$ subsumes $P(f(A)) \vee Q(A) \vee R(y)$

A clause in an unsatisfiable set that is subsumed by another clause in the set can be eliminated without affecting the unsatisfiability of the rest of the set. Eliminating clauses subsumed by others frequently leads to substantial reductions in the number of resolutions that need to be made in finding a refutation.

5.4. EXTRACTING ANSWERS FROM RESOLUTION REFUTATIONS

Many applications of predicate calculus theorem-proving systems involve proving formulas containing existentially quantified variables, and finding values or instances for these variables. That is, we might want to know if a wff such as $(\exists x)\, W(x)$, logically follows from S, and if it does, we want an instance of the "x" that exists. The problem of finding a proof for $(\exists x)\, W(x)$ from S is an ordinary predicate calculus theorem-proving problem, but producing the satisfying instance for x requires that the proof method be "constructive."

We note that the prospect of producing satisfying instances for existentially quantified variables allows the possibility for posing quite general questions. For example, we could ask "Does there exist a solution sequence to a certain 8-puzzle?" If a constructive proof can be found that a solution does exist, then we could produce the desired solution also. We could also ask whether there exist programs that perform desired computations. From a constructive proof of a program's existence, we could produce the desired program. (We must remember, though, that complex questions will generally have complex proofs, possibly so complex that our automatic proof-finding procedures will not find them.) In this section we describe a process by which a satisfying instance of an existentially quantified variable in a wff can be extracted from a resolution refutation for that wff.

5.4.1. AN EXAMPLE

Consider the following trivially simple problem: "If Fido goes wherever John goes and if John is at school, where is Fido?" Quite clearly the problem specifies two facts and then asks a question whose answer presumably can be deduced from these facts. The facts might be translated into the set S of wffs

$$(\forall x)[AT(JOHN, x) \Rightarrow AT(FIDO, x)]$$

and

$$AT(JOHN, SCHOOL).$$

175

The question "where is Fido?" can be answered if we first prove that the wff

$(\exists x) AT(FIDO, x)$

logically follows from S and then find an instance of the x "that exists." The key idea is to convert the question into a goal wff containing an existential quantifier such that the existentially quantified variable represents an answer to the question. If the question can be answered from the facts given, the goal wff created in this manner will logically follow from S. After obtaining a proof, we then try to extract an instance of the existentially quantified variable to serve as an answer. In our example we can easily prove that $(\exists x) AT(FIDO, x)$ follows from S. We can also show that a relatively simple process extracts the appropriate answer.

The resolution refutation is obtained in the usual manner, by first negating the wff to be proved, adding this negation to the set S, converting all of the members of this enlarged set to clause form, and then, by resolution, showing that this set of clauses is unsatisfiable. A refutation tree for our example is shown in Figure 5.6. The clauses resulting from the wffs in S are called *axioms*. Note that the negation of the goal wff $(\exists x) AT(FIDO, x)$ produces

$(\forall x)[\sim AT(FIDO, x)]$,

whose clause form is simply $\sim AT(FIDO, x)$.

Next we must extract an answer to the question "Where is Fido?" from this refutation tree. The process for doing so in this case is as follows:

(1) Append to each clause arising from the negation
     of the goal wff its own negation. Thus
     $\sim AT(FIDO, x)$ becomes the tautology
     $\sim AT(FIDO, x) \vee AT(FIDO, x)$.

(2) Following the structure of the refutation tree,
     perform the same resolutions as before until some
     clause is obtained at the root. (We make the phrase
     the same resolutions more precise later.)

(3) Use the clause at the root as an *answer statement*.

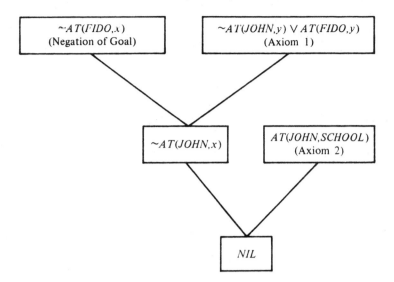

Fig. 5.6 Refutation tree for example problem.

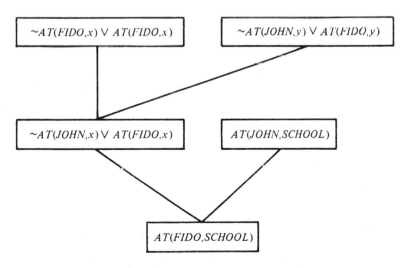

Fig. 5.7 The modified proof tree for example problem.

In our example, these steps produce the proof tree shown in Figure 5.7 with the clause $AT(FIDO, SCHOOL)$ at the root. This clause, then, is the appropriate answer to the problem.

We note that the answer statement has a form similar to that of the goal wff. In this case, the only difference is that we have a constant (the answer) in the answer statement in the place of the existentially quantified variable in the goal wff.

In the next sections, we deal more thoroughly with the answer extraction process, justify its validity, and discuss how it should be employed if the goal wff contains universal as well as existential quantifiers.

5.4.2. THE ANSWER EXTRACTION PROCESS

Answer extraction involves converting a refutation tree (with NIL at the root) to a proof tree with some statement at the root that can be used as an answer. Since the conversion involves converting every clause arising from the negation of the goal wff into a tautology, the converted proof tree is a resolution proof that the statement at the root logically follows from the axioms plus tautologies. Hence it also follows from the axioms alone. Thus, the converted proof tree itself justifies the extraction process!

Although the method is simple, there are some fine points that can be clarified by considering some additional examples.

EXAMPLE 1. Consider the following set of wffs:

1. $(\forall x)(\forall y)\{[P(x,y) \wedge P(y,z)] \Rightarrow G(x,z)\}$

and

2. $(\forall y)(\exists x)P(x,y)$.

We might interpret these as follows:

For all x and y, if x is the parent of y and y is the parent of z, then x is the grandparent of z.

and

Everyone has a parent.

Given these wffs as hypotheses, suppose we asked the question "Do there exist individuals x and y such that x is the grandparent of y?" The goal wff corresponding to this question is:

$(\exists x)(\exists y) G(x,y)$.

The goal wff is easily proved by a resolution refutation. The refutation tree is shown in Figure 5.8. The literals that are unified in each resolution are underlined. We call the subset of literals in a clause that is unified during a resolution the *unification set*.

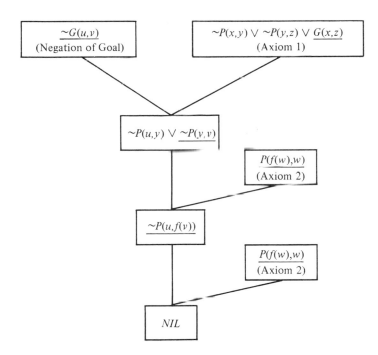

Fig. 5.8 A refutation tree for Example 1.

179

Note that the clause $P(f(w), w)$ contains a Skolem function, f, introduced to eliminate the existential quantifier in Axiom 2. (The function f can be interpreted as a function that is defined to name the parent of any individual.) The modified proof tree is shown in Figure 5.9. The negation of the goal wff is transformed into a tautology, and the resolutions follow those performed in the tree of Figure 5.8. *Each resolution in the modified tree uses unification sets that correspond precisely to the unification sets of the refutation tree.* Again, the unification sets are underlined.

The proof tree of Figure 5.9 has $G(f(f(v)), v)$ at the root. This clause represents the wff $(\forall v)[G(f(f(v)), v)]$, which is the answer statement. The answer statement provides an answer to the question "Are there x and y such that x is the grandparent of y?" The answer in this case involves the definitional function f. Any v and the parent of the parent of v are examples of individuals satisfying the conditions of the question. Again, the answer statement has a form similar to that of the goal wff.

EXAMPLE 2. Here we illustrate the way in which more complex clauses arising from the negation of the goal wff are transformed into tautologies.

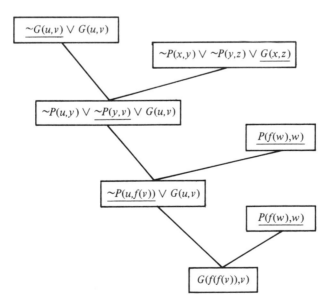

Fig. 5.9 The modified proof tree for Example 1.

Consider the following set of clauses or axioms:

$$\sim A(x) \vee F(x) \vee G(f(x))$$
$$\sim F(x) \vee B(x)$$
$$\sim F(x) \vee C(x)$$
$$\sim G(x) \vee B(x)$$
$$\sim G(x) \vee D(x)$$
$$A(g(x)) \vee F(h(x))$$

(In this example, we assume that the variables in these clauses are standardized apart before performing resolutions. For simplicity, we do not indicate this process explicitly.) We desire to prove, from these axioms, the goal wff

$$(\exists x)(\exists y)\{[B(x) \wedge C(x)] \vee [D(y) \wedge B(y)]\} \ .$$

The negation of this wff produces two clauses, each with two literals:

$$\sim B(x) \vee \sim C(x)$$
$$\sim B(x) \vee \sim D(x) \ .$$

A refutation tree for this combined set of clauses is shown in Figure 5.10.

Now, to transform this tree we must convert the clauses resulting from the negation of the goal wff (shown in double boxes in Figure 5.10) into tautologies, by appending their own negations. In this case, the negated clauses involve $\wedge$ symbols. For example, the clause $\sim B(x) \vee \sim C(x)$ is converted to the formula $\sim B(x) \vee \sim C(x) \vee [B(x) \wedge C(x)]$. This formula is not a clause because of the occurrence of the conjunction $[B(x) \wedge C(x)]$; nevertheless, we treat this conjunction as a single literal and proceed formally as if the formula were a clause (none of the elements of this conjunction are ever in any unification sets). Similarly, we transform the clause $\sim D(x) \vee \sim B(x)$ into the tautology $\sim D(x) \vee \sim B(x) \vee [D(x) \wedge B(x)]$.

Performing the resolutions dictated by corresponding unification sets, we then produce the proof graph shown in Figure 5.11. Here the root clause is the wff

$$(\forall x)\{[B(g(x)) \wedge C(g(x))] \vee [D(f(g(x))) \wedge B(f(g(x)))]$$

$$\vee [B(h(x)) \wedge C(h(x))]\} \ .$$

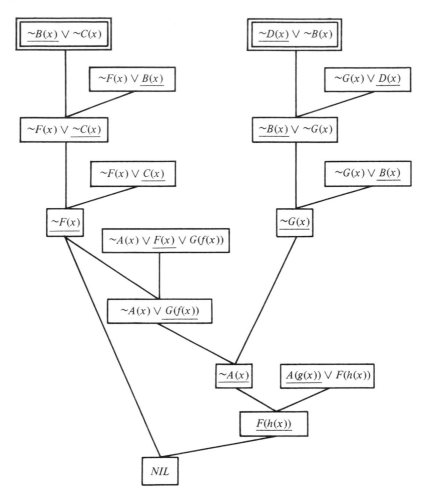

Fig. 5.10 A refutation tree for Example 2.

We note that, in this example, the answer statement has a form somewhat different from the form of the goal wff. The underlined part of the answer statement is obviously similar to the entire goal wff—with $g(x)$ taking the place of the existentially quantified variable x in the goal wff, and $f(g(x))$ taking the place of the existentially quantified variable y in the goal wff—but, in this example, there is the extra disjunct $[B(h(x)) \wedge C(h(x))]$ in the answer statement. This disjunct, however, is similar to one of the disjuncts of the goal wff, with $h(x)$ taking the place of the existentially quantified variable x of the goal wff.

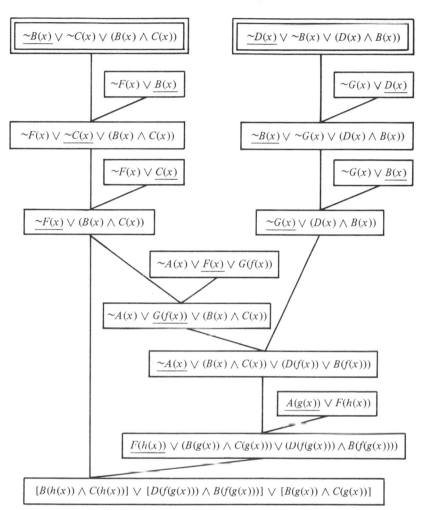

Fig. 5.11 The modified proof tree for Example 2.

In general, if the goal wff itself is in disjunctive normal form, then our answer-extraction process will produce a statement that is a disjunction of expressions, each of which is similar in form either to the entire goal wff or to one or more disjuncts of the entire goal wff. For this reason we claim that the root clause here can be used as an "answer" to the "question" represented by the goal wff.

5.4.3. GOAL WFFS CONTAINING UNIVERSALLY QUANTIFIED VARIABLES

A problem arises when the goal wff contains universally quantified variables. These universally quantified variables become existentially quantified in the negation of the goal wff, causing Skolem functions to be introduced. What is to be the interpretation of these Skolem functions if they should eventually appear as terms in the answer statement?

We illustrate this problem with another example. Let the clause form of the axioms be:

$C(x,p(x))$, meaning "For all x, x is the child of $p(x)$" (that is, p is a function mapping a child of an individual into the individual);

and

$\sim C(x,y) \vee P(y,x)$, meaning "For all x and y, if x is the child of y, then y is the parent of x."

Now suppose we wish to ask the question "For any x, who is the parent of x?" The goal wff corresponding to this question is:

$(\forall x)(\exists y)P(y,x)$.

Converting the negation of this goal wff to clause form, we obtain, first:

$(\exists x)(\forall y)[\sim P(y,x)]$,

and then:

$\sim P(y,A)$,

where A is a Skolem function of no arguments (i.e., a constant) introduced to eliminate the existential quantifier occurring in the negation of the goal wff. (The negation of the goal wff alleges that there is some individual, whom we call "A," that has no parent.) A modified proof tree with answer statement at the root is shown in Figure 5.12.

Here we obtain the somewhat obtuse answer statement $P(p(A),A)$, containing the Skolem function A. The interpretation should be that, regardless of the Skolem function A (hypothesized to spoil the validity of the goal wff), we are able to prove $P(p(A),A)$. That is, *any* individual A, thought to spoil the goal wff, actually satisfies the goal wff. The constant A could have been a variable without invalidating the proof shown in Figure 5.12. It can be shown [Luckham and Nilsson (1971)] that in the answer-extracting process it is correct to replace any Skolem functions in the clauses coming from the negation of the goal wff by new variables. These new variables will never be substituted out of the modified proof but will merely trickle down to occur in the final answer statement. Resolutions in the modified proof will still be limited to those defined by those unification sets corresponding to the unification sets occurring in the original refutation. Variables might be renamed during some resolutions so that, possibly, a variable used in place of a Skolem function may get renamed and thus might be the "ancestor" of several new variables in the final answer statement. We illustrate some of the things that might happen in the latter case by two simple examples.

EXAMPLE 3. Suppose S consists of the single axiom (in clause form):

$$P(B,w,w) \vee P(A,u,u),$$

and suppose we wish to prove the goal wff:

$$(\exists x)(\forall z)(\exists y)P(x,z,y).$$

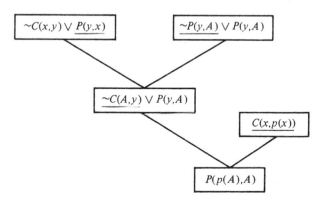

Fig. 5.12 *A modified proof tree for an answer statement.*

185

A refutation tree is shown in Figure 5.13. Here, the clause resulting from the negation of the goal wff contains the Skolem function $g(x)$. In Figure 5.13 we also show the modified proof tree in which the variable t is used in place of the Skolem function $g(x)$. Here we obtain a proof of the answer statement $P(A,t,t) \vee P(B,z,z)$ that is identical (except for variable names) to the single axiom. This example illustrates how variables introduced by renaming variables in one clause during a resolution can finally appear in the answer statement.

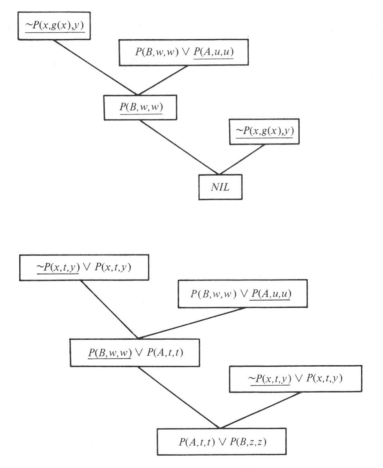

Fig. 5.13 Trees for Example 3.

EXAMPLE 4. As another example, suppose we wish to prove the same goal wff as before, but now from the single axiom $P(z,u,z) \lor P(A,u,u)$. The refutation tree is shown in Figure 5.14. Here the clause coming from the negation of the goal wff contains the Skolem function $g(x)$.

In Figure 5.14 we also show the modified proof tree in which the variable w is used in place of the Skolem function $g(x)$. Here we obtain a proof of the answer statement:

$$P(z,w,z) \lor P(A,w,w),$$

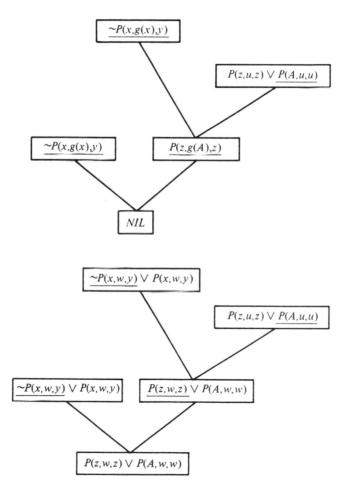

Fig. 5.14 Trees for Example 4.

which is identical (except for variable names) to the single axiom. Careful analysis of the unifying substitutions in this example will show that although the resolutions in the modified tree are constrained by corresponding unification sets, the substitutions used in the modified tree can be more general than those in the original refutation tree.

In conclusion, the steps of the answer extraction process can be summarized as follows:

1. A resolution-refutation tree is found by some search process. The unification subsets of the clauses in this tree are marked.

2. New variables are substituted for any Skolem functions occurring in the clauses that result from the negation of the goal wff.

3. The clauses resulting from the negation of the goal wff are converted into tautologies by appending to them their own negations.

4. A modified proof tree is produced modeling the structure of the original refutation tree. Each resolution in the modified tree uses a unification set determined by the unification set used by the corresponding resolution in the refutation tree.

5. The clause at the root of the modified tree is the answer statement extracted by this process.

Obviously, the answer statement depends upon the refutation from which it is extracted. Several different refutations might exist for the same problem; from each refutation we could extract an answer, and, although some of these answers might be identical, it is possible that some answer statements would be more general than others. Usually we have no way of knowing whether or not the answer statement extracted from a given proof is the most general answer possible. We could, of course, continue to search for proofs until we found one producing a sufficiently general answer. Because of the undecidability of the predicate calculus, though, we would not always know whether we had found all of the possible proofs for a wff, W, from a set, S.

5.5. BIBLIOGRAPHICAL AND HISTORICAL REMARKS

Various control strategies for resolution refutations are discussed in Loveland (1978) and Chang and Lee (1973). Ordering strategies have been proposed by Boyer (1971), Kowalski (1970), Reiter (1971), Kowalski and Kuehner (1971), Minker, Fishman, and McSkimin (1973), and Minker and Zanon (1979).

Some examples of large-scale resolution refutation systems are those of Guard et al. (1969), McCharen et al. (1976), Minker et al. (1974), and Luckham et al. (1978) [The latter is also described in Allen and Luckham (1970).] Unlike some of the very earliest resolution systems, many of these possess control knowledge adequate to prove some rather difficult theorems.

Our discussion of procedural attachment is based on the work of Weyhrauch (1980) on FOL. The process for extracting answers from resolution refutations was originally proposed by Green (1969b). Our treatment of answer extraction is based on work by Luckham and Nilsson (1971), who extended the method.

EXERCISES

5.1 Find a linear input form refutation for the following unsatisfiable set of clauses:

$$\sim P \vee \sim Q \vee R$$
$$\sim S \vee T$$
$$\sim T \vee P$$
$$S$$
$$\sim R$$
$$\sim S \vee U$$
$$\sim U \vee Q$$

5.2 Indicate which of the following clauses are subsumed by $P(f(x),y)$:

(a) $P(f(A),f(x)) \vee P(z,f(y))$
(b) $P(z,A) \vee \sim P(A,z)$
(c) $P(f(f(x)),z)$
(d) $P(f(z),z) \vee Q(x)$
(e) $P(A,A) \vee P(f(x),y)$

5.3 Show by a resolution refutation that *each* of the following formulas is a tautology:

(a) $(P \Rightarrow Q) \Rightarrow [(R \vee P) \Rightarrow (R \vee Q)]$
(b) $[(P \Rightarrow Q) \Rightarrow P] \Rightarrow P$
(c) $(\sim P \Rightarrow P) \Rightarrow P$
(d) $(P \Rightarrow Q) \Rightarrow (\sim Q \Rightarrow \sim P)$

5.4 Prove the validity of the following wffs using the method of resolution refutation:

(a) $(\exists x)\{[P(x) \Rightarrow P(A)] \wedge [P(x) \Rightarrow P(B)]\}$
(b) $(\forall z)[Q(z) \Rightarrow P(z)]$
        $\Rightarrow \{(\exists x)[Q(x) \Rightarrow P(A)] \wedge [Q(x) \Rightarrow P(B)]\}$
(c) $(\exists x)(\exists y)\{[P(f(x)) \wedge Q(f(B))]$
        $\Rightarrow [P(f(A)) \wedge P(y) \wedge Q(y)]\}$
(d) $(\exists x)(\forall y)P(x,y)$
        $\Rightarrow (\forall y)(\exists x)P(x,y)$
(e) $(\forall x)\{P(x) \wedge [Q(A) \vee Q(B)]\}$
        $\Rightarrow (\exists x)[P(x) \wedge Q(x)]$

5.5 Show by a resolution refutation that the wff $(\exists x)P(x)$ logically follows from the wff $[P(A1) \vee P(A2)]$. However, the Skolemized form of $(\exists x)P(x)$, namely, $P(A)$, does not logically follow from $[P(A1) \vee P(A2)]$. Explain.

5.6 Show that a production system using the resolution rule schema operating on a global database of clauses is commutative in the sense defined in chapter 1.

5.7 Find an ancestry-filtered form refutation for the clauses of EXAMPLE 2 in Section 5.4.2. Compare with the refutation graph of Figure 5.10.

5.8 Referring to the discussion in Section 3.3. on derivation graphs (and to Exercise 3.4) propose a heuristic search strategy for a resolution refutation system. On what factors would you base an h function?

5.9 In this exercise we preview a relationship between computation and deduction that will be more fully explored in chapter 6.

The expression $cons(x,y)$ denotes the list formed by inserting the element x at the head of the list y. We denote the empty list by NIL; the list (2) by $cons(2, NIL)$; the list (1,2) by $cons(1, cons(2, NIL))$; etc. The expression $LAST(x,y)$ is intended to mean that y is the last element of the list x. We have the following axioms:

$$(\forall u)\, LAST(cons(u, NIL), u)$$
$$(\forall x)(\forall y)(\forall z)[\, LAST(y,z) \Rightarrow LAST(cons(x,y),z)\,]$$

Prove the following theorem from these axioms by the method of resolution refutation:

$$(\exists v)\, LAST(cons(2, cons(1, NIL)), v)$$

Use answer extraction to find v, the last element of the list (2,1). Describe briefly how this method might be used to compute the last element of longer lists.

CHAPTER 6

RULE-BASED DEDUCTION SYSTEMS

The way in which a piece of knowledge about a certain field is expressed by an expert in that field often carries important information about how that knowledge can best be used. Suppose, for example, that a mathematician says:

If x and y are both greater that zero, so is the product of x and y.

A straightforward rendering of this statement into predicate calculus is:

$$(\forall x)(\forall y)\{[G(x,0) \wedge G(y,0)] \Rightarrow G(times(x,y),0)\} .$$

However, we could instead have used the following completely equivalent formulation:

$$(\forall x)(\forall y)\{[G(x,0) \wedge \sim G(times(x,y),0)] \Rightarrow \sim G(y,0)\} .$$

The logical content of the mathematician's statement is, of course, independent of the many equivalent predicate calculus forms that could represent it. But the way in which English statements are worded often carries extra-logical, or heuristic, control information. In our example, the statement seems to indicate that we are to use the fact that x and y are individually greater than zero to prove that x multiplied by y is greater than zero.

Much of the knowledge used by AI systems is directly representable by general implicational expressions. The following statements and expressions are additional examples:

(1) All vertebrates are animals.
$(\forall x)[VERTEBRATE(x) \Rightarrow ANIMAL(x)]$

(2) Everyone in the Purchasing Dept. over 30 is married.
$(\forall x)\,(\forall y)\,\{[\,WORKS\text{-}IN\,(PURCHASING\text{-}DEPT,x)$
$\wedge\,AGE\,(x,y)\,\wedge\,G\,(y,30)]\Rightarrow MARRIED\,(x)\}$

(3) There is a cube on top of every red cylinder.
$(\forall x)\{[\,CYLINDER\,(x)\,\wedge\,RED\,(x)]$
$\Rightarrow (\exists y)[\,CUBE\,(y)\,\wedge\,ON\,(y,x)]\}$

If we were to convert expressions such as these into clauses, we would lose the possibly valuable control information contained in their given implicational forms. The clausal expression $(A \vee B \vee C)$, for example, is logically equivalent to any of the implications $(\sim A \wedge \sim B)\Rightarrow C,$ $(\sim A \wedge \sim C)\Rightarrow B,$ $(\sim B \wedge \sim C)\Rightarrow A,$ $\sim A\Rightarrow(B \vee C),$ $\sim B\Rightarrow(A \vee C),$ or $\sim C\Rightarrow(A \vee B)$; but each of these implications carries its own, rather different, extra-logical control information not carried at all by the clause form. In this chapter we argue that implications should be used in the form originally given, as F-rules or B-rules of a production system.

The use of implicational wffs as rules in a production system prevents the system from making inferences directly from these rule wffs alone. All inferences made by a production system result from the application of production rules to the global database. Therefore each inference can involve only one rule wff at a time. This restriction has beneficial effects on the efficiency of the system. Additionally, we can show, in general, that converting wffs to clauses can lead to inefficiencies.

Consider the problem of attempting to prove the wff $P \wedge (Q \vee R)$. If we used a resolution refutation system, we would negate this wff and convert it to clause form through the following steps:

$\sim[\,P \wedge (Q \vee R)]$

$\sim P \vee \sim(Q \vee R)$

$\sim P \vee (\sim Q \wedge \sim R)$

(1) $\sim P \vee \sim Q$

(2) $\sim P \vee \sim R$

Suppose the base set also contains the following clauses:

(3) $\sim S \lor P$

(4) $\sim U \lor S$

(5) U

(6) $\sim W \lor R$

(7) W

One reasonable strategy for obtaining a refutation might involve selecting clause 1, say, and using it and its descendants in resolutions. We can resolve clauses 1 and 3 to produce $\sim S \lor \sim Q$, and then use clauses 4 and 5 in sequence to produce $\sim Q$. At this stage, we have "resolved away" the literal $\sim P$ from clause 1. Unfortunately, we now discover that we have no way to resolve away $\sim Q$, so our search must consider working with clause 2. The previous work in resolving away $\sim P$ is wasted because we must search for a way to resolve it away again, to produce the clause $\sim R$, which is on the way to a final solution. The fact that we had to resolve away $\sim P$ twice is an inefficiency caused by "multiplying out" a subexpression in the conversion to clause form. If we look at our original goal, namely, to prove $P \land (Q \lor R)$, it is obvious that the component P needs to be proved only once. Conversion to clauses makes this sort of duplication difficult to avoid.

The systems described in this chapter do not convert wffs to clauses; they use them in a form close to their original given form. Wffs representing assertional knowledge about the problem are separated into two categories: *rules* and *facts*. The rules consist of those assertions given in implicational form. Typically, they express *general* knowledge about a particular subject area and are used as production rules. The facts are the assertions that are not expressed as implications. Typically, they represent *specific* knowledge relevant to a particular case. The task of the production systems discussed in this chapter is to prove a *goal wff* from these facts and rules.

In forward systems, implications used as F-rules operate on a global database of facts until a termination condition involving the goal wff is achieved. In backward systems, the implications used as B-rules operate on a global database of goals until a termination condition involving the facts is achieved. Combined forward and backward operation is also possible. The details about rule operation and termination are explained in the next few pages.

This sort of theorem-proving system is a *direct* system rather than a refutation system. A direct system is not necessarily more efficient than a refutation system, but its operation does seem intuitively easier for people to understand.

Systems of this kind are often called *rule-based deduction systems*, to emphasize the importance of using rules to make deductions. AI research has produced many applications of rule-based systems.

6.1. A FORWARD DEDUCTION SYSTEM

6.1.1. THE AND/OR FORM FOR FACT EXPRESSIONS

We begin by describing a simple type of forward production system that processes fact expressions of arbitrary form. Then we consider a dual form of this system, namely, a backward system that is able to prove goal expressions of arbitrary form. Finally, we combine the two in a single system.

Our forward system has as its initial global database a representation for the given set of facts. In particular, we do not intend to convert these facts into clause form. The facts are represented as a predicate calculus wff that has been transformed into implication-free form that we call *AND/OR form*. To convert a wff into AND/OR form, the $\Rightarrow$ symbols (if there are any) are eliminated, using the equivalence of ($W1 \Rightarrow W2$) and ($\sim W1 \vee W2$). (Typically, there will be few $\Rightarrow$ symbols among the facts because implications are preferably represented as rules.) Next, negation symbols are moved in (using de Morgan's laws) until their scopes include at most a single predicate. The resulting expression is then Skolemized and prenexed; variables within the scopes of universal quantifiers are standardized by renaming, existentially quantified variables are replaced by Skolem functions, and the universal quantifiers are dropped. Any variables remaining are assumed to have universal quantification.

For example, the fact expression:

$$(\exists u)(\forall v)\{\, Q(v,u) \wedge \sim[[R(v) \vee P(v)] \wedge S(u,v)]\}$$

is converted to

$$Q(v,A) \wedge \{[\sim R(v) \wedge \sim P(v)] \vee \sim S(A,v)]\} \ .$$

Variables can be renamed so that the same variable does not occur in different (main) conjuncts of the fact expression. Renaming variables in our example yields the expression:

$$Q(w,A) \wedge \{[\sim R(v) \wedge \sim P(v)] \vee \sim S(A,v)\} \ .$$

Note that the variable v, in $Q(v,A)$, can be replaced by a new variable, w, but that neither occurrence of the variable v in the conjuncts of the embedded conjunction, $[\sim R(v) \wedge \sim P(v)]$, can be renamed because this variable also occurs in the disjunct $\sim S(A,v)$. An expression in AND/OR form consists of subexpressions of literals connected by $\wedge$ and $\vee$ symbols. Note that an expression in AND/OR form is not in clause form. It is much closer to the form of the original expression. In particular, subexpressions are not multiplied out.

6.1.2. USING AND/OR GRAPHS TO REPRESENT FACT EXPRESSIONS

An AND/OR graph can be used to represent a fact expression in AND/OR form. For example, the AND/OR tree of Figure 6.1 represents the fact expression that we just put into AND/OR form above. Each subexpression of the fact expression is represented by a node in the graph. Disjunctively related subexpressions, $E_1, \ldots, E_k$, of a fact, $(E_1 \vee \ldots \vee E_k)$, are represented by descendant nodes connected to their parent node by a k-connector. Each conjunctive subexpression, $E_1, \ldots, E_n$, of an expression, $(E_1 \wedge \ldots \wedge E_n)$, is represented by a single descendant node connected to the parent node by a 1-connector. It may seem surprising that we use k-connectors (a conjunctive notion) to separate *disjunctions* in fact expressions. We see later why we have adopted this convention.

The leaf nodes of the AND/OR graph representation of a fact expression are labeled by the literals occurring in the expression. We call that node in the graph labeling the entire fact expression, the *root node*. It has no ancestors in the graph.

An interesting property of the AND/OR graph representation of a wff is that the set of clauses into which that wff could have been converted can be read out as the set of solution graphs (terminating in leaf nodes) of the AND/OR graph. Thus, the clauses that result from the expression $Q(w,A) \wedge \{[\sim R(v) \wedge \sim P(v)] \vee \sim S(A,v)\}$ are:

$Q(w,A)$
$\sim S(A,v) \vee \sim R(v)$
$\sim S(A,v) \vee \sim P(v)$

Each clause is obtained as the disjunction of the literals at the leaf nodes of one of the solution graphs of Figure 6.1. We might therefore think of the AND/OR graph as a compact representation for a set of clauses. [The AND/OR graph representation for an expression is actually slightly less general than the clause representation, however, because not multiplying out common subexpressions can prevent certain variable renamings that are possible in clause form. In the last of the clauses above, for example, the variable v can be renamed u throughout the clause. This renaming cannot be expressed in the AND/OR graph, which results in loss of generality that can sometimes cause difficulties (discussed later in the chapter).]

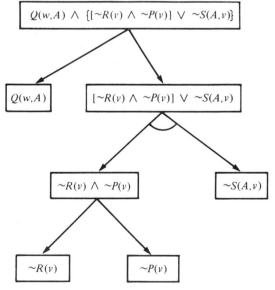

Fig. 6.1 An AND/OR tree representation of a fact expression.

Usually, we draw our AND/OR graph representations of fact expressions "upside down." Later we also use AND/OR graph representations of goal wffs; these are displayed in the usual manner, "rightside up."

When we represent wffs by AND/OR graphs, we are using AND/OR graphs for a quite different purpose than that described in chapters 1 and 3. There, AND/OR graphs were representations used by the control strategy to monitor the progress of decomposable production systems. Here we are using them as representational forms for the global database of a production system. Various of the processes to be described in this chapter involve transformations and tests on the AND/OR graph as a whole, and thus it is appropriate to use the entire AND/OR graph as the global database.

6.1.3. USING RULES TO TRANSFORM AND/OR GRAPHS

The production rules used by our forward production system are applied to AND/OR graph structures to produce transformed graph structures. These rules are based on the implicational wffs that represent general assertional knowledge about a problem domain. For simplicity of explanation, we limit the types of wffs that we allow as rules to those of the form:

$$L \Rightarrow W,$$

where L is a single literal, W is an arbitrary wff (assumed to be in AND/OR form), and any variables occurring in the implication are assumed to have universal quantification over the entire implication. Variables in the facts and rules are standardized apart so that no variable occurs in more than one rule and so that the rule variables are different than the fact variables.

The restriction to single-literal antecedents considerably simplifies the matching process in applying rules to AND/OR graphs. This restriction is a bit less severe than it appears because implications having antecedents consisting of a disjunction of literals can be written as multiple rules; for example, the implication $(L1 \lor L2) \Rightarrow W$ is equivalent to the pair of rules $L1 \Rightarrow W$ and $L2 \Rightarrow W$. In any case, the restrictions on rule forms that we impose in this chapter do not seem to cause practical limitations on the utility of the resulting deduction systems.

199

Any implication with a single-literal antecedent, regardless of its quantification, can be put in a form in which the scope of quantification is the entire implication by a process that first "reverses" the quantification of those variables local to the antecedent and then Skolemizes all existential variables. For example, the wff

$$(\forall x)\{[(\exists y)(\forall z)P(x,y,z)] \Rightarrow (\forall u)Q(x,u)\}$$

can be transformed through the following steps:

(1) *Eliminate (temporarily) implication symbol.*

$$(\forall x)\{\sim[(\exists y)(\forall z)P(x,y,z)] \\ \vee (\forall u)Q(x,u)\}$$

(2) *Reverse quantification of variables in first disjunct by moving negation symbol in.*

$$(\forall x)\{(\forall y)(\exists z)[\sim P(x,y,z)] \\ \vee (\forall u)Q(x,u)\}$$

(3) *Skolemize.*

$$(\forall x)\{(\forall y)[\sim P(x,y,f(x,y))] \\ \vee (\forall u)Q(x,u)\}$$

(4) *Move all universal quantifiers to the front and drop.*

$$\sim P(x,y,f(x,y)) \vee Q(x,u)$$

(5) *Restore implication.*

$$P(x,y,f(x,y)) \Rightarrow Q(x,u)$$

To explain how rules of this sort are applied to AND/OR graphs, we first consider the variable-free propositional calculus case. A rule of the form $L \Rightarrow W$ (where L is a literal and W is a wff in AND/OR form) can be applied to any AND/OR graph having a leaf node, n, labeled by literal L. The result is a new AND/OR graph in which node n now has an outgoing 1-connector to a descendant node (also labeled by literal L) which is the root node of that AND/OR graph structure representing W.

As an example, consider the rule

$$S \Rightarrow (X \wedge Y) \vee Z .$$

We can apply this rule to the AND/OR graph of Figure 6.2 at the leaf node labeled by S. The result is the graph structure shown in Figure 6.3. The two nodes labeled by S are connected by an arc that we call a *match arc*.

Before applying a rule, an AND/OR graph, such as that of Figure 6.2, represented a particular fact expression. (Its set of solution graphs terminating in leaf nodes represented the clause form of the fact expression.) We intend that the graph resulting after rule application represent both the original fact and a fact expression that is inferable from the original one and the rule.

Suppose we have a rule $L \Rightarrow W$, where L is a literal and W is a wff. From this rule and from the fact expression $F(L)$, we can infer the expression $F(W)$ derived from $F(L)$ by replacing all of the occurrences of L in F by W. When using a rule $L \Rightarrow W$ to transform the AND/OR graph representation of $F(L)$ in the manner described, we produce a new graph that can be considered to contain a representation of $F(W)$; that is, its set of solution graphs terminating in leaf nodes represents the set of clauses in the clause form of $F(W)$. This set of clauses includes the entire set that would be produced by performing *all* possible resolutions on L between the clause form of $F(L)$ and the clause form of $L \Rightarrow W$.

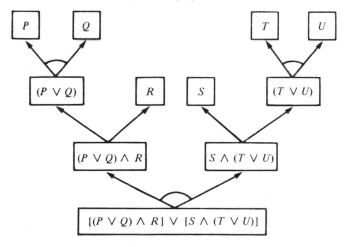

Fig. 6.2 An AND/OR graph with no variables.

201

Consider the example of Figure 6.3. The clause form of the rule $S \Rightarrow [(X \wedge Y) \vee Z]$ is:

$\sim S \vee X \vee Z$

and

$\sim S \vee Y \vee Z$.

Those clauses in the clause form of

$[(P \vee Q) \wedge R] \vee [S \wedge (T \vee U)]$

that would resolve (on S) with either of the two rule clauses are:

$P \vee Q \vee S$

and

$R \vee S$.

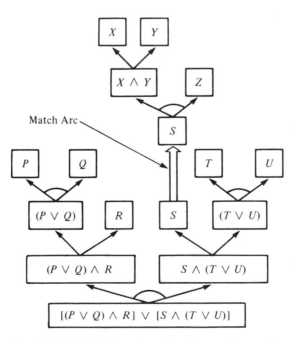

Fig. 6.3 An AND/OR graph resulting from applying a rule.

The complete set of resolvents that can be obtained from these four clauses by resolving on S is:

$$X \vee Z \vee P \vee Q$$
$$Y \vee Z \vee P \vee Q$$
$$R \vee Y \vee Z$$
$$R \vee X \vee Z$$

All of these are included in the clauses represented by the solution graphs of Figure 6.3.

From this example, and from the foregoing discussion, we see that the process of applying a rule to an AND/OR graph accomplishes in an extremely economical fashion what might otherwise have taken several resolutions.

We want the AND/OR graph resulting from a rule application to continue to represent the original fact expression as well as the inferred one. This effect is obtained by having identically labeled nodes on either side of the match arc. After a rule is applied at a node, this node is no longer a leaf node of the graph, but it is still labeled by a single literal and may continue to have rules applied to it. We call any node in the graph labeled by a single literal a *literal node*. The set of clauses represented by an AND/OR graph is the set that corresponds to the set of solution graphs terminating in literal nodes of the graph.

All of our discussion so far about rule applications has been for the propositional calculus case in which the expressions do not contain variables. Soon we will describe how expressions with variables are dealt with, but first we discuss the termination condition for the variable-free case.

6.1.4. USING THE GOAL WFF FOR TERMINATION

The object of the forward production system that we have described is to prove some goal wff from a fact wff and a set of rules. This forward system is limited in the type of goal expressions that it can prove; specifically, it can prove only those goal wffs whose form is a *disjunction* of literals. We represent this goal wff by a set of literals and assume that the members of this set are disjunctively related. (Later, we describe a backward system and a bidirectional system that are not limited to such

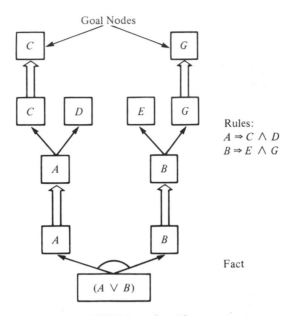

Fig. 6.4 An AND/OR graph satisfying termination.

simple goal expressions.) Goal literals (as well as rules) can be used to add descendants to the AND/OR graph. When one of the goal literals matches a literal labeling a literal node, n, of the graph, we add a new descendant of node n, labeled by the matching goal literal, to the graph. This descendant is called a *goal node*. Goal nodes are connected to their parents by match arcs. The production system successfully terminates when it produces an AND/OR graph containing a solution graph that terminates in goal nodes. (At termination, the system has essentially inferred a clause identical to some subpart of the goal clause.)

In our illustrations of AND/OR graphs, we represent matches between literal nodes and goal nodes in the same way that we represent matches between literal nodes and nodes representing rule antecedents. We show, in Figure 6.4, an AND/OR graph that satisfies a termination condition based on the goal wff ($C \lor G$). Note the match arcs to the goal nodes.

The AND/OR solution graph of Figure 6.4 can also be interpreted as a proof of the goal expression ($C \lor G$) using a "reasoning-by-cases" strategy. Initially, we have the fact expression, ($A \lor B$). Since we don't

204

know whether A or B is true, we might attempt first to prove the goal by assuming that A is true and then attempt to prove the goal assuming B is true. If *both* proofs succeed, we have a proof based simply on the disjunction $(A \lor B)$, and it wouldn't matter which of A or B was true. In Figure 6.4, the descendants of the node labeled by $(A \lor B)$ are connected to it by a 2-connector; thus both of these descendants must occur (as they indeed do) in the final solution graph. Now we can see the intuitive reason for using k-connectors to separate disjunctively related subexpressions in facts. If a solution graph for node n includes any descendant of n through a certain k-connector, it must include all of the descendants through this k-connector.

The production system that we have described, based on applying rules to AND/OR graphs, is commutative; therefore an irrevocable control regime suffices. The system continues to apply applicable rules until an AND/OR graph containing a solution graph is produced.

6.1.5. EXPRESSIONS CONTAINING VARIABLES

We now describe forward production systems that deal with expressions containing variables. We have already mentioned that variables in facts and rules have implicit universal quantification. We assume that any existential variables in facts and rules have been Skolemized.

For goal wffs containing existentially or universally quantified variables, we use a Skolemization process that is dual to that used for facts and rules. *Universal* variables in goals are replaced by Skolem functions of the existential variables in whose scopes these universal variables reside. Recall that in resolution refutation systems, goal wffs are negated, converting universal quantifiers into existential ones, and vice versa. Existential variables in these expressions are then replaced by Skolem functions. We achieve the same effect in direct proof systems if we replace *universally* quantified goal variables by Skolem functions. The existential quantifiers in the Skolemized goal wff can then be dropped, and variables remaining in goal expressions have assumed existential quantification.

We are still restricting our goal wffs to those that are a disjunction of literals. After Skolemizing a goal wff, we can rename its variables so that the same variable does not occur in more than one disjunct of the goal wff. (Recall the equivalence between the wff $(\exists x)[W1(x) \lor W2(x)]$ and the wff $[(\exists x)W1(x) \lor (\exists y)W2(y)]$.)

205

Now we consider the process of applying a rule of the form $(L \Rightarrow W)$ to an AND/OR graph, where L is a literal, W is a wff in AND/OR form, and all expressions might contain variables. The rule is applicable if the AND/OR graph contains a literal node L' that unifies with L. Suppose the mgu is u. Then, application of this rule extends the graph (just as in the propositional calculus case) by creating a match arc directed from the node labeled by L' in the AND/OR graph to a new descendant node labeled by L. This descendant node is the root node of the AND/OR graph representation of Wu. We also label the match arc by the mgu, u.

As an example, consider the fact expression

$$\{ P(x,y) \vee [Q(x,A) \wedge R(B,y)]\} \ .$$

The AND/OR graph representation for this fact is shown in Figure 6.5. Now, if we apply the rule:

$$P(A,B) \Rightarrow [S(A) \vee X(B)]$$

to this AND/OR graph, we obtain the AND/OR graph shown in Figure 6.6.

The AND/OR graph shown in Figure 6.6 has two solution graphs that terminate in leaf nodes and that include the newly added match arc. The clauses corresponding to these solution graphs are:

$$S(A) \vee X(B) \vee Q(A,A)$$

and

$$S(A) \vee X(B) \vee R(B,B) \ .$$

In constructing these clauses, we have applied the mgu, u, to the literals occurring at the leaf nodes of the solution graphs. These clauses are just those that could be obtained from the clause form of the fact and the rule wffs by performing resolutions on P.

The AND/OR graph of Figure 6.6 continues to represent the original fact expression, because we take it generally to represent all of those clauses corresponding to solution graphs terminating in *literal nodes*.

After more than one rule has been applied to an AND/OR graph, it contains more than one match arc. In particular, any solution graph (terminating in literal nodes) can have more than one match arc. In computing the sets of clauses represented by an AND/OR graph containing several match arcs, we count only those solution graphs terminating in literal nodes having *consistent* match arc substitutions. The clause represented by a consistent solution graph is obtained by applying a special substitution, called the *unifying composition,* to the disjunction of the literals labeling its terminal (literal) nodes.

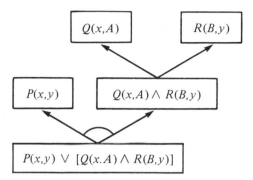

Fig. 6.5 An AND/OR graph representation of a fact expression containing variables.

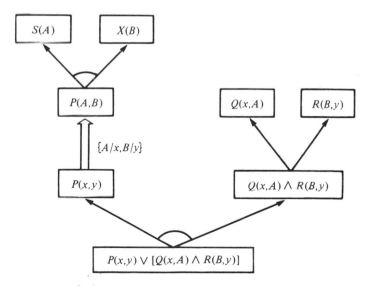

Fig. 6.6 An AND/OR graph resulting after applying a rule containing variables.

207

The notions of a consistent set of substitutions and a unifying composition of substitutions are defined as follows. Suppose we have a set of substitutions, $\{u_1, u_2, \ldots, u_n\}$. Each u_i is, in turn, a set of pairs:

$$u_i = \{t_{i1}/v_{i1}, \ldots, t_{im(i)}/v_{im(i)}\}$$

where the ts are terms and the vs are variables. From the $(u_1, \ldots, u_n)$, we define two expressions:

$$U_1 = (v_{11}, \ldots, v_{1m(1)}, \ldots, v_{n1}, \ldots, v_{nm(n)})$$

and

$$U_2 = (t_{11}, \ldots, t_{1m(1)}, \ldots, t_{n1}, \ldots, t_{nm(n)}).$$

The substitutions $(u_1, \ldots, u_n)$ are called *consistent* if and only if U_1 and U_2 are unifiable. The *unifying composition*, u, of $(u_1, \ldots, u_n)$ is the most general unifier of U_1 and U_2.

Some examples of unifying compositions [(Sickel (1976) and Chang and Slagle (1979)] are given in Table 6.1.

Table 6.1
Examples of Unifying Compositions of Substitutions

u_1	u_2	u
$\{A/x\}$	$\{B/x\}$	inconsistent
$\{x/y\}$	$\{y/z\}$	$\{x/y, x/z\}$
$\{f(z)/x\}$	$\{f(A)/x\}$	$\{f(A)/x, A/z\}$
$\{x/y, x/z\}$	$\{A/z\}$	$\{A/x, A/y, A/z\}$
$\{s\}$	$\{\}$	$\{s\}$
$\{g(y)/x\}$	$\{f(x)/y\}$	inconsistent
$\{f(g(x1))/x3,$ $f(x2)/x4\}$	$\{x4/x3, g(x1)/x2\}$	$\{f(g(x1))/x3,$ $f(g(x1))/x4, g(x1)/x2\}$

It is not difficult to show that the unifying composition operation is associative and commutative. Thus, the unifying composition associated with a solution graph does not depend on the order in which match arcs were generated while constructing the graph. (Recall that the *composition* of substitutions is associative but not commutative.)

It is reasonable to expect that a solution graph must have a set of consistent match arc substitutions in order for its corresponding clauses to be ones that can be inferred from the original fact expression and the rules. Suppose, for example, that we have the fact

$$P(x) \lor Q(x)$$

and the two rules

$$P(A) \Rightarrow R(A)$$

and

$$Q(B) \Rightarrow R(B).$$

Application of both of these rules would produce the AND/OR graph shown in Figure 6.7. Even though this graph contains a solution graph with literal nodes labeled by $R(A)$ and $R(B)$, this graph has inconsistent substitutions. Therefore, the clause $[R(A) \lor R(B)]$ is not one of those represented by the AND/OR graph shown in Figure 6.7. Of course, neither could this clause be derived by resolution from the clause form of the fact and rule wffs.

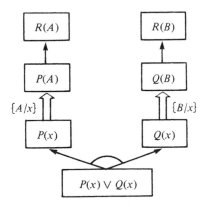

Fig. 6.7 An AND/OR graph with inconsistent substitutions.

209

The graph of Figure 6.7 does, however, contain a representation for the clause $[R(A) \lor Q(A)]$. It is the clause obtained by applying the substitution $\{A/x\}$ (which is the trivial unifying composition of the set containing the single element $\{A/x\}$) to the expression $[R(A) \lor Q(x)]$. This expression, in turn, corresponds to the solution graph terminating in the literal nodes labeled by $R(A)$ and $Q(x)$.

If the same rule is applied more than once, it is important that each application use renamed variables. Otherwise, we may needlessly over-constrain the substitutions.

The AND/OR graph can also be extended by using the goal literals. When a goal literal, L, unifies with a literal L' labeling a literal node, n, of the graph, we can add a match arc (labeled by the mgu) directed from node n to a new descendant *goal node* labeled by L. The same goal literal can be used a number of times, creating multiple goal nodes, but each use must employ renamed variables.

The process of extending the AND/OR graph by applying rules or by using goal literals successfully terminates when a consistent solution graph is produced having goal nodes for all of its terminal nodes. The production system has then proved that goal (sub)disjunction obtained by applying the unifying composition of the final solution graph to the disjunction of the literals labeling the goal nodes in the solution graph.

We illustrate how this forward production system operates by a simple example. Suppose we have the following fact and rules:

Fido barks and bites, or Fido is not a dog:

$$\sim DOG(FIDO) \lor [BARKS(FIDO) \land BITES(FIDO)]$$

All terriers are dogs:

> $R1: \quad \sim DOG(x) \Rightarrow \sim TERRIER(x)$
> (We use the contrapositive form of the implication here.)

Anyone who barks is noisy:

> $R2: \quad BARKS(y) \Rightarrow NOISY(y)$

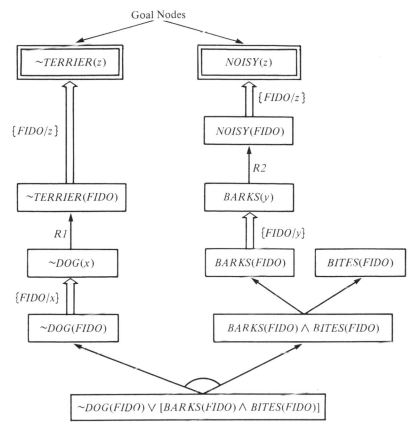

Fig. 6.8 An AND/OR graph for the "Terrier" problem.

Now suppose we want to prove that there exists someone who is not a terrier or who is noisy. The goal wff representing the statement to be proved is:

$$\sim TERRIER(z) \lor NOISY(z).$$

Recall that z is an existentially quantified variable.

The AND/OR graph for this problem is shown in Figure 6.8. The goal nodes are shown by double-boxed expressions, and rule applications are labeled by the rule numbers. A consistent solution graph within this

211

AND/OR graph has the substitutions $\{FIDO/x\}$, $\{FIDO/y\}$, $\{FIDO/z\}$. The unifying composition of these substitutions is simply $\{FIDO/x, FIDO/y, FIDO/z\}$. Applying this unifying composition to the goal literals used in the solution yields

$$\sim TERRIER(FIDO) \lor NOISY(FIDO),$$

which is the instance of the goal wff that our system has proved. This instantiated expression can thus be taken as the answer statement.

There are several extensions that we could make to this simple forward production system. We have not yet explained how we might achieve resolutions between components of the fact expressions—sometimes allowing certain intrafact resolutions is useful (and necessary); nor have we described how we might proceed in those cases in which a fact (sub)expression might be needed more than once in the same proof, with differently named variables in each usage. Of course, there is also the very important problem of controlling this production system so that it finds consistent solution graphs efficiently. We postpone further consideration of these matters until they arise again in the backward system, described next.

6.2. A BACKWARD DEDUCTION SYSTEM

An important property of logic is the duality between assertions and goals in theorem-proving systems. We have already seen an instance of this principle of duality in resolution refutation systems. There the goal wff was negated, converted to clause form, and added to the clause form of the assertions. Duality between assertions and goals allows the negated goal to be treated as if it were an assertion. Resolution refutation systems apply resolution to the combined set of clauses until the empty clause (denoting F) is produced.

We could also have described a dual resolution system that operates on goal expressions. To prepare wffs for such a system, we would first negate the wff representing the assertions, convert this negated wff to the dual of clause form (namely, a disjunction of conjunctions of literals), and add these clauses to the dual clause form of the goal wff. Such a system would then apply a dual version of resolution until the empty clause (now denoting T) was produced.

We can also imagine mixed systems in which three different forms of resolution are used, namely, resolution between assertions, resolution between goal expressions, and resolution between an assertion and a goal. The forward system described in the last section might be regarded as one of these mixed systems because it involved matching a fact literal in the AND/OR graph with a goal literal. The backward production system, described next, is also a mixed system that, in some respects, is dual to the forward system just described. Its operation involves the same sort of representations and mechanisms that were used in the forward system.

6.2.1. GOAL EXPRESSIONS IN AND/OR FORM

Our backward system is able to deal with goal expressions of arbitrary form. We first convert the goal wff to AND/OR form by the same sort of process used to convert a fact expression. We eliminate $\Rightarrow$ symbols, move negation symbols in, Skolemize *universal* variables, and drop existential quantifiers. Variables remaining in the AND/OR form of a goal expression have assumed existential quantification.

For example, the goal expression:

$$(\exists y)(\forall x)\{ P(x) \Rightarrow [Q(x,y) \wedge \sim[R(x) \wedge S(y)]]\}$$

is converted to

$$\sim P(f(y)) \vee \{ Q(f(y),y) \wedge [\sim R(f(y)) \vee \sim S(y)]\} ,$$

where $f(y)$ is a Skolem function.

Standardizing variables apart in the (main) disjuncts of the goal yields:

$$\sim P(f(z)) \vee \{ Q(f(y),y) \wedge [\sim R(f(y)) \vee \sim S(y)]\} .$$

(Note that the variable y cannot be renamed *within* the disjunctive subexpression to give each disjunct there a different variable.)

Goal wffs in AND/OR form can be represented as AND/OR graphs. But with goal expressions, k-connectors in these graphs are used to separate *conjunctively* related subexpressions. The AND/OR graph representation for the example goal wff used above is shown in Figure

213

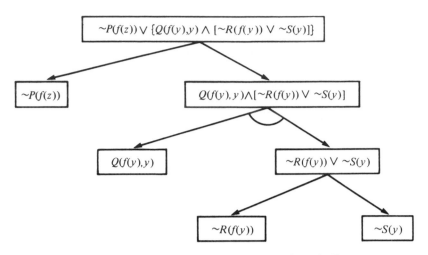

Fig. 6.9 An AND/OR graph representation of a goal wff.

6.9. The leaf nodes of this graph are labeled by the literals of the goal expression. In AND/OR goal graphs, we call any descendant of the root node, a *subgoal node*. The expressions labeling such descendant nodes are called *subgoals*.

The set of clauses in the clause form representation of this goal wff can be read from the set of solution graphs terminating in leaf nodes:

$$\sim P(f(z))$$
$$Q(f(y),y) \wedge \sim R(f(y))$$
$$Q(f(y),y) \wedge \sim S(y)$$

Goal clauses are *conjunctions* of literals and the disjunction of these clauses is the clause form of the goal wff.

6.2.2. APPLYING RULES IN THE BACKWARD SYSTEM

The B-rules for this system are based on assertional implications. They are assertions just as were the F-rules of the forward system. Now, however, we restrict these B-rules to expressions of the form

$$W \Rightarrow L ,$$

where W is any wff (assumed to be in AND/OR form), L is a literal, and the scope of quantification of any variables in the implication is the entire implication. [Again, restricting B-rules to implications of this form simplifies matching and does not cause important practical difficulties. Also, an implication such as $W \Rightarrow (L1 \wedge L2)$ can be converted to the two rules $W \Rightarrow L1$ and $W \Rightarrow L2$.]

Such a B-rule is applicable to an AND/OR graph representing a goal wff if that graph contains a literal node labeled by L' that unifies with L. The result of applying the rule is to add a match arc from the node labeled by L' to a new descendant node labeled by L. This new node is the root node of the AND/OR graph representation of Wu where u is the mgu of L and L'. This mgu labels the match arc in the transformed graph.

Our explanation of the appropriateness of this operation is dual to the explanation for applying an F-rule to a fact AND/OR graph. The assertional rule $W \Rightarrow L$ can be negated and added (disjunctively) to the goal wff. The negated form is $(W \wedge \sim L)$. Performing all (goal) resolutions on L between the clauses deriving from $(W \wedge \sim L)$ and the goal wff clauses produces a set of resolvents that are identical to clauses included among those associated with the consistent solution graphs of the transformed AND/OR graph.

6.2.3. THE TERMINATION CONDITION

The fact expressions used by our backward system are limited to those in the form of a conjunction of literals. Such expressions can be represented as a set of literals. Analogous to the forward system, when a fact literal matches a literal labeling a literal node of the graph, a corresponding descendant *fact node* can be added to the graph. This fact node is linked to the matching subgoal literal node by a match arc labeled by the mgu. The same fact literal can be used a multiple number of times (with different variables in each use) to create multiple fact nodes.

The condition for successful termination for our backward system is that the AND/OR graph contain a *consistent* solution graph terminating in fact nodes. Again, a consistent solution graph is one in which the match arc substitutions have a unifying composition.

Let us consider a simple example of how the backward system works.

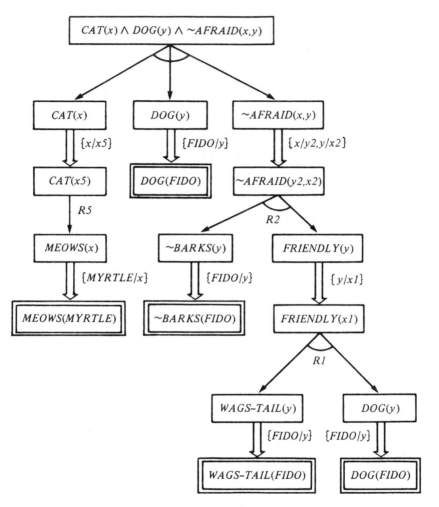

Fig. 6.10 A consistent solution graph for a backward system.

Let the facts be:

$F1$: $DOG(FIDO)$
$F2$: $\sim BARKS(FIDO)$
$F3$: $WAGS\text{-}TAIL(FIDO)$
$F4$: $MEOWS(MYRTLE)$

and let us use the following rules:

$R1$: $[WAGS\text{-}TAIL(x1) \wedge DOG(x1)] \Rightarrow FRIENDLY(x1)$
$R2$: $[FRIENDLY(x2) \wedge \sim BARKS(x2)]$
$\qquad \Rightarrow \sim AFRAID(y2, x2)$
$R3$: $DOG(x3) \Rightarrow ANIMAL(x3)$
$R4$: $CAT(x4) \Rightarrow ANIMAL(x4)$
$R5$: $MEOWS(x5) \Rightarrow CAT(x5)$

Suppose we want to ask if there are a cat and a dog such that the cat is unafraid of the dog. The goal expression is:

$$(\exists x)(\exists y)[CAT(x) \wedge DOG(y) \wedge \sim AFRAID(x,y)] .$$

We show a consistent solution graph for this problem in Figure 6.10. The fact nodes are shown double-boxed, and rule applications are labeled by the rule number. To verify the consistency of this solution graph, we compute the unifying composition of all of the substitutions labeling the match arcs in the solution graph. For Figure 6.10, we must compute the unifying composition of $(\{x/x5\}, \{MYRTLE/x\}, \{FIDO/y\}, \{x/y2, y/x2\}, \{FIDO/y\}, \{y/x1\}, \{FIDO/y\}, \{FIDO/y\})$. The result is $\{MYRTLE/x5, MYRTLE/x, FIDO/y, MYRTLE/y2, FIDO/x2, FIDO/x1\}$. This unifying composition applied to the goal expression yields the answer statement

$$[CAT(MYRTLE) \wedge DOG(FIDO) \\ \wedge \sim AFRAID(MYRTLE, FIDO)] .$$

6.2.4. CONTROL STRATEGIES FOR DEDUCTION SYSTEMS

Various techniques can be used to control the search for a consistent solution graph. We describe some of these as they might apply to a backward system; the same ideas can also be used with forward systems. The control strategy for our backward deduction system might attempt to find a consistent solution graph by first finding any solution graph and then checking it for consistency. If this *candidate* graph is not consistent, the search must continue until a consistent one is found.

A more sophisticated strategy would involve checking for consistency as the partial, candidate solution graphs are being developed (that is, before a complete candidate solution is found). Sometimes inconsistencies are revealed early in the process of developing a partial solution graph; these inconsistent partial solution graphs can be immediately ruled out, thus reducing the amount of search effort.

Consider the following example. Suppose that we want to prove the goal $P(x) \wedge Q(x)$ and that the facts include $R(A)$ and $Q(A)$. Suppose that the rules include

$$R1: \quad R(y) \Rightarrow P(y)$$

$$R2: \quad S(z) \Rightarrow P(B)$$

Now, at a certain stage, the backward system might have produced the AND/OR graph shown in Figure 6.11. There are two partial candidate solution graphs in Figure 6.11. One has the substitutions ($\{x/y\}$, $\{A/x\}$), and the other has the substitutions ($\{B/x\}$, $\{A/x\}$). The latter is inconsistent. Furthermore, if $Q(A)$ is the only match for the subgoal $Q(x)$, we can see that rule R2 could not possibly be a part of any solution. Thus, detecting inconsistencies early in the search process can lead to opportunities for pruning the AND/OR graph. In our example, we do not need to generate subgoals of $S(z)$.

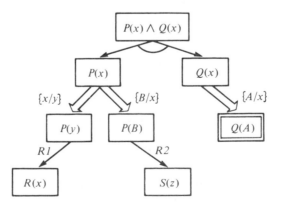

Fig. 6.11 An AND/OR graph with inconsistent substitutions.

Pruning operations that result from consistency checks among different levels of the graph are also possible. Consider the following example. Suppose the rules include:

$R1$: $[Q(u) \land R(v)] \Rightarrow P(u,v)$
$R2$: $W(y) \Rightarrow R(y)$
$R3$: $S(w) \Rightarrow R(w)$
$R4$: $U(z) \Rightarrow S(C)$
$R5$: $V(A) \Rightarrow Q(A)$

Now, in attempting to deduce the goal $P(x,x)$, we might produce the AND/OR graph shown in Figure 6.12. Note that rules $R4$ and $R5$ are in the same partial candidate solution graph and that their associated substitutions, namely, $\{A/x\}$ and $\{C/x\}$, are inconsistent. If rule $R5$ is the only possible match for subgoal $Q(x)$, this inconsistency would allow us to prune the subgoal $U(z)$ from the graph. Solving $U(z)$ cannot contribute to a consistent solution graph. Notice, however, that subgoal $S(x)$ can be left in the graph; it might still permit the substitution $\{A/x\}$. The general rule is that a match need not be attempted if it is inconsistent with the match substitutions in *all* other partial solution graphs containing it.

Another control strategy for backward, rule-based deduction systems involves building a structure called a *rule connection graph*. In this method, we precompute all possible matches among the rules and store the resulting substitutions. This precomputation is performed before solving any specific problems with the rules; the results are potentially useful in all problems so long as the set of rules is not changed. Such a process is, of course, only practical for rule sets that are not too large.

We show, in Figure 6.13, an example rule connection graph for the rules of our earlier "cat and dog" example. The graph is constructed by writing down each rule in AND/OR graph form and then connecting (with match arcs) literals in rule antecedents to all matching rule consequents. The match arcs are then labeled by the mgus.

When an actual problem is to be solved, we can connect the AND/OR goal graph and fact nodes to the rule connection graph by connecting the goal literal nodes to all matching rule consequents, and by connecting fact nodes to all matching literals in the rule antecedents. This enlarged connection graph can next be scanned to find candidate solution graphs within it. Once a candidate is found, we attempt to compute the unifying

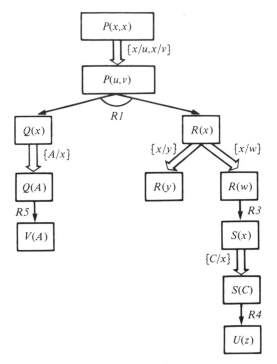

Fig. 6.12 Another AND/OR graph with inconsistent substitutions.

composition of the substitutions involved in this graph. If such a unifying composition exists, we have a consistent AND/OR solution graph and, thus, a solution. Otherwise, we must look for another candidate solution graph within the connection graph.

Using connection graphs of this sort, we are really producing AND/OR graphs largely from precomputed structure. There is one important complication, however, that we have not yet mentioned: We might need to use the same rule in the rule connection graph more than once in a candidate solution graph. Each time it is used, it must have differently named variables. These differently named variables must then also occur in the substitutions copied over to the candidate solution graph.

Let us consider a specific example. Suppose we have the rule $P(x) \Rightarrow P(f(x))$ and the fact $P(A)$. Suppose we want to prove the goal $P(f(f(A)))$. The rule connection graph for this problem is shown in Figure 6.14. Here we use an (unlabeled) match arc between the rule's consequent and antecedent to remind us that a new instance of the rule

220

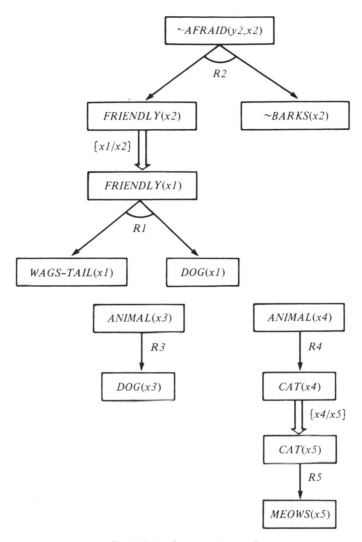

Fig. 6.13 A rule connection graph.

can have its consequent match the original antecedent, and so on. When the goal and fact nodes are connected, we have the graph shown in Figure 6.15. Scanning this connection graph for candidate solution graphs can produce the one shown in Figure 6.16. This graph uses the same rule twice (going around a loop in the rule connection graph), and, thus, the variables occurring in the rule and in the associated substitutions must be renamed. The substitutions in the solution graph have the unifying composition $\{ f(A)/x, A/y \}$.

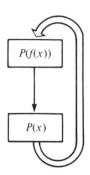

Fig. 6.14 Another rule connection graph.

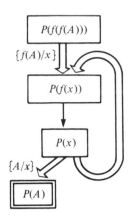

Fig. 6.15 A connection graph.

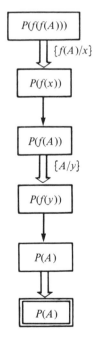

Fig. 6.16 A candidate solution graph.

6.2.5. EXAMPLES OF BACKWARD, RULE-BASED DEDUCTION SYSTEMS

To give a more concrete idea of the use of rule-based deduction systems in AI, we next describe some example systems. Each is illustrative only; practical versions of these systems would of course be much larger and need many additional features. It is interesting to note, however, that there are many important applications that can be attacked even with the restrictions we have imposed so far on the allowed forms for rules and facts in backward systems.

6.2.5.1. An Information Retrieval System. Let us imagine that our set of facts contains personnel data for a business organization and that we want an automatic system to answer various questions about personnel matters. A highly simplified example system might have facts such as the following:

> *MANAGER(P-D,JOHN-JONES)*
> John Jones is the manager of the Purchasing Dept.

> *WORKS-IN(P-D,JOE-SMITH)*
> Joe Smith works in the Purchasing Department.

> *WORKS-IN(P-D, SALLY-JONES)*

> *WORKS-IN(P-D, PETE-SWANSON)*

> *MANAGER(S-D, HARRY-TURNER)*
> Harry Turner is the manager of the Sales Department.

> *WORKS-IN(S-D, MARY-JONES)*

> *WORKS-IN(S-D, BILL-WHITE)*

> *MARRIED(JOHN-JONES, MARY-JONES)*

In order to provide certain commonsense information about personnel concepts and to allow the set of facts to be kept concise, we might have the following rules:

223

$R1$: $MANAGER(x,y) \Rightarrow WORKS\text{-}IN(x,y)$

$R2$: $[WORKS\text{-}IN(x,y) \wedge MANAGER(x,z)]$
$\Rightarrow BOSS\text{-}OF(y,z)$
(A more precise formulation might also state that a
person cannot be his own boss.)

$R3$: $[WORKS\text{-}IN(x,y) \wedge WORKS\text{-}IN(x,z)]$
$\Rightarrow \sim MARRIED(y,z)$
(Company policy does not allow married couples
to work in the same department.)

$R4$: $MARRIED(y,z) \Rightarrow MARRIED(z,y)$
(Marriage is symmetrical. A more precise formulation
might also state that persons cannot be married to
themselves.)

$R5$: $[MARRIED(x,y) \wedge WORKS\text{-}IN(P\text{-}D,x)]$
$\Rightarrow INSURED\text{-}BY(x,EAGLE\text{-}CORP)$
(All married employees of the Purchasing
Department are insured by the Eagle Corporation.)

With these facts and rules, a simple backward production system can
answer a variety of questions. For these examples, we assume that the
control strategy guides the generation of the AND/OR graph by
pursuing a depth-first search for a consistent solution graph. In selecting
a literal node within a partial solution graph to match against a B-rule
consequent or fact, we assume that a look-ahead process selects that
subgoal literal which has the fewest consistent matches.

Those queries that can be answered without using rules are handled
most simply. We show some example solution graphs in Figure 6.17. The
solution graph is shown in such a way that a depth-first, left-to-right
ordering of the literal nodes in the graph corresponds to the actual order
in which the control regime found matches for these literals. The
double-boxed nodes are fact nodes. In the second example, $MAR\text{-}RIED(y,x)$ has the fewest potential matches, so it is matched first. If we
apply the unifying composition of the substitutions occurring in the
solution graph to the query, we obtain the answer

$WORKS\text{-}IN(S\text{-}D, MARY\text{-}JONES)$
$\wedge MARRIED(JOHN\text{-}JONES, MARY\text{-}JONES).$

Name someone who works in the Purchasing Department.

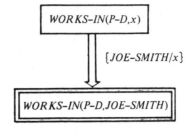

Name someone who is married and works in the Sales Department.

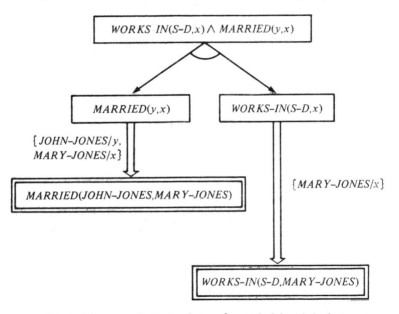

Fig. 6.17 Some simple queries that can be matched directly by facts.

Now let us try some more complex queries, ones that require using rules to answer. We show, in Figure 6.18, the solution graph for the query "Who is Joe Smith's Boss?"

The only rule that can be applied at the beginning is rule *R2*. Of the resulting new literal nodes, $MANAGER(x1,z1)$ has the fewest possible matches, so it is matched first. Matching this subgoal against *MAN-AGER(S-D, HARRY-TURNER)* cannot lead to a consistent solution graph, so ultimately the control process would have returned to try the match shown in Figure 6.18. (Notice that we have renamed the variables in rule *R2* so that they are standardized apart from the goal wff.) After a solution is obtained, we can apply the unifying composition of the substitutions to the query to obtain the answer *BOSS-OF(JOE-SMITH, JOHN-JONES)*.

As a more complex example, consider the request "Name someone insured by the Eagle Corporation." We show the solution graph for this query in Figure 6.19. The $MARRIED(x,y1)$ subgoal component is solved first, and then the rule *R1* is applied to $WORKS-IN(P-D,x)$ to set up the solution of the other subgoal component. Applying the unifying composition to the query produces the answer *INSURED-BY(JOHN-JONES, EAGLE-CORP)*.

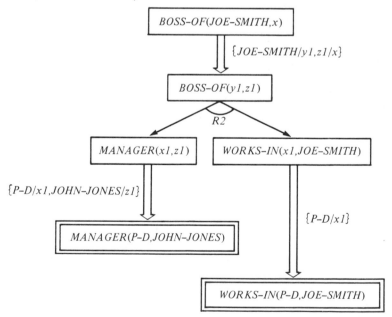

Fig. 6.18 The solution graph for "Who is Joe Smith's boss?".

Suppose we wanted to ask "Is John Jones married to Sally Jones?" The system might first try to prove *MARRIED(JOHN-JONES, SALLY-JONES)*. No matches with facts are possible, and the subgoal obtained by using rule *R4* doesn't help either. When no proof can be found, it is reasonable to attempt to prove the negation of the query. The solution graph for the negated goal is shown in Figure 6.20.

We can also use this example to illustrate how additional knowledge and capabilities can be added without extensive changes to the system. Suppose, for example, that we want to refine rule *R5* by introducing the notion of a temporary employee. The new rule, *R5′*, is:

$$R5': \ [\ MARRIED(x, y) \wedge WORKS\text{-}IN(P\text{-}D, x)$$
$$\wedge \sim TEMPORARY(x)]$$
$$\Rightarrow INSURED\text{-}BY(x, EAGLE\text{-}CORP)$$

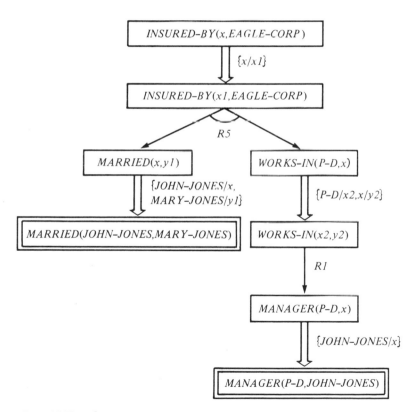

Fig. 6.19 The solution graph for "Name someone insured by the Eagle Corporation."

227

Now we must add to our set of facts the information about whether the employees are temporary or not. We might also have an additional definitional rule:

$R6: PERMANENT(x) \Rightarrow \sim TEMPORARY(x)$.

Additional facts might now include:

$PERMANENT(JOHN\text{-}JONES)$

$TEMPORARY(SALLY\text{-}JONES)$

The new rules and facts have little influence on the way in which previous queries are answered. As new rules are added to a deduction system, it is important, however, to check to see that they do not conflict with older rules. For example, suppose we were to add the rule:

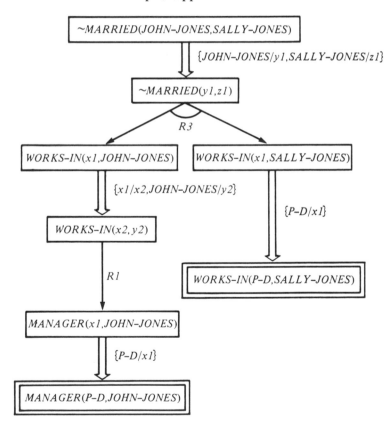

Fig. 6.20 The solution graph for "John Jones is Not Married to Sally Jones."

228

R7: $PREV\text{-}EMP(x, G\text{-}TEK)$
$\Rightarrow INSURED\text{-}BY(x, METRO\text{-}CORP)$
(Anyone previously employed by *G-TEK* is
insured by Metro Corporation.)

We would also add facts about the previous employment of employees. With these additions it now might be possible to derive conflicting *INSURED-BY*s. Resolution of such conflicts can usually be obtained by making the antecedents of the rules more precise.

One desirable feature involves *meta-rules* like "If the database does not say explicitly that an employee is temporary, then that employee is permanent." This rule makes a statement that refers to databases in addition to employees! To use rules like this, our system would need a linguistic expression that denoted its own database. Additionally, it would be desirable to have the appropriate attachments between these expressions and the computer code comprising the database. Such considerations, however, would involve us in interesting complexities slightly beyond the scope of this book. [But see Weyhrauch (1980).]

6.2.5.2. A System For Reasoning About Inequalities. Now let us turn our attention to some simple mathematics. We can use a system that reasons about inequalities to illustrate some additional points. This system will be able to show, for example, that if $C > E > 0$ and if $B > A > 0$, then $[B(A + C)/E] > B$. To simplify our present discussion we allow only one predicate, G. The intended meaning of $G(x, y)$ is that x is greater than y. (Sometimes we use the more familar infix notation $x > y$.) In this system we do not deal with equal or "less-than" relations, so we specifically exclude the negation of G.

The present system is not able to perform arithmetic operations, but it is able to represent their results by functional expressions. For addition and multiplication we use the expressions *plus* and *times*. Each of these takes as its single argument a *bag*, that is, an unordered group of elements. Thus, *plus* (3,4,3) is the same as *plus* (4,3,3), for example. (Most importantly, the two expressions are unifiable because they are regarded as the same expression.) We let the functions "*divides*" and "*subtracts*" have two arguments because their order is important. We represent x/y by *divides* (x, y), and $x - y$ by *subtracts* (x, y).

Using this notation, a typical expression might be $G[$*divides* (*times* (B, *plus* (A, C)), F), B] which is more familiarly represented as $[B(A + C)/E] > B$. The reason that we are using the more cumbersome prefix notation is to avoid possible sources of confusion when unifying terms. After one example of a deduction using prefix notation we revert to the more familiar infix convention.

Our system uses rules that express certain properties of inequalities. We begin with the following set of rules:

$R1$: $[G(x,0) \wedge G(y,0)] \Rightarrow G(times(x,y),0)$
that is, $[(x > 0) \wedge (y > 0)] \Rightarrow (xy > 0)$

$R2$: $[G(x,0) \wedge G(y,z)] \Rightarrow G(plus(x,y),z)$
that is, $[(x > 0) \wedge (y > z)] \Rightarrow [(x + y) > z]$

$R3$: $[G(x,w) \wedge G(y,z)] \Rightarrow G(plus(x,y), plus(w,z))$
that is, $[(x > w) \wedge (y > z)] \Rightarrow [(x + y) > (w + z)]$

$R4$: $[G(x,0) \wedge G(y,z)] \Rightarrow G(times(x,y), times(x,z))$
that is, $[(x > 0) \wedge (y > z)] \Rightarrow (xy > xz)$

$R5$: $[G(1,w) \wedge G(x,0)] \Rightarrow G(x, times(x,w))$
that is, $[(1 > w) \wedge (x > 0)] \Rightarrow (x > xw)$

$R6$: $G(x, plus(times(w,z), times(y,z)))$
   $\Rightarrow G(x, times(plus(w,y),z))$
that is, $[x > (wz + yz)] \Rightarrow [x > (w + y)z]$

$R7$: $[G(x, times(w,y)) \wedge G(y,0)] \Rightarrow G(divides(x,y), w)$
that is, $[(x > wy) \wedge (y > 0)] \Rightarrow [(x/y) > w]$

These, of course, are not the only rules that would be useful; in fact, we shall introduce more later. Our system uses these rules as B-rules only. Various control strategies might be used, but since the AND/OR graphs resulting from applying these rules are all relatively small, we present the entire graphs in our examples.

Our first problem is to prove $[B(A + C)]/E > B$ from the following facts: $E > 0, B > 0, A > 0, C > E$, and $C > 0$. The AND/OR graph for this problem is shown in Figure 6.21. The solution graph is indicated by heavy branches, and facts that match (sub)goals are drawn in double boxes. We note that rule $R2$ is used twice with different substitutions, but one of these applications leads to an unsolvable subgoal.

230

Examining the facts supporting this proof, we note some redundancy that could have been avoided by use of the transitive property of G. That is, from $C > E$ and $E > 0$, we ought to be able to derive $C > 0$ when needed, instead of having to represent it explicitly as a fact. Such a derivation could be made from a transitivity rule:

$$R8: \quad [(x > y) \wedge (y > z)] \Rightarrow (x > z) \ .$$

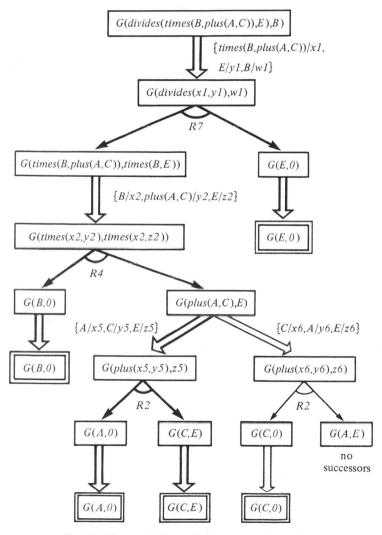

Fig. 6.21 The AND/OR graph for an inequality problem.

Comparing *R8* with the other rules, we note that its use is relatively unconstrained; it contains too many variables unencumbered by functions. Thus, it can participate in too many matches and will tend to get applied too often. Used as a B-rule, the consequent of *R8*, namely, $G(x, z)$, matches any subgoal produced by our system. Clearly, we don't want to use transitivity at every step.

Fortunately, there are ways to structure data so that special relations like transitivity can be implicitly encoded in the structure. For example, if the facts expressing an ordering relation are stored as nodes in a lattice-like structure, the desired consequences of transitivity (of the ordering) result automatically from simple computations on the lattice. These computations can be viewed as procedural attachments to the predicate denoting the ordering relation.

Let us consider a more difficult proof. From $B > 1$, $1 > A$, $A > 0$, $C > D$, and $D > 0$, prove:

$$(\exists u)[(Au + Bu) > D].$$

Also, from among the constants named in the facts, we would like an example of the u that satisfies the theorem.

Let us assume that the facts are stored in a lattice-like structure that makes the following derived facts readily evaluable: $B > A$, $B > 0$, $1 > 0$, and $C > 0$. In the following example, we assume that any of these facts can be used as needed.

The system first attempts to apply B-rules to the main goal. Only rule *R2* is applicable, but there are two alternative substitutions that can be used. For brevity, let's follow the derivation along just one of them. (The other one leads very quickly to some unsolvable subgoals, as the reader might want to verify for himself.)

Using just the rules *R1* through *R7*, our system would generate the AND/OR graph shown in Figure 6.22. Note the subgoal $(Bu > D)$ marked by an asterisk (*). No rules are applicable to this goal, so our present system would fail on this problem. What can be done to extend the power of the system?

Here again we see an example in which the power of a production system can be extended in an evolutionary manner without extensive redesign. We can add the following rule to our system:

$R9$: $[(y > 1) \wedge (x > z)] \Rightarrow (xy > z)$.

This rule is applicable to the goal ($Bu > D$), and its presence does not otherwise greatly diminish the efficiency of the system. [The reader may want to investigate the effect of $R9$ on the AND/OR graph of Figure 6.21. Its presence allows some additional—but ultimately futile—matches to the subgoal $G(times(B, plus(A, C)), times(B, E))$].

In Figure 6.23, we show the AND/OR graph produced by rule applications below $Bu > D$. Note that there are two 2-connectors below the top node. The left-hand one is futile, but the right-hand one is successful, with C substituted for u. We note that in Figure 6.22 the substitution $\{ C/u \}$ is one of the ones permitted under the goal $u > 0$. Thus our proof is complete, and a value of u that satisfies the theorem is $u = C$.

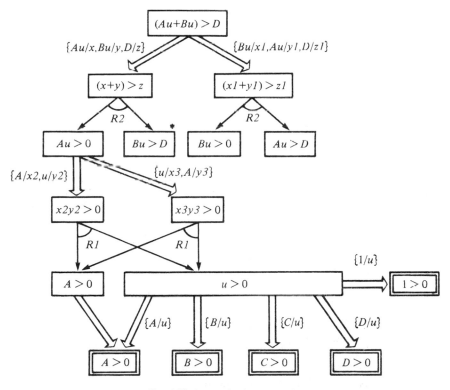

Fig. 6.22 A partial solution graph.

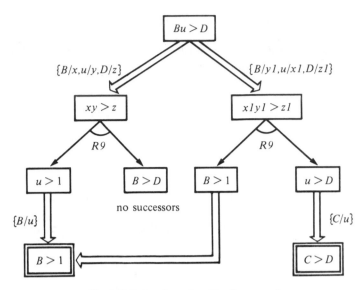

Fig. 6.23 Subgoals produced by the new rule.

Some additional extensions to our inequality reasoning system would increase its power further. One of the facts provided in our last example was $(1 > 0)$. We should not have to represent all possible inequalities between numbers as facts. What is needed is an attachment to a "greater-than" computation that would allow evaluation of ground instances of G literals. There should also be attachments to arithmetic programs so that $G(10, A)$ could be substituted for $G(plus(3,7), A)$, for example. A means should be provided to simplify algebraic expressions and to handle equality predicates. Some of the mechanisms for efficiently implementing improvements such as these depend on techniques to be discussed at the end of this chapter.

6.3. "RESOLVING" WITHIN AND/OR GRAPHS

The backward system we have described is not able to prove valid or tautological goal expressions such as $(\sim P \lor P)$ unless it can prove $\sim P$ or P separately. Neither can the forward system recognize contradictory fact expressions such as $(\sim P \land P)$. In order for these systems to overcome these deficiencies, they must be able to perform intragoal or intrafact inferences.

234

Let us describe how certain intragoal inferences might be performed. Consider, for example, the following expressions used by a backward system:

Goal

$$[P(x,y) \lor Q(x,y)] \land V(x,y)$$

Rules

$$R1: \quad [R(v) \land S(u,B)] \Rightarrow P(u,v)$$

$$R2: \quad [\sim S(A,s) \land W(r)] \Rightarrow Q(r,s)$$

Facts

$$R(B) \land W(B) \land V(A,B) \land V(B,B)$$

After rules *R1* and *R2* have been applied, we have the AND/OR graph shown in Figure 6.24. This graph has two complementary literals whose predicates unify with mgu $\{A/x, B/y\}$. We indicate this match in Figure 6.24 by an edge between the nodes representing the complementary literals. The edge is labeled by the mgu. The (goal) clause form of the expressions represented by this AND/OR graph include the clauses:

$$V(x,y) \land R(y) \land S(x,B)$$

and

$$V(x,y) \land W(x) \land \sim S(A,y).$$

If we were to perform a goal resolution (on S) between these two clauses (after standardizing variables apart), we would obtain the (goal) resolvent:

$$V(A,y) \land R(y) \land V(t,B) \land W(t).$$

We mentioned at the beginning of this chapter that the AND/OR graph representation for an expression is slightly less general than clause form because variables in the AND/OR graph cannot be fully standardized apart. This constraint makes it difficult to represent, with full generality, the expressions that can be obtained by resolving goal subexpressions.

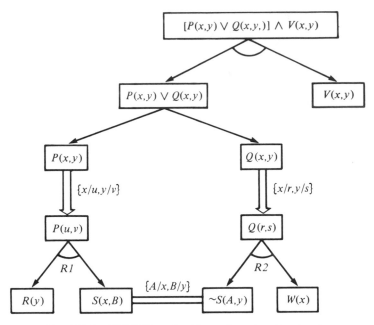

Fig. 6.24 An AND/OR graph with complementary literal nodes.

One way to represent a resolution operation performed between two goal clauses is to connect a literal in one partial solution graph with a complementary literal in another (as we have done in Figure 6.24). We take this connected structure to represent the clauses composed of the literal nodes in the *pairs* of all solution graphs (terminating in literal nodes) thus joined. We associate with a paired solution graph a substitution that is the unifying composition of the substitutions in each member of the pair plus the substitution associated with the match between the complementary literals. The substitution associated with a paired solution graph (terminating in literal nodes) is applied to its terminating literal nodes to obtain the clause that it represents.

Thus, the structure of Figure 6.24 includes a representation for the clause:

$$R(B) \land W(A) \land V(A,B).$$

This clause is not as general as the one we obtained earlier by goal resolution between goal clauses whose variables had been standardized apart, and this restricted generality can prevent us from finding certain proofs. (The expression $[R(B) \wedge W(A) \wedge V(A,B)]$ cannot be proved from the facts that we have given, whereas the expression $[V(A,y) \wedge R(y) \wedge V(t,B) \wedge W(t)]$ can.) We might say that this operation, of matching complementary pairs of literals in AND/OR goal graphs, is a *restricted goal resolution (RGR)*.

To use RGR in a backward production system, we must modify the termination criterion. We can assume, for the purposes of finding candidate solution graphs, that literals joined by an RGR match edge are terminal nodes. A pair of partial solution graphs thus joined constitutes a candidate solution if all of its other leaf nodes are terminal (that is, if they are either goal nodes or if they participate in other RGR matches). Such a candidate solution graph is a final solution graph if its associated substitution is consistent.

In our example, matching the remaining nonterminal leaf nodes of Figure 6.24 with facts fails to produce a consistent solution graph because the solution of this problem requires more generality than can be obtained by applying RGR to the AND/OR graph representation of the goal expression. The required generality can be obtained in this case by multiplying out the goal expression into clauses and standardizing the variables apart between the two clauses, producing the expression:

$$[P(x1,y1) \wedge V(x1,y1)] \vee [Q(x2,y2) \wedge V(x2,y2)].$$

Now this expression can be represented as an AND/OR graph, and rules and RGR can be applied to produce the consistent solution graph shown in Figure 6.25. The unifying composition associated with this solution includes the substitution $\{B/y1, A/x1, B/x2, B/y2\}$. Applying this substitution to the root node of the graph yields the answer statement:

$$[P(A,B)] \wedge V(A,B)] \vee [Q(B,B) \wedge V(B,B)].$$

To avoid conflicting substitutions when using RGR, it is sometimes necessary to multiply out part or all of the goal expression into clause form. A reasonable strategy for deduction systems of this type might be to attempt first to find a proof using the original goal expression. If this attempt fails, the system can convert (part of) the goal expression to clause form, standardize variables, and try again. In the example above, we had to multiply out the *entire* goal expression into clause form in order to find a proof. In general, it suffices to multiply out just that subexpression of the goal that contains *all* of the occurrences of the variables that

237

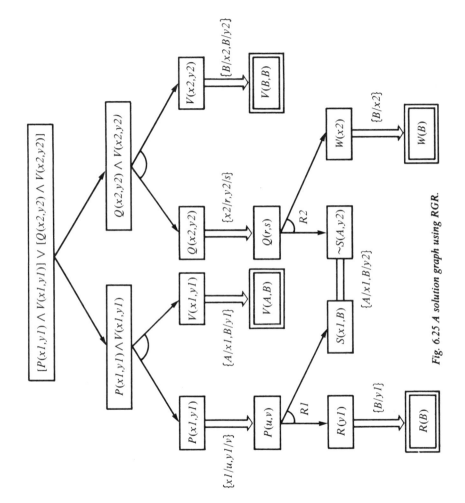

Fig. 6.25 A solution graph using RGR.

238

need renaming. These variables are those for which substitution inconsistencies were detected in the first proof attempt. Comparing Figure 6.24 and Figure 6.25 reveals that the second proof attempt can be guided by the structure of the first.

We can sometimes avoid multiplying out into clause form by using *conditional substitutions*. The idea of conditional substitutions is important in program synthesis applications. A conditional substitution is one that contains a conditional expression. The conditions that we use in conditional substitutions are ones based on a complementary pair of unifiable literals in alternative partial solution graphs. For example, in Figure 6.24, the literals $S(x, B)$ and $\sim S(A, y)$ are in two different partial solution graphs and their predicates unify with mgu $\{A/x, B/y\}$. Applying this mgu to $S(x, B)$ yields $S(A, B)$; applying it to $\sim S(A, y)$ yields $\sim S(A, B)$. We could match the node labeled by $S(x, B)$ with a fact node if $S(A, B)$ had value T. In a sense, the conditional substitution $\{(\text{if } S(A, B), \text{ then } A/x)\}$ unifies $S(x, B)$ with T. Also, the conditional substitution $\{(\text{if } \sim S(A, B), \text{ then } B/y)\}$ unifies $\sim S(A, y)$ with T.

Using these two substitutions permits us to find the two consistent solution graphs shown in Figure 6.26. The unifying composition of the substitutions in the graph on the left includes the substitution $\{(\text{if } S(A, B), A/x, B/y)\}$. The unifying composition of the substitutions in the graph on the right includes the substitution $\{(\text{if } \sim S(A, B), B/y, B/x)\}$. Since either $S(A, B)$ or $\sim S(A, B)$ must be true, we can combine these two solutions into one, with the unifying composition $\{B/y, (\text{if } S(A, B), A/x; \text{ else } B/x)\}$. Such a substitution might well provide a useful answer statement to associate with the goal wff if $S(A, B)$ is a literal that can be evaluated by the user at the time the answer is needed.

Dual processes could be described for restricted resolutions within AND/OR graphs representing facts, but we omit an explicit description because we do not usually expect to encounter contradictions among the facts of an AI system. (Tautologies among goals or subgoals is more common.)

In the next section, we show how we can make use of the version of RGR using conditional expressions in systems that synthesize computer programs. First, though, we describe an alternative method for dealing with implicational goal wffs. Ordinarily we convert a goal wff of the form $P1 \Rightarrow P2$ to its AND/OR form $(\sim P1 \vee P2)$. Suppose, for simplicity,

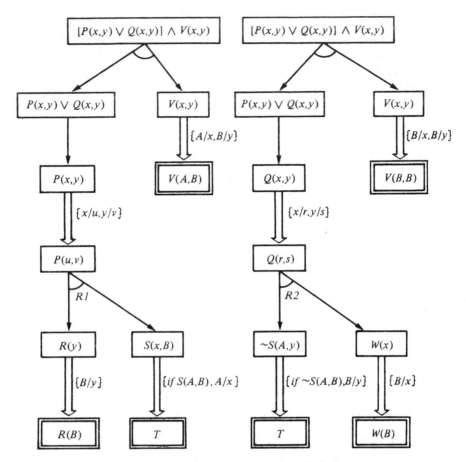

Fig. 6.26 Two solution graphs with conditional substitutions.

that *P1* is a literal. If the system then generates some subgoal of *P2* that contains the literal *P1*, it can use RGR between ∼*P1* and *P1*.

An alternative treatment of a goal of the form *P1* ⇒ *P2* involves converting this goal to the subgoal *P2* while adding *P1* to the set of facts that can be used in proving *P2* or its subgoals. Then, if the system generates *P1* as a subgoal of *P2*, this subgoal can be matched against the assumed fact *P1*.

The process of converting goal antecedents to assumed facts can be applied repeatedly so long as the subgoals contain implications, but the system must maintain a separate set of assumed facts for each subgoal that is created in this manner. Also, the goal antecedents must be in the form of a conjunction of literals, because we are still restricted to fact expressions of that form.

The logical justification for treating an implicational goal in this manner rests on the *deduction theorem* of logic, which states that if *W2* logically follows from *W1*, then $W1 \Rightarrow W2$ is valid. We have occasion to use this method in one of the examples in the next section.

6.4. COMPUTATION DEDUCTIONS AND PROGRAM SYNTHESIS

We next show how backward, rule-based deduction systems can be used for performing computations and for synthesizing certain kinds of computer programs. For such applications, we use a predicate calculus expression to denote the relationship between the input and output of the computation or of the program to be synthesized. For example, suppose the input to a program is denoted by the variable "x," and the output is denoted by the variable "y." Now suppose that we want to synthesize a program such that the relationship P holds between input and output. We can state the synthesis problem as the problem of finding a constructive proof for the expression $(\forall x)(\exists y)P(x,y)$. If we prove that such a y exists by one of our theorem-proving methods, then we can exhibit y as some composition of functions of x. This composition of functions is then the program that we wished to synthesize. The elementary functions comprising the composition are the primitives of the particular programming language being used. "Pure" LISP is a convenient language for this sort of approach because its operations can all be defined in terms of functional expressions.

Let us illustrate this approach by some examples. First, we show how we might compute an expression that bears a given relation to a given input expression. Then we illustrate how a recursive program can be synthesized for arbitrary inputs.

Suppose we simply want to reverse the list (1,2). That is, we want a computation that takes the list (1,2) as input and produces the list (2,1) as output. We show how a rule-based deduction system can perform this computation. First, we specify the relationship between input and output by a two-place predicate *"REVERSED"* whose arguments are terms denoting lists. *REVERSED* is defined, in turn, in terms of other predicates and primitive LISP expressions.

We adopt the convention used in LISP for representing lists as nested *dotted pairs*. In LISP notation, the list (A, B, C, D), for example, is represented as $A.(B.(C.(D.NIL)))$. The dots can be regarded as a special infix function symbol whose prefix form we call *cons*. Thus, the prefix form of $A.B$ is $cons(A, B)$. We prefer the prefix form because that is the form we have been using for functional terms in our predicate calculus language. Using this convention for representing lists, we show how the desired computation can be performed by a system that attempts to prove the goal expression:

$$(\exists y) REVERSED(cons(1, cons(2, NIL)), y).$$

In specifying rules and facts to use in our proof, we use the three-place predicate *"APPENDED."* $APPENDED(x, y, z)$ has the value T just when z is the list formed by appending the list x onto the front of the list y. [For example, appending the list (1,2) onto the list (3,4) produces the list (1,2,3,4).]

The facts that we need in proving the goal expression are:

$F1$: $REVERSED(NIL, NIL)$

$F2$: $APPENDED(NIL, x1, x1)$

We express certain relationships involving *REVERSED* and *AP-PENDED* by the following rules:

$R1$: $APPENDED(x2, y2, z2)$
$\Rightarrow APPENDED(cons(u1, x2), y2, cons(u1, z2))$

$R2$: $[REVERSED(x3, y3)$
$\land APPENDED(y3, cons(u2, NIL), v1)]$
$\Rightarrow REVERSED(cons(u2, x3), v1)$

Rule $R1$ states that the list created by appending a list, whose first element is $u1$ and whose tail is $x2$, to a list $y2$ is the same as the list created by adding the element $u1$ to the front of the list formed by appending $x2$

to $y2$. Rule $R2$ states that the reverse of a list formed by adding an element $u2$ to the front of a list $x3$ is the same as appending the reverse of $x3$ onto the list consisting of the single element $u2$.

Let us show how a backward production system might go about reversing the list (1,2) given these facts and B-rules. We do not attempt to explain here how a control strategy for this system might efficiently decide which applicable rule ought to be applied. Much of the control knowledge needed to make these sorts of choices intelligently is special to the domain of automatic programming and outside the scope of our present discussion of general mechanisms.

We first look for facts and rules that match the goal RE-$VERSED(cons(1,cons(2,NIL)),y)$. We can apply B-rule $R2$ with mgu $\{1/u2, cons(2,NIL)/x3, y/v1\}$. Applying this mgu to the antecedent of $R2$ yields new literal nodes labeled by

$$REVERSED(cons(2,NIL),y3)$$

and

$$APPENDED(y3,cons(1,NIL),y).$$

We can apply B-rule $R2$ to the subgoal $REVERSED(cons(2,NIL),y3)$, creating two new literal nodes. (We rename the variables in $R2$ before application to avoid confusion with the variables used in the previous application.)

A consistent solution graph for this problem is shown in Figure 6.27. The output expression that results from this proof is obtained by combining substitutions to find the term substituted for y, namely, $cons(2,cons(1,NIL))$. This expression represents the list that is the reverse of the input list (1,2).

It is interesting to compare the computations involved in the search for the proof shown in Figure 6.27 with the computations involved in executing the following LISP program for reversing an arbitrary list:

```
reverse( x ):
    if null( x ), NIL
    else, append(reverse(cdr( x )), cons(car( x ), NIL )))
```

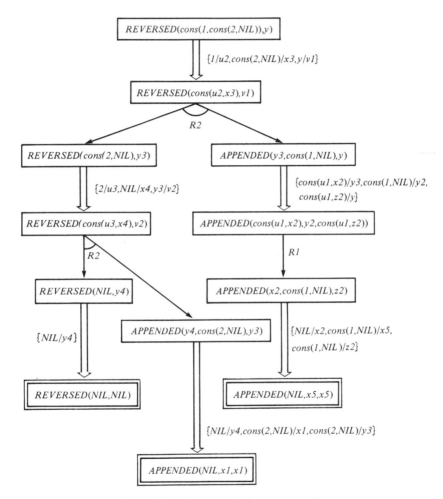

Fig. 6.27 The solution graph for reversing a list.

append(x, y):
  if null(x), y
  else, cons(car(x **), append(cdr(** x **),** y **))**

If the search process of our backward production system is sufficiently well-guided by an appropriate control strategy, then the steps in the search process correspond quite closely to the steps involved in executing the LISP program on the input list (1,2).

We can control the production system search process by specifying which applicable fact or rule should be used at any stage, and in which order, to solve the component subgoals. A "language" for specifying this control information can be based on conventions about the order in which rules and facts are tested for possible matches and the order in which literals appear in rule antecedents. When a rule or fact must be selected for use, we select the first one in this ordering that can be matched. When a subgoal component must be selected for solution, we select according to the ordering in which literals are written in rule antecedents. It turns out that the order (*F1*, *F2*, *R1*, *R2*) for rule and fact matching and the order in which we have written the antecedents of rules *R1* and *R2* provide a very efficient control strategy for our example problem. With this control strategy, the steps performed in the *search process* for a proof mirror almost exactly the computational steps of executing the LISP program.

To see the parallel, let us trace out just a few steps of the search process. Beginning with the goal $REVERSED(cons(1, cons(2, NIL)), y)$, we first check (in the order *F1*, *F2*, *R1*, *R2*) for a match. There might be a match against *F1*, so we check to see if $cons(1, cons(2, NIL))$ unifies with NIL. [Compare with **if null**(x) in the program.] Failing this test, we check for a match against the consequent of *R2*. This test involves matching $cons(u2, x3)$ against $cons(1, cons(2, NIL))$. This match succeeds with the substitution $\{1/u2, \; cons(2, NIL)/x3\}$. [Compare with computing **car(** x **)** and **cdr(** x **)** in the second line of the reverse program.] The first subgoal component [namely, $REVERSED(cons(2, NIL), y)$] of the antecedent of *R2* is worked on first. [Compare with the recursive call to **reverse(cdr(** x **))** in the program.] Again, we check for a match against *F1* by checking to see if $cons(2, NIL)$ equals NIL. Failing in this test again, we pass to another level of subgoal generation in the proof search (and of recursion in the program). At this level, we succeed in our match against *F1* (with mgu $\{NIL/y4\}$), so we work on the next subgoal *AP-*

$PENDED(y4, cons(2, NIL), y3)$. [In the program, we call the subroutine **append**(NIL,**cons**(2, NIL)).] This same parallelism holds between the rest of the proof search and the program.

In many cases, it is possible to control the search process sufficiently so that it mimics efficient computation, and, for this reason, it has been said that computation is controlled deduction [Hayes (1973b)]. In fact, a programming language, called PROLOG, is based on this very idea. PROLOG "programs" consist of a sequence of "facts" and "rules." The rules are implications just like our rules except that, in PROLOG, the rule antecedents are restricted to conjunctions of literals. A program is "called" by a goal expression. The fact and rule statements in the program are scanned to find the first match for the first component in the goal expression. The substitutions found in the match correspond to variable binding, and control is transferred to the first subgoal component of the rule. Thus, the "interpreter" for a PROLOG program corresponds to a backward, rule-based production system with very specific control information about what to do next. (The PROLOG interpreter is a bit less flexible than our backward system, because in PROLOG the substitutions used in matching one literal of a conjunctive subgoal are straightaway applied to the other conjuncts. The subgoal instances thus created might not have solutions, so PROLOG incorporates a backtracking mechanism that can try other matches.)

The example that we have been considering has involved a fixed input list, namely, (1,2). If this fixed list were different, the theorem-proving system would have produced a different proof and a different answer. (Presumably, though, our PROLOG program would continue to function analogously to the general LISP program.) Rather than perform the search process each time we "run the program" (even though, apparently, this search can be made quite efficient), we are led to ask if we could automatically synthesize one general program (like the LISP one, for example) that would accept *any* input list. To do so we must find a proof for the goal:

$$(\forall x)(\exists y) REVERSED(x, y).$$

(Of course, we don't literally mean "for *all* x" because the program doesn't have to be defined for all possible inputs. We only require that it be defined for lists. We could have expressed this input restriction in the formula to be proved, but our illustrative example is simpler if we merely assume that the domain of x is limited to lists.)

246

Since we already know that the final program for any given input list has a repetitive character, we might guess that the program we are seeking for arbitrary input lists is recursive. The introduction of recursive functions in program synthesis comes about by using mathematical induction in the proof. It turns out that in reversing a list by using an **append** function, we have double recursion, once in **reverse** and once in **append**. As a simpler example, let's consider just the problem of producing a program to append one list to (the front of) another. That is, our goal is to prove:

$$(\forall x)(\forall y)(\exists z)\,APPENDED\,(x,y,z)\,.$$

In this case, we have two input lists, x and y, and one output list, z.

Skolemizing the goal wff yields

$$APPENDED\,(A,B,z)\,,$$

where A and B are Skolem constants. To prove this goal, we'll need fact *F2* and rule *R1* from our previous example. (The presence of the other unneeded fact and rule does no harm, however.) Our explanation of this example is simplified if we re-represent *F1* and *R1* as the following rules:

$$R3:\quad NULL(u)\Rightarrow APPENDED\,(u,x1,x1)$$

$$R4:\quad [\sim NULL(v)\wedge APPENDED\,(cdr(v),y0,z1)]$$
$$\Rightarrow APPENDED\,(v,y0,cons(car(v),z1))$$

In these expressions, we introduce the primitive LISP functions, namely, *cons*, *car*, and *cdr*, out of which our program will be constructed. These LISP expressions could have been introduced instead by the rule

$$\sim NULL(x)\Rightarrow EQUAL(x,cons(car(x),cdr(x)))\,.$$

This alternative, however, would have involved us in some additional complexities regarding special techniques for using equality axioms. We avoid these difficulties, and simplify our example, by using rules *R3* and *R4* instead. The needed equality substitutions are already contained in these rules.

As already mentioned, to synthesize a recursive program using theorem-proving methods requires the use of induction. We use the

247

method of *structural induction* for lists. To do so, we need the concept of a list as a sublist of a given list. This relation is denoted by the predicate $SUBLIST(u,x)$. The principal property of $SUBLIST$ on which our inductive argument depends can be expressed as the rule:

$$R5: \quad \sim NULL(x) \Rightarrow SUBLIST(cdr(x),x)) \ ,$$

that is, the tail of any nonempty list, x, is a sublist of x.

To prove

$$(\forall y1)(\forall y2)(\exists z1)APPENDED(y1,y2,z1) \ ,$$

using structural induction for lists, we would proceed as follows:

1. Assume the *induction hypothesis*

$$(\forall u1)(\forall u2)[\,SUBLIST(u1,x1)$$
$$\Rightarrow (\exists z2)APPENDED(u1,u2,z2)] \ .$$

That is, we assume our goal expression true for all input lists $u1$ and $u2$ such that $u1$ is a sublist of some arbitrary list $x1$.

2. Next, given the induction hypothesis, we attempt to prove our goal expression true for all input lists $x1$ and $x2$ where $x1$ is the arbitrary list of the induction hypothesis.

If step 2 is successful, then our goal expression is true for all input lists, $y1$ and $y2$.

We can capture this argument in a single formula, which we call the *induction rule*.

$$\{(\forall x1)(\forall x2)$$
$$\{(\forall u1)(\forall u2)[\,SUBLIST(u1,x1)$$
$$\Rightarrow (\exists z2)APPENDED(u1,u2,z2)]\}$$
$$\Rightarrow (\exists z3)APPENDED(x1,x2,z3)\}$$
$$\Rightarrow (\forall y1)(\forall y2)(\exists z1)APPENDED(y1,y2,z1)$$

Although this rule looks rather complicated, we use it in a straightforward manner. Ignoring quantifiers, the rule is of the form:

$$[(A \Rightarrow C1) \Rightarrow C2] \Rightarrow C3 \ .$$

248

We will be using this rule as a B-rule to prove C3. Such a use creates the subgoal of proving

$$[(A \Rightarrow C1) \Rightarrow C2] \ .$$

We elect to prove this subgoal by proving $C2$ while having available (only for use on $C2$ and its descendant subgoals) the B-rule $(A \Rightarrow C1)$. (This manner of treating an implicational goal was discussed earlier. Now, however, rather than assume the goal's antecedent as a *fact*, we assume it as a *rule*.) A diagram that illustrates this strategy is shown in Figure 6.28.

Alternatively, we could transform the antecedent of the induction rule into AND/OR form and use the rule to create the subgoal $[(A \wedge \sim C1) \vee C2]$. This use of the induction rule is entirely equivalent, but it is a bit less intuitive and more difficult to explain, because an RGR step between $\sim C1$ and $C2$ would ultimately be required to prove the subgoal.

The induction rule can be Skolemized as follows:

$$\{[\,SUBLIST(u1,A1) \Rightarrow APPENDED(u1,u2,sk1(u1,u2))] \\ \Rightarrow APPENDED(A1,A2,z3)\} \\ \Rightarrow APPENDED(y1,y2,sk2(y1,y2)) \ .$$

Note the Skolem constants and functions $A1, A2, sk1$, and $sk2$. The program that we seek will, in fact, turn out to be either of the Skolem functions $sk1$ or $sk2$. Thus, it is reasonable now to represent both of them by the single function symbol *append*. With this renaming, our induction rule, in the form in which we use it, is:

$$RI: \quad \{[\,SUBLIST(u1,A1) \\ \Rightarrow APPENDED(u1,u2,append(u1,u2))] \\ \Rightarrow APPENDED(A1,A2,z3)\} \\ \Rightarrow APPENDED(y1,y2,append(y1,y2)) \ .$$

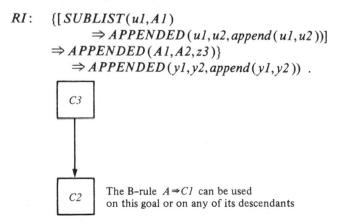

The B-rule $A \Rightarrow C1$ can be used on this goal or on any of its descendants

Fig. 6.28 Using the induction rule.

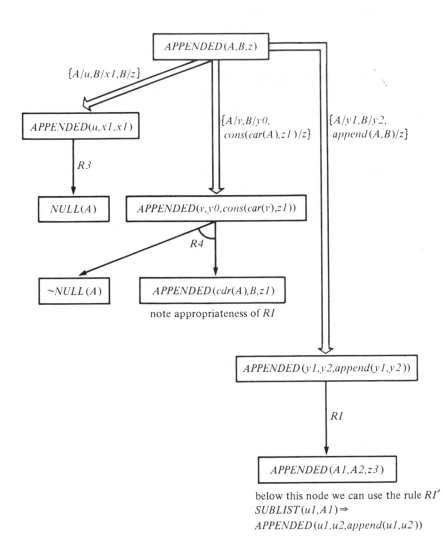

note appropriateness of *RI*

below this node we can use the rule *RI'*
SUBLIST(u1,A1) ⇒
APPENDED(u1,u2,append(u1,u2))

(continued on next page)

Fig. 6.29 A search graph for the APPENDED problem.

(continued from preceding page)

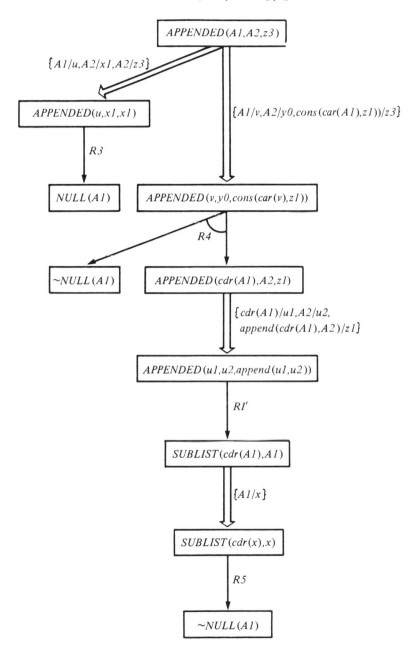

An AND/OR search graph for the problem of proving *AP-PENDED*(A,B,z) is shown in Figure 6.29. In our example, search begins by applying rules *R3* and *R4* to the main goal. One of the subgoals produced by *R4* is recognized as similar to the main goal. Producing a subgoal having this sort of similarity suggests, to the control strategy, the appropriateness of applying the induction rule, *RI*, to the main goal. (Of course, it is logically correct to apply the induction rule to the main goal at any time. Since proof by induction is relatively complicated, the induction rule should not be used unless it is judged heuristically appropriate. When a straightforward proof attempt produces this sort of "instance" of the main goal as a subgoal, induction is usually appropriate.)

Applying *RI* to the main goal produces the subgoal *AP-PENDED*($A1,A2,z3$) and the rule:

RI': $SUBLIST(u1,A1) \Rightarrow APPENDED(u1,u2,append(u1,u2))$.

This rule can be used only in the proof of *APPENDED*($A1,A2,z3$) or its subgoals.

Next, the control strategy applies the same rules as were applied earlier to the main goal (namely, *R3* and *R4*) to the subgoal produced by the induction rule. Ultimately, two different solution graphs are produced that are complete except for the occurrence of *NULL*($A1$) in one and $\sim NULL(A1)$ in the other. An RGR step completes the solution and yields the conditional substitution:

{(if null($A1$), $A2/z3$;
  else $cons(car(A1),append(cdr(A1),A2))/z3$)} .

This substitution produces a term for variable $z3$, which occurred in a subgoal of the maingoal. This subgoal, which we have now proved, is

$APPENDED(A1,A2,$(if null($A1$), $A2$;
  else $cons(car(A1),append(cdr(A1),A2))))$.

Since *A1* and *A2* are Skolem constants originating from universal variables in a goal expression, they can be replaced by universally quantified variables when constructing an answer. Thus, we have proved:

$(\forall x1)(\forall x2)APPENDED(x1,x2,$(if null($x1$), $x2$;
  else $cons(car(x1),append(cdr(x1),x2))))$.

Now we recognize that the third argument of *APPENDED* in the above expression is a recursive program satisfying our input/output condition.

There are many subtleties involved in using induction in program synthesis. A full account of the process is beyond the scope of this book and would involve an explanation of methods for constructing auxiliary functions, recursion within recursive programs, and the use of induction hypotheses that are more general or "stronger" than the theorem to be proved. The special induction rule for *APPENDED* that we used in our example could be replaced by more general structural induction rule schemas. These would use *well-founded ordering* conditions more general than *SUBLIST* [see Manna and Waldinger (1979)].

6.5. A COMBINATION FORWARD AND BACKWARD SYSTEM

Both the forward and the backward rule-based deduction systems had limitations. The backward system could handle goal expressions of arbitrary form but was restricted to fact expressions consisting of conjunctions of literals. The forward system could handle fact expressions of arbitrary form but was restricted to goal expressions consisting of disjunctions of literals. Can we combine these two systems into one that would have the advantages of each without the limitations of either?

We next describe a production system that is based on a combination of the two we have just described. The global database of this combined system consists of two AND/OR graph structures, one representing goals and one representing facts. These AND/OR structures are initially set to represent the given goal and fact expressions whose forms are now unrestricted.

These structures are modified by the B-rules and F-rules, respectively, of our two previous systems. The designer must decide which rules are to work on the fact graph and which are to work on the goal graph. We continue to call these rules B-rules and F-rules even though our new production system is really only proceeding in one direction as it modifies its bipartite global database. We continue to restrict the B-rules to single-literal consequents, and the F-rules to single-literal antecedents.

The major complication introduced by this combined production system is its termination condition. Termination must involve the proper kind of abutment between the two graph structures. These structures can be joined by match edges at nodes labeled by literals that unify. We label the match edges themselves by the corresponding mgus. In the initial graphs, match edges between the fact and goal graphs must be between leaf nodes. After the graphs are extended by B-rule and F-rule applications, the matches might occur at any literal node.

After all possible matches between the two graphs are made, we still have the problem of deciding whether or not the expression at the root node of the goal graph has been proved from the rules and the expression at the root node of the fact graph. Our proof procedure should terminate only when such a proof is found (or when we can conclude that one cannot be found within given resource limits).

One simple termination condition is a straightforward generalization of the procedure for deciding whether the root node of an AND/OR graph is "solved." This termination condition is based on a symmetric relationship, called *CANCEL*, between a fact node and a goal node. *CANCEL* is defined recursively as follows:

> Two nodes n and m *CANCEL* each other if one of (n,m) is a fact node and the other a goal node,
>
> and
>
> if n and m are labeled by unifiable literals, or n has an outgoing k-connector to a set of successors $\{s_i\}$, such that $CANCEL(s_i, m)$ holds for each member of the set.

When the root node of the goal graph and the root node of the fact graph *CANCEL* each other, we have a *candidate solution*. The graph structure, within the goal and fact graphs, that demonstrates that the goal and fact root nodes *CANCEL* each other is called a candidate *CANCEL graph*. The candidate solution is an actual solution if all of the match mgus in the candidate *CANCEL* graph are consistent.

As an example, we show the matches between an initial fact graph and an initial goal graph in Figure 6.30. A consistent candidate *CANCEL*

254

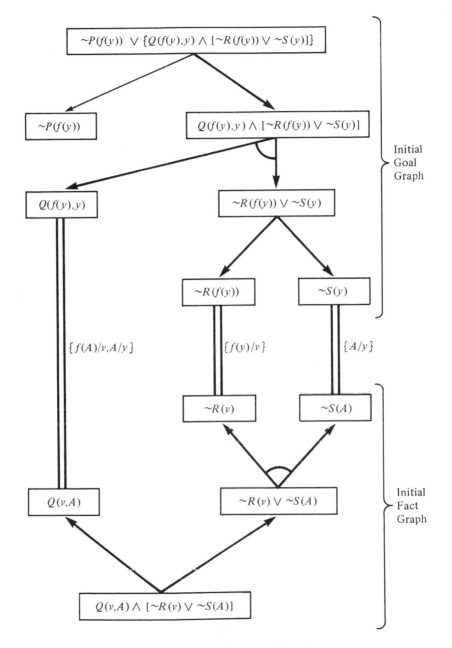

Fig. 6.30 An example CANCEL graph.

graph is indicated by the darkened arcs. The mgus of each of the fact-goal node matches are shown next to the match edges, and the unifying composition of all of these mgus is $\{f(A)/v, A/y\}$.

Note that our *CANCEL* graph method treats conjunctively related goal nodes correctly. Each conjunct must be proved before the parent is proved. Disjunctively related fact nodes are treated in a similar manner. In order to use one member of a disjunction in a proof, we must be able to prove the same goal using each of the disjuncts separately. This process implements the "reasoning-by-cases" strategy.

As the AND/OR search graphs are developed by application of B-rules and F-rules, substitutions are associated with each rule application. All substitutions in a solution graph, including the mgus obtained in rule matches and the mgus obtained between matching fact and goal literals, must be consistent.

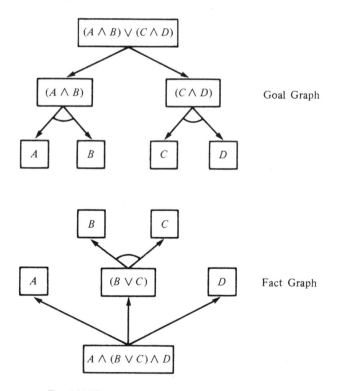

Fig. 6.31 *The termination check fails to detect a proof.*

We note that pruning the AND/OR graphs by detecting inconsistent substitutions may be impossible in systems that use both B-rules and F-rules because, for these, both the fact and goal graphs change dynamically, making it impossible to tell at any stage whether all possible matches have already been made for a given literal node. Also, when using F-rules and B-rules simultaneously, it may be important to treat the appropriate instances of solved goals as facts, so that F-rules can be applied to them. (A solved goal is one that is *CANCEL*led by the root node of the fact graph.)

The termination condition we have just described is adequate for many problems but would fail to detect that the goal graph follows from the fact graph in Figure 6.31. A more general sort of "fact-goal" resolution operation would be needed for this problem than that embodied in our simple *CANCEL*-based termination check.

An alternative way of dealing with both arbitrary fact and goal expressions is to use a (unidirectional) refutation system that processes facts only. The goal expression is first negated and then converted to AND/OR form and conjoined with the fact expression. F-rules, the contrapositive forms of B-rules, and restricted resolution operations are then applied to this augmented fact graph until a contradiction is produced.

6.6. CONTROL KNOWLEDGE FOR RULE-BASED DEDUCTION SYSTEMS

Earlier we divided the knowledge needed by AI systems into three categories: declarative knowledge, procedural knowledge, and control knowledge. The production systems discussed in this chapter make it relatively easy to express declarative and procedural knowledge. Experts in various fields such as medicine and mathematics, who might not be familiar with computers, have found it quite convenient and natural to express their expertise in the form of predicates and implicational rules.

Nevertheless, there is still the need to supply control knowledge for deduction systems. Efficient control strategies for the production systems we describe might need to be rather complex. Embedding these strategies into control programs requires a large amount of programming skill. Thus, there is the temptation to leave the control strategy design entirely to the AI expert. But much important control knowledge is specific to the domain in which the AI program is to operate. It is often just as important for the physicians, chemists, and other domain experts to supply control knowledge as it is for them to supply declarative and procedural knowledge.

There are several examples of control knowledge that might be specific to a particular application. Separating the rules into B-rules and F-rules relieves the control strategy of the burden of deciding on the direction of rule application. The best direction in which to apply a rule sometimes depends on the domain. As an example of the importance of the direction in which a rule is applied, consider rules that express taxonomic information such as "all cats are animals," and "all dogs are animals":

$$CAT(x) \Rightarrow ANIMAL(x)$$

$$DOG(x) \Rightarrow ANIMAL(x)$$

If we had several such rules, one for each different type of animal, it would be extremely inefficient to use any of them in the backward direction. That is, one should not go about attempting to prove that Sam, say, is an animal by first setting up the subgoal of proving that he is a cat and, failing in that, trying the other subgoals. The taxonomic hierarchy branches out too extensively in the direction of search.

Whenever possible, the direction of reasoning ought to be in the direction of a decreasing number of alternatives. The rules above can safely be used in the forward direction. When we learn that Sam is a cat, say, we can efficiently assert that he is also an animal. Following the hierarchy in this direction does not lead to a combinatorial explosion because search is pinched off by the ever-narrowing number of categories.

The *contrapositive* form of $CAT(x) \Rightarrow ANIMAL(x)$ is $\sim ANIMAL(x) \Rightarrow \sim CAT(x)$. This rule should be used in the backward direction only. That is, to prove that Sam is not a cat, it is efficient to attempt to prove that he is not an animal. Again, search is pinched off by the narrow end of the taxonomic hierarchy.

There is other important control information that might depend on the domain. In a rule of the form $[P1 \wedge P2 \wedge \ldots \wedge PN] \Rightarrow Q$, used as a

B-rule, the domain expert may want to specify the order in which the subgoals should be attacked. For each of these subgoals, he may further want to specify explicitly a set of B-rules to be used on them and the order in which these B-rules should be applied. Similarly, whenever a rule of the form $P \Rightarrow [Q1 \wedge \ldots \wedge QN]$ is used as an F-rule, he may want to specify an additional set of F-rules that can now be applied and the order in which these F-rules ought to be applied.

It may be appropriate for the control strategy to make other tests before deciding whether to apply a B-rule or an F-rule. In an earlier example, the transitivity of the "greater-than" predicate played an important role. It would typically be inefficient to apply a transitivity rule in the backward direction; but there may be specific cases in which it is efficient to do so. Recall that the transitivity rule was of the form:

$$[(x > y) \wedge (y > z)] \Rightarrow (x > z) \, .$$

We might want to apply this rule as a B-rule if one of the subgoal conjuncts could match an existing fact, for example. This *conditional application* would greatly restrict the use of the rule. Application conditions comprise important control knowledge.

In order to use this sort of control knowledge, we need suitable formalisms in which to represent it. There seem to be several approaches to the problem. First, we could consider the control strategy problem itself as a problem to be solved by another AI production system. The *object-level* AI system would have declarative and procedural knowledge about the applications domain; the *meta-level* AI system would have declarative and procedural knowledge relevant to the control of the object-level system. Such a scheme might conveniently allow the formulation of object-level control knowledge as meta-level rules.

A second approach involves embedding some of the control knowledge into evaluation functions used by the control strategy. When a domain expert specifies that some conjunctive subgoal A, say, is to be solved before B, then we must arrange that the function used to order the AND nodes of a partial AND/OR solution graph places A before B in the ordering. This approach has not been thoroughly explored.

A third method involves embedding the relevant control knowledge right into the rules. This approach has been embodied in several high-level AI programming languages. We attempt to describe the essence of this approach in the following section.

6.6.1.   F-RULE AND B-RULE PROGRAMS

Control knowledge specifies the order in which operations should be performed: Do this before that, do this first, do this if that is true, and so on. It is natural to attempt to represent this sort of knowledge in programs. F-rules and B-rules can be considered programs that operate on facts and goals. The most straightforward solution to the control problem is to embed control responsibility directly into the F-rules and B-rules.

Just how much control should be given to the F-rules and B-rules? So far, we have been considering one extreme (production systems) in which a separate global control system retained total control and none was given to the rules. Let us now briefly investigate another extreme in which all control is given over to the rules (with a consequent atrophying of the global control system).

We want to retain the basic character of the F-rules and B-rules. That is, F-rules should be called only when they can be applied to facts, and B-rules should be called only when they can be applied to goals. The calling mechanism should invoke rules only when new goals or facts are derived. This type of mechanism might be called *goal- (fact-) directed function invocation.* An extremely simple scheme for performing this invocation involves the following: When a new goal (fact) is created, all of the rules that are applicable to this new goal (fact) are collected. One of these is then selected and given complete control. This program is then executed; it may set new goals (invoking other B-rules) or it may assert new facts (invoking other F-rules). In either case, the control structure is otherwise much like that of conventional programs. A rule program runs until it encounters a **RETURN** statement. It then returns control to the program from which it was invoked. While it is running, a rule program has complete control. If an executing rule program *fails* (for one of several reasons to be discussed later), control automatically backtracks to the next highest choice point where another selection is made. Thus, the scheme we are describing corresponds to a simple backtrack control regime in which all of the control information is embedded in the rules.

We elaborate later on the mechanism by which one of the many possible applicable rules is selected for invocation. We must also describe how consequents and antecedents of rules are represented in programs and how matching is to be handled.

260

We next present a simplified syntax for our F- and B-rule programs. (This syntax is related to, but not identical to, syntaxes of the high-level AI languages PLANNER, QLISP, and CONNIVER.)

A goal or subgoal is introduced by a **GOAL** statement; for example, **GOAL** $(ANIMAL\ ?x)$. This statement is equivalent to the predicate calculus goal expression $(\exists x)ANIMAL(x)$. The variable x with a ? prefix is existentially quantified when it occurs in **GOAL** statements.

A new or inferred fact is added to the set of facts by an **ASSERT** statement; for example,

ASSERT $(CAT\ SAM)$

or

ASSERT $(DOG\ ?x)$.

The latter is equivalent to the predicate calculus expression $(\forall x)DOG(x)$. The variable x with a ? prefix is universally quantified when it occurs in facts or in **ASSERT** statements.

F-rule and B-rule programs each have triggering expressions that are called their *patterns*. For F-rule programs, the pattern is the antecedent of the corresponding rule; for B-rule programs, the pattern is the consequent. For simplicity, we assume that a pattern consists of a single literal only. Patterns can contain ?-variables, and these variables can be matched against anything when invoking a program. Since F-rule patterns are used only to match facts and B-rule patterns are used only to match goals, the use of ?-variables in both patterns is consistent with our assumptions about variable quantifications in facts and goals.

The body of rule programs contains, besides control information, that part of the corresponding rule not in the pattern. Thus, F-rule programs contain **ASSERT** statements corresponding to consequents, and B-rule programs contain **GOAL** statements corresponding to antecedents. Any variables in these statements that are the same as pattern variables are preceded by a $ and are called $-variables. When a pattern is matched to a fact or goal, the ?-variables are bound to the terms that they match. The corresponding $-variables in the body of the program receive the same bindings. These bindings also apply locally to subsequent statements in the calling program that contained the **GOAL** or the **ASSERT** statement that caused the match. Pattern matching then takes the place of unification, and variable binding takes the place of substitution.

Using this syntax, we could represent the rule $CAT(x) \Rightarrow ANIMAL(x)$ by the following simple F-rule program:

> **FR1** $(CAT\,?x)$
>   **ASSERT** $(ANIMAL\,\$x)$
>   **RETURN**

The pattern, $(CAT\,?x)$, occurs immediately after the name of the program **FR1**. In this case, the body of the program consists only of an **ASSERT** statement. The variable $\$x$ is bound to that entity to which $?x$ was matched when the pattern $(CAT\,?x)$ was matched against a fact.

Consider the rule, $ELEPHANT(x) \Rightarrow GRAY(x)$. This rule can be written as a B-rule program as follows:

> **BR1** $(GRAY\,?x)$
>   **GOAL** $(ELEPHANT\,\$x)$
>   **ASSERT** $(GRAY\,\$x)$
>   **RETURN**

The variable $\$x$ is bound to whatever individual matched $?x$ during the pattern match.

Mechanisms for applying rules to facts and goals can be simply captured in programs, but we must also be able to match goals directly against facts. This objective is accomplished simply by checking the facts (in addition to the B-rule patterns) whenever a **GOAL** statement is encountered. Ordinarily we would check the facts first.

Let's look at a simple example to see how these programs work and to gain familarity with the syntax.

Suppose we have the following programs:

> **BR1** $(BOSS\text{-}OF\,?y\,?z)$
>   **GOAL** $(WORKS\text{-}IN\,?x\,\$y)$
>   **GOAL** $(MANAGER\,\$x\,\$z)$
>   **ASSERT** $(BOSS\text{-}OF\,\$y\,\$z)$
>   **RETURN**

(If y works in x and z is the manager of x, then z is the boss of y).

(Note that the B-rule program allows us naturally to specify the order in which conjunctive goals are to be solved. The variable $\$x$ in the second subgoal is bound to whatever is matched against $?x$ in the first subgoal.)

> **BR2** (*HAPPY* $?x$)
> **GOAL** (*MARRIED* $\$x\ ?y$)
> **GOAL** (*WORKS-IN* $?z\ \$y$)
> **ASSERT** (*HAPPY* $\$x$)
> **RETURN**

(Happy is the person with a working spouse.)

> **BR3** (*HAPPY* $?x$)
> **GOAL** (*WORKS-IN P-D* $\$x$)
> **ASSERT** (*HAPPY* $\$x$)
> **RETURN**

(If x works in the Purchasing Department, x is happy.)

> **BR4** (*WORKS-IN* $?x\ ?y$)
> **GOAL** (*MANAGER* $\$x\ \$y$)
> **ASSERT** (*WORKS-IN* $\$x\ \$y$)
> **RETURN**

(If y is the manager of x, y works in x.)

Suppose the facts are as follows:

> *F1*: *MANAGER(P-D,JOHN-JONES)*
> *F2*: *WORKS-IN(P-D,JOE-SMITH)*
> *F3*: *WORKS-IN(S-D,SALLY-JONES)*
> *F4*: *MARRIED(JOHN-JONES,MARY-JONES)*

Consider the problem of finding the name of an employee who has a happy boss. The query can be expressed by the following program:

> **BEGIN**
> **GOAL** (*BOSS-OF* $?u\ ?v$)
> **GOAL** (*HAPPY* $\$v$)
> **PRINT** $\$u$ "has happy boss" $\$v$
> **END**

Let us trace a typical execution. We first encounter **GOAL** (*BOSS-OF* ? *u* ? *v*). Since no facts match this goal, we look for B-rules and find **BR1**. The pattern match merely passes along the existential variables. The computational environment is now as shown in Figure 6.32. The asterisk marks the next statement to be executed, and the bindings that apply for a sequence of statements are shown at the top of the sequence. The next statement encountered (after binding variables) is:

GOAL (*WORKS-IN* ? *x* ? *u*).

Here we have a match against *F2* with ? *x* bound to *P-D* and ? *u* bound to *JOE-SMITH*. Following the sequence of Figure 6.32, we next meet:

GOAL (*MANAGER P-D* ? *v*).

This statement matches *F1*, binding ? *v* to *JOHN-JONES*. We can now assert *BOSS-OF*(*JOE-SMITH, JOHN-JONES*) and return to the query program to encounter **GOAL** (*HAPPY JOHN-JONES*). Now there are two different sequences of programs that might be used. **GOAL** (*HAPPY JOHN-JONES*) might invoke either **BR2** or **BR3**. We leave it to the reader to trace through either or both of these paths.

A **GOAL** statement can **FAIL** if there are no facts or B-rules that match its pattern. Suppose, for example, that we matched **GOAL** (WORKS-IN ? *x* ? *u*) against *F3* instead of against *F2*. This match would have led to an attempt to execute **GOAL** (*MANAGER S-D* ? *v*). The set of facts does not include any information about the manager of the Sales Department.

BEGIN   (bindings: *?u/?y, ?v/?z*)

——————————————————————▶

*   **GOAL** (*WORKS–IN* ?x $y)
    GOAL (*MANAGER* $x $z)
    ASSERT (*BOSS–OF* $y $z)
    RETURN

◀——————————————————————

GOAL (*HAPPY* $v)
PRINT $u "has happy boss" $v
END

Fig. 6.32 A state in the execution of a query.

No B-rule applies either, so the **GOAL** statement **FAILS**. In such a case, control backtracks to the previous choice point, namely, the pattern match for **GOAL** (*WORKS-IN* ?*x* ?*u*). In addition to transferring control, all bindings made since this choice point are undone. Now we can use the ultimately successful match against *F2*.

Because rules are now programs, we can augment them with other useful control statements. For example, we can include tests to decide whether an F-rule or B-rule program ought to be applied. If the test indicates inappropriateness of the program, we can execute a special **FAIL** statement that causes backtracking. The general form of such a condition statement is:

IF <condition> **FAIL** .

The <condition> can be an arbitrary program that evaluates to true or false. Such statements are usually put at the beginning of the program to trap cases where the program ought not to continue.

An important category of conditions involves testing to see if there is a fact that matches a particular pattern. This testing is done by an **IS** statement. The general form is:

IS <pattern> .

If <pattern> matches a fact, bindings are made (that apply locally to any following statements) and the program continues. Otherwise, the statement **FAILS** and backtracking occurs.

Recall that earlier we mentioned that the transitivity rule for the "greater-than" predicate might be used as a B-rule if one of the antecedents was already a fact. We could implement such a B-rule as follows:

> **BTRANS** (*G* ?*x* ?*z*)
>   **IS** (*G* $*x* ?*y*)
>   **GOAL** (*G* $*y* $*z*)
>   **RETURN**

Now if $G(A, B)$ and $G(B, C)$ were facts, we could use **BTRANS** to prove $G(A, C)$ as follows: First, we match **BTRANS** against **GOAL** (*G A C*) and thus attempt to execute **IS** (*G A* ?*y*). This test is

265

successful, $?y$ is bound to B, and we next encounter **GOAL** (G B C). This goal matches one of the facts directly, and we are finished. If the **IS** test failed, we would not have used this transitivity B-rule and, thus, would have avoided generating the subgoal. We'll see additional examples later of the usefulness of applicability conditions.

Another important type of control information might be called "advice." At the time a **GOAL** statement is made, we may want to give advice about the B-rules that might be used in attempting to solve it. This advice can be in the form of a list of B-rules to be tried in order. Similarly, **ASSERT** statements can be accompanied by a list of F-rules to be tried in order. These lists can be dynamically modified by other programs, thus enabling quite flexible operation.

There are other advantages of rule programs beyond those related to control strategies. We can write very general procedures to transform certain goals into subgoals, to evaluate goals, and to assert new facts. To achieve these same effects by ordinary production rules could sometimes be cumbersome.

Suppose, for example, that in doing inequality reasoning we encounter the subgoal $G(8,5)$. Now, as mentioned earlier, we certainly do not want to include G predicates for all pairs of numbers. The effect of procedural attachment to a "greater-than" computation can be achieved by the following B-rule:

> **BG** (G $?x$ $?y$)
>   **IF (NOTNUM** $\$x$) **FAIL**
>   **IF (NOTNUM** $\$y$) **FAIL**
>   **IF (NOTG** $\$x$ $\$y$) **FAIL**
>   **ASSERT** (G $\$x$ $\$y$)
>   **RETURN**

In this program, **NOTNUM** tests to see if its argument is not a number. If **NOTNUM** returns T (i.e., if its argument is not a number), we **FAIL** out of this B-rule. If both **NOTNUM**s return F, we stay in the B-rule and use the program **NOTG** to see if the first numerical argument is greater than the second. If it is, we successfully bypass another **FAIL** and return.

Similar examples could be given of procedural attachment in the forward direction. Suppose that in a circuit analysis problem, it has been computed that a 1/2 ampere current flows through a certain 1000 ohm

266

resistor named *R3*. After the current has been computed (but not before), we may want to **ASSERT** the value of the voltage across this resistor. Such an assertion could be appropriately made by the following general F-rule:

> **FV** (*CURRENT* ? *R* ? *I*)
>   **IF (NOTNUM (VALUE** $ *R*)) **FAIL**
>   **IF (NOTNUM** $ *I*) **FAIL**
>   **SET** ? *V* **(TIMES** $ *I* **(VALUE** $ *R*))
>   **ASSERT** (*VOLTAGE* $ *R* $ *V*)
>   **RETURN**

Now when the statement (**ASSERT** *CURRENT R3* 0.5) is made, **FV** is invoked. We compute **VALUE**(*R3*) to be 1000, so we pass through the first **NOTNUM**. Similarly, since $ *I* is bound to 0.5, we pass through the second **NOTNUM** and encounter the **SET** statement. This binds ? *V* to 500, we assert *VOLTAGE* (*R3* 500) and return. In this case we have attached a multiplication procedure that implements Ohm's law to the predicate *VOLTAGE*.

6.7. BIBLIOGRAPHICAL AND HISTORICAL REMARKS

One of the reasons for the inefficiency of early resolution theorem-proving systems is that they lacked domain-specific control knowledge. The AI languages **PLANNER** [Hewitt (1972), Sussman, Winograd, and Charniak (1971)], **QA4** [Rulifson, Derksen, and Waldinger (1972)], and **CONNIVER** [McDermott and Sussman (1972)] are examples of attempts to develop deduction and problem-solving formalisms in which control information could be explicitly represented. Moore (1975a) discusses some of the logical inadequacies of these languages and proposes some remedies. Among other points, Moore notes: (a) clause form is an inefficient representation for many wffs, (b) general implicational wffs should be used as rules and these rules should be kept separate from facts, and (c) the direction of rule use (forward or backward) is often an important factor in efficiency.

Other researchers, too, moved away from resolution after its early popularity. Bledsoe (1977) presents a thorough discussion of "nonresolution" theorem proving. Examples of some nonresolution systems include those of Bledsoe and Tyson (1978), Reiter (1976), Bibel and Schreiber (1975), Nevins (1974), Wilkins (1974), and Weyhrauch (1980). Many of the techniques for enhancing efficiency used by these nonresolution systems can be used in the rule-based systems described in this chapter, where the relationship with resolution is clear.

Unifying compositions of substitutions and their properties are discussed by van Vaalen (1975) and by Sickel (1976), both of whom discuss the importance of the use of these substitutions in theorem proving with AND/OR graphs. Kowalski (1974b, 1979b) discusses the related process of finding *simultaneous unifiers*.

The forward and backward rule-based deduction systems discussed in this chapter are intended to be models of various rule-based systems used in AI. The use of AND/OR graph structures (often called AND/OR goal trees) in theorem proving has a long history; however, many systems that have used them have important logical deficiencies. Our versions of these systems have a stronger logical base than most existing systems. The RGR operation used in our backward system is based on a similar operation proposed by Moore (1975a). Loveland and Stickel (1976) and Loveland (1978) also propose systems based on AND/OR graphs and discuss relationships with resolution.

Human experts in some subject domains seem to be able to deduce useful conclusions from rules and facts about which they are less than completely certain. Extensions to rule-based deduction systems that allow use of only partially certain rules and facts were made by Shortliffe (1976) in the MYCIN system, for medical diagnosis and therapy selection. We might describe MYCIN as a backward, rule-based deduction system (without RGR) for the propositional calculus, augmented by the ability to handle partially certain rules and facts. A technique based on the use of Bayes' rule and subjective probabilities for dealing with uncertain facts and rules is described by Duda, Hart, and Nilsson (1976).

Checking the consistency of substitutions as search proceeds derives from a paper by Sickel (1976). The use of connection graphs was originally suggested by Kowalski (1975). Other authors who have used various forms of connection graphs are Cox (1977), Klahr (1978), Chang and Slagle (1979), and Chang (1979). Cox (1977) proposes an interesting technique for modifying inconsistent solutions to make them consistent.

Most of these ideas were originally proposed as control strategies for resolution refutation systems rather than for rule-based deduction systems.

The use of a metasystem, with its own rules, to control a deduction system has been suggested by several researchers, including Davis (1977), de Kleer et al. (1979), and Weyhrauch (1980). Hayes (1973b) proposes a related idea.

Using deduction systems for intelligent information retrieval is discussed in several papers in the volume by Gallaire and Minker (1978). Wong and Mylopoulos (1977) discuss the relationships between data models in database management and predicate calculus knowledge representations in AI.

Bledsoe, Bruell, and Shostak (1978) describe a theorem-proving system for inequalities. A system developed by Waldinger and Levitt (1974) is able to prove certain inequalities arising in program verification problems.

Our use of conditional substitutions is related to an idea proposed by Tyson and Bledsoe (1979). Manna and Waldinger (1979) employ the idea of conditional substitutions in their program synthesis system.

Green (1969a) described how theorem-proving systems could be used both for performing computations and for synthesizing programs. Program synthesis through deduction was also studied by Waldinger and Lee (1969) and by Manna and Waldinger (1979). [For approaches to program synthesis based on techniques other than deduction, see the survey by Hammer and Ruth (1979). For a discussion of programming "knowledge" needed by an automatic programming system, see Green and Barstow (1978).] Our use of induction to introduce recursion is based on a technique described in Manna and Waldinger (1979).

Using deduction systems to perform computations (and predicate logic as a programming language) was advocated by Kowalski (1974a). Based on these ideas, a group at the University of Marseille [see Roussel (1975), and Warren (1977)] developed the PROLOG language. Warren and Pereira (1977) describe PROLOG and compare it with LISP. Van Emden (1977) gives a clear tutorial account of these ideas. One of the appealing features of PROLOG is that it separates control information from logic information in programming. This idea, first advocated by Hayes (1973b), has also been advanced in Kowalski (1979a) and by Pratt (1977). [For a contrary view, see Hewitt (1975, pp. 195ff.)]

The combined forward/backward deduction system and the *CAN-CEL* relation for establishing termination is based on a paper by Nilsson (1979).

Our section on F-rule and B-rule programs is based on ideas in the AI languages **PLANNER** [Hewitt (1972), Sussman, Winograd, and Charniak (1971)] and **QLISP** [Sacerdoti et al. (1976)]. [See also the paper by Bobrow and Raphael (1974).]

EXERCISES

6.1 Represent the following statements as production rules for a rule-based geometry theorem-proving system:

(a) Corresponding angles of two congruent triangles are congruent.

(b) Corresponding sides of two congruent triangles are congruent.

(c) If the corresponding sides of two triangles are congruent, the triangles are congruent.

(d) The base angles of an isoceles triangle are congruent.

6.2 Consider the following piece of knowledge: Tony, Mike, and John belong to the Alpine Club. Every member of the Alpine Club who is not a skier is a mountain climber. Mountain climbers do not like rain, and anyone who does not like snow is not a skier. Mike dislikes whatever Tony likes and likes whatever Tony dislikes. Tony likes rain and snow.

Represent this knowledge as a set of predicate calculus statements appropriate for a backward rule-based deduction system. Show how such a system would answer the question. "Is there a member of the Alpine Club who is a mountain climber but not a skier?"

6.3 A blocks-world situation is described by the following set of wffs:

$ONTABLE(A)$ $CLEAR(E)$
$ONTABLE(C)$ $CLEAR(D)$
$ON(D,C)$ $HEAVY(D)$
$ON(B,A)$ $WOODEN(B)$
$HEAVY(B)$ $ON(E,B)$

Draw a sketch of the situation that these wffs are intended to describe.

The following statements provide general knowledge about this blocks world:

Every big, blue block is on a green block.
Each heavy, wooden block is big.
All blocks with clear tops are blue.
All wooden blocks are blue.

Represent these statements by a set of implications having single-literal consequents. Draw a consistent AND/OR solution tree (using B-rules) that solves the problem: "Which block is on a green block?"

6.4 Consider the following restricted version of a backward rule-based deduction system: Only leaf nodes of the AND/OR graph can be matched against rule consequents or fact literals, and the mgu of the match is then applied to all leaf nodes in the graph. Explain why the resulting system is not commutative. Show how such a system would solve the problem of reversing the list (1, 2), using the facts and rules of Section 6.4. What sort of control regime did you use?

6.5 Discuss how a backward rule-based deduction system should deal with each of the following possibilities:

(a) A subgoal literal is generated that is an instance of a higher goal (i.e., one of its ancestor goals in the AND/OR graph).

(b) A subgoal literal is generated such that a higher goal is an instance of the subgoal.

(c) A subgoal literal is generated that unifies with the negation of a higher goal.

271

(d) A subgoal literal is generated that is
identical to another subgoal literal in the
same potential solution graph.

6.6 Show how RGR can be used in a backward deduction system to obtain a proof for the goal wff:

$$[(\exists x)(\forall y)P(x,y) \Rightarrow (\forall y)(\exists x)P(x,y)]$$

6.7 Propose a heuristic search method to guide rule selection in rule-based deduction systems.

6.8 Although we have used AND/OR graphs in this chapter to represent formulas, we have not advocated the use of decomposable production systems for theorem proving. What is wrong with the idea of decomposing a conjuctive goal formula, for example, and processing each conjunct independently? Under what circumstances might decom-position be a reasonable strategy?

6.9 Describe how to use a formula like $EQUALS(f(x), g(h(x)))$ as a "replacement rule" in a rule-based deduction system. What heuristic strategies might be useful in using replacement rules?

6.10 Critically examine the following proposal:

An implication of the form $(L1 \wedge L2) \Rightarrow W$,
where $L1$ and $L2$ are literals, can be used as
an F-rule if it is first converted to the
equivalent form $L1 \Rightarrow (L2 \Rightarrow W)$. The rule
can be applied when $L1$ matches a fact literal,
and the effect of the rule is to add the new
F-rule $L2 \Rightarrow W$.

6.11 Deduction systems based on rule programs cannot (easily) perform resolutions between facts or between goals. Why not?

6.12 Consider the following electrical circuit diagram:

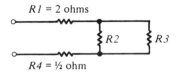

$R1 = 2$ ohms

$R4 = ½$ ohm

We represent the fact that resistors *R1* and *R4* are in series by the assertion (*SERIES R1 R4*). We represent the fact that the current through *R1* is 2 amperes by the assertion (*CURRENT R1* 2). We represent the fact that *R1* has resistance 2 ohms by the assertion (*RESISTANCE R1* 2), etc.

Write a forward rule program that expresses the fact that if a current *I* flows through a resistor *R*, then that same current flows through any resistor in series with *R*.

Write a backward rule program that expresses the fact that the voltage across a resistor is equal to the current through it multiplied by its resistance. Assuming that the forward program executes first (triggered by the assertion about the current in *R1*), trace the effect of the following **GOAL** statement:

GOAL (*VOLTAGE R4 ? V*) .

6.13 Propose facts and rules involving the predicate $MEMBER(x,y)$, which is intended to mean that atom x is a member of the list of atoms y. Use these facts and rules in a rule-based deduction system to prove the goal wff $MEMBER(3, cons(4, cons(2, cons(3, NIL))))$. What control information results in an efficient search for a proof? What fact would be needed in order to prove $\sim MEMBER(3, cons(4, NIL))$?

CHAPTER 7

BASIC PLAN-GENERATING SYSTEMS

In chapters 5 and 6 we saw that a wide class of deduction tasks could be solved by commutative production systems. For many other problems of interest in AI, however, the most natural formulations involve noncommutative systems. Typical problems of this sort are ones where goals are achieved by a sequence (or *program*) of actions. Robot problem solving and automatic programming are two domains in which these kinds of problems occur.

7.1. ROBOT PROBLEM SOLVING

Research on robot problem solving has led to many of our ideas about problem solving systems. Since robot problems are simple and intuitive, we use examples from this domain to illustrate the major ideas. In the typical formulation of a "robot problem" we have a robot that has a repertoire of primitive actions that it can perform in some easy-to-understand world. In the "blocks world," for example, we imagine a world of several labeled blocks (like children's blocks) resting on a table or on each other and a robot consisting of a moveable hand that is able to pick up and move blocks. Many other types of robot problems have also been studied. In some problems the robot is a mobile vehicle that performs tasks such as moving objects from place to place through an environment containing other objects.

Programming a robot involves integrating many functions, including perception of the world around it, formulation of plans of action, and monitoring of the execution of these plans. Here, we are concerned mainly with the problem of synthesizing a sequence of robot actions that will (if properly executed) achieve some stated goal, given some initial situation.

The action synthesis part of the robot problem can be solved by a production system. The global database is a description of the situation, or state, of the world in which the robot finds itself, and the rules are computations representing the robot's actions.

7.1.1. STATE DESCRIPTIONS AND GOAL DESCRIPTIONS

State descriptions and goals for robot problems can be constructed from predicate calculus wffs, as discussed in chapter 4. As an example, consider the robot hand and configuration of blocks shown in Figure 7.1. This situation can be represented by the conjunction of formulas shown in the figure. The formula $CLEAR(B)$ means that block B has a clear top; that is, no other block is on it. The ON predicate is used to describe which blocks are (directly) on other blocks. The "robot" in this situation is a simple hand that can move blocks about in a manner to be described momentarily. The predicate $HANDEMPTY$ has value T just when the robot hand is empty, as in the situation depicted. Of course, any finite conjunction of formulas actually describes a *family* of different world situations, where each member can be regarded as an *interpretation* satisfying the formulas (as discussed in chapter 4). For brevity, however, we usually use the phrase "*the* situation" rather than "the family of situations."

Goal descriptions also can be expressed as predicate logic formulas. For example, if we wanted the robot of Figure 7.1 to construct a stack of blocks in which block B was on block C, and block A was on block B, we might describe the goal as:

$$ON(B,C) \land ON(A,B).$$

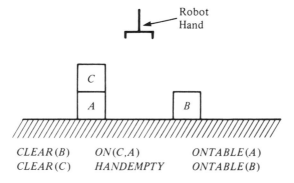

$$
\begin{array}{lll}
CLEAR(B) & ON(C,A) & ONTABLE(A) \\
CLEAR(C) & HANDEMPTY & ONTABLE(B)
\end{array}
$$

Fig. 7.1 A configuration of blocks.

Such a formula describes a family of world states, any one of which suffices as a goal.

For ease of exposition, we place certain restrictions on the kinds of formulas that we allow for descriptions of world states and goals. (Many of these restrictions could be lifted by using some of the techniques described in the last chapter for dealing with complex wffs.) For goal (and subgoal) expressions, we allow conjunctions of literals only, and any variables in goal expressions are assumed to have existential quantification. For initial and intermediate state descriptions, we allow only conjunctions of *ground* literals (i.e., literals without variables). The formulas in Figure 7.1 clearly satisfy these restrictions.

7.1.2. MODELING ROBOT ACTIONS

Robot actions change one state, or configuration, of the world into another. We can model these actions by F-rules that change one state description into another. One simple, but extremely useful technique for representing robot actions was employed by a robot problem-solving system called STRIPS. This technique can be contrasted with our use of implicational rules as production rules, discussed in chapter 6. There, when an implicational rule was applied to a global database, the database was changed, by appending additional structure, but nothing was *deleted* from the database. In modeling robot actions, however, F-rules must be able to delete expressions that might no longer be true. Suppose, for example, that the robot hand of Figure 7.1 were to pick up block B. Then certainly the expression $ONTABLE(B)$ would no longer be true and should be deleted by any F-rule modeling this pick-up action. F-rules of the STRIPS type specify the expressions to be deleted by listing them explicitly.

STRIPS-form F-rules consists of three components. The first is the *precondition formula*. This component is like the antecedent of an implicational rule. It is a predicate calculus expression that must logically follow from the facts in the state description in order for the F-rule to be applicable to that state description. Consistent with our restrictions on the form of goal wffs, we assume here that the preconditions of our F-rules consist of a conjunction of literals. Variables in these precondition formulas are assumed to have existential quantification. To decide whether or not a conjunction of literals (the precondition formula) logically follows from another conjunction of literals (the facts) is straightforward: It follows if there are literals among the facts that unify with each of the precondition literals and if all of the mgu's are consistent (that is, if these mgu's have a unifying composition). If such a match can be found, we say that the precondition of the F-rule *matches* the facts. We call the unifying composition, the *match substitution*. For a given F-rule and state description, there may be many match substitutions. Each leads to a different instance of F-rule that can be applied.

The second component of the F-rule is a list of literals (possibly containing free variables) called the *delete list*. When an F-rule is applied to a state description, the match substitution is applied to the literals in the delete list; and the ground instances thus obtained are deleted from the old state description as the first step of constructing the new one. We assume that all of the free variables in the delete list occur as (existentially quantified) variables in the precondition formula. This restriction ensures that any match instance of a delete list literal is a ground literal.

The third component is the *add formula*. It consists of a conjunction of literals (possibly containing free variables) and is like the consequent of an implicational F-rule. When an F-rule is applied to a state description, the match substitution is applied to the add formula and the resulting match instance is added to the old state description (after the literals in the delete list are deleted) as the final step in constructing the new state description. Again we assume that all of the free variables in the add formula occur in the precondition formula so that any match instance of an add formula will be a conjunction of ground literals. Again, it is possible to lift some of these restrictions on F-rule components; we use them solely because they make our presentation much simpler.

As an example of an F-rule, we model the action of picking up a block from a table. Let us say that the *preconditions* for executing this action are that the block be on the table, that the hand be empty, and that the block have nothing on top of it. The effect of the action is that the hand is holding the block. We might represent such an action as follows:

pickup(x)
    Precondition: $ONTABLE(x) \land HANDEMPTY$
                     $\land CLEAR(x)$
    Delete list: $ONTABLE(x), HANDEMPTY, CLEAR(x)$
    Add formula: $HOLDING(x)$

Since, with our restrictions, the precondition and add formulas are conjunctions of literals, we can represent each of them by a set or list of literals. Sometimes, as in the above example, the precondition formula and the delete list contain identical literals. In our example, we have chosen to include only $HOLDING(x)$ in the add formula rather than, additionally, the negations of literals in the delete list. For our purposes, it will suffice merely to delete these literals from the state description.

We see that we can apply **pickup**(x) to the situation of Figure 7.1 only if B is substituted for x. The new state description, in this case, would be given by:

$CLEAR(C)$ $ON(C,A)$
$ONTABLE(A)$ $HOLDING(B)$

Production systems using STRIPS-form F-rules are not, in general, commutative because these rules may delete certain literals from a state description. Such F-rules change one set of states to another set of states, in contrast to rules based on implications, whose application merely restricts the original set of states. Special methods must be used with STRIPS-form rules. These methods are the main focus of this chapter and chapter 8.

7.1.3. THE FRAME PROBLEM

To use a familiar analogy, the changes between one state description and another can be compared to changes between frames in an animated film. In very simple animations, certain characters move in a fixed background from frame to frame. In more realistic (and expensive) animations, many changes occur in the background also. A STRIPS F-rule (with short delete and add lists) treats most of the wffs in a state description as fixed background.

The problem of specifying which wffs in a state description should change and which should not is usually called *the frame problem* in AI. The best approach to dealing with the frame problem depends on the sort of world states and actions that we are modeling. Speaking loosely, if the components of a world state are very closely coupled or unstable, then each action might have profound and global effects on the world state. In such a world, picking up the top block from a stack of blocks, for example, might topple the whole stack of blocks, causing other stacks to topple also, in domino fashion. A simple STRIPS F-rule would not be an appropriate action model in that kind of world.

279

Typically, the components of a world state are sufficiently decoupled to permit us to assume that the effects of actions are relatively local. When such an assumption is justified, STRIPS F-rules are efficient and appropriate models of many types of actions.

Applying an F-rule to a state description can be regarded as *simulating* the action represented by the F-rule. Simulations vary with respect to the level of detail and accuracy with which they model actions. The F-rule **pickup**(x), for example, is a much more approximate representation of the pick-up action than a simulation program that took into account such factors as the weight and size of blocks, friction in robot arm joints, ambient temperature, etc. In the next chapter we argue that it is useful to have models of actions at several levels of detail. Gross and approximate models are useful for computing high-level plans; more accurate models are necessary for computing detailed plans. Typically, the frame problem is more critical for the detailed models because they must take into account couplings among world state components that might be ignored at higher levels.

Another aspect of the frame problem concerns how to deal with anomalous conditions. We can regard the F-rule **pickup**(x) as being an appropriate model for the *normal operation* of a picking-up action. But suppose the robot arm is broken, or that the block being picked up is too heavy, or that there is a power failure that prevents the motors in the arm from operating, or that the block being picked up is glued to the table, etc. Of course, we could include the negation of each of these anomalous conditions in the precondition of the F-rule to render the rule inapplicable as appropriate. But there are too many such conditions (an infinite number might be imagined), and normally the deviant conditions do not hold. Yet, if any of them do hold, the simple F-rule model is inaccurate.

Several approaches to the problem of anomalous conditions have been suggested, but none of these, so far, is compelling. If a hierarchy of action models is used, it seems that the most detailed and accurate simulations automatically take into account all of the conditions of which the system can (by definition) be aware.

Let us leave the frame problem now and make use of the representations that we have been discussing in systems for solving robot problems. We begin with a forward production system.

7.2. A FORWARD PRODUCTION SYSTEM

The simplest type of robot problem-solving system is a production system that uses the state description as the global database and the rules modeling robot actions as F-rules. In such a system, we select applicable F-rules to apply until we produce a state description that matches the goal expression. Let us examine how such a system might operate in a concrete example.

Consider the F-rules given below, in STRIPS-form, corresponding to a set of actions for the robot of Figure 7.1.

1) **pickup(x)**
    P & D: $ONTABLE(x), CLEAR(x), HANDEMPTY$
    A: $HOLDING(x)$

2) **putdown(x)**
    P & D: $HOLDING(x)$
    A: $ONTABLE(x), CLEAR(x), HANDEMPTY$

3) **stack(x,y)**
    P & D: $HOLDING(x), CLEAR(y)$
    A: $HANDEMPTY, ON(x,y), CLEAR(x)$

4) **unstack(x,y)**
    P & D: $HANDEMPTY, CLEAR(x), ON(x,y)$
    A: $HOLDING(x), CLEAR(y)$

Note that in each of these rules, the precondition formula (expressed as a list of literals) and the delete list happen to be identical. The first rule is the same as the rule that we used as an example in the last section. The others are models of actions for putting down, stacking, and unstacking blocks.

Suppose our goal is the state shown in Figure 7.2. Working forward from the initial state description shown in Figure 7.1, we see that **pickup(B)** and **unstack(C,A)** are the only applicable F-rules. Figure 7.3 shows the complete state-space for this problem, with a solution path indicated by the dark branches. The initial state description is labeled

281

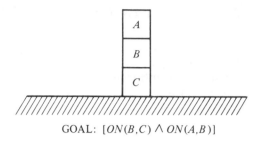

GOAL: $[ON(B,C) \wedge ON(A,B)]$

Fig. 7.2 Goal for a robot problem.

SO, and a state matching the goal is labeled *G* in Figure 7.3. (Contrary to custom and merely to reveal symmetries in the problem, *SO* is not the top node in Figure 7.3.) Note that in this example, each F-rule has an inverse.

In this very simple example (with only 22 states in the entire state-space), a forward production system, with an unsophisticated control strategy, can quickly find a path to a goal state. For more complex problems, we would expect, however, that a forward search to the goal would generate a rather large graph and that such a search would be feasible only if combined with a well-informed evaluation function.

7.3. A REPRESENTATION FOR PLANS

We can construct the desired sequence of actions for achieving the goal in our example by referring to the F-rules labeling the arcs along the branch to the goal state. The sequence is: {**unstack**(*C*,*A*), **putdown**(*C*), **pickup**(*B*), **stack**(*B*,*C*), **pickup**(*A*), **stack**(*A*,*B*)}. We call such a sequence a *plan* for achieving the goal. (In this case all of the elements of the plan refer to "primitive" actions. In chapter 8 we consider plans whose elements might themselves be intermediate level goals requiring further and more detailed problem solving before being reduced to primitive actions.)

For many purposes, it is useful to have additional information included in a specification of a plan. We might want to know, for example, what the relationships are between the F-rules and the preconditions that they provide for other F-rules. Such contextual information can be provided conveniently by a triangular table whose entries correspond to the preconditions and additions of the F-rules in the plan.

282

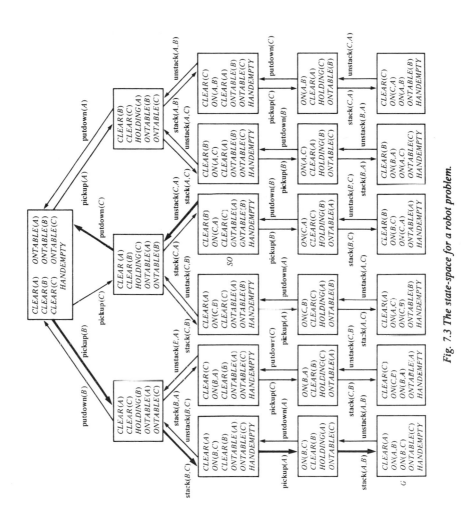

Fig. 7.3 The state-space for a robot problem.

An example of a *triangle table* is shown in Figure 7.4. It is a table whose columns are headed by the F-rules in the plan. Let the leftmost column be called the zero-th column; then the j-th column is headed by the j-th F-rule in the sequence. Let the top row be called the first row. If there are N F-rules in the plan sequence, then the last row is the $(N + 1)$-th row. The entries in cell (i,j) of the table, for $j > 0$ and $i < N + 1$, are those literals added to the state description by the j-th F-rule that survive as preconditions of the i-th F-rule. The entries in cell $(i,0)$, for $i < N + 1$, are those literals in the initial state description that survive as preconditions of the i-th F-rule. The entries in the $(N + 1)$-th row of the table are then those literals in the original state description, and those added by the various F-rules, that are components of the goal (and that survive the entire sequence of F-rules).

Triangle tables can easily be constructed from the initial state description, the F-rules in the sequence, and the goal description. These tables are concise and convenient representations for robot plans. The entries in the row to the left of the i-th F-rule are precisely the preconditions of the F-rule. The entries in the column below the i-th F-rule are precisely the add formula literals of that F-rule that are needed by subsequent F-rules or that are components of the goal.

Let us define the i-th *kernel* as the intersection of all rows below, and including, the i-th row with all columns to the left of the i-th column. The 4th kernel is outlined by double lines in Figure 7.4. The entries in the i-th kernel are then precisely the conditions that must be matched by a state description in order that the sequence composed of the i-th and subsequent F-rules be applicable and achieve the goal. Thus, the first kernel, that is, the zero-th column, contains those conditions of the initial state needed by subsequent F-rules and by the goal; the $(N + 1)$-th kernel [i.e., the $(N + 1)$-th row] contains the goal conditions themselves. These properties of triangle tables are very useful for monitoring the actual execution of robot plans.

Since robot plans must ultimately be executed in the real world by a mechanical device, the execution system must acknowledge the possibility that the actions in the plan may not accomplish their intended effects and that mechanical tolerances may introduce errors as the plan is executed. As actions are executed, unplanned effects might either place us unexpectedly close to the goal or throw us off the track. These problems could be dealt with by generating a new plan (based on an updated state description) after each execution step, but obviously, such

284

	0	1	2	3	4	5	6
1	*HANDEMPTY* *CLEAR(C)* *ON(C,A)*	1 **unstack**(*C,A*)					
2		*HOLDING(C)*	2 **putdown**(*C*)				
3	*ONTABLE(B)* *CLEAR(B)*		*HANDEMPTY*	3 **pickup**(*B*)			
4			*CLEAR(C)*	*HOLDING(B)*	4 **stack**(*B,C*)		
5	*ONTABLE(A)*	*CLEAR(A)*			*HANDEMPTY*	5 **pickup**(*A*)	
6					*CLEAR(B)*	*HOLDING(A)*	6 **stack**(*A,B*)
7					*ON(B,C)*		*ON(A,B)*

Fig. 7.4 A triangle table.

a strategy would be too costly, so we instead seek a scheme that can intelligently monitor progress as a given plan is being executed.

The kernels of triangle tables contain just the information needed to realize such a plan execution system. At the beginning of a plan execution, we know that the entire plan is applicable and appropriate for achieving the goal because the literals in the first kernel are matched by the initial state description, which was used when the plan was created. (Here we assume that the world is static; that is, no changes occur in the world except those initiated by the robot itself.) Now suppose the system has just executed the first $i - 1$ actions of a plan sequence. Then, in order for the remaining part of the plan (consisting of the i-th and subsequent actions) to be both applicable and appropriate for achieving the goal, the literals in the i-th kernel must be matched by the new current state description. (We presume that a sensory perception system continuously updates the state description as the plan is executed so that this description accurately models the current state of the world.) Actually, we can do better than merely check to see if the expected kernel matches the state description after an action; we can look for the highest numbered matching kernel. Then, if an unanticipated effect places us closer to the goal, we need only execute the appropriate remaining actions; and if an execution error destroys the results of previous actions, the appropriate actions can be re-executed.

To find the appropriate matching kernel, we check each one in turn starting with the highest numbered one (which is the last row of the table) and work backward. If the goal kernel (the last row of the table) is matched, execution halts; otherwise, supposing the highest numbered matching kernel is the i-th one, then we know that the i-th F-rule is applicable to the current state description. In this case, the system executes the action corresponding to this i-th F-rule and checks the outcome, as before, by searching again for the highest numbered matching kernel. In an ideal world, this procedure merely executes in order each action in the plan. In a real-world situation, on the other hand, the procedure has the flexibility to omit execution of unnecessary actions or to overcome certain kinds of failures by repeating the execution of appropriate actions. Replanning is initiated when there are no matching kernels.

As an example of how this process might work, let us return to our block-stacking problem and the plan represented by the triangle table in Figure 7.4. Suppose the system executes actions corresponding to the first four F-rules and that the results of these actions are as planned. Now suppose the system attempts to execute the pick-up-block-A action, but the execution routine (this time) mistakes block B for block A and picks up block B instead. [Assume again that the perception system accurately updates the state description by adding $HOLDING(B)$ and deleting $ON(B, C)$; in particular, it does not add $HOLDING(A)$.] If there were no execution error, the 6th kernel would now be matched; the result of the error is that the highest numbered matching kernel is now kernel 4. The action corresponding to **stack**(B, C) is thus re-executed, putting the system back on the track.

The fact that the kernels of triangle tables overlap can be used to advantage to scan the table efficiently for the highest numbered matching kernel. Starting in the bottom row, we scan the table from left to right, looking for the first cell that contains a literal that does not match the current state description. If we scan the whole row without finding such a cell, the goal kernel is matched; otherwise, if we find such a cell in column i, the number of the highest numbered matching kernel cannot be greater than i. In this case, we set a *boundary* at column i and move up to the next-to-bottom row and begin scanning this row from left to right, but not past column i. If we find a cell containing an unmatched literal, we reset the column boundary and move up another row to begin scanning that row, etc. With the column boundary set to k, the process terminates by finding that the k-th kernel is the highest numbered matching kernel when it completes a scan of the k-th row (from the bottom) up to the column boundary.

7.4. A BACKWARD PRODUCTION SYSTEM

7.4.1. DEVELOPMENT OF THE B-RULES

In order to construct robot plans in an efficient fashion, we often want to work backward from a goal expression to an initial state description, rather than vice versa. Such a system starts with a goal description (again a conjunction of literals) as its global database and applies B-rules to this database to produce subgoal descriptions. It successfully terminates when it produces a subgoal description that is matched by the facts in the initial state description.

Our first step in designing a backward production system is to specify a set of B-rules that transform goal expressions into subgoal expressions. One strategy is to use B-rules that are based on the F-rules that we have just discussed. A B-rule that transforms a goal G into a subgoal G' is logically based on the corresponding F-rule that when applied to a state description matching G' produces a state description matching G.

We know that the application of an F-rule to any state description produces a state description that matches the add list literals. Therefore, if a goal expression contains a literal, L, that unifies with one of the literals in the add list of an F-rule, then we know that if we produce a state description that matches appropriate instances of the preconditions of that F-rule, the F-rule can be applied to produce a state description matching L. Thus, the subgoal expression produced by a backward application of an F-rule must certainly contain instances of the preconditions of that F-rule. But if the goal expression contains other literals (besides L), then the subgoal expression must also contain other literals, which after application of the F-rule, become those other literals (i.e., other than L) in the goal expression.

7.4.2. REGRESSION

To formalize what we have just stated, suppose that we have a goal given by a conjunction of literals $[L \wedge G1 \wedge \ldots \wedge GN]$ and that we want to use some F-rule (backward) to produce a subgoal expression. Suppose an F-rule with precondition formula, P, and add formula, A, contains a literal L' in A that unifies with L, with most general unifier u. Application of u to the components of the F-rule creates an instance of the F-rule. Certainly the literals in Pu are a subset of the literals of the subgoal that we seek. We must also include the expressions $G1', \ldots, GN'$ in the complete subgoal. The expressions $G1', \ldots, GN'$ must be such that the application of the instance of the F-rule to any state description matching these expressions produces a state description matching $G1, \ldots, GN$. Each Gi' is called the *regression* of Gi through the instance of the F-rule. The process of obtaining Gi' from Gi is called *regression*.

For F-rules specified in the simple STRIPS-form, the regression procedure is quite easily described for ground instances of rules. (A *ground instance* of an F-rule is an instance in which all of the literals in the precondition formula, the delete list, and the add formula are ground literals.) Let $R[Q;Fu]$ be the regression of a literal Q through a ground instance Fu of an F-rule with precondition, P, delete list, D, and add list, A. Then,

if Qu is a literal in Au,

$R[Q;Fu] = T$ (True)

else, if Qu is a literal in Du,

$R[Q;Fu] = F$ (False)

else, $R[Q;Fu] = Qu$

In simpler terms, Q regressed through an F-rule is trivially T if Q is one of the add literals, it is trivially F if Q is one of the deleted literals; otherwise, it is Q itself.

Regressing expressions through incompletely instantiated F-rules is slightly more complicated. We describe how we deal with incompletely instantiated F-rules by some examples. Suppose the F-rule is **unstack**, given earlier and repeated here:

unstack(x,y)
    P & D: $HANDEMPTY, CLEAR(x), ON(x,y)$
    A: $HOLDING(x), CLEAR(y)$

In particular, suppose we are considering the instance **unstack**(B,y), perhaps because our goal is to produce $HOLDING(B)$. This instance is not fully instantiated. If we were to regress $HOLDING(B)$ through this F-rule instance, we would obtain T, as expected. (The literal $HOLDING(B)$ is unconditionally true in the state resulting after applying the F-rule.) If we were to regress $HANDEMPTY$ through this F-rule instance, we would obtain F. (The literal $HANDEMPTY$ can never be true *immediately* after applying **unstack**.) If we were to regress $ONTABLE(C)$, we would obtain $ONTABLE(C)$. (The literal $ONTABLE(C)$ is unaffected by the F-rule.)

Suppose we attempt to regress $CLEAR(C)$ through this incompletely instantiated instance of the F-rule. Note that if y were equal to C, $CLEAR(C)$ would regress to T; otherwise, it would simply regress to

$CLEAR(C)$. We could summarize this result by saying that $CLEAR(C)$ regresses to the disjunction $(y = C) \lor CLEAR(C)$. (In order for $CLEAR(C)$ to hold after applying any instance of **unstack**(B, y), either y must be equal to C or $CLEAR(C)$ had to have held before applying the F-rule.) Unfortunately, to accept a disjunctive subgoal expression would violate our restrictions on the allowed forms of goal expressions. Instead, when such a case arises, we produce two alternative subgoal expressions. In the present example, one subgoal expression would contain the precondition of **unstack**(B, C), and the other would contain the uninstantiated precondition of **unstack**(B, y) conjoined with the literal $\sim(y = C)$.

A related complication occurs when we regress an expression matching an incompletely instantiated literal in the delete list. Suppose, for example that we want to regress $CLEAR(C)$ through **unstack**(x, B). If x were equal to C, then $CLEAR(C)$ would regress to F; otherwise, it would regress to $CLEAR(C)$. We could summarize this result by saying that $CLEAR(C)$ regressed to

$$[(x = C) \Rightarrow F] \land [\sim(x = C) \Rightarrow CLEAR(C)] .$$

As a goal, this expression is equivalent to the conjunction $[\sim(x = C) \land CLEAR(C)]$.

The reader might ask what would happen if we were to regress $CLEAR(B)$ through **unstack**(B, y). In our example, we would obtain T for the case $y = B$. But $y = B$ corresponds to the instance **unstack**(B, B), which really ought to be impossible because its precondition involves $ON(B, B)$. Our simple example would be made more realistic by adding the precondition $\sim(x = y)$ to **unstack**(x, y).

In summary, a STRIPS-form F-rule can be used as a B-rule in the following manner. The applicability condition of the B-rule is that the goal expression contain a literal that unifies with one of the literals in the add list of the F-rule. The subgoal expression is created by regressing the other (the nonmatched) literals in the goal expression through the match instance of the F-rule and conjoining these and the match instance of the precondition formula of the F-rule.

Let's consider a few more examples to illustrate the regression process. Suppose our goal expression is $[ON(A, B) \land ON(B, C)]$. Referring to the F-rules given earlier, there are two ways in which **stack**(x, y) can be used on this expression as a B-rule. The mgu's for these two cases are $\{A/x, B/y\}$ and $\{B/x, C/y\}$. Let's consider the first of these. The subgoal description is constructed as follows:

(1) Regress the (unmatched) expression $ON(B, C)$
      through **stack**(A, B) yielding $ON(B, C)$.

(2) Add the expressions $HOLDING(A)$, $CLEAR(B)$
      to yield, finally, the subgoal
      $[ON(B, C) \wedge HOLDING(A) \wedge CLEAR(B)]$.

Another example illustrates how subgoals having existentially quantified variables are created. Suppose our goal expression is $CLEAR(A)$. Two F-rules have $CLEAR$ on their add list. Let's consider **unstack**(x, y). As a B-rule, the mgu is $\{A/y\}$, and the subgoal expression created is $[HANDEMPTY \wedge CLEAR(x) \wedge ON(x, A)]$. In this expression, the variable x is interpreted as existentially quantified. That is, if we can produce a state in which there is a block that is on A and whose top is clear, we can apply the F-rule, **unstack**, to this state to achieve a state that matches the goal expression, $CLEAR(A)$.

A final example illustrates how we might generate "impossible" subgoal descriptions. Suppose we attempt to apply the B-rule version of **unstack** to the goal expression $[CLEAR(A) \wedge HANDEMPTY]$. The mgu is $\{A/y\}$. The regression of $HANDEMPTY$ through **unstack**(x, A) is F. Since no conjunction containing F can be achieved, we see that the application of this B-rule has created an impossible subgoal. [That is, there is no state from which the application of an instance of **unstack**(x, A) produces a state matching $CLEAR(A) \wedge HANDEMPTY$.]

Impossible goal states might be detected in other ways also. In general, we could use some sort of theorem prover to attempt to deduce a contradiction. If a goal expression is contradictory, it cannot be achieved. Checking for the consistency of goals is important in order to avoid wasting effort attempting to achieve those that are impossible.

Sometimes the mgu of a match between a literal on the add list of an F-rule and a goal literal does not further instantiate the F-rule. Suppose, for example, that we want to use the STRIPS rule **unstack**(u, C) as a B-rule applied to the goal $[CLEAR(x) \wedge ONTABLE(x)]$. The mgu is $\{C/x\}$. Now, even though this substitution does not further instantiate

291

unstack(u, C), the substitution is used in the regression process. When $ONTABLE(x)$ is regressed through this instance of **unstack**(u, C), we obtain $ONTABLE(C)$.

7.4.3. AN EXAMPLE SOLUTION

Let us show how a backward production system, using the STRIPS rules given earlier, might achieve the goal:

$$[ON(A,B) \wedge ON(B,C)] .$$

In this particular example, the subgoal space generated by applying all applicable B-rules is larger than the state space that we produced using F-rules. Many of the subgoal descriptions, however, are "impossible," that is, either they contain F explicitly or rather straightforward theorem proving would reveal their impossibility. Pruning impossible subgoals greatly reduces the subgoal space.

In Figure 7.5 we show the results of applying some B-rules to our example goal. (The tail of each B-rule arc is adjacent to that goal literal used to match a literal in the add list of the rule.) Note in Figure 7.5 that when **unstack** was matched against $CLEAR(B)$, it was not fully instantiated. As we discussed earlier, if a possible instantiation allows a literal in the add list of the rule to match a literal in the goal expression, we make this instantiation explicit by creating a separate subgoal node using it.

All but one of the tip nodes in this figure can be pruned. The tip nodes marked "*" all represent impossible goals. That is, no state description can possibly match these goals. In one of them, for example, we must achieve the conjunct $[HOLDING(B) \wedge ON(A,B)]$, an obvious impossibility. We assume that our backward reasoning system has some sort of mechanism for detecting such unachievable goals.

The tip node marked "**" can be viewed as a further specification of the original goal (that is, it contains all of the literals in the original goal plus some additional ones.) Heuristically, we might prune (or at least delay expansion of) this subgoal node, because it is probably harder to achieve than the original goal. Also, this subgoal is one of those produced by matching $CLEAR(B)$ against the add list of a rule. Since $CLEAR(B)$ is already true in the initial state, there are heuristic grounds against

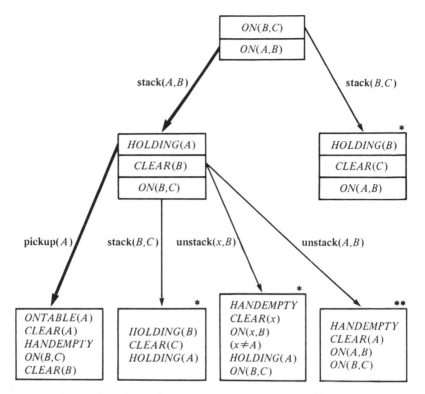

Fig. 7.5 Part of the backward (goal) search graph for a robot problem.

attempting to achieve it when it occurs in subgoal descriptions. (Sometimes, of course, goal literals that already match literals in the initial state might get deleted by early F-rules in the plan and need to be reachieved by later F-rules. Thus, this heuristic is not always reliable.)

The pruning operations leave just one subgoal node. The immediate successors of this subgoal are shown numbered in Figure 7.6. In this figure, nodes 1 and 6 contain conditions on the value of the variable x. (Conditions like these are inserted by the regression process when the delete list of the rule contains literals that might match regressed literals.) Both nodes 1 and 6 can be pruned in any case, because they contain the literal F, which makes them impossible to achieve. Note also that node 2 is impossible to achieve because of the conjunction $HOLD\text{-}ING(B) \land ON(B,C)$. Node 4 is identical to one of its ancestors (in Figure 7.5), so it can be pruned also. (If a subgoal description is merely implied by one of its ancestors instead of being identical to one of them,

293

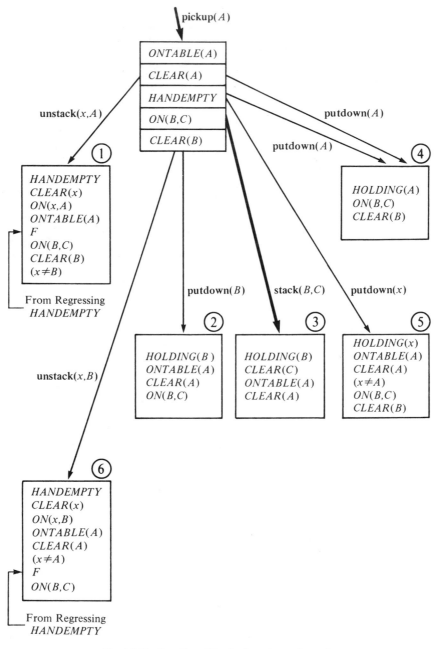

Fig. 7.6 Continuation of the backward search graph.

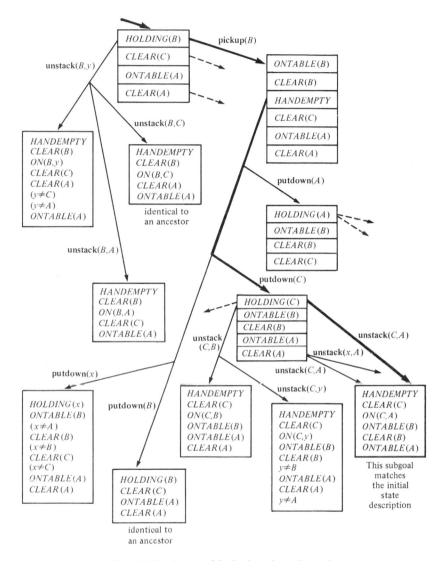

Fig. 7.7 Conclusion of the backward search graph.

we cannot, in general, prune it. Some of the successors generated by the ancestor might have been impossible because literals in the ancestor, but not in the subgoal node, might have regressed to *F*.)

These pruning operations leave us only nodes 5 and 3. Let's examine node 5 for a moment. Here we have an existential variable in the goal description. Since the only possible instances that can be substituted for *x* (namely, *B* and *C* in this case) lead to impossible goals, we are justified in pruning node 5 also.

In Figure 7.7 we show part of the goal space below node 3, the sole surviving tip node from Figure 7.6. This part of the space is a bit more branched than before, but we soon find a solution. (That is, we produce a subgoal description that matches the initial state description.) If we follow the B-rule arcs back to the top goal (along the darkened branches), we see that the following sequence of F-rules solves our problem: {**unstack**(*C*,*A*), **putdown**(*C*), **pickup**(*B*), **stack**(*B*,*C*), **pickup**(*A*), **stack**(*A*,*B*)}.

7.4.4. INTERACTING GOALS

When literals in a goal description survive into descendant descriptions, some of the same B-rules are applicable to the descendants as were applicable to the original goal. This situation can involve us in a search through all possible orderings of a sequence of rules before one that is acceptable is found. In problems for which several possible orderings of the different rules are acceptable, such a search is wastefully redundant. This efficiency problem is the same one that led us to the concept of decomposable systems.

One way to avoid the redundancy of multiple solutions to the same goal component in different subgoals is to isolate a goal component and work on it alone until it is solved. After solving one of the components, by finding an appropriate sequence of F-rules, we can return to the compound goal and select another component, and so on. This process is related to splitting or decomposing compound (i.e., conjunctive) goals into single-literal components and suggests the use of decomposable systems.

If we attempted to use a decomposable system to solve our example block-stacking problem, the compound goal would be split as shown in Figure 7.8. Suppose the initial state of the world is as shown in Figure 7.1.

If we work on the component goal $ON(B,C)$ first, we easily find the solution sequence {**pickup**(B), **stack**(B,C)}. But if we apply this sequence, the state of the world would change, so that a solution to the other component goal, $ON(A,B)$, would become more difficult. Furthermore, any solution to $ON(A,B)$ from this state must "undo" the achieved goal, $ON(B,C)$. On the other hand, if we work on the goal $ON(A,B)$ first, we find we can achieve it by the sequence {**unstack**(C,A), **putdown**(C), **stack**(A,B)}. Again, the state of the world would change to one from which the other component goal, $ON(B,C)$, would be harder to solve. There seems no way to solve this problem by selecting one component, solving it, and then solving the other component without undoing the solution to the first.

We say that the component goals of this problem *interact*. Solving one goal undoes an independently derived solution to the other. In general, when a forward production system is noncommutative, the corresponding backward system is not decomposable and cannot work on component goals independently. Interactions caused by the noncommutative effects of F-rule applications prevent us from being able to use successfully the strategy of combining independent solutions for each component.

In our example problem, the component goals are highly interactive. But in more typical problems, we might expect that component goals would occasionally interact but often would not. For such problems, it might be more efficient to assume initially that the components of compound goals can be solved separately, handling interactions, when they arise, by special mechanisms—rather than assuming that all compound goals are likely to interact. In the next section we describe a problem-solving system named **STRIPS** that is based on this general strategy.

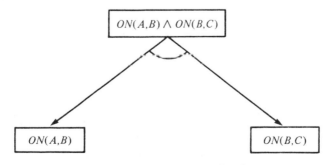

Fig. 7.8 Splitting a compound goal.

297

7.5. STRIPS

The STRIPS system was one of the early robot problem-solving systems. STRIPS maintains a "stack" of goals and focuses its problem-solving effort on the top goal of the stack. Initially, the goal stack contains just the main goal. Whenever the top goal in the goal stack matches the current state description, it is eliminated from the stack, and the match substitution is applied to the expressions beneath it in the stack. Otherwise, if the top goal in the goal stack is a compound goal, STRIPS adds each of the component goal literals, in some order, above the compound goal in the goal stack. The idea is that STRIPS works on each of these component goals in the order in which they appear on the stack. When all of the component goals are solved, it reconsiders the compound goal again, re-listing the components on the top of the stack if the compound goal does not match the current state description. This reconsideration of the compound goal is the (rather primitive) safety feature that STRIPS uses to deal with the interacting goal problem. If solving one component goal undoes an already solved component, the undone goal is reconsidered and solved again if needed.

When the top (unsolved) goal on the stack is a single-literal goal, STRIPS looks for an F-rule whose add list contains a literal that can be matched to it. The match instance of this F-rule then replaces the single-literal goal at the top of the stack. On top of the F-rule is then added the match instance of its precondition formula, P. If P is compound and does not match the current state description, its components are added above it, in some order, on the stack.

When the top item on the stack is an F-rule, it is because the precondition formula of this F-rule was matched by the current state description and removed from the stack. Thus, the F-rule is applicable, and it is applied to the current state description and removed from the top of the stack. The new state description is now used in place of the original one, and the system keeps track of the F-rule that has been applied for later use in composing a solution sequence.

We can view STRIPS as a production system in which the global database is the combination of the current state description and the goal stack. Operations on this database produce changes to either the state description or to the goal stack, and the process continues until the goal stack is empty. The "rules" of this production system are then the rules

298

that transform one global database into another. They should not be confused with the STRIPS rules that correspond to the models of robot actions. These top-level rules change the global database, consisting of both state description and goal stack. STRIPS rules are named in the goal stack and are used to change the state description.

The operation of the STRIPS system with a graph-search control regime produces a graph of global databases, and a solution corresponds to a path in this graph leading from the start to a termination node. (A termination node is one labeled by a database having an empty goal stack.)

Let us see how STRIPS might solve a rather simple block-stacking problem. Suppose the goal is [$ON(C,B)$ and $ON(A,C)$], and the initial state is as shown in Figure 7.1. We note that this goal can be simply accomplished by putting C on B and then putting A on C. We use the same STRIPS rules as before.

In Figure 7.9 we show part of a graph that might be generated by STRIPS during the solution of this example problem. (For clarity, we show a picture of the state of the blocks along with each state description.) Since this problem was very simple, STRIPS quite easily obtains the solution sequence {**unstack**(C,A), **stack**(C,B), **pickup**(A), **stack**(A,C)}.

STRIPS has somewhat more difficulty with the problem whose goal is [$ON(B,C) \land ON(A,B)$]. Starting from the same initial configuration of blocks, it is possible for STRIPS to produce a solution sequence longer than needed, namely, {**unstack**(C,A), **putdown**(C), **pickup**(A), **stack**(A,B), **unstack**(A,B), **putdown**(A), **pickup**(B), **stack**(B,C), **pickup**(A), **stack**(A,B)}. The third through sixth rules represent an unnecessary detour. This detour results in this case because STRIPS decided to achieve $ON(A,B)$ before achieving $ON(B,C)$. The interaction between these goals then forced STRIPS to undo $ON(A,B)$ before it could achieve $ON(B,C)$.

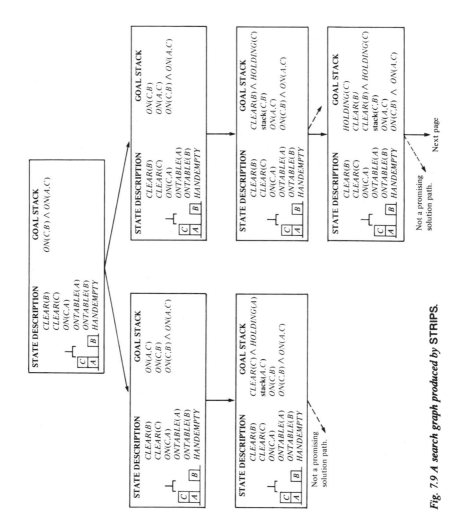

Fig. 7.9 A search graph produced by STRIPS.

From previous page

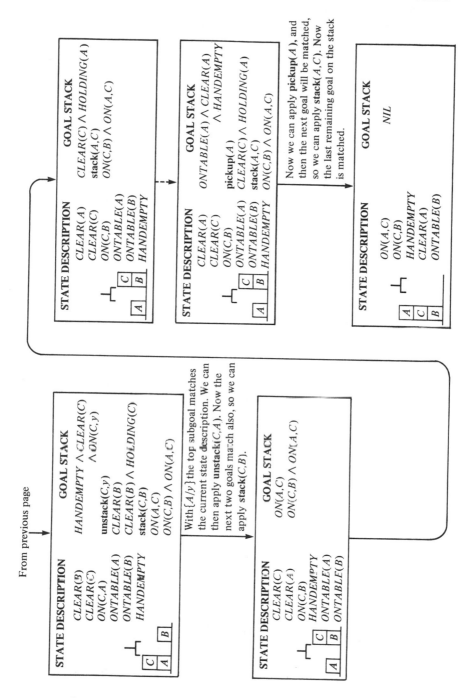

STATE DESCRIPTION

```
    C
A   B
```

CLEAR(B)
CLEAR(C)
ON(C,A)
ONTABLE(A)
ONTABLE(B)
HANDEMPTY

GOAL STACK

HANDEMPTY ∧ CLEAR(C)
            ∧ ON(C,y)
unstack(C,y)
CLEAR(B)
CLEAR(B) ∧ HOLDING(C)
stack(C,B)
ON(A,C)
ON(C,B) ∧ ON(A,C)

With {A/y} the top subgoal matches the current state description. We can then apply unstack(C,A). Now the next two goals match also, so we can apply stack(C,B).

STATE DESCRIPTION

```
    C
A   B
```

CLEAR(C)
CLEAR(A)
ON(C,B)
HANDEMPTY
ONTABLE(A)
ONTABLE(B)

GOAL STACK

ON(A,C)
ON(C,B) ∧ ON(A,C)

STATE DESCRIPTION

```
    C
A   B
```

CLEAR(A)
CLEAR(C)
ON(C,B)
ONTABLE(A)
ONTABLE(B)
HANDEMPTY

GOAL STACK

CLEAR(C) ∧ HOLDING(A)
stack(A,C)
ON(C,B) ∧ ON(A,C)

STATE DESCRIPTION

```
    C
A   B
```

CLEAR(A)
CLEAR(C)
ON(C,B)
ONTABLE(A)
ONTABLE(B)
HANDEMPTY

GOAL STACK

ONTABLE(A) ∧ CLEAR(A)
            ∧ HANDEMPTY
pickup(A)
CLEAR(C) ∧ HOLDING(A)
stack(A,C)
ON(C,B) ∧ ON(A,C)

Now we can apply pickup(A), and then the next goal will be matched, so we can apply stack(A,C). Now the last remaining goal on the stack is matched.

STATE DESCRIPTION

```
A
C
B
```

ON(A,C)
ON(C,B)
HANDEMPTY
CLEAR(A)
ONTABLE(B)

GOAL STACK

NIL

7.5.1. CONTROL STRATEGIES FOR STRIPS

Several decisions must be made by the control component of the STRIPS system. We'll mention some of these briefly. First, it must decide how to order the components of a compound goal above the compound goal in the goal stack. A reasonable approach is first to find all of those components that match the current state description. (Conceptually, they are put on the top of the stack and then immediately stripped off.) This step leaves only the unmatched goals to be ordered. We could create a new successor node for each possible ordering (as we did in our examples) or we could select just one of them arbitrarily (perhaps that goal literal heuristically judged to be the hardest) and create a successor node in which only that component goal is put on the stack. The latter approach is probably adequate because after this single goal is solved, we'll confront the compound goal again and have the opportunity to select another one of its unachieved components.

When (existentially quantified) variables occur in the goal stack, the control component may need to make a choice from among several possible instantiations. We can assume that a different successor can be created for each possible instantiation.

When more than one STRIPS F-rule would achieve the top goal on the goal stack, we are again faced with a choice. Each relevant rule can produce a different successor node.

A graph-search control strategy must be able to make a selection of which leaf node to work on in the problem-solving graph. Any of the methods of chapter 2 might be used here; in particular, we might develop a heuristic evaluation function over these nodes taking into account, for example, such factors as length of the goal stack, difficulty of the problems on the goal stack, cost of the STRIPS F-rules, etc.

An interesting special case of STRIPS can be developed if we decide to use a backtracking control regime instead of a graph-search control regime. Here we can imagine a recursive function called **STRIPS** that calls itself to solve the top goal on the stack. In this case, the explicit use of a goal stack can be supplanted by the built-in stack mechanism of the language (such as LISP) in which recursive STRIPS is implemented.

The program for recursive STRIPS would look something like the following:

First, we set S, a global variable, to the initial state description. (We call the program initially with the argument, G, the goal that STRIPS is trying to achieve.)

> *Recursive Procedure* **STRIPS(G)**
>
> 1 **until** S matches G, **do:;** the main loop of
>   STRIPS is iterative
>
> 2 **begin**
>
> 3 $g \leftarrow$ a component of G that does not match
> S; a nondeterministic selection and
>   therefore a backtracking point
>
> 4 $f \leftarrow$ an F-rule whose add list contains a
>   literal that matches g; another backtracking
>   point
>
> 5 $p \leftarrow$ precondition formula of appropriate
>   instance of f
>
> 6   **STRIPS(p);** a recursive call to solve the
>   subproblem
>
> 7 $S \leftarrow$ result of applying appropriate instance
>   of f to S
>
> 8 **end**

7.5.2. MEANS-ENDS ANALYSIS AND GPS

An early problem-solving system called GPS (standing for General Problem Solver) used methods similar to those later used by STRIPS. GPS used a technique for identifying some key F-rules, given a state description, S, and a goal, G. The identification process first attempted to calculate a *difference* between S and G. This difference-calculating process was performed by a function that needed to be written especially for cach domain of application.

303

Differences were used to select "relevant" F-rules by accessing a "difference table" in which F-rules were associated with differences. The F-rules associated with a given difference are those F-rules that are "relevant to reducing that difference." The F-rules associated with each difference were ordered according to relevance. A difference table had to be provided for each domain of application. Once an F-rule was selected as relevant to removing a difference, GPS worked recursively on the preconditions for that F-rule. When these had been satisfied, the F-rule was applied to the current state description, and the process continued.

Thus, we see that recursive GPS is very similar to (if slightly more general than) recursive STRIPS. (Historically, the design of STRIPS was motivated by GPS.) The program for recursive GPS might look something like the following:

First, we set S, a global variable, to the initial state description. (We call the program initially with the argument, G, the goal that GPS is trying to achieve.)

Recursive Procedure **GPS**(G)

1 **until** S matches G, **do:**; the main loop of **GPS**
      is iterative

2   **begin**

3     $d \leftarrow$ a difference between S and G;
        a backtracking point

4     $f \leftarrow$ an F-rule relevant to reducing d;
        another backtracking point

5     $p \leftarrow$ precondition formula of appropriate
        instance of f

6   **GPS**(p); a recursive call to solve the subproblem

7     $S \leftarrow$ result of applying appropriate instance
        of f to S

8   **end**

The process of identifying differences and selecting F-rules to reduce them is called *means-ends analysis*. Recursive STRIPS can be regarded as a special case of GPS, where differences between S and G are those components of G unmatched by S and where all F-rules whose add list contains a literal L are considered relevant to reducing the difference, L.

Although, originally, GPS worked recursively, as we have described, we could also easily imagine a GPS system having a graph-search control regime similar to that discussed for STRIPS.

7.5.3. A PROBLEM THAT STRIPS CANNOT SOLVE

STRIPS produces straightforward solutions to many problems, but, as we have seen, there are some problems for which STRIPS may produce solutions longer than necessary. Also, there are some very simple problems for which it is impossible for STRIPS (as described) to produce any solution at all. An example of a problem that STRIPS cannot solve is the problem of generating a program to switch the contents of two memory registers in a computer.

Suppose we have two memory registers X and Y whose initial contents are A and B respectively. We might represent this situation by the state description $[CONT(X,A) \wedge CONT(Y,B)]$ where $CONT(X,A)$, for example, means that register X has content A (i.e., program variable X has value A). In this example we must try not to be confused by the fact that a program "variable," like X, is really a constant symbol of our predicate calculus language that refers to a definite object (a particular memory register). Predicate calculus variables, like x and y, are used to denote arbitrary program variables (like X) and their "values" (like A). To help avoid confusion, we purposely use the terms "register" and "content" instead of "program variables" and "values."

Our goal for STRIPS is the expression $[CONT(X,B) \wedge CONT(Y,A)]$. The only operation that we allow is the assignment statement in which one register is "assigned" to another, that is, its content is replaced by the content of the other. We can represent such an assignment statement by an F-rule:

assign(u,r,t,s)
      P: $CONT(r,s) \wedge CONT(u,t)$
      D: $CONT(u,t)$
      A: $CONT(u,s)$

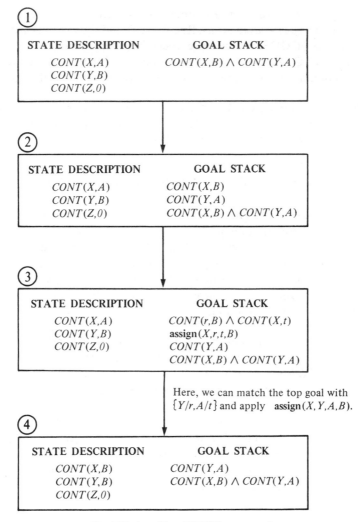

Fig. 7.10 A problem **STRIPS** *cannot solve.*

This assignment statement might be read: Assign the register *u* (with current content *t*) to the register *r* (with current content *s*). The result is that the current content of register *u* will be *s*, and the content of *r* will remain *s*. The original content of *u*, namely *t*, is lost in this process.

A production system using this F-rule is noncommutative, because a *CONT* relation is deleted by **assign**. Well-known to beginning programming students, the destructive property of the assignment statement requires that one must store the content of either X or Y in a third register before attempting an exchange. To make the problem more than fair for STRIPS, we explicitly name this needed third register at the beginning of the problem. This naming can be done by adding the fact $CONT(Z, O)$ to the initial state description. (In the next chapter we discuss a way in which additional registers could be created if the system decides it needs them.)

In Figure 7.10 we show an attempt by STRIPS at the solution to this problem. Since the initial problem is completely symmetrical, it makes no difference how we order the components of the initial compound goal in node 1. At node 2, STRIPS quite reasonably decides to apply the instance **assign**(X, r, t, B). This operation creates node 3. Now we see STRIPS' fatal flaw: It is too anxious! It immediately decides that the top goal of node 3 can be matched by the current state description with mgu $\{ Y/r, A/t \}$. This instance of **assign** unfortunately loses A, making the top goal in node 4 unsolvable. Furthermore, there is no other match for the top goal in node 3 with node 3's state description.

The only way that this problem could be solved would be to defer temporarily matching the top goal of node 3, and to create a successor node with top goal $CONT(r, B)$. Then perhaps in some ultimate descendant, Z would be substituted for r. But to add this mechanism, of deferring goal matching, would greatly complicate STRIPS. Instead we describe in the next chapter some problem-solving systems that are inherently more powerful than STRIPS.

7.6. USING DEDUCTION SYSTEMS TO GENERATE ROBOT PLANS

From the examples given in this chapter, we see that the problem of composing a sequence of actions has a straightforward formulation involving STRIPS-form rules. A forward production system using these rules is typically noncommutative because certain expressions may be deleted when a rule is applied. We stress again that there is nothing *inherently* commutative or noncommutative about robot problems themselves: Commutativity (or its lack) depends entirely on the details of the production system used to solve a problem. It is perfectly possible, for example, to formulate robot problems so that they can be solved by commutative production systems. One way to achieve such a commutative formulation is to pose robot problems as theorems to be proved and then use one of our commutative deduction systems. Formulating a robot problem as a problem of deduction is, perhaps, a bit more complex and awkward than using STRIPS-form rules, but theorem-proving formulations have considerable theoretical interest and preceded STRIPS historically. We describe two alternative approaches for posing robot problems as theorem-proving problems.

7.6.1. GREEN'S FORMULATION

One of the first attempts to solve robot problems was by Green (1969a), who formulated them in such a way that a resolution theorem-proving system (a commutative system) could solve them. This formulation involved one set of assertions that described the initial state and another set that described the effects of the various robot actions on states. To keep track of which facts were true in which state, Green included a "state" or "situation" variable in each predicate. The goal condition was then described by a formula with an existentially quantified state variable. That is, the system would attempt to prove that there existed a state in which a certain condition was true. A constructive proof method, then, could be used to produce the set of actions that would create the desired state. In Green's system, all assertions (and the negation of the goal condition) were converted to clause form for a resolution theorem prover, although other deduction systems could have been used as well.

An example problem will help to illustrate exactly how this method works. Unfortunately, the notation needed in these theorem-proving formulations is a bit cumbersome, and the block-stacking examples that we have been using need to be simplified somewhat to keep the examples manageable.

Suppose we have the initial situation depicted in Figure 7.11. There are just four discrete positions on a table, namely, D, E, F and G; and there are three blocks, namely, A, B and C, resting on three of the positions as shown. Suppose we name this initial state SO. Then we denote the fact that block A is on position D in SO by the literal $ON(A, D, SO)$. The state name is made an explicit argument of the predicate. The complete configuration of blocks in the initial state is then given by the following set of formulas:

$$ON(A, D, SO)$$
$$ON(B, E, SO)$$
$$ON(C, F, SO)$$
$$CLEAR(A, SO)$$
$$CLEAR(B, SO)$$
$$CLEAR(C, SO)$$
$$CLEAR(G, SO)$$

Now we need a way to express the effects that various robot actions might have on the states. In theorem-proving formulations, we express these effects by logical implications rather than by STRIPS-form rules. For example, suppose the robot has an action that can "transfer" a block x from position y to position z, where y and z might be either the names of other blocks that block x might be resting on or the names of positions on the table that block x might be resting on. Let us assume that both block x and position z (the target position) must be clear in order to execute this action. We model this action by the expression "$trans(x, y, z)$."

When an action is executed in one state, the result is a new state. We use the special functional expression "$do(action, state)$" to denote the function that maps a state into the one resulting from an action. Thus, if $trans(x, y, z)$ is executed in state, s, the result is a state given by $do[trans(x, y, z), s]$.

The major effect of the action modeled by *trans* can then be formulated as the following implication:

$$[CLEAR(x, s) \land CLEAR(z, s) \land ON(x, y, s) \land DIFF(x, z)]$$
$$\Rightarrow [CLEAR(x, do[trans(x, y, z), s])$$
$$\land CLEAR(y, do[trans(x, y, z), s])$$
$$\land ON(x, z, do[trans(x, y, z), s])] .$$

(All variables in assertions have implicit universal quantification.)

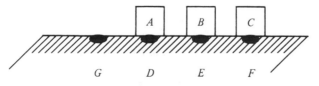

Fig. 7.11 An initial configuration of blocks.

309

This formula states that if x and z are clear and if x is on y in state s, and if x and z are different, then x and y will be clear and x will be on z in the state resulting from performing the action trans(x,y,z) in state s. (The predicate *DIFF* does not need a state variable because its truth value is independent of state.)

But this formula alone does not completely specify the effects of the action. We must also state that certain relations are *unaffected* by the action. In systems like STRIPS, the F-rules use the convention that relations not explicitly named in the rule are unaffected. But here the effects and "non-effects" alike need to be stated explicitly.

Unfortunately, in Green's formulation, we must have assertions for *each* relation not affected by an action. For example, we need the following assertion to express that the blocks that are not moved stay in the same position:

$$[ON(u,v,s) \land DIFF(u,x)]$$
$$\Rightarrow ON(u,v,do[trans(x,y,z),s]) \ .$$

And we would need another formula to state that block u remains clear if block u is clear when a block v (not equal to u) is put on a block w (not equal to u).

These assertions, describing what stays the same during an action, are sometimes called the *frame assertions*. In large systems, there may be many predicates used to describe a situation. Green's formulation would require (for each action) a separate frame assertion for each predicate. This representation could be condensed if we used a higher order logic, in which we could write a formula something like:

$$(\forall P)[P(s) \Rightarrow P[do(action,s)]].$$

But higher order logics have their own complications. (Later, we examine another first-order logic formulation that does allow us to avoid multiple frame assertions.)

After all of the assertions for actions are expressed by implications, we are ready to attempt to solve an actual robot problem.

Suppose we wanted to achieve the simple goal of having block A on block B. This goal would be expressed as follows:

$(\exists s)\, ON(A,B,s)$.

The problem can now be solved by finding a constructive proof of the goal formula from the assertions. Any reasonable theorem-proving method might be used.

As already mentioned, Green used a resolution system in which the goal was negated and all formulas were then put into clause form. The system then would attempt to find a contradiction, and an answer extraction process would find the goal state that exists. This state would, in general, be expressed as a composition of *do* functions, naming the actions involved in producing the goal state. We show a resolution refutation graph for our example problem in Figure 7.12 (the *DIFF* predicate is evaluated, instead of resolved against). Applying answer extraction to the graph of Figure 7.12 yields:

$s1 = do[trans(A,D,B), SO]$,

which names the single action needed to accomplish the goal in this case.

Instead of resolution, we could have used one of the rule-based deduction systems discussed in chapter 6. The assertions describing the initial state might be used as facts, and the action and frame assertions might be used as production rules.

The example just cited is trivially simple, of course—we didn't even need to use any of the frame assertions in this case. (We certainly would have had to use them if, for example, our goal had been the compound goal $[ON(A,B,s) \wedge ON(B,C,s)]$. In that case, we would have had to prove that B stayed on C while putting A on B.) However, in even slightly more complex examples, the amount of theorem-proving search required to solve a robot problem using this formulation can grow so explosively that the method becomes quite impractical. These search problems together with the difficulties caused by the frame assertions were the major impetus behind the development of the STRIPS problem-solving system.

7.6.2. KOWALSKI'S FORMULATION

Kowalski has suggested a different formulation. It simplifies the statement of the frame assertions. What would ordinarily be predicates in Green's formulation are made terms.

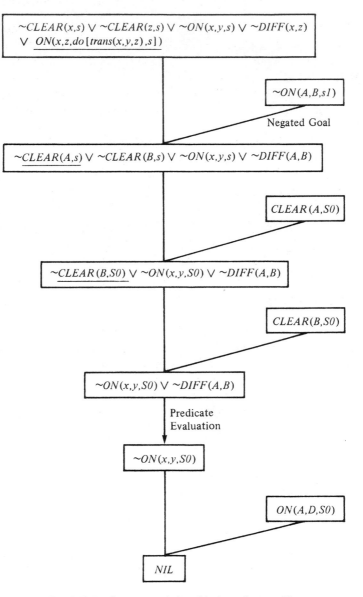

Fig. 7.12 A refutation graph for a block-stacking problem.

For example, instead of using the literal $ON(A, D, SO)$ to denote the fact that A is on D in state SO, we use the literal $HOLDS[on(A, D), SO]$. The term $on(A, D)$ denotes the "concept" of A being on D; such concepts are treated as individuals in our new calculus. Representing what would normally be relations as individuals is a way of gaining some of the benefits of a higher order logic in a first-order formulation.

The initial state shown in Figure 7.11 is then given by the following set of expressions:

1 $POSS(SO)$
2 $HOLDS[on(A, D), SO]$
3 $HOLDS[on(B, E), SO]$
4 $HOLDS[on(C, F), SO]$
5 $HOLDS[clear(A), SO]$
6 $HOLDS[clear(B), SO]$
7 $HOLDS[clear(C), SO]$
8 $HOLDS[clear(G), SO]$

The literal $POSS(SO)$ means that the state SO is a possible state, that is, one that can be reached. (The reason for having the $POSS$ predicate will become apparent later.)

Now we express part of the effects of actions (the "add-list" literals) by using a separate HOLDS literal for each relation made true by the action. In the case of our action $trans(x, y, z)$, we have the following expressions:

9   $HOLDS[clear(x), do[trans(x, y, z), s]]$
10 $HOLDS[clear(y), do[trans(x, y, z), s]]$
11 $HOLDS[on(x, z), do[trans(x, y, z), s]]$

(Again, all variables in the assertions are universally quantified.)

Another predicate, $PACT$, is used to say that it is possible to perform a given action in a given state, that is, the preconditions of the action match that state description. $PACT(a, s)$ states that it is possible to perform action a in state s. For our action $trans$, we thus have:

12 $\{HOLDS[clear(x), s] \wedge HOLDS[clear(z), s]$
    $\wedge HOLDS[on(x, y), s] \wedge DIFF(x, z)\}$
    $\Rightarrow PACT[trans(x, y, z), s]$

313

Next we state that if a given state is possible and if the preconditions of an action are satisfied in that state, then the state produced by performing that action is also possible:

$$13 \quad [POSS(s) \land PACT(u,s)] \Rightarrow POSS[do(u,s)]$$

The major advantage of Kowalski's formulation is that we need only one frame assertion for each action. In our example, the single frame assertion is:

$$14 \quad \{HOLDS(v,s) \land DIFF[v, clear(z)] \land DIFF[v, on(x,y)]\}$$
$$\Rightarrow HOLDS[v, do[trans(x,y,z),s]]$$

This expression quite simply states that all terms different than $clear(z)$ and $on(x,y)$ still $HOLD$ in all states produced by performing the action $trans(x,y,z)$.

A goal for the system is given, as usual, by an expression with an existentially quantified state variable. If we wanted to achieve B on C and A on B, our goal would be:

$$(\exists s)\{POSS(s) \land HOLDS[on(B,C),s] \land HOLDS[on(A,B),s]\}$$

The added conjunct, $POSS(s)$, is needed to require that state s be reachable.

Assertions 1-14, then, express the basic knowledge needed by a problem solver for this example. If we were to use one of the rule-based deduction systems of chapter 6 to solve problems using this knowledge, we might use assertions 1-11 as facts and use assertions 12-14 as rules. The details of operation of such a system would depend on whether the rules were used in a forward or backward manner and on the specific control strategy used by the system. For example, to make the rule-based system "simulate" the steps that would be performed by a backward production system using STRIPS-form rules, we would force the control strategy of the deduction system, first, to match one of assertions 9-11 (the "adds") against the goal. (This step would establish the action through which we were attempting to work backward.) Next, assertions 13 and 12 would be used to set up the preconditions of that action. Subsequently, the frame assertion, number 14, would be used to regress the other goal conditions through this action. All $DIFF$ predicates should be evaluated whenever possible. This whole sequence would then be repeated on one of the subgoal predicates until a set of subgoals was produced that would unify with fact assertions 1-8.

Other control strategies could, no doubt, be specified that would allow a rule-based deduction system to "simulate" the steps of STRIPS and other more complex robot problem-solving systems, to be discussed in the next chapter. One way to specify the appropriate control strategies would be to use the ordering conventions on facts and rules that are used by the PROLOG language discussed in chapter 6.

Comparing deduction systems with a STRIPS-like system, we must not be tempted to claim that one type can solve problems that the other cannot. In fact, by suitable control mechanisms, the problem-solving traces of different types of systems can be made essentially identical. The point is that to solve robot problems efficiently with deduction systems requires specialized and explicit control strategies that are implicitly "built-into" the conventions used by systems like STRIPS. STRIPS-like robot problem-solving systems would appear, therefore, to be related to the deduction-based systems in the same way that a higher level programming language is related to lower level ones.

7.7. BIBLIOGRAPHICAL AND HISTORICAL REMARKS

Modeling robot actions by STRIPS-form rules was proposed, as a partial solution to the frame problem, in a paper by Fikes and Nilsson (1971). A similar approach is followed in the PLANNER-like AI languages [Bobrow and Raphael (1974); Derksen, Rulifson, and Waldinger (1972)]. The frame problem is discussed in McCarthy and Hayes (1969), Hayes (1973a), and Raphael (1971). The problem of dealing with anomalous conditions is discussed in McCarthy and Hayes (1969) and in McCarthy (1977). McCarthy calls this problem the *qualification problem* and suggests that it may subsume the frame problem. Fahlman (1974) and Fikes (1975) avoid some frame problems by distinguishing between primary and secondary relationships. Models of actions are defined in terms of their effects on primary relationships; secondary relationships are deduced (as needed) from the primary ones. Waldinger (1977, part 2) contains a clear discussion of frame problems not overcome by **STRIPS**-form rules. Hendrix (1973) proposes a technique for modeling continuous actions.

The robot actions used in the examples of this chapter are based on those of Dawson and Siklóssy (1977). The use of triangle tables to represent the structure of plans was proposed in a paper by Fikes, Hart, and Nilsson (1972b). Execution strategies using triangle tables were also discussed in that paper.

The use of regression for computing the effects of B-rules is based on a similar use by Waldinger (1977). The **STRIPS** problem-solving system is described in Fikes and Nilsson (1971). The version of **STRIPS** discussed in this chapter is somewhat simpler than the original system. Fikes, Hart, and Nilsson (1972b) describe how solutions to specific robot problems can be generalized and used as components of plans for solving more difficult problems. Triangle tables play a key role in this process.

The **GPS** system was developed by Newell, Shaw, and Simon (1960) [see also Newell and Simon (1963)]. Ernst and Newell (1969) describe how later versions of **GPS** solve a variety of problems. Ernst (1969) presents a formal analysis of the properties of **GPS**.

For an interesting example of applying "robot" problem-solving ideas to a domain other than robotics, see Cohen (1978), who describes a system for planning *speech acts*.

The use of formal methods for solving robot problems was proposed in the "advice taker" memoranda of McCarthy (1958, 1963). Work toward implementing such a system was undertaken by Black (1964). Green (1969a) was the first to develop a full-scale formal system. McCarthy and Hayes (1969) contains proposals for formal problem-solving methods. Kowalski (1974b, 1979b) presents an alternative formulation that escapes some of the frame problems of first-order systems. Simon (1972a) discusses the general problem of reasoning about actions.

EXERCISES

7.1 In LISP, **rplaca**(x,y) alters the list structure x by replacing the *car* part of x by y. Similarly, **rplacd**(x,y) relaces the *cdr* part of x by y. Represent the effects on list structure of these two operations by STRIPS rules.

7.2 Let *right* (x) denote the cell to the right of cell x (when there is such a cell) in the 8-puzzle. Define similarly *left*(x), *up*(x), and *down*(x). Write STRIPS rules to model the actions move B (blank) up, move B down, move B left, move B right.

7.3 Write simple English sentences that express the intended meanings of each of the literals in Figure 7.1. Devise a set of context-free rewrite rules to describe the syntax of these sentences.

7.4 Describe how the two STRIPS rules **pickup**(x) and **stack**(x,y) could be combined into a macro-rule **put**(x,y). What are the preconditions, delete list and add list of the new rule. Can you specify a general procedure for creating macro-rules from components?

7.5 Referring to the blocks-world situation of Figure 7.1, let us define the predicate $ABOVE$ in terms of ON as follows:

$$ON(x,y) \Rightarrow ABOVE(x,y)$$
$$ABOVE(x,y) \wedge ABOVE(y,z) \Rightarrow ABOVE(x,z).$$

The frame problems caused by the explicit occurrence of such derived predicates in state descriptions make it difficult to specify STRIPS F-rules. Discuss the problem and suggest some remedies.

7.6 Consider the following pictures:

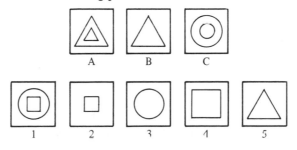

317

Describe each by predicate calculus wffs and devise a **STRIPS** rule that is applicable to both the descriptions of A and C; and when applied to a description of A, produces a description of B; and when applied to a description of C, produces a description of just *one* of pictures 1 through 5. Discuss the problem of building a system that could produce such descriptions and rules automatically.

7.7 Two flasks, $F1$ and $F2$, have volume capacities of $C1$ and $C2$, respectively. The wff $CONT(x,y)$ denotes that flask x contains y volume units of a liquid. Write **STRIPS** rules to model the following actions:

    (a)   Pour the entire contents of $F1$ into $F2$.
    (b)   Fill $F2$ with (part of) the contents of $F1$.

Can you see any difficulties that might arise in attempting to use these rules in a backward direction? Discuss.

7.8 The "monkey-and bananas" problem is often used to illustrate AI ideas about plan generation. The problem can be stated as follows:

> A monkey is in a room containing a box and
> a bunch of bananas. The bananas are hanging
> from the ceiling out of reach of the monkey.
> How can the monkey obtain the bananas?

Show how this problem can be represented so that **STRIPS** would generate a plan consisting of the following actions: go to the box, push the box under the bananas, climb the box, grab the bananas.

7.9 Referring to the block-stacking problem solved by **STRIPS** in Figure 7.9, suggest an evaluation function that could be used to guide search.

7.10 Write a **STRIPS** rule that models the action of interchanging the contents of two registers. (Assume that this action can be performed directly without explicit use of a third register.) Show how **STRIPS** would produce a program (using this action) for changing the contents of registers X, Y, and Z from A, B, and C, respectively, to C, B, and A, respectively.

7.11 Suppose the initial state description of Figure 7.1 contained the expression $HANDEMPTY \lor HOLDING(D)$ instead of $HAND$-

EMPTY. Discuss how STRIPS might be modified to generate a plan containing a "runtime conditional" that branches on *HANDEMPTY*. (Conditional plans are useful when the truth values of conditions not known at planning time can be evaluated at execution time.)

7.12 Discuss how rule programs (similar to those described at the end of chapter 6) can be used to solve block-stacking problems. (A **DELETE** statement will be needed.) Illustrate with an example.

7.13 Find a proof for the goal wff:

$$(\exists s)\{ POSS(s) \wedge HOLDS[on(B,C),s] \wedge HOLDS[on(A,B),s]\}$$

given the assertions 1-14 of Kowalski's formulation described in Section 7.6.2. Use any of the deduction systems described in chapters 5 and 6.

7.14 A robot pet, Rover, is currently outside and wants to get inside. Rover cannot open the door to let itself in; but Rover can bark, and barking usually causes the door to open. Another robot, Max, is inside. Max can open doors and likes peace and quiet. Max can usually still Rover's barking by opening the door. Suppose Max and Rover each have STRIPS plan-generating systems and triangle-table based plan-execution systems. Specify STRIPS rules and actions for Rover and Max and describe the sequence of planning and execution steps that bring about equilibrium.

CHAPTER 8

ADVANCED PLAN-GENERATING SYSTEMS

In this chapter we continue our discussion of systems for generating robot plans. First, we discuss two systems that can deal with interacting goals in a more sophisticated manner than STRIPS. Then, we discuss various hierarchical methods for plan generation.

8.1. RSTRIPS

RSTRIPS is a modification of STRIPS that uses a goal regression mechanism for circumventing goal interaction problems. A typical use of this mechanism prevents RSTRIPS from applying an F-rule, *F1*, that would interfere with an achieved precondition, *P*, needed by another F-rule, *F2*, occurring later in the plan. Because *F2* occurs later than *F1*, it must be that *F2* has some additional unachieved precondition, *P'*, that led to the need to apply *F1* first. Instead of applying *F1*, RSTRIPS rearranges the plan by regressing *P'* through the F-rule that achieves *P*. Now, the achievement of the regressed *P'* will no longer interfere with *P*.

Some of the techniques and conventions used by RSTRIPS can best be introduced while discussing an example problem in which the goals do not happen to interact. After these have been explained, we shall describe in detail how RSTRIPS handles interacting goals.

EXAMPLE 1. Let us use one of the simpler blocks-world examples from the last chapter. Suppose the goal is [$ON(C, B) \land ON(A, C)$] and that the initial state is as shown in Figure 7.1. Until the first F-rule is applied, RSTRIPS operates in the same manner as STRIPS. It does use some special conventions in the goal stack, however. Specifically, when it orders the components above a compound goal in the stack, it groups these components along with their compound goal within a *vertical parenthesis* in the stack. We shall see the use of this grouping shortly.

The goal stack portion of the global database produced by RSTRIPS at the time that the first F-rule, namely, **unstack(** C, A **)**, can be applied is as follows:

$$
\begin{aligned}
&[HANDEMPTY \wedge CLEAR(C) \wedge ON(C,y) \\
&\text{ } \text{unstack}(C,y) \\
&[HOLDING(C) \\
&\text{ } CLEAR(B) \\
&\text{ } HOLDING(C) \wedge CLEAR(B) \\
&\text{ } \text{stack}(C,B) \\
&[ON(C,B) \\
&\text{ } ON(A,C) \\
&\text{ } ON(C,B) \wedge ON(A,C)
\end{aligned}
$$

This goal stack is the same as the one produced by STRIPS at this stage of the problem's solution. (See Figure 7.9 of chapter 7.) For added clarity in the examples of this section, we retain the condition achieved by applying an F-rule just under the F-rule that achieved it in the goal stack. Note the vertical parentheses grouping goal components with compound goals.

With the substitution $\{A/y\}$, RSTRIPS can apply **unstack(** C, A **)** because its precondition (at the top of the stack) is matched by the initial state description. Rather than removing the satisfied precondition and the F-rule from the goal stack (as STRIPS did), RSTRIPS leaves these items on the stack and places a marker just below $HOLDING(C)$ to indicate that $HOLDING(C)$ has just been achieved by the application of the F-rule. As the system tests conditions on the stack, it adjusts the position of the marker so that the marker is just above the next condition in the stack that still needs to be satisfied. After applying **unstack(** C, A **)** the goal stack is as follows:

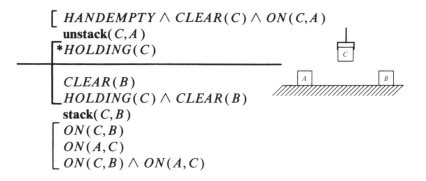

$$\left[\begin{array}{l} HANDEMPTY \wedge CLEAR(C) \wedge ON(C,A) \\ \textbf{unstack}(C,A) \\ *HOLDING(C) \end{array}\right.$$

$$\left[\begin{array}{l} CLEAR(B) \\ HOLDING(C) \wedge CLEAR(B) \end{array}\right.$$

stack(C, B)

$$\left[\begin{array}{l} ON(C,B) \\ ON(A,C) \\ ON(C,B) \wedge ON(A,C) \end{array}\right.$$

The horizontal line running through the stack is the marker. All of the F-rules above the marker have been applied, and the condition just under the marker, namely, $CLEAR(B)$, must now be tested. (For clarity, we include next to our goal stacks a picture of the state produced by applying the F-rules above the marker.)

When the marker passes through a vertical parenthesis (as it does in the goal stack shown above), there are goals above the marker that have already been achieved that are components of a compound goal below the marker at the end of the parenthesis. RSTRIPS notes these components and "protects" them. Such protection means that RSTRIPS will ensure that no F-rule can be applied within this vertical parenthesis that deletes or falsifies the protected goal components. Protected goals are indicated by asterisks (*) in our goal stacks.

In the last chapter, whenever STRIPS satisfied the preconditions of an F-rule in the goal stack, it applied that F-rule to the then current state description to produce a new state description. RSTRIPS does not need to perform this process explicitly. Rather, that part of the goal stack above the marker indicates the sequence of F-rules applied so far. From this sequence of F-rules, RSTRIPS can always compute what the state description would be if this sequence were applied to the initial state. Actually, RSTRIPS never needs to compute such a state description. At most it needs to be able to compute whether or not certain subgoals match the then current state description. This computation can be made by regressing the subgoal to be tested backward through the sequence of F-rules applied so far. For example, in the goal stack above, RSTRIPS must next decide whether or not $CLEAR(B)$ matches the state description achieved after applying **unstack**(C,A). Regressing $CLEAR(B)$ through this F-rule produces $CLEAR(B)$, which matches the initial state description, so, therefore, it must also match the subsequent description. (If $CLEAR(B)$ did not match, RSTRIPS would next have had to insert into the goal stack the F-rules for achieving it.)

At this stage, RSTRIPS notes that both of the preconditions for **stack**(C,B) are satisfied, so this F-rule is applied (by moving the marker), and $ON(C,B)$ is protected. [Since the parenthesis of the compound goal $HOLDING(C) \wedge CLEAR(B)$ is now entirely above the marker, the system removes its protection of $HOLDING(C)$.] Next, RSTRIPS attempts to achieve $ON(A,C)$. Finally, it produces the goal stack shown below:

$$\begin{array}{l} [\ HANDEMPTY \wedge CLEAR(C) \wedge ON(C,A) \\ \quad \textbf{unstack}(C,A) \\ [\ HOLDING(C) \\ \quad CLEAR(B) \\ \quad HOLDING(C) \wedge CLEAR(B) \\ \quad \textbf{stack}(C,B) \\ [\ *ON(C,B) \end{array}$$

$$\begin{array}{l} [\ HANDEMPTY \wedge CLEAR(A) \wedge ONTABLE(A) \\ \quad \textbf{pickup}(A) \\ [\ HOLDING(A) \\ \quad CLEAR(C) \\ \quad HOLDING(A) \wedge CLEAR(C) \\ \quad \textbf{stack}(A,C) \\ \quad ON(A,C) \\ \quad ON(C,B) \wedge ON(A,C) \end{array}$$

The preconditions of **pickup**(A) match the *current* state description, as can be verified by regressing them through the sequence of F-rules applied so far, namely, {**unstack**(C,A), **stack**(C,B)}. (The condition $CLEAR(A)$ did not match the initial state, but it becomes true in the current one by virtue of applying **unstack**(C,A). The condition $HAND$-$EMPTY$ matched the initial state, was deleted after applying **unstack**(C,A), and becomes true again after applying **stack**(C,B). The regression process reveals that these conditions are true currently.)

Before the F-rule, **pickup**(A), can be applied, RSTRIPS must make sure that it does not violate any protected subgoals. At this stage $ON(C,B)$ is protected. A violation check is made by regressing $ON(C,B)$ through **pickup**(A). A violation of the protected status of $ON(C,B)$ would occur only if it regressed through to F [that is, only if $ON(C,B)$ were *deleted* by application of the F-rule, **pickup**(A)]. Since no protections are violated, the F-rule, **pickup**(A), can be applied. The marker is moved to just below $HOLDING(A)$, and $HOLDING(A)$ is protected. [$ON(C,B)$ retains its protected status.]

Regression through the sequence of F-rules of the other precondition of **stack**(A,C), namely, $CLEAR(C)$, reveals that it matches the now current state description. Thus, the compound precondition of **stack**(A,C) is satisfied. Regression of the previously solved main goal component, $ON(C,B)$, through **stack**(A,C) reveals that its protected status would not be violated, so RSTRIPS applies **stack**(A,C) and moves the marker below the last condition in the stack. RSTRIPS can now terminate because all items in the stack are above the marker. The F-rules in the goal stack at this time yield the solution sequence {**unstack**(C,A), **stack**(C,B), **pickup**(A), **stack**(A,C)}.

This example was straightforward because there were no protection violations. When goals interact, however, we will have protection violations; next we describe how RSTRIPS deals with these.

EXAMPLE 2. Suppose the same initial configuration as before, namely, that of Figure 7.1. Here, however, we attempt to solve the more complicated goal [$ON(A,B) \wedge ON(B,C)$]. All goes well until the point at which RSTRIPS has produced the goal stack on the following page.

325

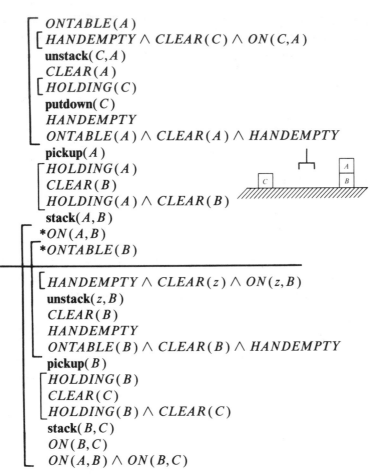

$$\begin{array}{l}
ONTABLE(A) \\
\left[HANDEMPTY \wedge CLEAR(C) \wedge ON(C,A) \right. \\
\textbf{unstack}(C,A) \\
CLEAR(A) \\
\left[HOLDING(C) \right. \\
\textbf{putdown}(C) \\
HANDEMPTY \\
ONTABLE(A) \wedge CLEAR(A) \wedge HANDEMPTY \\
\textbf{pickup}(A) \\
\left[HOLDING(A) \right. \\
CLEAR(B) \\
HOLDING(A) \wedge CLEAR(B) \\
\textbf{stack}(A,B) \\
*ON(A,B) \\
\left[*ONTABLE(B) \right.
\end{array}$$

$$\begin{array}{l}
\left[HANDEMPTY \wedge CLEAR(z) \wedge ON(z,B) \right. \\
\textbf{unstack}(z,B) \\
CLEAR(B) \\
HANDEMPTY \\
ONTABLE(B) \wedge CLEAR(B) \wedge HANDEMPTY \\
\textbf{pickup}(B) \\
\left[HOLDING(B) \right. \\
CLEAR(C) \\
HOLDING(B) \wedge CLEAR(C) \\
\textbf{stack}(B,C) \\
ON(B,C) \\
ON(A,B) \wedge ON(B,C)
\end{array}$$

The F-rule sequence that has been applied to the initial state description can be seen from the goal stack above the marker: {**unstack**(C,A), **putdown**(C), **pickup**(A), **stack**(A,B)}. The subgoals $ON(A,B)$ and $ONTABLE(B)$ are currently solved by this sequence and are protected. We note that the preconditions of F-rule **unstack**(A,B) are currently satisfied, but its application would violate the protection of the goal $ON(A,B)$. What should be done?

RSTRIPS first checks to see whether or not $ON(A,B)$ might be reachieved by the sequence of F-rules below the marker and above the end of its parenthesis. It is only at the end of its parenthesis that $ON(A,B)$ needs to be true. Perhaps one of the F-rules within its parenthesis might happen to reachieve it; if so, such "temporary" violations can be tolerated. In this case none of these F-rules reachieves $ON(A,B)$, so RSTRIPS must take steps to avoid the protection violation.

RSTRIPS notes that the compound goal at the end of the parenthesis of the violated goal is $ON(A,B) \land ON(B,C)$. An F-rule needed to solve one of these components, namely, $ON(B,C)$, would violate the other's protection. We call $ON(B,C)$ the *protection violating* component. RSTRIPS attempts to avoid the violation by regressing the protection violating component, $ON(B,C)$, back through the sequence of F-rules (above the marker) that have already been applied until it has regressed it through the F-rule that achieved the protected subgoal. Since the last F-rule to be applied, **stack**(A,B), was also the rule that achieved $ON(A,B)$, RSTRIPS regresses $ON(B,C)$ through **stack**(A,B) to yield $ON(B,C)$. In this case, the subgoal was not changed by regression, and RSTRIPS now attempts to achieve this regressed goal at the point in the plan just prior to the application of **stack**(A,B). This regression process leaves RSTRIPS with the following goal stack:

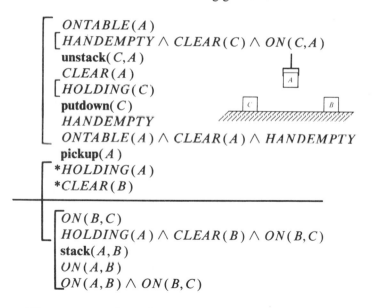

$$\begin{bmatrix} ONTABLE(A) \\ \begin{bmatrix} HANDEMPTY \land CLEAR(C) \land ON(C,A) \\ \textbf{unstack}(C,A) \\ CLEAR(A) \\ \begin{bmatrix} HOLDING(C) \\ \textbf{putdown}(C) \\ HANDEMPTY \\ ONTABLE(A) \land CLEAR(A) \land HANDEMPTY \\ \textbf{pickup}(A) \\ \begin{bmatrix} *HOLDING(A) \\ *CLEAR(B) \end{bmatrix} \end{bmatrix} \end{bmatrix} \end{bmatrix}$$

$$\begin{bmatrix} ON(B,C) \\ HOLDING(A) \land CLEAR(B) \land ON(B,C) \\ \textbf{stack}(A,B) \\ ON(A,B) \\ ON(A,B) \land ON(B,C) \end{bmatrix}$$

The compound goal $ON(A,B) \land ON(B,C)$ at the end of the parenthesis in which the potential violation was detected, is retained in the stack. The other items below $ON(A,B)$ in the stack of page 326 were part of the now discredited plan to achieve $ON(B,C)$. These items are eliminated from the stack. The plan to achieve $ON(A,B)$ by applying

stack(A,B) is still valid and is left in the stack. Note that we have combined the regressed goal $ON(B,C)$ with the compound precondition just above the F-rule, **stack**(A,B). Since the marker crosses a parenthesis, the subgoals $HOLDING(A)$ and $CLEAR(B)$ are protected.

RSTRIPS begins again with this goal stack and does not discover any additional potential protection violations until the following goal stack is produced:

$$
\begin{array}{l}
ONTABLE(A) \\
[HANDEMPTY \wedge CLEAR(C) \wedge ON(C,A) \\
\textbf{unstack}(C,A) \\
CLEAR(A) \\
[HOLDING(C) \\
\textbf{putdown}(C) \\
HANDEMPTY \\
ONTABLE(A) \wedge CLEAR(A) \wedge HANDEMPTY \\
\textbf{pickup}(A) \\
*HOLDING(A) \\
*CLEAR(B) \\
*ONTABLE(B) \\
*CLEAR(B) \\
\hline
[HOLDING(\text{x}) \\
\textbf{putdown}(\text{x}) \\
HANDEMPTY \\
ONTABLE(B) \wedge CLEAR(B) \wedge HANDEMPTY \\
\textbf{pickup}(B) \\
HOLDING(B) \\
CLEAR(C) \\
HOLDING(B) \wedge CLEAR(C) \\
\textbf{stack}(B,C) \\
ON(B,C) \\
HOLDING(A) \wedge CLEAR(B) \wedge ON(B,C) \\
\textbf{stack}(A,B) \\
ON(A,B) \\
ON(A,B) \wedge ON(B,C)
\end{array}
$$

RSTRIPS notes, by regression, that the precondition of **putdown**(A) matches the current state description but that the application of **putdown**(A) would violate the protection of $HOLDING(A)$. The violation is not temporary. To avoid this violation, RSTRIPS regresses the protection violating component, $ON(B,C)$, further backward, this time through the F-rule **pickup**(A).

After regression, the goal stack is as follows:

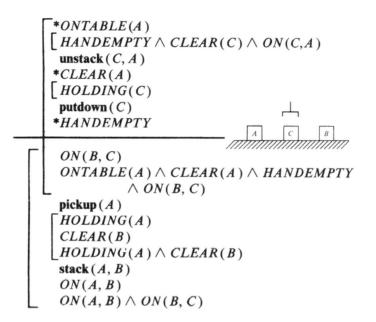

```
┌ *ONTABLE(A)
│ [ HANDEMPTY ∧ CLEAR(C) ∧ ON(C,A)
│   unstack(C, A)
│   *CLEAR(A)
│ [ HOLDING(C)
│   putdown(C)
│   *HANDEMPTY
─────────────────────────────────
┌   ON(B, C)
│   ONTABLE(A) ∧ CLEAR(A) ∧ HANDEMPTY
│              ∧ ON(B, C)
│   pickup(A)
│ [ HOLDING(A)
│ │ CLEAR(B)
│ [ HOLDING(A) ∧ CLEAR(B)
│   stack(A, B)
│   ON(A, B)
└   ON(A, B) ∧ ON(B, C)
```

The plan for achieving $ON(A, B)$ is retained, but the protection violating plan for achieving $ON(B, C)$ is eliminated.

Beginning again with the resulting goal stack, RSTRIPS finds another potential protection violation when the following goal stack is produced:

$\begin{bmatrix} *ONTABLE(A) \\ [HANDEMPTY \wedge CLEAR(C) \wedge ON(C,A) \\ \quad \textbf{unstack}(C,A) \\ *CLEAR(A) \\ [HOLDING(C) \\ \quad \textbf{putdown}(C) \\ *HANDEMPTY \end{bmatrix}$

$\begin{bmatrix} [ONTABLE(B) \wedge CLEAR(B) \wedge HANDEMPTY \\ \quad \textbf{pickup}(B) \\ [HOLDING(B) \\ CLEAR(C) \\ HOLDING(B) \wedge CLEAR(C) \\ \quad \textbf{stack}(B,C) \\ ON(B,C) \\ ONTABLE(A) \wedge CLEAR(A) \wedge HANDEMPTY \\ \qquad \wedge ON(B,C) \\ \quad \textbf{pickup}(A) \\ [HOLDING(A) \\ CLEAR(B) \\ HOLDING(A) \wedge CLEAR(B) \\ \quad \textbf{stack}(A,B) \\ ON(A,B) \\ ON(A,B) \wedge ON(B,C) \end{bmatrix}$

If **pickup**(B) were to be applied, the protection of *HANDEMPTY* would be violated. But this time the violation is only temporary. A subsequent F-rule, namely, **stack**(B,C) (within the relevant stack parenthesis) reachieves *HANDEMPTY*, so we can tolerate the violation and proceed directly to a solution.

In this case, RSTRIPS finds a shorter solution sequence than STRIPS could have found on this problem. The F-rules in the solution found by RSTRIPS are those above the marker in its terminal goal stack, namely, {**unstack**(C,A), **putdown**(C), **pickup**(B), **stack**(B,C), **pickup**(A), **stack**(A,B)}.

330

EXAMPLE 3. As another example, let us apply RSTRIPS to the problem of interchanging the contents of two registers. The F-rule is:

assign(u,r,t,s)
    P: $CONT(r,s) \wedge CONT(u,t)$
    D: $CONT(u,t)$
    A: $CONT(u,s)$

Our goal is to achieve $[CONT(X,B) \wedge CONT(Y,A)]$ from the initial state $[CONT(X,A) \wedge CONT(Y,B) \wedge CONT(Z,O)]$.

A difficulty is encountered at the point at which RSTRIPS has produced the following goal stack:

$$
\begin{array}{l}
\left[CONT(Y,B) \wedge CONT(X,A) \right. \\
\quad \textbf{assign}(X,Y,A,B) \\
\left[{}^*CONT(X,B) \right. \\
\hline
\left[CONT(r1,A) \right. \\
\quad CONT(Y,t1) \\
\left. CONT(r1,A) \wedge CONT(Y,t1) \right. \\
\quad \textbf{assign}(Y,r1,t1,A) \\
\quad CONT(Y,A) \\
\left. CONT(X,B) \wedge CONT(Y,A) \right.
\end{array}
\qquad Z{:}0 \quad X{:}B \quad Y{:}B
$$

(We indicate the effect of applying **assign**(X,Y,A,B) by the notation next to the goal stack.) The condition $CONT(r1,A)$ cannot be satisfied because after applying **assign**(X,Y,A,B) there is no register having A as its contents. Here RSTRIPS has confronted an impossible goal rather than a potential protection violation. Goal regression is a useful tactic in this situation as well. The impossible goal is regressed through the last F-rule; perhaps there its achievement will be possible.

Regressing $CONT(r1,A)$ through **assign**(X,Y,A,B) yields the expression:

$$[CONT(r1,A) \wedge \sim EQUAL(r1,X)].$$

331

The resulting goal stack is:

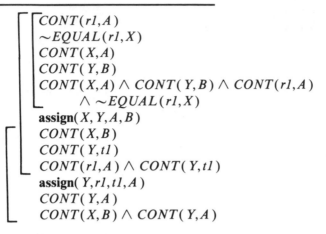

Next, RSTRIPS attempts to solve $CONT(r1,A)$. It cannot simply match this subgoal against the fact $CONT(X,A)$ because the substitution $\{X/r1\}$ would make the next goal, $\sim EQUAL(X,X)$, impossible. The only alternative is to apply the F-rule **assign** again. This operation produces the following goal stack:

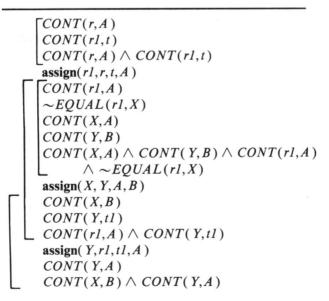

Now RSTRIPS can match $CONT(r,A)$ against the fact $CONT(X,A)$. Next, it can match $CONT(r1,t)$ against the fact $CONT(Z,0)$. These matches allow application of **assign**$(Z,X,0,A)$. The next subgoal in the stack, namely, $\sim EQUAL(Z,A)$ is evaluated to T; and all of the other subgoals above **assign**(X,Y,A,B) match facts. Next, RSTRIPS matches $CONT(Y,t1)$ against $CONT(Y,B)$ and applies **assign**(Y,Z,B,A). The marker is then moved to the bottom of the stack, and the process terminates with the sequence $\{$**assign**$(Z,X,0,A)$, **assign**(X,Y,A,B), **assign**$(Y,Z,B,A)\}$.

The reader might object that we begged the question in this example by explicitly providing a third register. It is perfectly straightforward to provide another F-rule, perhaps called **genreg**, that can generate new registers when needed. Then, instead of matching $CONT(r1,t)$ against $CONT(Z,0)$ as we have done in this example, RSTRIPS could apply **genreg** to $CONT(r1,t)$ to produce a new register. The effect of applying **genreg** would be to substitute the name of the new register for $r1$, and 0 (say) for t.

8.2. DCOMP

We call our next system for dealing with interacting goals DCOMP. It operates in two main phases. In phase 1, DCOMP produces a tentative "solution," assuming that there are *no* goal interactions. Goal expressions are represented as AND/OR graphs, and B-rules are applied to literal nodes that do not match the *initial* state description. This phase terminates when a consistent solution graph is produced with leaf nodes that match the initial state description. This solution graph serves as a tentative solution to the problem; typically, it must be processed by a second phase to remove interactions.

A solution graph of an AND/OR graph imposes only a *partial ordering* on the solution steps. If there were no interactions, then rules in the solution graph that are not ancestrally related could be applied in parallel, rather than in some sequential order. Sometimes the robot hardware permits certain actions to be executed simultaneously. For example, a robot may be able to move its arm while it is locomoting. To the extent that parallel actions are possible, it is desirable to express robot action sequences as partial orderings of actions. From the standpoint of achieving some particular goal, the least commitment possible about the order of actions is best. A solution graph of an AND/OR graph thus appears to be a good format with which to represent the actions for achieving a goal.

In phase 2, DCOMP examines the tentative solution graph for goal interactions. Certain rules, for example, destroy the preconditions needed by rules in other branches of the graph. These interactions force additional constraints on the order of rule application. Often, we can find a more constrained partial ordering (perhaps a strict linear sequence) that satisfies all of these additional constraints. In this case, the result of this second phase is a solution to the problem. When the additional ordering constraints conflict, there is no immediate solution, and DCOMP must make more drastic alterations to the plan found in phase 1.

These ideas can best be illustrated by some examples. Suppose we use the simpler example from chapter 7 again. The initial state description is as shown in Figure 7.1, and the goal is $[ON(C,B) \wedge ON(A,C)]$. In phase 1, DCOMP applies B-rules until all subgoals are matched by the initial state description. There is no need to regress conditions through F-rules, because DCOMP assumes no interactions.

A consistent solution graph that might be achieved by phase 1 is shown in Figure 8.1. (In Figure 8.1, we have suppressed match arcs; consistency of substitutions is not an issue in these examples. A substitution written near a leaf node unifies the literal labeling that node with a fact literal.) The B-rules in the graph are labeled by the F-rules from which they stem, because we will be referring to various properties of these F-rules later. All rule applications in the graph have been numbered (in no particular order) for reference in our discussion. Note also that we have numbered, by 0, the "operation" in which the goal $[ON(A,C) \wedge ON(C,B)]$ is split into the two components $ON(A,C)$ and $ON(C,B)$. We might imagine that this backward splitting rule is based on an imaginary "join" F-rule that, in the final plan, assembles the two components into the final goal.

We see that the solution consists of two sequences of F-rules to be executed in parallel, namely, {**unstack**(C,A), **stack**(C,B)} and {**unstack**(C,A), **pickup**(A), **stack**(A,C)}. Because of interactions, we obviously cannot execute these sequences in parallel. For example, F-rule 5 deletes a precondition, namely, $HANDEMPTY$, needed by F-rule 2. Thus, we cannot apply F-rule 5 immediately prior to F-rule 2. Worse, F-rule 5 deletes a precondition, namely, $HANDEMPTY$, needed by the

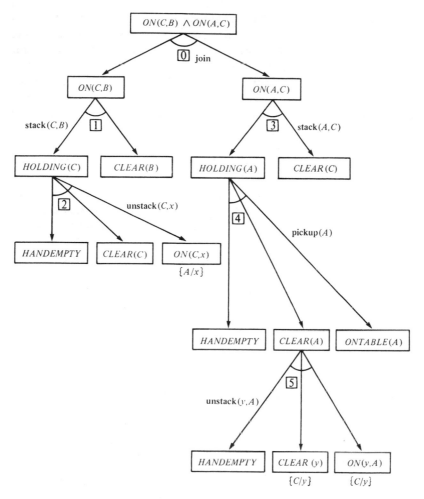

Fig. 8.1 A first-phase solution.

immediately subsequent F-rule 4. The graph of Figure 8.1 has several such interaction defects.

The process for recognizing a *noninteractive partial order* involves examination of every F-rule mentioned in the solution graph (including the fictitious join rule) to see if its preconditions are matched by the state description at the time that it is to be applied. Suppose we denote the i-th precondition literal of the j-th F-rule in the graph as C_{ij}. For each such C_{ij} in the graph, we compute two (possibly empty) sets. The first set, D_{ij},

335

is the set of F-rules specified in the graph that delete C_{ij} and that are not ancestors of rule j in the graph nor rule j itself. This set is called the *deleters* of C_{ij}. Any deleter of C_{ij} might (as an F-rule) destroy this precondition for F-rule j; thus the order in which deleters occur relative to F-rule j is important. If the deleter is a descendant of rule j in the graph, we have special problems. (We are not concerned about rule j itself or any of its ancestors that might delete C_{ij}, since the "purpose" of C_{ij} has by then already been served.)

The second set, A_{ij}, computed for the condition C_{ij}, is the set of F-rules specified by the graph that add C_{ij} and are not ancestors of rule j in the graph nor j itself. This set is called the *adders* of C_{ij}. Any adder of C_{ij} is important because it might be ordered such that it occurs after a deleter and before F-rule j, thus vitiating the effect of the deleter. Also, if some rule, say rule k, was used in the original solution graph to achieve condition C_{ij}, we might be able to apply one of the other adders before F-rule j instead of F-rule k and thus eliminate rule k (and all of its descendants!). Obviously F-rule j and any of its ancestors that might add condition C_{ij} are not of interest to us because they are applied *after* condition C_{ij} is needed.

In Figure 8.2 we show all of the adders and deleters for all of the conditions in the graph.

A partial order is *noninteractive* if, for each C_{ij} in the graph, either of the following two conditions holds:

> 1) F-rule j occurs before all members of D_{ij}
> (In this case the condition, C_{ij}, is not deleted
> until after F-rule j is applied); or
>
> 2) There exists a rule in A_{ij}, say rule k, such
> that F-rule k occurs before F-rule j and no
> member of D_{ij} occurs between F-rule k and
> F-rule j.

According to the above criteria, the solution graph of Figure 8.2 is *not* noninteractive because, for example, F-rule 2 does not precede F-rule 5 in the ordering (and F-rule 5 deletes the preconditions of F-rule 2).

In its second phase, DCOMP attempts to transform the partial ordering to one which is noninteractive. Often, such a transformation can be made. There are two principal techniques for transforming the ordering. We can further constrain the ordering so as to satisfy one of the two conditions for noninteraction stated above, or we can eliminate an F-rule (and its descendants) from the graph if its effect can be achieved by constraining the order of one of the other adders.

For example, in Figure 8.2, F-rule 3 is a deleter of condition *CLEAR(C)* of F-rule 2. If we order F-rule 2 before F-rule 3, then F-rule 3 would no longer be a deleter of this condition. Also F-rule 5 is a deleter of condition *HANDEMPTY* of F-rule 4. Obviously, we cannot make F-rule 4 occur before F-rule 5; it is already an ancestor of F-rule 5 in the partial ordering.

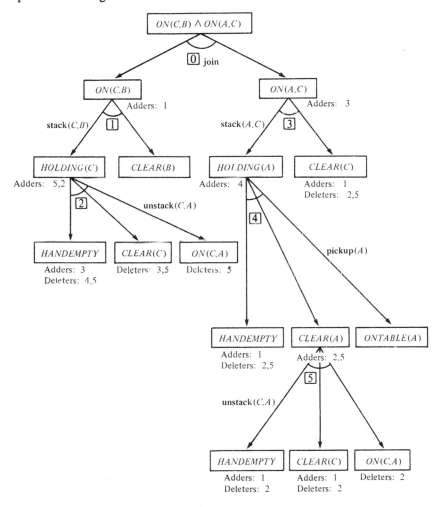

Fig. 8.2 First-phase solution with adders and deleters listed.

337

But we might be able to insert an adder, F-rule 1, between F-rule 5 and F-rule 4. Or if F-rule 2 occurs before F-rule 4 and after any deleters of this *CLEAR(A)* condition, we eliminate F-rule 5 entirely since *CLEAR(A)* is added by F-rule 2.

DCOMP attempts to render the phase 1 ordering noninteractive by further constraining it or by eliminating F-rules. The general problem of finding an acceptable set of manipulations seems rather difficult, and we discuss it here only informally. The additional ordering constraints imposed on the original solution graph must themselves be consistent. In some cases, DCOMP is not able to find appropriate orderings. In our example, however, DCOMP constructs an ordering by the following steps:

1) Place F-rule 2 before F-rule 4 and
eliminate F-rule 5. Note that F-rule 4 cannot
now delete any preconditions of F-rule 2.
Also because F-rule 2 now occurs before
F-rule 3, F-rule 3 cannot delete any
preconditions of F-rule 2 either.

2) Place F-rule 1 before F-rule 4. Since F-rule
1 occurs after F-rule 2 and before F-rules 4
and 3 it reestablishes conditions needed by
F-rules 4 and 3 deleted by F-rule 2.

These additional constraints give us the ordering {2,1,4,3}, corresponding to the sequence of F-rules {**unstack**(*C,A*), **stack**(*C,B*), **pickup**(*A*), **stack**(*A,C*)}.

In this case, the ordering of the F-rules in the plan produced a strict sequence. In fact, the F-rules that we have been using for these blocks-world examples are such that they can only be applied in sequence; the robot has only one hand, and this hand is involved in each of the actions. Suppose we had a robot with two hands and that each was capable of performing all four of the actions modeled by our F-rules. These rules could be adapted to model the two-handed robot by providing each of them with an extra "hand" argument taking the values "1" or "2." Also the predicates *HANDEMPTY* and *HOLDING* would need to have this hand argument added. (We won't allow interactions between the hands, such as one of them holding the other.) The F-rules for the two-handed robot are then as follows:

1) **pickup**(x, h)
   P & D: $ONTABLE(x)$, $CLEAR(x)$, $HANDEMPTY(h)$
   A: $HOLDING(x,h)$

2) **putdown**(x, h)
   P & D: $HOLDING(x,h)$
   A: $ONTABLE(x)$, $CLEAR(x)$, $HANDEMPTY(h)$

3) **stack**(x, y, h)
   P & D: $HOLDING(x,h)$, $CLEAR(y)$
   A: $HANDEMPTY(h)$, $ON(x,y)$, $CLEAR(x)$

4) **unstack**(x, y, h)
   P & D: $HANDEMPTY(h)$, $CLEAR(x)$, $ON(x,y)$
   A: $HOLDING(x,h)$, $CLEAR(y)$

With the rules just cited, we ought to be able to generate partially ordered plans in which hands "1" and "2" could be performing actions simultaneously. Let's attempt to solve the very same block-stacking problem just solved [that is, the goal is [$ON(A,C) \land ON(C,B)$], from the initial state shown in Figure 7.1. [The $HANDEMPTY$ predicate in that state description is now, of course, replaced by $HAND$-$EMPTY(1) \land HANDEMPTY(2)$.] In Figure 8.3, we show a possible DCOMP first-phase solution with the adders and deleters listed for each condition. Note that, compared with Figure 8.2, there are fewer deleters of the $HANDEMPTY$ predicates because we have two hands.

During the second phase of this problem, DCOMP might specify that F-rule 2 occur before F-rule 4 so that we can delete rule 5. Further, F-rule 2 should occur before F-rule 3 to avoid deleting the $CLEAR(C)$ condition of F-rule 2. Now if F-rule 1 occurs between F-rules 2 and 3, the $CLEAR(C)$ condition of F-rule 3 would be re-established. These additional constraints give us the partially ordered plan shown in Figure 8.4.

It is convenient to be able to represent any partially ordered plan in a form similar to solution graphs of AND/OR graphs. If there were no interactions at all among the subgoals of a solution graph produced by the first phase, then that graph itself would be a perfectly acceptable representation for the partially ordered plan. If the interactions were such that there could be no parallel application of F-rules, than a solution path like that shown in Figures 7.5 through 7.7 would be required. What about cases between these extremes, such as that of our present two-handed robot? We show in Figure 8.5 one way of representing the plan of Figure 8.4. Starting from the goal condition, we work backward along the plan producing the appropriate subgoal states. When the plan splits, it is because the subgoal condition at that point can be split into components. Such a split occurs at the point marked "*" in Figure 8.5. These components can be solved separately until they join again at the point marked "**". Notice that *CLEAR(C)* in node 1 regresses to *T*, as does *CLEAR(A)* in node 2. Structures similar to those of Figure 8.5 have been called *procedural nets* by Sacerdoti (1977).

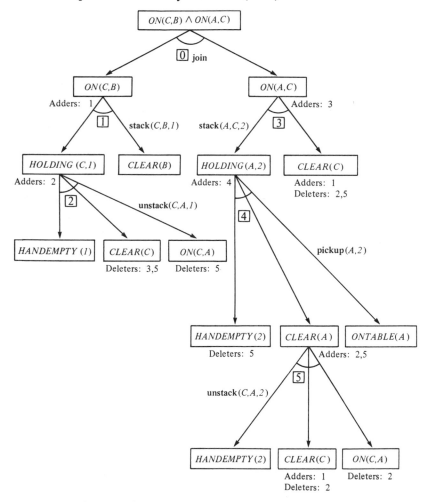

Fig. 8.3 A first-phase solution to a problem using two hands.

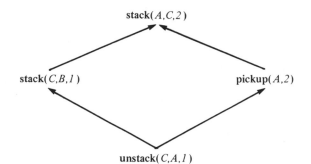

Fig. 8.4 *A partially ordered plan for a two-handed block stacking problem.*

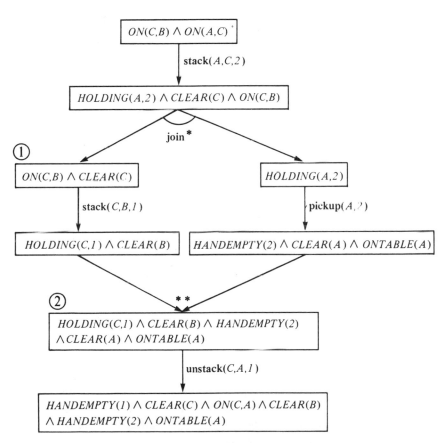

Fig. 8.5 *Goal graph form for partially ordered plan.*

8.3.   AMENDING PLANS

Sometimes it is impossible to transform the phase-1 solution into a noninteractive ordering merely by adding additional ordering constraints. The general situation, in this case, is that the phase-2 process can do no better than leave us with a partially ordered plan in which some of the preconditions are unavoidably deleted. We assume that phase 2 produces a plan having as few such deletions as possible and that the deletions that are left are those that are estimated to be easy to reachieve. After producing some such "approximate plan," DCOMP calls upon a *phase-3* process to develop plans to reachieve the deleted conditions and then to "patch" those plans into the phase-2 (approximate) plan in such a way that the end result is noninteractive.

The main task of phase 3, then, is to amend an existing (and faulty) plan. The process of amending plans requires some special explanation so we consider this general subject next.

We begin our discussion by considering another example. Suppose we are trying to achieve the goal [$CLEAR(A) \land HANDEMPTY$] from the initial state shown in Figure 7.1 (with just one hand now). In Figure 8.6, we show the result of phase 1, with the adders and deleters listed. Here, we obviously have a solution that cannot be put into noninteractive form by adding additional constraints; there is only one F-rule, and it deletes a "precondition" of the join rule, number 0. The only remedy to this situation is to permit the deletion and to plan to reachieve *HAND-EMPTY* in such a way that $CLEAR(A)$ remains true.

Our strategy is to insert a plan, say P, between F-rule 1 and the join. The requirements on P are that its preconditions must regress through F-rule 1 to conditions that match the initial state description and that $CLEAR(A)$ regress through P unchanged (so that it can be achieved by F-rule 1). The structure of the solution that we are seeking is shown in Figure 8.7.

If we apply the B-rule version of **putdown**(x) to $HANDEMPTY$, we obtain the subgoal $HOLDING(x)$. This subgoal regresses through **unstack**(C, A) to T, with the substitution $\{ C/x \}$. Furthermore, $CLEAR(A)$ regresses through **putdown**(C) unchanged, so **putdown**(C) is the appropriate patch. The final solution is shown in Figure 8.8.

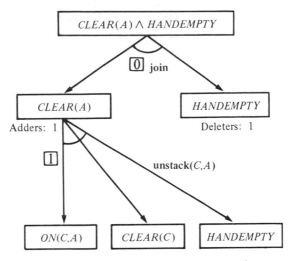

Fig. 8.6 *First-phase solution requiring a patch.*

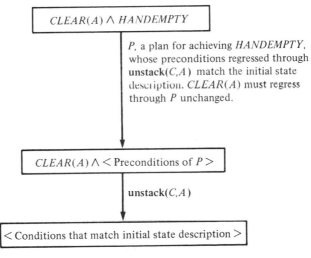

Fig. 8.7 *The form of the patched solution.*

343

When interactions occur that cannot be removed by additional ordering constraints, the general situation is often very much like this last example. In these cases, DCOMP attempts to insert patches as needed starting with the patch that is to be inserted earliest in the plan (closest to the initial state). This patching process is applied iteratively until the entire plan is free of interactions.

We illustrate the patching process by another example. Now we consider the familiar, and highly interactive block-stacking problem that begins with the initial configuration of Figure 7.1 and whose goal is $[ON(A,B) \land ON(B,C)]$. The first-phase solution, shown in Figure 8.9, has interactions that cannot be removed by adding additional ordering constraints. The ordering $3 \to 5 \to 4 \to 2 \to 1$ is a good approximate solution even though F-rule 3 deletes a precondition of F-rule 4, namely, $CLEAR(C)$, and it also deletes a precondition of F-rule 5, namely, $HANDEMPTY$. Our patching process attempts to reachieve these deleted conditions and works on the earliest one, $HANDEMPTY$, first.

The path of the approximate solution is shown in Figure 8.10; we do not split the initial compound goal because neither of the components can be achieved in an order-independent fashion. Note that regression must be used to create successor nodes and that some of the goal components regress to T and thus disappear. Here, we use the convention that the tail of the B-rule arc adjoins the condition used to match a literal in the add list of the rule. The conditions marked with asterisks (*) are conditions that our approximate plan does not yet achieve.

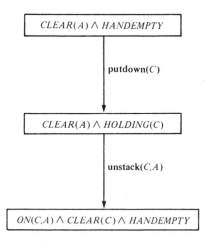

Fig. 8.8 *The patched solution.*

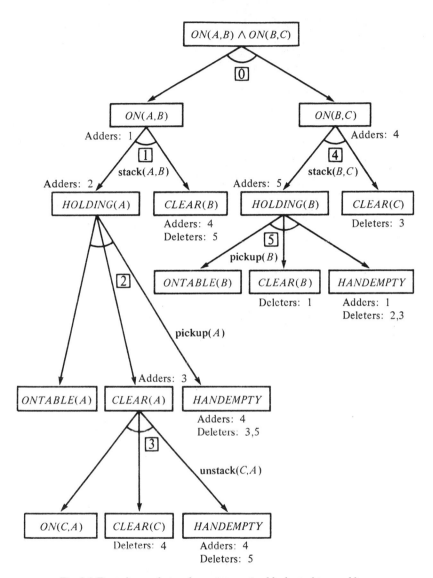

Fig. 8.9 First-phase solution for an interactive block-stacking problem.

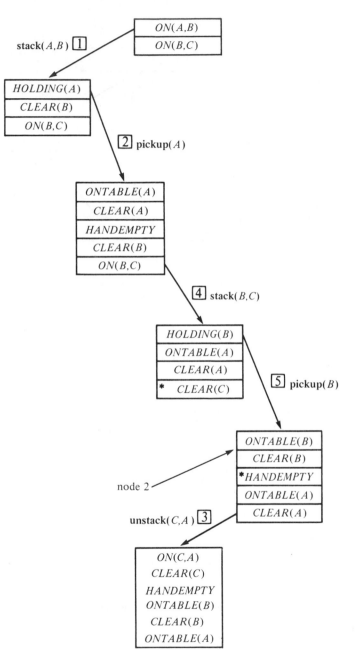

Fig. 8.10 An approximate solution.

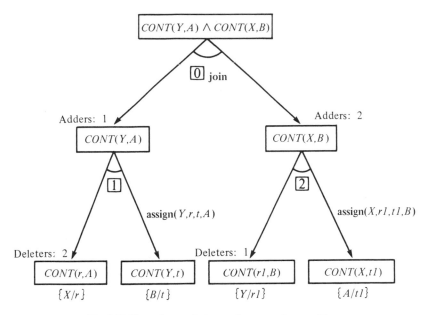

Fig. 8.11 First-phase solution to the two-register problem.

We first attempt to insert a patch between F-rule 3 and F-rule 5 to achieve *HANDEMPTY*. (Note the similarity of this situation with that depicted in Figure 8.7.) The rule **putdown**(x) with the substitution $\{ C/x \}$ is an appropriate patch. Its subgoal, *HOLDING*(C), regresses through **unstack**(C, A) to T. Furthermore, all of the conditions of node 2 [except *HANDEMPTY*, which is achieved by **putdown**(C)] regress unchanged through **putdown**(C).

Now, we can consider the problem of finding a patch for the other deleted precondition, namely, *CLEAR*(C). Note, that in this case, however, *CLEAR*(C) regresses unchanged through F-rule 5, **pickup**(B), and then it regresses through our newly inserted rule, **putdown**(C), to T. Therefore no further modifications of the plan are necessary, and we have the usual solution {**unstack**(C, A), **putdown**(C), **pickup**(B), **stack**(B, C), **pickup**(A), **stack**(A, B)}.

The process of patching can be more complicated than our examples have illustrated. If the preconditions of the patched plan have only to regress through a strict sequence (as in this last example), the process is straightforward, but how are conditions to be regressed through a *partial* ordering? Some conditions may regress through to conditions that match

347

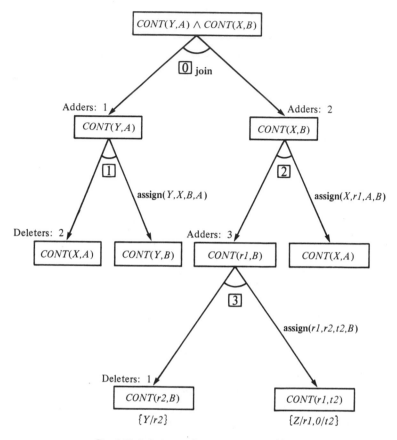

Fig. 8.12 Solution to the two-register problem.

the initial state description for all strict orderings consistent with the partial ordering; others may do so for none of these strict orderings. Or we may be able to impose additional constraints on the partial ordering such that the preconditions of a patched plan may regress through it to conditions that are satisfied by the initial state description. The general problem of patching plans into partial orderings appears rather complex and has not yet received adequate attention.

As a final example of DCOMP, we consider again the problem of interchanging the contents of two registers. From the initial state

348

$[CONT(X,A) \wedge CONT(Y,B) \wedge CONT(Z,O)]$, we want to achieve the goal $[CONT(Y,A) \wedge CONT(X,B)]$. The first phase produces the solution shown in Figure 8.11. The adders and deleters are indicated as usual. This first-phase solution has unavoidable deletions. F-rule 1 deletes a precondition of F-rule 2, and vice versa. They cannot both be first! [Sacerdoti (1977) called this type of conflict a "double cross."]

The blame for the unavoidable deletion conflict might be assigned to the substitutions used in one of the rules, say, rule 2. If Y were not substituted for rl in rule 2, then F-rule 1 would not have deleted $CONT(rl,B)$. Then F-rule 1 could be ordered before F-rule 2 to avoid the deletion of the precondition, $CONT(X,A)$, of F-rule 1 by F-rule 2. In this manner, DCOMP is led to continue the search for a solution by establishing the precondition, $CONT(rl,B)$, of F-rule 2 but now prohibiting the substitution $\{Y/rl\}$.

Continued search results in the tentative solution shown in Figure 8.12. From this tentative solution, DCOMP can compute that the ordering $3 \rightarrow 1 \rightarrow 2$ produces a noninteractive solution. The final solution produced is $\{\textbf{assign}(Z,Y,O,B), \textbf{assign}(Y,X,B,A), \textbf{assign}(X,Z,A,B)\}$.

8.4. HIERARCHICAL PLANNING

The methods that we have considered so far for generating plans to achieve goals have all operated on "one level." When working backward, for example, we investigated ways to achieve the goal condition and then to achieve all of the subgoals, and so on. In many practical situations, we might regard some goal and subgoal conditions as mere *details* and postpone attempts to solve them until the *major* steps of the plan are in place. In fact, the goal conditions that we encounter and the rules to achieve them might be organized in a hierarchy with the most detailed conditions and fine-grained actions at the lowest level and the major conditions and their rules at the highest level.

Planning the construction of a building, for example, involves the high level tasks of site preparation, foundation work, framing, heating and electrical work, and so on. Lower level activities would detail more precise steps for accomplishing the higher level tasks. At the very lowest

349

level, the activities might involve nail-driving, wire-stripping, and so on. If the entire plan had to be synthesized at the level of the most detailed actions, it would be impossibly long. Developing the plan level by level, in hierarchical fashion, allows the plans at each level to be of reasonable length and thus increases the likelihood of their being found. Such a strategy is called *hierarchical planning*.

8.4.1. POSTPONING PRECONDITIONS

One simple method of planning hierarchically is to identify a hierarchy of conditions. Those at the lower levels of the hierarchy are relatively unimportant details compared to those at the higher levels, and achievement of the former can be postponed until most of the plan is developed. The general idea is that plan synthesis should occur in stages, dealing with the highest level conditions first. Once a plan has been developed to achieve the high-level conditions (and their high-level preconditions, and so on), other steps can be added in place to the plan to achieve lesser conditions, and so on. This method does not require that the rules themselves be graded according to a hierarchy. We can still have one set of rules.

Hierarchical planning is achieved by constructing a plan in levels, using any of the single-level methods previously described. During each level, certain conditions are regarded as details and are thus postponed until a subsequent level. A condition regarded as a detail at a certain level is effectively invisible at that level. When details suddenly become visible at a lower level, we must have a means of patching the higher level plans to achieve them.

8.4.2. ABSTRIPS

The patching process is relatively straightforward with a STRIPS-type problem solver, so we illustrate the process of hierarchical planning first by using STRIPS as the basic problem solver. When STRIPS is modified in this way, it is called ABSTRIPS.

For an example problem, let us again use the goal $[ON(C,B) \land ON(A,C)]$, and the initial state depicted in Figure 7.1. This goal is one that the single-level STRIPS can readily solve but we use it here merely to illustrate how ABSTRIPS works.

The F-rules that we use are those that we have been using, but for purposes of postponing preconditions we must specify a hierarchy of conditions (including goal conditions). To be realistic, this hierarchy ought to reflect the intrinsic difficulty of achieving the various conditions. Clearly, the major goal predicate, *ON*, should be on the highest level of the hierarchy; and perhaps *HANDEMPTY* should be at the lowest level, since it is easy to achieve. In this simple example, we use only three hierarchical levels and place the remaining predicates, namely, *ON-TABLE*, *CLEAR*, and *HOLDING*, in the middle level.

The hierarchical level of each condition can be simply indicated by a *criticality value* associated with the condition. Small numbers indicate a low hierarchical level or small criticality, and large numbers indicate a high hierarchical level or large criticality. The F-rules for ABSTRIPS, with criticality values indicated above the preconditions, are shown below:

1) **pickup**(x)
$$\qquad\qquad\quad 2 \qquad\quad 2 \qquad\quad 1$$
P & D: $ONTABLE(x)$, $CLEAR(x)$, $HANDEMPTY$
A: $HOLDING(x)$

2) **putdown**(x)
$$\qquad\qquad\qquad 2$$
P & D: $HOLDING(x)$
A: $ONTABLE(x)$, $CLEAR(x)$, $HANDEMPTY$

3) **stack**(x,y)
$$\qquad\qquad\quad 2 \qquad\qquad 2$$
P & D: $HOLDING(x)$, $CLEAR(y)$
A: $HANDEMPTY$, $ON(x,y)$, $CLEAR(x)$

4) **unstack**(x,y)
$$\qquad\qquad\quad 1 \qquad\quad 2 \qquad\quad 3$$
P & D: $HANDEMPTY$, $CLEAR(x)$, $ON(x,y)$
A: $HOLDING(x)$, $CLEAR(y)$

Note that criticality values appear on both the preconditions and on the delete-list literals. They do not appear on the add-list literals. When an F-rule is applied, all of the literals in the add list are added to the state description.

ABSTRIPS begins by considering only conditions of highest criticality, namely, those with criticality value 3 in this example. All conditions having criticality values below this *threshold* value are invisible, that is, they are ignored. Since our main goal contains two conditions of value 3, ABSTRIPS considers one of them, say, $ON(C, B)$, and adds **stack**(C, B) to the goal stack. (If ABSTRIPS had selected the other component to work on first, it would later have had to back up; the reader might want to explore this path on his own.) No preconditions (of **stack**) are added to the goal stack, because they have a criticality value of only 2 (below threshold) and are thus invisible at this level.

ABSTRIPS can therefore apply the F-rule **stack** (C, B), resulting in a new state description. Next, it considers the other goal component $ON(A, C)$ and adds **stack**(A, C) to the goal stack. (Again, the preconditions of this rule are invisible.) Then ABSTRIPS applies **stack**(A, C) to the current state resulting in a state description that matches the entire goal. We show the solution path for this level of the operation of ABSTRIPS in Figure 8.13. Note that when delete literals of rules are invisible, certain items that ought to be deleted from a state description are not deleted. A contradictory state description may result, but this causes no problems.

The first level solution, obtained by ignoring certain details, is the sequence {**stack**(C, B), **stack**(A, C)}. (An equally valid solution at the first level, obtained by a different ordering of goal components, is {**stack**(A, C), **stack**(C, B)}. This solution will run into difficulties at a lower level causing the need to return to this first level to produce the appropriately ordered sequence.) Our first-level solution can be regarded as a high-level plan for achieving the goal. From this view, the block-stacking operations are considered most important, and a lower level of planning can be counted on to fill in details.

We now pass down our first-level solution, namely, {**stack**(C, B), **stack**(A, C)}, to the second level. In this level we consider conditions of criticality value 2 or higher so that we begin to consider some of the details. We can effectively pass down the higher level solution by beginning the process at the next level with a goal stack that includes the sequence of F-rules in the higher level solution together with any of their *visible* preconditions. The last item in the beginning goal stack is the main goal. In this case the beginning goal stack for the second level is:

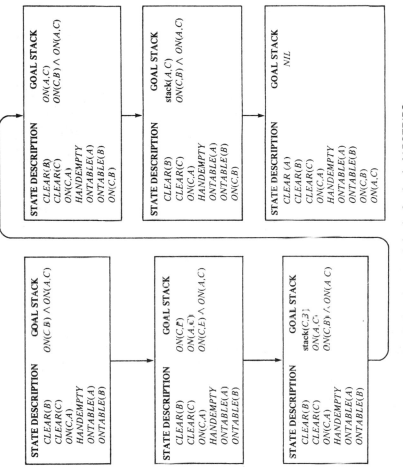

Fig. 8.13 The solution path for the first level of ABSTRIPS.

$HOLDING(C) \wedge CLEAR(B)$
stack(C,B)
$HOLDING(A) \wedge CLEAR(C)$
stack(A,C)
$ON(C,B) \wedge ON(A,C)$

Because STRIPS works with a goal stack, it is easy for a subsequent level to patch in rules for achieving details. The plan passed down from higher levels effectively constrains the search at lower levels, enhancing efficiency and diminishing the combinatorial explosion.

The reader can verify for himself that one possible solution produced by this second level is the sequence {**unstack**(C,A), **stack**(C,B), **pickup**(A), **stack**(A,C)}. If no solution can be found during one of the levels, the process can return to a higher level to find another solution. In this case our second-level solution is a good one and is complete except that in its construction we have ignored the condition $HANDEMPTY$.

During the next or third level, we lower to 1 the threshold on criticality values. We start with a goal stack containing the sequence of F-rules from the second-level solution together with (now *all* of) their preconditions. The work at this level, for our present example, merely verifies that the second-level solution is a correct solution even to the most detailed level of the problem.

ABSTRIPS is thus a completely straightforward process for accomplishing hierarchical planning. All that is required is a grading of the importance of predicates accomplished by assigning them criticality values. In problems more complex than this example, ABSTRIPS is a much more efficient problem solver than the single-level STRIPS.

8.4.3. VARIATIONS

There are several variations on this particular theme of hierarchical problem solving. First, the basic problem solver used at each level does not have to be STRIPS. Any problem-solving method can be used so long as it is possible for the method at one level to be guided by the solution produced at a higher level. For example, we could use RSTRIPS or DCOMP at each level augmented by an appropriate patching process.

A minor variation on this hierarchical planning scheme involves only two levels of precondition criticality and a slightly different way of using the criticality levels. Since this variant is important, we illustrate how it works with an example using the set of F-rules given below:

1) **pickup**(x)
    P & D: *ONTABLE* (x), *CLEAR* (x), *P-HANDEMPTY*
    A: *HOLDING* (x)

2) **putdown**(x)
    P & D: *HOLDING* (x)
    A: *ONTABLE* (x), *CLEAR* (x), *HANDEMPTY*

3) **stack**(x,y)
    P & D: *P-HOLDING* (x), *CLEAR* (y)
    A: *HANDEMPTY, ON* (x,y), *CLEAR* (x)

4) **unstack**(x,y)
    P & D: *P-HANDEMPTY, CLEAR* (x), *ON* (x,y)
    A: *HOLDING* (x), *CLEAR* (y)

The special *P-* prefix before a predicate indicates that achievement of the corresponding precondition is *always* postponed until the next lower level. We call these preconditions *P-conditions*. This scheme allows us to specify, for each F-rule, which preconditions are the most important (to be achieved during the current planning level) and which are details (to be achieved in the immediately lower level).

In this example, we use **STRIPS** as the basic problem solver at each level. Let us consider the same problem solved earlier, namely, to achieve the goal [$ON(C,B) \land ON(A,C)$] from the initial state shown in Figure 7.1. In Figure 8.14, we show a **STRIPS** solution path for the first level. Note again that the state description may contain inconsistencies because details are not deleted. The first level solution is the sequence { **stack**(C,B), **stack**(A,C)}.

We begin the second-level solution attempt with a goal stack containing the sequence of F-rules just obtained and their preconditions. Now, however, the P-conditions previously postponed must be included as conditions and be achieved at this level. Also, when *these* F-rules are applied, we delete these preconditions from the current state description. Any *new* F-rules inserted at this level are treated as before.

355

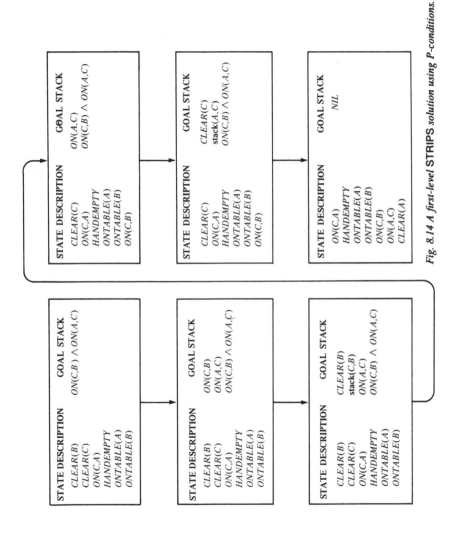

Fig. 8.14 A first-level STRIPS solution using P-conditions.

The beginning goal stack for the next level of problem solving is given below. To distinguish the F-rules inherited from a previous level from those that might be inserted at the present level, we precede the inherited ones by an asterisk (*).

$HOLDING(C) \land CLEAR(B)$
*stack(C, B)
$HOLDING(A) \land CLEAR(C)$
*stack(A, C)
$[ON(C, B) \land ON(A, C)]$

The STRIPS solution at this level is the sequence {**unstack**(C, A), **stack**(C, B), **pickup**(A), **stack**(A, C)}. Even though there were post-poned conditions at this level, namely, $HANDEMPTY$, this sequence is a valid solution. The goal stack set up for the next lower level causes no additional F-rules to be inserted in the plan. The problem-solving process for this level merely verifies the correctness of the second-level plan when all details are included.

8.5. BIBLIOGRAPHICAL AND HISTORICAL REMARKS

RSTRIPS is based on systems for dealing with interacting goals developed by Warren (1974) and by Waldinger (1977). [Warren's system, WARPLAN, is clearly and economically implemented in PROLOG.] A similar scheme was proposed by Rieger and London (1977).

DCOMP is based on Sacerdoti's (1975, 1977) and Tate's (1976, 1977) ideas for developing "nonlinear" plans. Sussman (1975) discusses several of the problems of simultaneously achieving interacting goals and recommends the strategy of creating a plan that tolerates a few bugs and then debugging this plan in preference to the strategy of synthesizing a perfect plan.

The ABSTRIPS system for hierarchical planning was developed by Sacerdoti (1974). The LAWALY system of Siklóssy and Dreussi (1973) also used hierarchies of subtasks. Our variation of ABSTRIPS using "P-conditions" is based on Sacerdoti's (1977) NOAH system. NOAH combines hierarchical and nonlinear planning; thus it might be thought of as an **AB-DCOMP** using *P*-conditions. Tate's (1977) system for generating project networks can be viewed as an elaboration of **NOAH**. See also a hierarchical planning and execution system proposed by Nilsson (1973).

Extensions to the capabilities of robot problem solving-systems have been proposed by Fikes, Hart, and Nilsson (1972a). Feldman and Sproull (1977) discuss problems caused by uncertainty in robot planning and recommend the use of decision-theoretic methods.

EXERCISES

8.1 Starting with the initial state description shown in Figure 7.1, show how **RSTRIPS** would achieve the goal $[ON(B,A) \wedge ON(C,B)]$.

8.2 Use any of the plan generating systems described in chapters 7 and 8 to solve the following block-stacking problem:

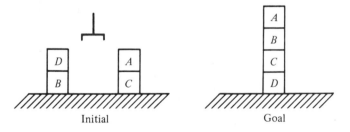

8.3 Show how **DCOMP** would solve the following blocks-world problem:

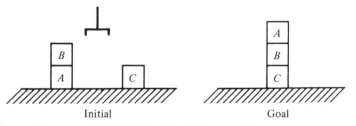

Use the predicates and **STRIPS** rules of chapter 7 to represent states and actions.

8.4 An initial blocks-world situation is described as follows:

$CLEAR(A)$ $ONTABLE(A)$
$CLEAR(B)$ $ONTABLE(B)$
$CLEAR(C)$ $ONTABLE(C)$

There is just one F-rule, namely:

puton(x,y)
  P: $CLEAR(x), CLEAR(y), ONTABLE(x)$
  D: $CLEAR(y), ONTABLE(x)$
  A: $ON(x,y)$

Show how DCOMP would achieve the goal $[ON(A,B) \land ON(B,C)]$.

8.5 Sketch out the design of a hierarchical version of DCOMP that bears the same relationship to DCOMP that ABSTRIPS bears to STRIPS. (We might call the system AB-DCOMP.) Show how the system might work on an example problem.

WARNING: There are some conceptual difficulties in designing AB-DCOMP. Describe any that you encounter even if you do not solve them.

8.6 If certain nodes in the graph of Figure 7.3 were combined, it would have the following structure:

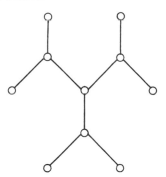

Specify a hierarchical planning system based on the form of this structure and illustrate its operation by an example.

8.7 Suppose a hierarchical planning system fails to find a solution at one of its levels. What sort of information about the reason for the failure might be useful in searching for an alternative higher level plan? Illustrate with an example.

8.8 Can you think of any ways in which the ideas about hierarchical problem solving described in this chapter might be used in rule-based deduction systems? Test your suggestions by applying them to a deduction-system solution of a robot problem using Kowalski's formulation.

8.9 Can you find a counter-example to the following statement?

> Any plan that can be generated by STRIPS
> can also be generated by ABSTRIPS.

8.10 Discuss the "completeness" properties of RSTRIPS and DCOMP. That is, can these planning systems find plans whenever plans exist?

CHAPTER 9

STRUCTURED OBJECT
REPRESENTATIONS

As we discussed in chapter 4, there are many ways to represent a body of knowledge in the predicate calculus. The appropriateness of a representation depends on the application. After deciding on a particular form of representation, the system designer must also decide on how predicate calculus expressions are to be encoded in computer memory. Efficient storage, retrieval, and modification are key concerns in selecting an implementation design. Up to now in this book, we have not been concerned with these matters of efficiency. We have treated each predicate calculus statement, whether fact, rule, or goal, as an individual entity that could be accessed as needed without concern for the actual mechanisms or costs involved in this access. Yet, ease of access is such an important consideration that it has had a major effect on the style of predicate calculus representation used in large AI systems. In this chapter, we describe some of the specialized representations that address some of these concerns. We also confront certain representational questions that might also have been faced earlier, say in chapter 6, but seem more appropriate in this chapter.

The representations discussed here aggregate several related predicate calculus expressions into larger structures (sometimes called *units*) that are identified with important objects in the subject domain of the system. When information about one of these objects is needed by the system, the appropriate unit is accessed and all of the relevant facts about the object are retrieved at once. We use the phrase *structured objects* to describe these representational schemes, because of the heavy emphasis on the *structure* of the representation. Indeed, the structure carries some of the representational and computational burden. Certain operations that might otherwise have been performed by explicit rule applications (in other representations) can be performed in a more automatic way by mechanisms that depend on the structure of the representation. These representational schemes are the subject of this chapter.

9.1.   FROM PREDICATE CALCULUS TO UNITS

Suppose we want to represent the following sentences as predicate calculus facts:

John gave Mary the book.

John is a programmer.

Mary is a lawyer.

John's address is 37 Maple St.

The following wffs appear to be a reasonable representation:

GIVE(JOHN, MARY, BOOK)

OCCUPATION(JOHN, PROGRAMMER)

OCCUPATION(MARY, LAWYER)

ADDRESS(JOHN,37-MAPLE-ST)

In this small database, we have used individual constant symbols to refer to six entitities, namely, *JOHN, MARY, BOOK, PROGRAMMER, LAWYER*, and 37-*MAPLE-ST*. If the database were enlarged, we would presumably mention more entities, but we would also probably add other information about these same entities. For retrieval purposes, it would be helpful if we gathered together all of the facts about a given entity into a single group, which we call a *unit*. In our simple example, the unit *JOHN* has associated with it the following facts:

JOHN

  GIVE(JOHN, MARY, BOOK)
  OCCUPATION(JOHN, PROGRAMMER)
  ADDRESS(JOHN,37-MAPLE-ST)

Similarly, we associate the following facts with the unit *MARY*:

MARY

$$GIVE(JOHN, MARY, BOOK)$$
$$OCCUPATION(MARY, LAWYER)$$

(It is possible to have the same fact associated with terms denoting different entities in our domain.)

A representational scheme in which the facts are indexed by terms denoting entities or objects of the domain is called an *object-centered* representation.

Most notations for structured objects involve the use of binary (two-argument) predicates for expressing facts about the objects. A simple conversion scheme can be used to rewrite arbitrary wffs using only binary predicates. To convert the three argument formula *GIVE(JOHN, MARY, BOOK)*, for example, to one involving binary predicates, we postulate the existence of a particular "giving event" and a set of such giving events. Let us call this set *GIVING-EVENTS*. For each argument of the original predicate, we invent a new binary predicate that relates the value of the argument to the postulated event. Using this scheme, the formula *GIVE(JOHN, MARY, BOOK)* would be converted to:

$$(\exists x)[EL(x, GIVING\text{-}EVENTS) \wedge GIVER(x, JOHN)$$
$$\wedge RECIP(x, MARY) \wedge OBJ(x, BOOK)]$$

The predicate *EL* is used to express set membership. Skolemizing the existential variable in the above formula gives a name, say *G1*, to our postulated giving event:

$$EL(G1, GIVING\text{-}EVENTS) \wedge GIVER(G1, JOHN)$$
$$\wedge RECIP(G1, MARY) \wedge OBJ(G1, BOOK)$$

Thus, we have converted a three-argument predicate to the conjunction of four binary ones.

The relations between *G1* and the original arguments of *GIVE* could just as well be expressed as functions over the set *GIVING-EVENTS* instead of as predicates. With this additional notational change, the sentence "John gave Mary the book" can be represented by the following formula:

$$EL(G1, GIVING\text{-}EVENTS)$$
$$\wedge\ EQ[giver(G1), JOHN]$$
$$\wedge\ EQ[recip(G1), MARY]$$
$$\wedge\ EQ[obj(G1), BOOK]$$

The predicate *EQ* is meant to denote the equality relation. The expression above uses certain functions, defined over the set *GIVING-EVENTS*, whose values name other objects that participate in *G1*.

There are some advantages in converting to a representation that uses events and binary relations. For our purposes, the primary advantage is modularity. Suppose, for example, that we want to add some information about *when* a giving event takes place. Before converting to our binary form, we would need to add a fourth (time) argument to the predicate *GIVE*. Such a change might require extensive changes to the production rules that referenced *GIVE* and to the control system. If, instead, giving is represented as a domain entity, then additional information about it can easily be incorporated by adding new binary relations, functions, and associated rules.

In this part of the book we represent all but a small number of propositions as terms denoting "events" or "situations" that are considered entities of our domain. The only predicates that we need are *EQ*, to say that two entities are the same; *SS*, to say that one set is a subset of another; and *EL*, to say that an entity is an element of a set. For our example sentences above, we had events in which persons had occupations and an event in which a person had an address. These sentences are represented as follows:

$$G1$$

$$EL(G1, GIVING\text{-}EVENTS)$$
$$EQ[giver(G1), JOHN]$$
$$EQ[recip(G1), MARY]$$
$$EQ[obj(G1), BOOK]$$

OC1

$$EL(OC1, OCCUPATION\text{-}EVENTS)$$
$$EQ[\,worker(OC1), JOHN\,]$$
$$EQ[\,profession(OC1), PROGRAMMER\,]$$

OC2

$$EL(OC2, OCCUPATION\text{-}EVENTS)$$
$$EQ[\,worker(OC2), MARY\,]$$
$$EQ[\,profession(OC2), LAWYER\,]$$

ADR1

$$EL(ADR1, ADDRESS\text{-}EVENTS)$$
$$EQ[\,person(ADR1), JOHN\,]$$
$$EQ[\,location(ADR1), 37\text{-}MAPLE\text{-}ST\,]$$

In these units, we have freely invented functions to relate events with other entities.

❧ We notice that the units above share a common structure. First, an *EL* predicate is used to state that the object described by the unit is a member of some set. (If the object described by the unit had been a set itself, then an *SS* predicate would have been used to state that it was a subset of some other set.) Second, the values of the various functions of the object described by the unit are related to other objects. We next introduce a special unit notation based on this general structure.

As an abbreviation for a formula like $EQ[\,giver(G1), JOHN\,]$, we use the expression or pair "*giver*: *JOHN*." All of the EQ predicates that relate functions of the object described by the unit to other objects are expressed by such pairs grouped below the unit name. Thus, drawing from our example, we have:

G1
  giver: *JOHN*
  recip: *MARY*
  obj: *BOOK*

In AI systems using unit notation, constructs like *"giver: JOHN"* are often called *slots*. The first expression, *giver*, is called the *slotname*, and the second expression, *JOHN*, is called the *slotvalue*.

Sometimes the slotvalue is not a constant symbol (such as *JOHN*) but a functional expression. In particular, the function may correspond to the slotname of another unit. Consider, for example, the sentences "John gave the book to Mary," and "Bill gave the pen to the person to whom John gave the book." We express this pair of sentences by the following units:

> G1
>> $EL(G1, GIVING\text{-}EVENTS)$
>> *giver*: *JOHN*
>> *recip*: *MARY*
>> *obj*: *BOOK*

> G2
>> $EL(G2, GIVING\text{-}EVENTS)$
>> *giver*: *BILL*
>> *recip*: *recip(G1)*
>> *obj*: *PEN*

In these examples, *recip(G1)* and *MARY* are two different ways of describing the same person. Later, we discuss a process for "evaluating" a functional expression like *recip(G1)* by finding the slotvalue of *recip* in the unit *G1*.

Slotvalues can also be existential variables. For example, a predicate calculus version of the sentence "Someone gave Mary the book" might include the formula $(\exists x) EQ[giver(G3), x]$. We might Skolemize the existential variable to get an expression like $EQ[giver(G3), S]$. Usually, we have some information about the existential variable. In our current example, we would know that "someone" referred to a person. A better rendering of "Someone gave Mary the book" would involve the formula:

$$(\exists x)\{ EQ[giver(G3), x] \wedge EL(x, PERSONS)]\}$$

or simply,

$$EL[giver(G3), PERSONS].$$

In order to handle this sort of formula in our unit notation, we invent the special form "(*element-of PERSONS*)" as a kind of pseudo-slot-value. This form serves as an abbreviation for the formula that used the *EL* predicate. An expression using the abbreviated form can be thought of as an *indefinite description* of the slotvalue.

To complete our set of abbreviating conventions, we use the "(*element-of*)" form in a slotname called "self" to state that the object described by the unit is an element of a set. With these conventions, our set of units that were originally written as groups of predicate calculus formulas can be rewritten as follows:

> *G1*
> > *self*: (*element-of GIVING-EVENTS*)
> > *giver*: *JOHN*
> > *recip*: *MARY*
> > *obj*: *BOOK*
>
> *OC1*
> > *self*: (*element-of OCCUPATION-EVENTS*)
> > *worker*: *JOHN*
> > *profession*: *PROGRAMMER*
>
> *OC2*
> > *self*: (*element-of OCCUPATION-EVENTS*)
> > *worker*: *MARY*
> > *profession*: *LAWYER*
>
> *ADR1*
> > *self*: (*element-of ADDRESS-EVENTS*)
> > *person*: *JOHN*
> > *location*: 37-MAPLE-ST

Other entities in our domain might similarly be described by the following units:

> *JOHN*
> > *self*: (*element-of PERSONS*)
>
> *MARY*
> > *self*: (*element-of PERSONS*)

367

BOOK
  self: (*element-of PHYS-OBJS*)

PROGRAMMER
  self: (*element-of JOBS*)

LAWYER
  self: (*element-of JOBS*)

37-MAPLE-ST
  self: (*element-of ADDRESSES*)

PERSONS
  self: (*subset-of ANIMALS*)

This set of units represents explicitly certain information (about set membership) that was merely implicit in our original sentences. Note that in the last unit, *PERSONS*, we use the form "(*subset-of AN-IMALS*)." This form is analogous to the "(*element-of*)" form; within the *PERSONS* unit it stands for *SS*(*PERSONS,ANIMALS*).

It should be clear how to translate any of the above units back into conventional predicate calculus notation.

We can also accommodate universally quantified variables in units. Consider, for example, the sentence "John gave something to everyone." In predicate calculus, this sentence might be represented as follows:

$$(\forall x)(\exists y)(\exists z)\{\ EL(y, GIVING\text{-}EVENTS)$$
$$\wedge\ EQ[giver(y), JOHN] \wedge EQ[obj(y), z]$$
$$\wedge\ EQ[recip(y), x]\}\ .$$

Skolemization replaces the variables y and z by functions of x. In particular, the giving event, y, is now a Skolem function of x and not a constant. The family of giving events represented by this function can be described by the functional unit:

$g(x)$
  self: (*element-of GIVING-EVENTS*)
  giver: *JOHN*
  obj: *sk*(x)
  recip: x

In this unit, the slotvalue of *obj* is the Skolem function, $sk(x)$. The scope of universal variables in units is the entire unit. (We assume that all predicate calculus formulas represented in unit notation are in prenex Skolem form. That is, all negation signs are moved in, variables are standardized apart, existential variables are Skolemized, and all universal quantifiers apply to the entire expression. Thus, when translating unit notation back into predicate calculus, the universal variables all have maximum scopes.)

Since ideas about sets and set membership play such a prominent role in the representations being discussed in this chapter, it will be helpful to have some special functions for describing sets. To describe a set composed of certain individuals, we use the function *the-set-of*; for example, *the-set-of*(*JOHN, MARY, BILL*). We also use functions *intersection*, *union*, and *complement* to describe sets composed of the intersection, union, or complement of sets, respectively.

These set-describing functions can be usefully employed as a way to represent certain sentences expressing disjunctions and negations. For example, consider the sentences: "John bought a car," "It was either a Ford or a Chevy," and "It was not a convertible." These sentences could be described by the following unit:

B1
> *self*: (*element-of BUYING-EVENTS*)
> *buyer*: *JOHN*
> *bought*: (*element-of intersection*(*union*(*FORDS, CHEVYS*),
> > *complement*(*CONVERTIBLES*))) .

As another example, the sentence "John gave the book to either Bill or Mary" might be represented by:

G4
> *self*: (*element-of GIVING-EVENTS*)
> *giver*: *JOHN*
> *recip*: (*element-of the-set-of*(*BILL, MARY*))
> *obj*: *BOOK*

We postpone the discussion of how to represent implications in unit notation. It is not our intention here to develop the unit notation into a completely adequate alternative syntax for predicate calculus. A complete syntax might be quite cumbersome; indeed, various useful AI systems have employed quite restricted versions of unit languages.

9.2. A GRAPHICAL REPRESENTATION: SEMANTIC NETWORKS

The binary-predicate version of predicate calculus introduced in the last section lends itself to a graphical representation. The terms of the formalism (namely, the constant and variable symbols and the functional expressions) can be represented by nodes of a graph. Thus, in our examples above, we would have nodes for *JOHN, G1, MARY, LAW-YER, ADR1*, etc. The predicates *EQ, EL*, and *SS* can be represented by arcs; the tail of the arc leaves the node representing the first argument, and the head of the arc enters the node representing the second argument. Thus, the expression *EL(G1, GIVING-EVENTS)* is represented by the following structure:

The nodes and arcs of such graphs are labeled by the terms and predicates that they denote.

When an *EQ* predicate relates a term and a unary function of another term, we represent the unary function expression by an arc connecting the two terms. For example, to represent the formula *EQ[giver(G1), JOHN]*, we use the structure:

A collection of predicate calculus expressions of the type we have been discussing can be represented by a graph structure that is often called a *semantic network*. A network representation of our example collection of sentences is shown in Figure 9.1. Semantic networks of this sort are useful for descriptive purposes because they give a simple, structural picture of a body of facts. They also depict some of the indexing structure used in many implementations of predicate calculus representations. Of course, whether we choose to describe the computer representation of a certain body of facts by a semantic network, by a set of units, or by a collection of linear formulas is mainly a matter of taste. The underlying computer data structures may well be the same! We use all three types of descriptions more or less interchangeably in this chapter.

We show another semantic net example in Figure 9.2. It represents the same set of facts that were represented as predicate calculus expressions in an information retrieval example in chapter 6.

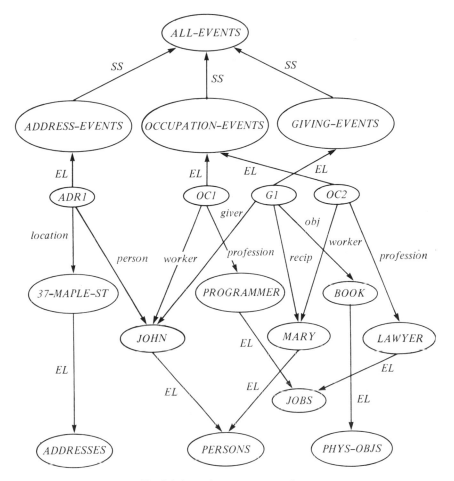

Fig. 9.1 A simple semantic network.

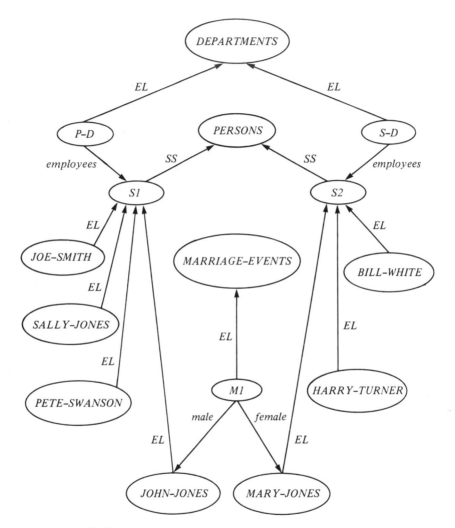

Fig. 9.2 *A semantic network representing personnel information.*

The nodes in the networks of Figures 9.1 and 9.2 are all labeled by constant symbols. We can also accommocate variable nodes; these are labeled by lower case letters near the end of the alphabet (e.g., . . ., x, y, z). Again, the variables are standardized apart and are assumed to be universally quantified. The scope of these quantifications is the entire fact network.

We follow the same conventions converting predicate calculus formulas to network form as we did converting them to unit notation. Existentially quantified variables are Skolemized, and the resulting Skolem functions are represented by nodes labeled by functional expressions. Thus the sentence "John gave something to everyone" can be represented by the network in Figure 9.3. In this figure, "x" is universally quantified. The nodes labeled by "$g(x)$" and "$sk(x)$" are Skolem-function nodes. (Computer implementations of nodes labeled by functional expressions would probably have some sort of pointer structure between the dependent nodes and the independent ones. For simplicity, we suppress explicit display of these pointers in our semantic networks; although some net formalisms include them.)

We next discuss how to represent the propositional connectives graphically. Representing conjunctions is easy: The multiple nodes and EL and SS arcs in a semantic network represent the conjunction of the associated atomic formulas. To represent a disjunction, we need some way of setting off those nodes and arcs that are the disjuncts. In a linear notation, we use parentheses or brackets to delimit the disjunction. For semantic networks, we employ a graphical version of the parentheses, an *enclosure*, represented by a closed, dashed line in our illustrations. For a disjunction, each disjunctive predicate is drawn within the enclosure, and the enclosure is labeled *DIS*. Thus, the expression $[EL(A,B) \lor SS(B,C)]$ is represented as in Figure 9.4.

To set off a conjunction nested within a disjunction, we can use an enclosure labeled *CONJ*. (By convention, we omit the implied conjunctive enclosure that surrounds the entire semantic network.) Arbitrary nesting of enclosures within enclosures can be handled in this manner. As an example, Figure 9.5 shows the semantic network version of the sentence "John is a programmer or Mary is a lawyer."

In converting predicate calculus expressions to semantic network form, negation symbols are typically moved in, so that their scopes are limited to a single predicate. In this case, expressions with negation symbols can be represented in semantic network form simply by allowing $\sim EL$, $\sim SS$, and $\sim EQ$ arcs. More generally, we can use enclosures to delimit the scopes of negations also. In this case, we label the enclosure by *NEG*. We show, in Figure 9.6, a graphical representation of $\sim[EL(A,B) \wedge SS(B,C)]$. To simplify the notation we assume, by convention, that the predicates within a negative enclosure are conjunctive.

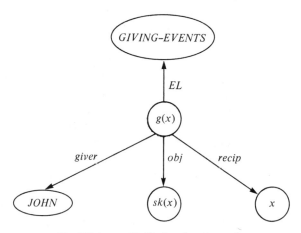

Fig. 9.3 A net with Skolem-function nodes.

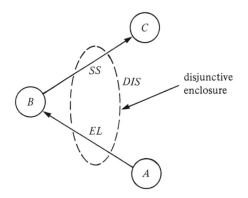

Fig. 9.4 Representing a disjunction.

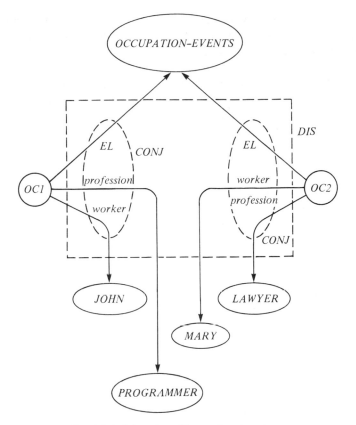

Fig. 9.5 A disjunction with nested conjunctions.

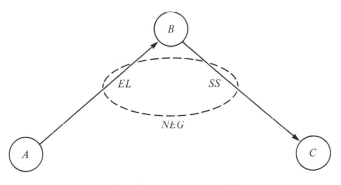

Fig. 9.6 Representing a negation.

In Figure 9.7 we show an example of a semantic network with both a disjunctive and a negative enclosure. This semantic network is equivalent to the following logical formula:

$$\{ EL(B1, BUYING\text{-}EVENTS) \wedge EQ[buyer(B1), JOHN]$$
$$\wedge EQ[bought(B1), X] \wedge \sim EL(X, CONVERTIBLES)$$
$$\wedge [EL(X, FORDS) \vee EL(X, CHEVYS)]$$
$$\wedge SS(FORDS, CARS) \wedge SS(CHEVYS, CARS)$$
$$\wedge SS(CONVERTIBLES, CARS)\}$$

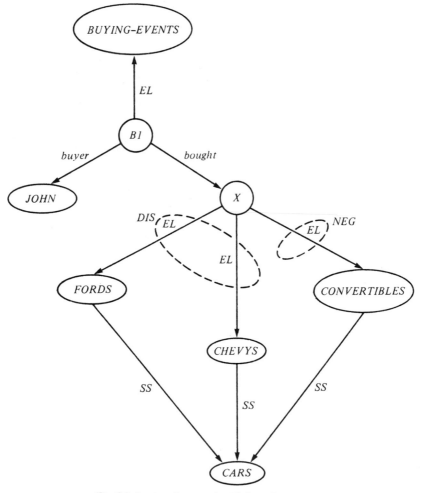

Fig. 9.7 A semantic network with logical connectives.

If we negate an expression with a leading existentially quantified variable and then move the negation symbol in past the quantifier, the quantification is changed to universal. Thus, the statement "Mary is not a programmer" might be represented as

$$\sim\{(\exists x)\,EL(x, OCCUPATION\text{-}EVENTS)$$
$$\wedge\; EQ[profession(x), PROGRAMMER]$$
$$\wedge\; EQ[worker(x), MARY]\}\;,$$

which is equivalent to

$$(\forall x)\sim\{\,EL(x, OCCUPATION\text{-}EVENTS)$$
$$\wedge\; EQ[profession(x), PROGRAMMER]$$
$$\wedge\; EQ[worker(x), MARY]\}\;.$$

The network representation for the latter formula is shown in Figure 9.8.

Enclosures can also be used to represent semantic network implications. For this purpose, we have a linked pair of enclosures, one labeled *ANTE* and one labeled *CONSE*. For example, the sentence "Everyone who lives at 37 Maple St. is a programmer" might be represented by the net in Figure 9.9. In this figure, $o(x,y)$ is a Skolem function naming an occupation event dependent on x and y. A dashed line links the *ANTE* and *CONSE* enclosures to show that they belong to the same implication. We discuss network implications in more detail later when we introduce rules for modifying databases.

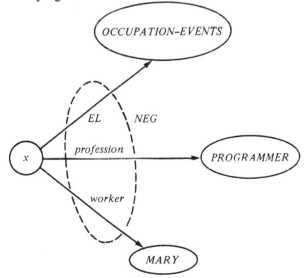

Fig. 9.8 One representation of a negated existential statement.

377

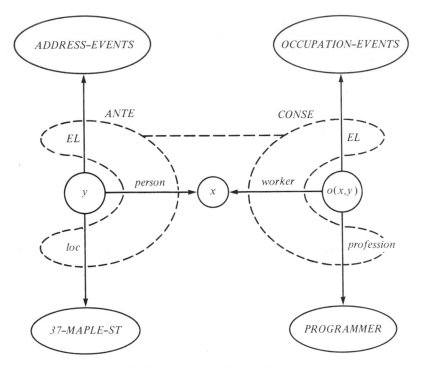

Fig. 9.9 A network with an implication.

In all of these examples, enclosures are used to set off a group of *EL*, *SS*, and function arcs and thus are drawn so as to enclose only arcs. (Whether or not they enclose nodes has no consequence in our semantic net notation.)

9.3. MATCHING

A matching operation, analogous to unification, is fundamental to the use of structured objects as the global database of a production system. We turn to this subject next.

To help us define what we mean by saying that two structured objects "match," we must remember the fact that structured objects are merely an alternative kind of predicate calculus formalism. The appropriate definition must be something like: Two objects match if and only if the predicate calculus formula associated with one of them unifies with the predicate calculus formula associated with the other. We are interested in a somewhat weaker definition of match, because our match operations are not usually symmetrical. That is, we usually have a *goal object* that we want to match against a *fact object*. We say that a goal object matches a fact object if the formula involving the goal object unifies with some sub-conjunction of the formulas of the fact object. (Matching occurs only if the goal object formulas are provable from the fact-object formulas.)

Let us look at some example matches between units using this definition. Suppose we have the fact unit:

> *M1*
> *self*: (*element-of MARRIAGE-EVENTS*)
> *male*: *JOHN-JONES*
> *female*: *MARY-JONES*

The predicate calculus formula associated with this unit is:

> $EL(M1, MARRIAGE-EVENTS)$
> $\wedge\ EQ[male(M1), JOHN-JONES]$
> $EQ[female(M1), MARY-JONES]$.

This fact unit would match the goal unit:

> *M1*
> *self*: (*element-of MARRIAGE-EVENTS*)
> *male*: *JOHN-JONES*

It would not match the goal unit:

> *M1*
> *self*: (*element-of MARRIAGE-EVENTS*)
> *male*: *JOHN-JONES*
> *female*: *MARY-JONES*
> *duration*: 10

For semantic networks, the situation is quite similar. In Figures 9.10 and 9.11 we show the fact and goal networks that correspond to the units examples above. In these figures, we separate the fact and goal arcs by a dashed line. (Again, only the location of the *arcs*, with respect to the

379

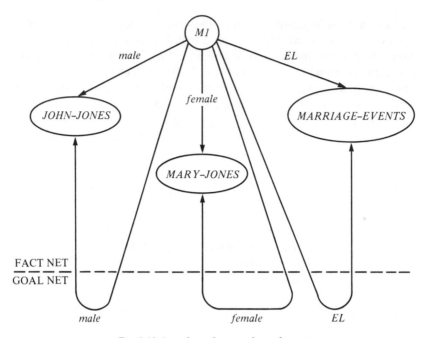

Fig. 9.10 A goal net that matches a fact net.

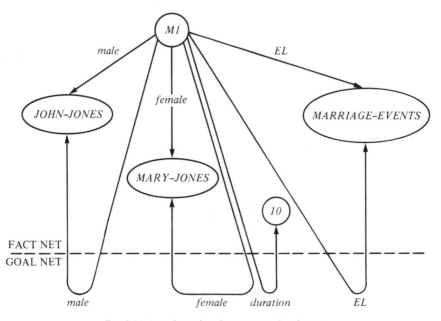

Fig. 9.11 A goal net that does not match a fact net.

380

dashed line, is important; the location of nodes is irrelevant in our formulation.) In order for a goal network structure to match a fact network structure, the formula associated with the goal structure must unify with some sub-conjunction of the formulas associated with the fact structure. In these examples, we merely have to find fact arcs that match each of the goal arcs. The match is successful in Figure 9.10, but it is unsuccessful in Figure 9.11.

In any representational scheme there are often several alternative representations for basically the same information. Since our definition of structure matching depends on the exact form of the structure, such alternatives do not strictly match. Consider the network examples of Figure 9.12. There we show two alternatives for representing "John Jones is married to Mary Jones." One of these uses a "marriage-event," and the other uses the special *wife-of* function. (Ordinarily, our preference is not to use functions like *wife-of* unless their values are truly independent of other parameters, such as time.) Syntactically, the two structures of Figure 9.12 do not match even though they semantically "say" the same thing. Such a circumstance corresponds to the fact that two predicate calculus forms for representing the same idea do not unify when they contain different predicate or function symbols. We show a somewhat more complex example of equivalent forms in Figure 9.13.

Some AI systems that use structured objects have elaborate matchers that use special knowledge about the domain of application to enable direct matches between structures like those shown in Figure 9.12 and Figure 9.13. These systems have what are often described as "semantic matchers," that is, matchers that decide that two structures are the same if they "mean" the same thing.

It is perhaps a matter of taste as to where one wants to draw the line between matching and object manipulation computations and deductions. Our preference is to prohibit operations in the matcher that require specialized domain knowledge or that might involve combinatorial computations. In these cases, we would prefer to use rule-based deductive machinery to establish the semantic equivalence between different syntactic forms. Such a strategy retains, for the control system, the responsibility of managing all potentially combinatorial searches. It permits the matcher to be a general-purpose routine that does not have to be specially designed for each application. We postpone a discussion of deductive machinery until later, when we talk about operations on structured objects.

A common cause of syntactic differences between network structures are the different ways of setting up chains of *EL* and *SS* arcs. Consider the example of Figure 9.14. The goal structure can be derived from the fact structure using a fundamental theorem from set theory. Because this derivation occurs so often with structured objects, it is usually built into the matcher. In fact, one of the advantages of structured objects is that their pointer structures allow easy computation of element/subset/set relationships. Thus, we say that the two structures in Figure 9.14 *do* match.

So far, we have only discussed matching between two constant structures. Usually, one or both of the structures contain variables that can have terms substituted for them during the matching process. Variables that occur in fact structures have implicit universal quantification in all formulas in which they appear, and variables that occur in goal structures have implicit existential quantification in all formulas in which they appear. Our structured-object systems are first-order, so variables can only occur as labels for nodes, units, or slotvalues.

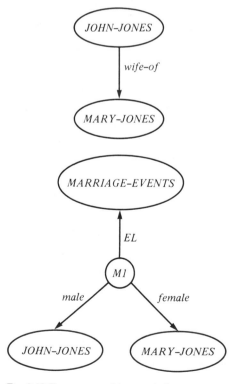

Fig. 9.12 Two non-matching, equivalent structures.

John or Bill gave Mary the pen.

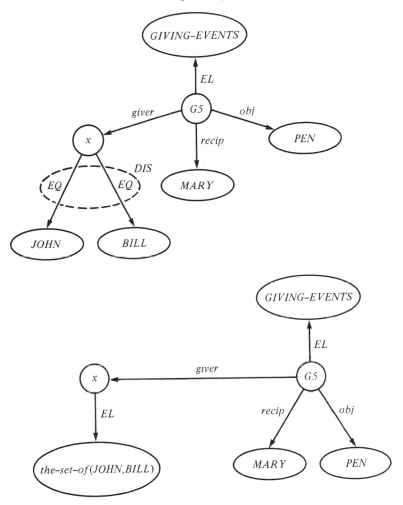

Fig. 9.13 Another example of equivalent networks.

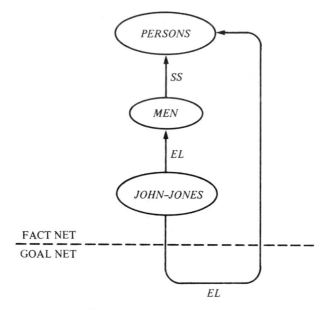

Fig. 9.14 Nets with EL and SS arcs.

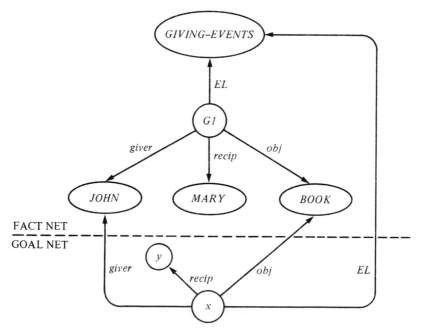

Fig. 9.15 Matching nets.

A typical use of structures with variables is as goal structures. Suppose, for example, that we wanted to ask the question "To whom did John give the book?" This question could be represented by the following goal unit:

x
    self: (*element-of GIVING-EVENTS*)
    giver: *JOHN*
    recip: *y*
    obj: *BOOK*

Matching this goal unit against the fact unit, *G1*, yields the substitution $\{G1/x, MARY/y\}$, which can be used to generate an answer to the question. In network notation, we show the corresponding matching fact and goal structures in Figure 9.15. In order for a goal net to be matched, each of its elements (arcs and nodes) must unify with corresponding fact-net elements.

In matching objects that contain functional expressions for slotvalues, we assume that these functional expressions are evaluated whenever possible. Evaluation is performed by reference to the object named by the argument of the function. Suppose, for example, that we want to ask the question: "Did Bill give Mary the pen?" This query can be expressed as the goal unit:

x
    self: (*element-of GIVING EVENTS*)
    giver: *BILL*
    recip: *MARY*
    obj: *PEN*

Suppose our fact units include:

G1
    self: (*element-of GIVING-EVENTS*)
    giver: *JOHN*
    recip: *MARY*
    obj: *BOOK*

G2
    self: (*element-of GIVING-EVENTS*)
    giver: *BILL*
    recip: *recip*(*G1*)
    obj: *PEN*

Because *recip*(*G1*) can be evaluated to *MARY*, by reference to *G1*, our goal unit matches *G2*; and we can answer "yes" to the original query. We permit the matcher to perform these kinds of evaluations because they can be handled without domain-specific strategies and do not cause combinatorial computations.

It might also be desirable to allow the matcher to use certain common equivalences between units. One such equivalence involves the special descriptive form (*element-of*). For example, the sentence "Joe bought a car" might be represented either by the unit:

> *B2*
> > *self*: (*element-of BUYING-EVENTS*)
> > *buyer*: *JOE*
> > *bought*: (*element-of CARS*)

or by the pair of units:

> *B2*
> > *self*: (*element-of BUYING-EVENTS*)
> > *buyer*: *JOE*
> > *bought*: *X*

and

> *X*
> > *self*: (*element-of CARS*)

(The first unit could be considered an abbreviated form for the pair of units.) We could build information about this abbreviation into the matcher so that, for example, the pair of units would match the goal unit:

> *y*
> > *self*: (*element-of BUYING-EVENTS*)
> > *buyer*: *JOE*
> > *bought*: (*element-of CARS*)

9.4. DEDUCTIVE OPERATIONS ON STRUCTURED OBJECTS

9.4.1. DELINEATIONS

Structured object representations can be used in production systems for performing deductions. As in our earlier discussions of predicate calculus deduction systems, the production rules are based on implications. Before talking about how implications are used in general, we consider a frequently occurring special use: when an implication asserts properties about every member of a given set.

Consider, for example, the sentence "All computer science students have graduate standing." From this assertion and the sentence, "John is a computer science student," we should be able to deduce that "John has graduate standing." We could represent these statements in the predicate calculus as follows:

$Fact$: $EL(JOHN, CS\text{-}STUDENTS)$

$Rule$: $EL(x, CS\text{-}STUDENTS) \Rightarrow EQ[class(x), GRAD]$

$Goal$: $EQ[class(JOHN), GRAD]$

An ordinary predicate calculus production system might use the rule (in either direction) to prove the goal.

In unit language, our fact might be represented as:

> $JOHN$
> $\quad$ $self$: ($element\text{-}of$ $CS\text{-}STUDENTS$)

and our goal might be represented as:

> $JOHN$
> $\quad$ $class$: $GRAD$

Our problem now is how to represent and use the implicational rule in a system based on unit notation.

387

In the unit formalism, we represent implications that assert properties about every member of a set by a special kind of unit called a *delineation unit*. Such a unit describes (delineates) each of the individuals in a set denoted by another unit. For example, suppose we have a unit denoting the set of computer science students:

> *CS-STUDENTS*
> > *self*: (*subset-of STUDENTS*)

A delineation unit for this set is used to describe each of the individuals in the set. We let this delineation unit be a *sorted* universal variable whose domain of universal quantification is the set. The sort of the variable, that is, the name of its domain set, follows the variable after a vertical bar, "|". Thus, to describe each computer science student, we have the delineation unit:

> $x \mid$ *CS-STUDENTS*
> > *major*: *CS*
> > *class*: *GRAD*

We must be careful not to confuse delineation units describing each individual in a set with the unit describing the set itself, or with any particular individuals in the set! Some AI systems using a unit formalism have entities called *prototype* units that seem to play the same role as our delineation units. In these systems, prototype units seem to be treated as if they were a special kind of constant, representing a mythical "typical" member of a set. The prototype units are then related to other members of the set by an "instance" relation. But such prototype units might cause confusion—because substituting a constant for a variable (instantiation) should properly be thought of as a metaprocess rather than as a relation in the formalism itself. It seems more reasonable to think of a delineation unit as a special form of implicational rule.

Delineation units can be used in the forward direction to create new fact units or to add properties to existing fact units. For example, suppose we had the fact unit:

> *JOHN*
> > *self*: (*element-of CS-STUDENTS*)

To use the delineation unit in the forward direction, we note that $x \mid$ *CS-STUDENTS* matches the fact unit *JOHN*. The sorted variable, x, matches any term that is an element of *CS-STUDENTS*. Applying the delineation unit to the fact unit involves adding, to the fact unit, the slots "*major*: *CS*" and "*class*: *GRAD*." Thus extended, the fact unit *JOHN* matches our goal unit *JOHN*.

Used in the backward direction on the goal unit, the delineation unit sets up the subgoal unit:

> *JOHN*
>> *self*: (*element-of CS-STUDENTS*)

Since this subgoal unit matches the original fact unit, we again have a proof.

In the *CS*-student example, the goal unit did not contain any variables. Allowing (existential) variables in goals is perfectly straightforward. Suppose we want to find out which individual has graduate standing. A goal unit for this query might be:

> y
>> *class*: *GRAD*

Reasoning in the backward direction, this goal unit can be matched against the delineation unit $x \mid CS\text{-}STUDENTS$ to create the subgoal unit:

> y
>> *self*: (*element-of CS-STUDENTS*)

This subgoal unit, in turn, matches the fact unit *JOHN*, so the answer to our original query can be constructed from the substitution $\{JOHN/y\}$.

Delineations can be represented in the network formalism by sorted variable nodes. The variable is assumed to have universal quantification over the individuals in the sort set. The network representation for the delineation of *CS-STUDENTS*, analogous to the unit representation just discussed, is shown in Figure 9.16.

In addition to representations for a set of objects and characterizations of the properties of every member of a set, we often use the idea of an *abstract individual* in relation to members of the set. For example,

389

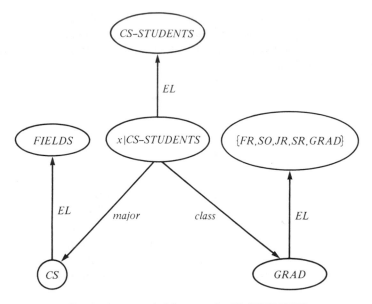

Fig. 9.16 A network delineation for CS-STUDENTS.

consider the net shown in Figure 9.17. This net refers to the set of all autos, describes some properties of each member of the set, and also mentions a particular member, "car 54." Suppose we wanted a representation of the sentence "The auto was invented in 1892." We could easily construct a node representing an "invention situation" with function arcs pointing to the inventor, the thing invented, etc. But to which node would the *thing-invented* arc point? It wasn't car 54 or even the *set* of all autos that was invented in 1892. Just what was invented?

We can answer this question satisfactorily for many purposes by using the idea of an *abstract* auto, denoted by the node *AB-AUTO*. This abstract individual is then related to the rest of the network as shown in Figure 9.18. In that figure, the properties of each member of the set of autos (as expressed by the delineation) are augmented to include the fact that the abstract auto is the abstraction of every member of the set of autos.

Note that the *abstraction-of* function does not have an inverse; the function is many-to-one. In systems that treat a delineation as if it were an individual constant representing a typical set member, it would be possible to have an inverse function of *abstraction-of*, say, *reification-prototype-of*, whose value would be the prototype individual. Since the

390

prototype confers all of its properties on every member of the set, *each* would have the absurd property that it was *the* reification prototype of the abstract individual. Treating prototypes as universally quantified implications instead of as constants avoids this difficulty.

Some constant objects, such as *LAWYER* and *PROGRAMMER*, that were used in our earlier examples are probably best interpreted as abstract individuals. We'll see more examples of abstract individuals in the examples to follow.

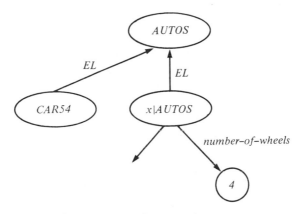

Fig. 9.17 Some information about autos.

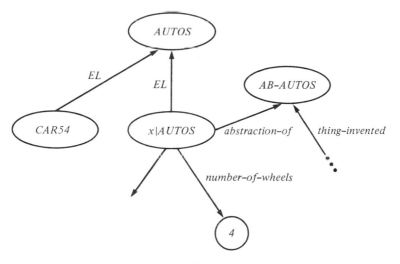

Fig. 9.18 A net with a node denoting an abstract individual.

9.4.2. PROPERTY INHERITANCE

In many applications, the structured objects denoting individuals and sets form a taxonomic hierarchy. A common example is the tree-like taxonomic division of the animals into species, families, orders, etc. The taxonomies used in ordinary reasoning might be somewhat more "convoluted" than those used in formal biology—an individual may be an element of more than one set, for example. Usually, though, useful hierarchies narrow toward a small number of sets at the top and, in any case, the various sets form a partial order under the subset relation.

Consider the hierarchy shown in Figure 9.19. Learning that Clyde is an elephant, we could use the delineations (together with some set theory) to make several forward inferences. Specifically, we could derive that Clyde is gray and wrinkled, that he likes peanuts, that he is warm-blooded, etc. The results of these operations could be used to augment the structured object denoting Clyde. In any given reasoning problem, efficiency considerations demand that we do not derive all of these facts about Clyde explicitly.

Similar efficiency problems arise when delineations in a taxonomic hierarchy are used to reason backward. Suppose that we want to prove that Clyde was gray (when we didn't know this fact explicitly). Using the delineations of Figure 9.19, we might set up several subgoals including showing that Clyde was a shark, a sperm whale, or an elephant. If the facts had included the assertion that Clyde was an elephant, we ought to be able to reason more efficiently, since, then, we should be able at least to avoid subgoals like Clyde being a shark. There is evidence that humans are able to perform these sorts of reasoning tasks rapidly without being overwhelmed by combinatorial considerations.

Some of the forward uses of delineations in taxonomic hierarchies can be efficiently built into the matcher without risking severe combinatorial problems. We describe how this might be done for some simple examples using the network formalism.

In taxonomic hierarchies that narrow toward a small number of sets at the top, there is little harm in building into the matcher itself the ability to apply certain delineations in the forward direction. Consider the problem of trying to find a match for a goal arc a between two fact nodes $N1$ and $N2$. We show this situation in Figure 9.20. If there is a fact arc a between $N1$ and $N2$ (as shown by one of the dashed arcs in Figure 9.20), then we have an immediate match. We could restrict the matcher by permitting it

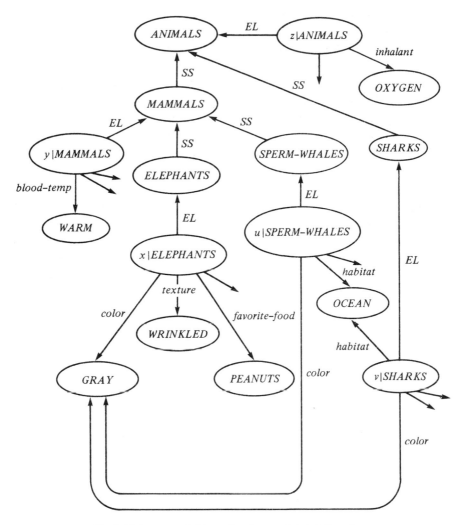

Fig. 9.19 A taxonomic hierarchy of sets and their delineations.

to look only for such immediate matches. If none were found, we could apply production rules, like the delineation shown in Figure 9.20, to solve the problem.

For the example of Figure 9.20, if the matcher could not find an explicit *a* arc in the fact network between *N1* and *N2*, then it would ascend the taxonomic hierarchy from *N1* checking for the presence of *a* arcs to *N2* from delineations of the sets (and supersets) to which *N1*

393

belongs. In Figure 9.20 we show, by dashed arcs, some of the possible *a* arcs that the matcher is permitted to seek. If it can find such an arc, the match is successful. Unless all of the goal arcs can be matched, the matcher terminates with failure.

A system with an extended matcher of this type operates as if an object automatically *inherited* all of the (needed) properties of its sets and supersets. The ease with which properties can be inherited is one of the advantages of using a structured object formalism. As an illustration of this process, let's consider the following examples based on Figure 9.19.

First, suppose we want to prove that Clyde is gray when we know that Clyde is an elephant (but we don't know explicitly that Clyde is gray). This problem is represented in Figure 9.21, where we have included part of the net shown in Figure 9.19. Since there is no *color* arc within the fact net pointing from *CLYDE* to *GRAY*, we cannot obtain an immediate match. So we move up to the *ELEPHANTS* delineation where we do have a *color* arc to *GRAY*. The matcher notes that *CLYDE* inherits this *color* arc and finishes with a successful match.

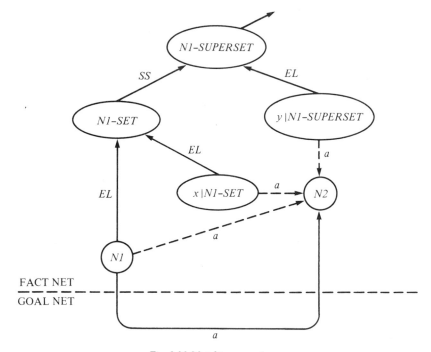

Fig. 9.20 Matching a goal arc.

394

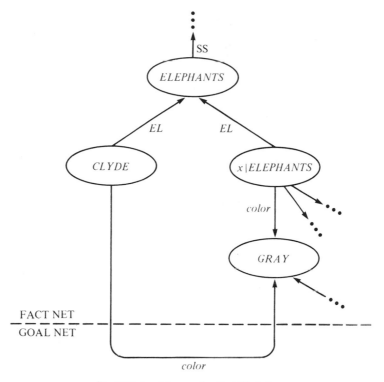

Fig. 9.21 A net for proving that Clyde is gray.

Next, suppose we want to prove that Clyde is warm-blooded when we know only that Clyde is an elephant. Again, we move up the taxonomic hierarchy to the delineation unit for *MAMMALS* where a match is readily determined.

Finally, suppose we want to prove that Clyde breathes oxygen and is gray and warm-blooded, given only that Clyde is a mammal. Ascending the delineation hierarchy picks up a *blood-temp* arc to *WARM* and an *inhalant* arc to *OXYGEN*, but not a complete match. These two properties are added explicitly to *CLYDE* before attempting to prove the goal by rule-based means.

One might also want to build one other important operation into the matcher, namely, an operation in which an inherited Skolem function node must be proved equal to a constant node. Consider the example of Figure 9.22. Our goal there is to show that Henry is a member of the computer science faculty. Using the delineation *x | CS-STUDENTS* in

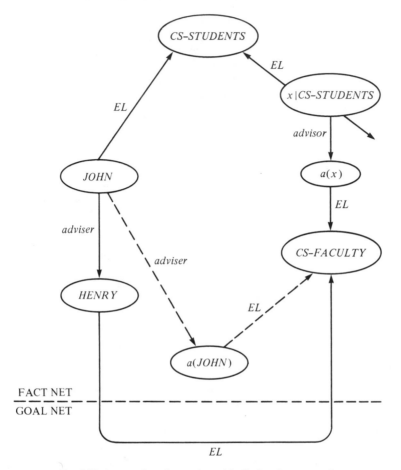

Fig. 9.22 A network with an inheritable Skolem-function node.

the forward direction on *JOHN* creates the structure shown in dashes in Figure 9.22. Now, since the *adviser* arc represents a function, *HENRY* must be equal to *a*(*JOHN*), and our match is complete.

One could use the following scheme for building this sort of reasoning process into the matcher. Using the example of Figure 9.22 as an illustration, we first attempt an immediate match by looking for a fact *EL* arc between *HENRY* and *CS-FACULTY*. Failing to find one, we then look in the taxonomic hierarchy above *HENRY* to see if there is an *EL* arc to be inherited. In our example, we fail again. Next, we look for function arcs pointing to *HENRY* from constant nodes. Suppose we find an arc, *ai*, pointing to *HENRY* from a node, *Ni*. (That is,

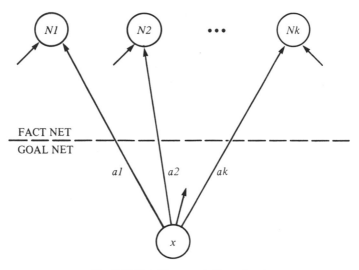

Fig. 9.23 Matching a variable goal node.

$EQ[ai(Ni), HENRY]$.) Then, we look in the taxonomic hierarchy above each such node Ni to see if Ni inherits an ai arc to some Skolem function node that has an *EL* arc directly to *CS-FACULTY*. If we find such an inheritance, our extended matcher succeeds.

Strategies for matching a variable goal node against facts in the database also depend on the structure of the net. In the simplest case, the variable goal node, say, x, is tied to constant fact nodes, $N1, N2, \ldots, Nk$, by arcs labeled $a1, a2, \ldots, ak$, respectively. The situation is depicted in Figure 9.23. The constant nodes $N1, \ldots, Nk$ also have other arcs incident on them. Our attempt to find a match must look back through $a1$ arcs incident on $N1$, $a2$ arcs incident on $N2$, etc. (We assume that our implementation of the network makes it easy to trace through arcs in the "reverse" direction.) Some of these arcs originate from constant nodes and some from delineations.

A good strategy is to look first for a constant node, because the set of possible nodes in the fact net that might match x can be quite large if the delineations are considered. Suppose node Ni has the smallest set of constant nodes sending ai arcs to Ni. We attempt to match x against the nodes in this set and allow the matcher to use delineations in matching the other arcs. In Figure 9.24, we show a simple example. In this case, there is only one constant node, namely, *CLYDE*, having the desired properties. In attempting a match against *CLYDE*, we must next find an *EL* arc between *CLYDE* and *MAMMALS*, and a *blood-temp* arc

397

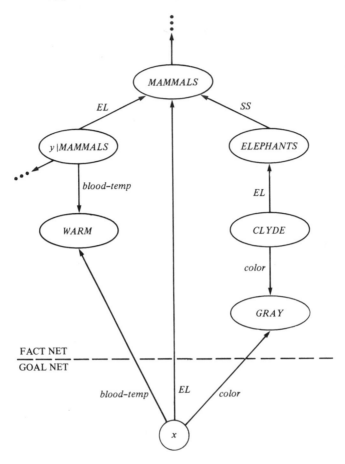

Fig. 9.24 An example with a variable goal node.

between *CLYDE* and *WARM*. The first of these arcs is inferred by a subset chain, and the second is established by inheritance; so the match succeeds.

We can always find at least one constant node to use as a candidate if we allow the matcher to look backward down through *SS* and *EL* chains. Consider, for example, the problem shown in Figure 9.25. In this net, there is no "immediate" constant node to serve as a candidate match, but working down from *MAMMALS* through an *SS* and an *EL* chain puts us at the constant node, *CLYDE*. The rest of the match is easily handled by property inheritance. We can assume that a variable goal node always has

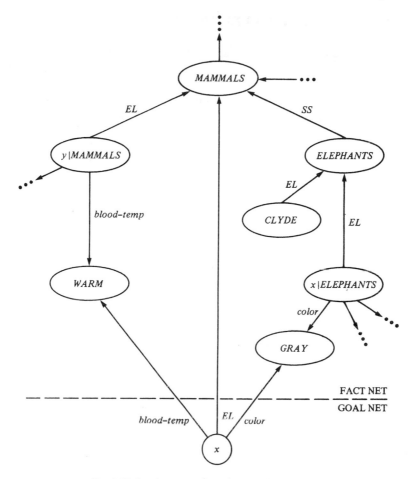

Fig. 9.25 Another example with a variable goal node.

an *EL* (or *SS*) arc pointing to something in the fact net (every entity is at least a member of the universal set).

This matching strategy can be elaborated to deal with cases in which the goal net structure is more complex, where it contains more than one variable node. Each variable node must be properly matched in order for the whole goal structure to be matched. In any case, if no match can be obtained, either delineation rules must be used in the backward direction or other rules must be used to change the fact or the goal structures. We discuss rule use in a later section.

9.4.3. PROCEDURAL ATTACHMENT

In some applications, we can associate computer programs with the slots of delineations. Executing these programs, for properly instantiated arguments, produces slotvalues for instances of the delineation. Suppose, just as a simple example, that we wanted to use a unit-based system to multiply two numbers. One method is to provide such a system with a large set of facts such as:

> *M1*
>> *self* : (*element-of MULTIPLICATIONS*)
>> *multiplicand1* : 1
>> *multiplicand2* : 1
>> *product* : 1

> *M2*
>> *self* : (*element-of MULTIPLICATIONS*)
>> *multiplicand1* : 1
>> *multiplicand2* : 2
>> *product* : 2

> .

> .

> .

> etc.

These units are a way of encoding a multiplication table. When we want to know the product of two numbers, 3 and 6, we query the system with the goal unit:

> *z*
>> *multiplicand1* : 3
>> *multiplicand2* : 6
>> *product* : *x*

This goal would match some stored fact unit having a slot "*product* : 18."

400

Rather than store all the required facts explicitly, we could provide a computer program, say, **TIMES** and "attach" it to the delineation of *MULTIPLICATIONS*, thus:

$x \mid MULTIPLICATIONS$
    multiplicand1 : (*element-of NUMERALS*)
    multiplicand2 : (*element-of NUMERALS*)
    product : **TIMES**[*multiplicand1* (x), *multiplicand2* (x)]

Delineation units with attached procedures are used just as ordinary delineation units. Procedures occurring in substitutions are executed as soon as their instantiations permit. To illustrate how all of this might work, suppose again that we want to find the product of 3 and 6. First, we introduce as a fact unit the existence of the multiplication situation for which we want an answer:

M
    self : (*element-of MULTIPLICATIONS*)
    multiplicand1 : 3
    multiplicand2 : 6

Next, we pose the goal unit:

M
    product : y

When we attempt a match between goal M and fact M, the matcher uses the delineation for multiplications to allow fact M to inherit the "*product*" slot. This process produces the substitution {**TIMES**(3,6)/y}. The correct answer is then obtained by executing the **TIMES** program.

A completely analogous example could have been given using the network formalism.

9.4.4. UNIT RULES

Some implicational statements are not easily interpreted as expressing information solely about members of a set. For these, we introduce the concept of a *unit rule* having an *antecedent* and a *consequent*. The antecedent (*ANTE*) and consequent (*CONSE*) are lists of units (possibly containing variables). When a unit rule is used in the forward direction, if *all* of the units in the *ANTE* (regarded as goal units) are matched by fact units, then the units in the *CONSE* (properly instantiated) can be added to the set of fact units. (When *ANTE* units are regarded as goals, their variables are, of course, existential.) If some of the added fact units already exist, the addition operation need only involve adding those properties mentioned in the *CONSE* units. This usage is consistent with how implications were used in the rule-based deduction systems of chapter 6.

When a unit rule is used in the backward direction against a single goal unit, one of the *CONSE* units (regarded as a fact unit) must match the goal unit. (When *CONSE* units are regarded as facts, their variables are universal.) If the match succeeds, the units in the *ANTE* (properly instantiated) are set up as subgoal units. A backward unit rule applied to a (conjunctive) set of goal units is a slightly more complex operation; the process is analogous to the methods discussed in chapter 6 involving AND/OR graphs and substitution consistency tests. For simplicity of explanation in this chapter, we confine ourselves to examples that do not require these added mechanisms.

We'll next show some simple examples of the use of unit rules. The reader might like to refer to our information retrieval example using personnel data in chapter 6. There we had the rule:

$$R1 : MANAGER(x,y) \Rightarrow WORKS\text{-}IN(x,y)$$

Expressed in the predicate calculus system being used in this part of the book, this rule becomes:

$$\{ EL(x, DEPARTMENTS) \wedge EQ[manager(x), y]\}$$
$$\Rightarrow EQ[works\text{-}in(y), x]$$

Using our syntax for unit rules, we would express this rule as follows:

R1

ANTE: *x*

        self: (*element-of DEPARTMENTS*)
        manager: *y*

$CONSE: y$

$works\text{-}in: x$

Another rule used in our personnel problem example was:

$R2: [WORKS\text{-}IN(x,y) \land MANAGER(x,z)] \Rightarrow BOSS\text{-}OF(y,z)$

Restated, this piece of information might be represented as:

$\{ EQ[works\text{-}in(y),x] \land EQ[manager(x),z]\}$
$\quad \Rightarrow EQ[boss\text{-}of(y),z]$

As a unit rule, we might represent it as follows:

$R2$

$ANTE: y$

$works\text{-}in: x$

x

$manager: z$

$CONSE: y$

$boss\text{-}of: z$

A variety of implications can be represented by unit rules of this kind. These rules, in turn, can be used as production rules for manipulating fact and goal units in deduction systems.

Earlier, we spoke of the fact that there are often many different ways of representing the same knowledge. Complex systems might not limit themselves to one alternative; thus there is a need to be able to translate freely among them. Consider the example in Figure 9.12. There we showed two alternatives for representing "John Jones is married to Sally Jones." The equivalence between these forms might be represented as follows:

$EQ[y, wife\text{-}of(x)] \equiv (\exists z)\{ EL(z, MARRIAGE\text{-}EVENTS)$
$\quad \land EQ[x, male(z)] \land EQ[y, female(z)]\}$

(Here, we use a wff of the form $W1 \equiv W2$ as an abbreviation for $[W1 \Rightarrow W2] \land [W2 \Rightarrow W1]$.) Using the "left-to-right" implication, we

403

have an existential variable within the scope of two universals. Skole-mizing yields:

$$EQ[y, wife\text{-}of(x)] \Rightarrow \{ EL[\mathrm{m}(x,y), MARRIAGE\text{-}EVENTS]$$
$$\wedge\ EQ[x, male(m(x,y))]$$
$$\wedge\ EQ[y, female(m(x,y))]\}$$

We represent this implication as the following unit rule:

R-M

ANTE: x
        wife-of: y

CONSE: m(x,y)
        self: (*element-of MARRIAGE-EVENTS*)
        male: x
        female: y

To use this rule in the forward direction, we match the *ANTE* to a fact unit and then create a new constant unit corresponding to the instantiated unit in the *CONSE*.

The simplicity of the unit syntax makes representing implications that are much more complex than those we have used in our examples awkward. Even with this limitation, the formalism that has been developed so far is quite useful for a wide variety of problems.

9.4.5. NET RULES

Earlier we mentioned the use of enclosures to represent network implications. These implications can be used as forward or backward rules in semantic network-based production systems. For example, the implication:

$$\{ EL(x, DEPARTMENTS) \wedge EQ[manager(x), y] \}$$
$$\Rightarrow EQ[works\text{-}in(y), x]$$

might be represented by the network structure shown in Figure 9.26.

To use a network implication as a forward rule, the *ANTE* structure (regarded as a goal) must match existing network fact structures. The

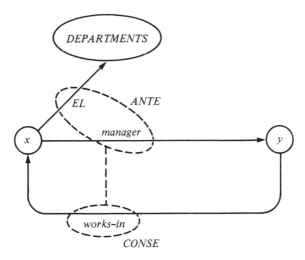

Fig. 9.26 Representing an implication.

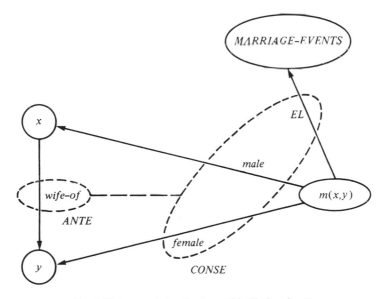

Fig. 9.27 A network implication with a Skolem function.

CONSE structure (appropriately instantiated) can then be added to the fact network. To use a network implication as a backward rule, the *CONSE* structure (regarded as a fact) must match the goal structure. Then, the *ANTE* structure (appropriately instantiated) is the subgoal produced by the rule application. Again, the situation is more complex (involving AND/OR graphs and substitution consistency testing) when the goal structure is first broken into component structures, and when these are matched individually by rule *CONSE* structures.

As a more complex example we show, in Figure 9.27, the network version of an implication used earlier:

$$EQ[y, wife\text{-}of(x)] \Rightarrow$$
$$\{ EL[m(x,y), MARRIAGE\text{-}EVENTS]$$
$$\wedge EQ[x, male(m(x,y))]$$
$$\wedge EQ[y, female(m(x,y))]\}$$

The node labeled $m(x,y)$ is a Skolem function node. Every forward application of the rule in Figure 9.27 creates a newly instantiated $m(x,y)$ node.

9.4.6. APPENDING ADVICE TO DELINEATIONS

In order to minimize combinatorial difficulties, rule applications must be guided by an intelligent control strategy. One way to specify useful control information is to add advice about rule applications to delineations. We mention two forms for such advice: the "to-fill" form, and the "when-filled" form. The former gives advice about which rules should be used in the backward direction when attempting to match existential variables in goals. The latter gives advice about which rules should be used in the forward direction to create new fact units.

As an illustration of the use of such advice, consider the rules *R1* and *R2* used above in our personnel data example. We repeat these rules here for convenience:

R1

ANTE: *x*

> *self*: (*element-of DEPARTMENTS*)
> *manager*: *y*

CONSE: *y*

      works-in : *x*

R2

ANTE: *y*

      works-in : *x*

    x

      manager : *z*

CONSE: *y*

      boss-of : *z*

The following delineations contain advice about when to use these rules:

> *u* | *EMPLOYEES*
>   *boss-of* : (*element-of EMPLOYEES*)
>   < *to-fill* : *R2* >
>   *works-in* : (*element-of DEPARTMENTS*)

> *r* | *DEPARTMENTS*
>   *manager* : (*element-of EMPLOYEES*)
>   < *when-filled* : *R1* >

The notation < *to-fill* : *R2* > in *u* | *EMPLOYEES* states that whenever a goal has a *boss-of* slotvalue that is a variable, rule *R2* should be used in the backward direction (when there is no direct match against a fact unit). The notation < *when-filled* : *R1* > in *r* | *DEPARTMENTS* states that whenever a fact unit whose *self* slot contains "(*element-of DEPART-MENTS*)" and whose *manager* slot has a value, rule *R1* should be used.

Suppose we have the fact units:

> *JOE-SMITH*
>   *self*: (*element-of EMPLOYEES*)
>   *works-in*: *P-D*

P-D
    self: (*element-of DEPARTMENTS*)
    manager: *JOHN-JONES*

When the second of these is asserted, a check of the delineation *r*|*DEPARTMENTS* indicates that rule *R1* should be applied in the forward direction. This application produces the fact unit:

JOHN-JONES
    works-in: *P-D*

Suppose we want to ask "Who is Joe Smith's boss?" This query is represented by the goal unit:

JOE-SMITH
    boss-of: *u*

An attempt at a direct match against fact unit *JOE-SMITH* fails; but one of the delineations, containing the *boss-of* slot, advises the system to use rule *R2* in the backward direction; and doing so produces the subgoal units:

JOE-SMITH
    works-in: *x*

x
    manager: *u*

The first of these can be matched against fact *JOE-SMITH*, to produce the substitution { *P-D/x* }. The instantiated second subgoal unit can then be matched against fact *P-D*, to produce the substitution { *JOHN-JONES/u* }, which contains the answer to our original query.

9.5. DEFAULTS AND CONTRADICTORY INFORMATION

Many descriptive statements of the form "All *x*s have property *P*" must be regarded as only approximately true. Perhaps most *x*s do have property *P*, but typically we will come across exceptions. Examples of these kinds of exceptions abound: All birds can fly (except ostriches); all insects have six legs (except juveniles like caterpillars); all lemons are yellow (except unripe green ones or mutant orange ones); etc. It appears that many general synthetic (as opposed to analytic or definitional) statements that we might make about the world are incorrect unless qualified. Furthermore these qualifications probably are so numerous that the formalism would become unmanageable if we attempted to include them all explicitly. Is there a way around this difficulty that would still preserve the simplicity of a predicate-calculus language?

One approach to preserving simplicity is to allow *implicit* exceptions to the domain of universal quantification in certain implicational statements. Thus, the statement "All elephants are gray" might initially be given without listing any exceptions. Such a statement would allow us to deduce that Clyde is gray when we learn that Clyde is an elephant. Later, if we learn that Clyde is actually white, we must retract our deduction about his grayness and change the universal statement about elephants so that it excludes Clyde. After making this change, it is no longer possible to deduce erroneous conclusions about Clyde's color.

The way in which the matcher uses property inheritance provides an automatic mechanism for dealing with exceptions like Clyde's being white. The matcher uses inheritance to deduce a property of an object from a delineation of its class only if specific information about the property of that object is lacking. Suppose, for example, that we want to know the color of Clyde. Such a query might be stated as the following goal unit:

> *CLYDE*
>   *color* : *x*

To answer this query, we first attempt a direct match with a fact unit. Suppose we have a fact unit describing Clyde:

> *CLYDE*
>   *self* : (*element-of ELEPHANTS*)
>   *color* : *WHITE*

In this case, the match substitution is { *WHITE*/*x* }, and *WHITE* is our answer.

409

If our fact unit states only that Clyde is an elephant, the matcher automatically uses the delineation of *ELEPHANTS* to answer our query. Such a delineation might be as follows:

$y\,|\,ELEPHANTS$
  color: *GRAY*

This scheme, of countermanding general information by conflicting specific information, can be extended to several hierarchical levels. For example, we might have the following delineation for *MAMMALS*:

$u\,|\,MAMMALS$
  texture: *FUZZY*

Now, in order to avoid deducing that elephants are fuzzy, we need only include with the *ELEPHANTS* delineation a property such as "*texture*: *WRINKLED*." Clyde, however, may be a fuzzy elephant, and this property can be added to the unit *CLYDE* to override the *ELEPHANTS* delineation. (The hierarchy may contain several such property reversals.)

For such a scheme to work, the use of delineations to deduce properties needs always to proceed from the most specific to the more general. With this built-in ordering on matching and retrieval processes, information at the more specific levels protects the system from making possibly contradictory deductions based on higher level delineations. It is as if the universal quantifiers of delineations specifically exclude, from their domains, all of the more specific objects that would contradict the delineation.

Schemes of this sort do have certain problems, however. Suppose, for example, that an object in the taxonomic hierarchy belongs to two different sets and that the delineations of these sets are contradictory. We show a network example in Figure 9.28. In this figure, we do not show an explicit *color* arc for *CLYDE*, but *CLYDE* inherits contradictory color values [assuming that $\sim EQ(GRAY, WHITE)$]. A possible way to deal with this problem is to indicate something about the *quality* of each arc or slot in a delineation. In our example, if the *color* arc in the *ALBINOS* delineation were to dominate the *color* arc in the *ELEPHANTS* delineation, then we would always attempt to inherit the *color* value from the *ALBINOS* delineation first.

410

We can indicate that the arc or slot of a delineation is of low priority by marking it as a *default*. Default delineations can be used only if there is no other way to derive the needed information. In general, though, we need an ordering on the default markers. If both of the delineations in Figure 9.28 were marked simply as defaults, for example, we would be at an impasse: We could prove that Clyde was gray only if we could not prove that he was any other color. However, we could prove that he was another color, namely, white, if we could not prove that he was any other color. And so on.

We must also be careful when we use default delineations as forward rule applications, because then we risk adding objects to the fact database that contradict existing or subsequent specific facts. The forward use of delineations must be coupled with "truth maintenance" techniques to ensure that contradictory facts (and facts that might be derived from them) are either purged or otherwise inactivated.

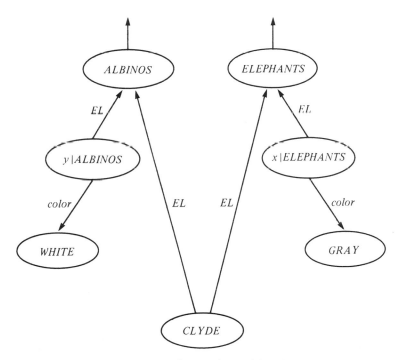

Fig. 9.28 A net with contradictory delineations.

9.6. BIBLIOGRAPHICAL AND HISTORICAL REMARKS

Structured object representations are related to frames (no relation to the frame problem) proposed by Minsky (1975); *scripts* proposed by Schank and Abelson (1977); and beta-structures proposed by Moore and Newell (1973). Bobrow et al. (1977) implemented a system called GUS which used a frame-like representation. Roberts and Goldstein (1977) implemented a simple frame language called FRL, and Goldstein and Roberts (1979) describe a system for automatic scheduling written in FRL. Stefik (1979) and Friedland (1979) describe a frame-based representation used by a computer system for planning experiments in molecular genetics.

KRL-*0* and KRL-*1* are frame-based knowledge representation languages developed by Bobrow and Winograd (1977a). [See also Bobrow and Winograd (1977b), Lehnert and Wilks (1979), and Bobrow and Winograd (1979) for discussion and criticisms of KRL.] Winograd (1975) presents a readable discussion of some of the advantages of frame-based representations.

Hayes (1977, 1979) discusses the relationships between predicate logic and frame-based representations. Our treatment of structured objects in this chapter, stressing relationships with the predicate calculus, leans toward Hayes' point of view. Converting to binary predicates is discussed by Deliyanni and Kowalski (1979c).

Work on semantic networks stems from many sources. In cognitive psychology, Quillian (1968), Anderson and Bower (1973), and Rumelhart and Norman (1975) have all proposed memory models based on networks. In computer science, Raphael's (1968) SIR system is based on networks of property lists; Winston (1975) used networks for representing and learning information about configurations of blocks; and Simmons (1973) discusses the uses of networks in natural language processing. Woods (1975) discusses some of the logical inadequacies of early semantic networks. It is interesting that Frege's (1879) original symbolism for the predicate calculus involved two-dimensional diagrams.

Several semantic network "languages" have now been proposed that have the full expressive power of predicate calculus. Shapiro's (1979a)

412

SNePS system, Hendrix's (1975b, 1979) *partitioned semantic network* formalism and Schubert's (1976) [see also Schubert, Goebel and Cercone (1979)] network formalism are examples. Papers in the volume edited by Findler (1979) describe several different types of semantic networks. The semantic network formalism described in this chapter seems to capture the main ideas of those that use binary predicates.

Example applications of semantic networks include natural language processing [Walker (1978, Section 3)], database management [Mylopoulos et al. (1975)], and computer representation of geological (ore-prospecting) knowledge [Duda et al. (1978a)].

We base much of our discussion about matching network goal structures against network fact structures on a matcher developed by Fikes and Hendrix (1977) and, partially, on ideas of Moore (1975a). Various mechanisms for inheritance of properties in unit systems or in net formalisms have been suggested as approaches to what some have called the *symbol-mapping problem*. This problem is discussed at length in two issues of the SIGART newsletter. [See McDermott (1975a,b), Bundy and Stone (1975), Fahlman (1975), and Moore (1975b).] Fahlman (1979) recommends using special-purpose hardware to solve the set intersection problems required to perform property inheritance efficiently.

Representing and using default information is discussed by Bobrow and Winograd (1977a) and by Reiter (1978). Attempts to formalize inferences of the form *assume X unless ~X can be proved* have led to *non-monotonic* logics. McDermott and Doyle (1980) discuss the history of these attempts, propose a specific formalism of their own, and prove its soundness and completeness. "Maintaining" databases by purging or modifying derived expressions, as appropriate, in response to changes in the truth values of primitive expressions, is discussed by Doyle (1979). Stallman and Sussman's (1977) system for reasoning about circuits uses a "truth-maintenance" scheme to make backtracking more efficient.

Other complex representational schemes, related to those discussed in this chapter, have been proposed by Martin (1978), Schank and Abelson (1977), Srinivasan (1977), and Sridharan (1978).

413

EXERCISES

9.1 Represent the situation of Figure 7.1 as a semantic network and represent the STRIPS rule **pickup**(x) as a production rule for changing networks. Explain how the rule **pickup**(B) is tested for applicability and how it changes the network representation of Figure 7.1.

9.2 The predicate $D(x,y)$ is intended to mean that sets x and y have an empty intersection. Explain how this predicate might be used to label arcs in a semantic network. Illustrate by an example. Can you think of any other useful arc predicates?

9.3 Represent the following sentences as semantic network delineations:

> (a) All men are mortal.

> (b) Every cloud has a silver lining.

> (c) All roads lead to Rome.

> (d) All branch managers of G-TEK
> participate in a profit-sharing plan.

> (e) All blocks that are on top of blocks that
> have been moved have also been moved.

9.4 Use *EL* and *SS* predicates to rewrite each of the following wffs as a binary-predicate wff. Rewrite them also as sets of units and as semantic networks.

> (a) $[ON(C,A) \wedge ONTABLE(A) \wedge ONTABLE(B)$
> $\wedge HANDEMPTY \wedge CLEAR(B) \wedge CLEAR(C)]$
> (b) $[DOG(FIDO) \wedge \sim BARKS(FIDO)$
> $\wedge WAGS\text{-}TAIL(FIDO) \wedge MEOWS(MYRTLE)]$
> (c) $(\forall x)HOLDS[clear(x), do[trans(x,y,z),s]]$

9.5 Represent the major ideas about search techniques in a semantic network taxonomic hierarchy. (Search techniques might first be divided into uninformed ones and heuristic ones, for example.) Include a delineation for each set represented in your network.

PROSPECTUS

We have seen in this book that generalized production systems (especially those that process expressions in the first-order predicate calculus) play a fundamental role in Artificial Intelligence. The organization and control of AI production systems and the ways in which these systems are used to solve several varieties of problems have been discussed in some detail. Lest the reader imagine that all of these details—the formalisms and the mathematical and empirical results—constitute an already mature engineering discipline routinely supporting extensive applications, we attempt here a perspective on the entire AI enterprise and point out several areas where further research is needed. In fact, we might say that our present knowledge of the mechanisms of intelligence consists of small islands in a large ocean of speculation, hope, and ignorance.

The viewpoint presented in this book is just one window on the core ideas of AI. The specialist will also want to be familiar with AI programming languages such as LISP and AI programming techniques. We have not attempted to discuss these topics in this book, but there are other books that concentrate on just these subjects [see Winston (1977); Shapiro (1979); and Charniak, Riesbeck, and McDermott (1979)]. Serious students of AI will also want to be familiar with a variety of large-scale AI applications. We have cited many of these in the bibliographical remarks sections of this book.

In this prospectus, we give brief descriptions of problem areas that seem to be very important for future progress in AI. Some work has already been done on most of these problems, but results are typically tentative, controversial, or limited. We organize these problems into three main categories. The first category concerns novel AI system architectures and the challenges of parallel and distributed processing. The second category deals with the problems of knowledge acquisition and learning. Last, there are the problems concerned with the adequacy of AI processes and representational formalisms for dealing with topics such as knowledge, goals, beliefs, plans, and self-reference.

417

10.1. AI SYSTEM ARCHITECTURES

10.1.1. MEMORY ORGANIZATION

One of the most important design questions facing the implementer of AI systems concerns how to structure the knowledge base of facts and rules so that appropriate items can be efficiently accessed. Several techniques have been suggested. The QA3 resolution theorem-proving system [Green (1969b)] partitioned its list of clauses into an active list and a secondary storage list. Clauses were brought from the secondary list into the active list only if no resolutions were possible within the active list. The PLANNER-like AI languages generally had special methods for storing and accessing expressions. McDermott (1975c) describes the special indexing features used by many of these languages. The discrimination net used by QA4 [Rulifson, Derksen, and Waldinger (1972)] is an example of such a feature.

Probably the most important aspect of the frame-like representations (unit systems and semantic networks) is their built-in mechanisms for indexing. Indeed, the authors of KRL [Bobrow and Winograd (1977a)] speak specifically of permitting system designers to organize memory into those *chunks* that are most appropriate for the specific task at hand. We can expect that work will continue along these lines as systems are developed that must use the equivalent of hundreds of thousands of facts and rules.

10.1.2. PARALLEL AND DISTRIBUTED SYSTEMS

Our discussion of AI production systems was based on the tacit assumption of a single serial processor that applied one rule at a time to a database. Yet, there are several ways in which our production systems could be extended to utilize parallel processing. First, some of the primitive operations of the system could be performed by parallel hardware. For example, Fahlman (1979) has suggested a parallel system for performing the set intersections needed for efficient property inheritance computations.

Second, in tentative control regimes, a system capable of parallel processing could apply several rules simultaneously rather than backtracking or developing a search tree one node at a time. If the number of successors to be generated exceeds the number of parallel rule-application modules, the control system must attempt to apportion the available rule-application modules as efficiently as possible.

Third, in decomposable production systems, parallel processors could be assigned to each component database, and these processors (and their descendants) could work independently until all databases were processed to termination. These three methods of using parallelism do not alter the basic production-system paradigm for AI systems presented in this book; they merely involve *implementing* this paradigm with parallel processing.

A third use of parallelism involves an expansion of the ideas presented here. One could imagine a large community of more-or-less independent systems. (Each of these systems could be a production system or a system of some different style, with internal processes either serial or parallel.) The systems communicate among themselves in order to solve problems cooperatively. If each of the component systems is relatively simple, the communication protocols and the procedures for control and cooperation must be specified in rather precise detail by the designer of the community. The augmented Petri nets of Zisman (1978) and the *actor* formalism of Hewitt (1977) seem to be examples of this type. [See also Hewitt and Baker (1977) and Kornfeld (1979).] On the other hand, if each of the systems is itself a complex AI system, then the situation is analogous to a society of humans or other higher animals who must plan their own communication and cooperation strategies. We have little experience with complexes of interacting AI systems, but the work of Lesser and Erman (1979), Lesser and Corkill (1979), and of Corkill (1979) are steps in that direction. Related work by Smith (1978, 1979) also involves networks of cooperating problem-solving components. Crane (1978) treats analogies between parallel computer systems and human societies in a provocative manner.

10.2. KNOWLEDGE ACQUISITION

Formalizing knowledge and implementing knowledge bases are major tasks in the construction of large AI systems. The hundreds of rules and thousands of facts required by many of these systems are generally obtained by interviewing experts in the domain of application. Representing expert knowledge as facts or rules (or as expressions in any other

419

formalism) is typically a tedious and time-consuming process. Techniques for automating this knowledge acquisition process would constitute a major advance in AI technology.

We shall briefly discuss three ways in which knowledge acquisition might be automated. First, special editing systems might be built that allow persons who possess expert knowledge about the domain of application (but who are not themselves computer programmers) to interact directly with the knowledge bases of AI systems. Second, advances in natural language processing techniques will allow humans to instruct and teach computer systems through ordinary conversations (augmented, perhaps, with diagrams and other nontextual material). Third, AI systems might learn important knowledge directly from their experiences in their problem domains.

Virtually all large AI systems must have a knowledge base editing system of some sort to facilitate the processes of adding, deleting, and changing facts and rules as the systems evolve. Davis (1976) designed a system called TEIRESIAS that allowed physicians to interact directly with the knowledge base of the MYCIN medical diagnosis system. Friedland (1979) reports on a representation system that contains expert knowledge about molecular genetics; a key feature of this system is its family of editors for interacting with the knowledge base. Duda et al. (1979) describes a knowledge-base editing system for the PROSPECTOR system. As systems of these kinds become capable of conversing with their designers in natural language, knowledge entry and modification processes will become much more efficient. One must remember, however, that computer systems will be incapable of truly flexible dialogues about representations and the concepts to be used in these representations until designers are able to give these systems useful meta-knowledge about representations themselves. Unfortunately, we do not even have a very clear outline yet of a general theory of knowledge representation.

It has often been hoped that the knowledge acquisition task could be eased somewhat by automatic learning mechanisms built into AI systems. Humans and other animals seem to have impressive capacities for learning from experience. Indeed, some early work in AI was based on the strategy of constructing intelligent machines that could learn how to perform tasks.

There are, of course, several varieties of learning. Almost any change to an AI system, such as the entry of a single new fact, the addition of a new component to a control strategy, or a profound reorganization of system architecture, might be called an instance of learning. Furthermore, these changes might be caused either directly by a programmer (design changes) or indirectly through conversation with a human or other system (teaching) or through response to experience in an environment (adaptive learning). Evolutionary design changes already play an important role in the development of AI systems. Some work has also been done on developing techniques for teaching AI systems. Strategies for adaptive learning, however, have so far met with only limited success. It can be expected that all of these varieties of learning will be important in future AI systems. The subject is an important area for AI research.

Early work in adaptive learning concentrated on systems for pattern classification [Nilsson (1965)] and for game playing [Samuel (1959, 1967)]. This work involved automatic adjustment of the parameters of simple classification and evaluation functions. Winston (1975) developed a system that could learn reasonably complex predicates for category membership; as with many learning systems, efficiency depended strongly on appropriately sequenced experiences. Mitchell (1979) and Dietterich and Michalski (1979) give good discussions of their own and other approaches to the problem of *concept learning* and *induction*.

Some efforts have also been made to save the results of AI computations (such as proofs of theorems and robot plans) in a form that permits their use in later problems. For example, Fikes, Hart, and Nilsson (1972b) proposed a method for generalizing and saving triangle tables so that they could be used as macro-operators in the construction of more complex plans.

One of the most powerful ways of using learned or remembered material involves the ability to recognize *analogies* between current problems and those previously encountered. An early program by Evans (1968) was able to solve geometric analogy problems of the sort found in standard intelligence tests. Kling (1971) used an analogy-based method to improve the efficiency of a theorem-proving system. Ulrich and Moll (1977) describe a system that uses analogies in program synthesis. Winston (1979) describes a theory (accompanied by a program) about the use of analogy in learning, and McDermott (1979) discusses how a program might learn analogies.

A system described by Vere (1978) is able to learn STRIPS-like rules by observing state descriptions before and after actions that modify them.

Buchanan and Mitchell (1978) describe a process for learning the production rules used by the DENDRAL chemical-structure computing system. A report by Soloway (1978) describes a system that learns some of the rules of baseball by observing the (simulated) actions of players.

Last, we might mention the AM system of Lenat (1976) that uses a stock of simple, primitive concepts in mathematics and discovers concepts (such as prime numbers).

10.3. REPRESENTATIONAL FORMALISMS

The example problems that we have considered in this book demonstrate that the first-order predicate calculus can be used to represent much of the knowledge needed by AI systems. There are varieties of knowledge, however, that humans routinely use in solving problems and in interacting with other humans that present certain difficulties for first-order logic in particular and for AI systems in general. Examples include knowledge that is uncertain or indefinite in various ways, commonsense knowledge about cause and effect, knowledge about plans and processes, knowledge about the beliefs, knowledge, and goals of ourselves and others, and knowledge about knowledge. McCarthy (1977) discusses these and other *epistemological problems* of AI.

Some workers have concluded that logical formalisms are fundamentally inadequate to deal with these sorts of concepts and that some radically different representational schemes will have to be invented [see, for example, Winograd (1980b)]. Citing previous successes of formal methods, others maintain that certain augmentations of first-order logic, or suitably complex theories represented in first-order logic, or perhaps more complex logical formalisms will ultimately prove adequate to capture the knowledge and processes used in human-like reasoning.

10.3.1. COMMONSENSE REASONING

Many of the existing ideas about AI techniques have been refined on "toy" problems, such as problems in the "blocks world," in which the necessary knowledge is reasonably easy to formalize. AI applications in more difficult domains such as medicine, geology, and chemistry require extensive effort devoted to formalizing the appropriate knowledge. Hayes (1978a) and others have argued that AI researchers should now begin an attempt to formalize fundamental "commonsense knowledge about the everyday physical world: about objects; shape; space; movement; substances (solids and liquids); time, etc." Hayes (1978b) has begun this task with an essay about the formalization of the properties of liquids. Kuipers (1978,1979) describes a system for modeling commonsense knowledge of space.

Formalizing commonsense physics must be distinguished from the rather precise mathematical models of the physics of solids, liquids and gases. The latter are probably too cumbersome to support commonsense reasoning about physical events. (McCarthy argues, for example, that people most likely do not—even unconsciously—perform complex hydrodynamic simulation computations in order to decide whether or not to move in order to avoid getting burned by a spilled cup of hot coffee.)

Formalizing commonsense physics is important because many applications require reasoning about space, materials, time, etc. Also, much of the content of natural language expressions is about the physical world; certainly many metaphors have a physical basis. Indeed, in order to make full use of analogical reasoning, AI systems will need a thorough, even if somewhat inexact, understanding of simple physics.

Much commonsense reasoning (and even technical reasoning) is inexact in the sense that the conclusions and the facts and rules on which it is based are only approximately true. Yet, people are able to use uncertain facts and rules to arrive at useful conclusions about everyday subjects or about specialized subjects such as medicine. A basic characteristic of such approximate reasoning seems to be that a conclusion carries more conviction if it is independently supported by two or more separate arguments.

We have previously cited the work of Shortliffe (1976) on MYCIN and of Duda, Hart, and Nilsson (1976) on PROSPECTOR and referred to their related methods for dealing with uncertain rules and facts. Their techniques have various shortcomings, however, especially when the facts and rules are not independent; furthermore, it is not clear that the MYCIN/PROSPECTOR methods can easily be extended to rules and facts containing quantified variables.

423

Collins (1978) stresses the importance of meta-knowledge in plausible reasoning. (We discuss the subject of meta-knowledge below.) Zadeh (1979) invokes the ideas of *fuzzy sets* to deal with problems of approximate reasoning. The work on default reasoning and non-monotonic logic, cited at the end of chapter 9, offers additional approaches to plausible reasoning.

Another important component of commonsense reasoning is the ability to reason about actions, processes and plans. To do so, we first need ways of representing these concepts. In the bibliographic remarks sections of chapters 7 and 8, we cited several sources relevant to the problem of modeling actions and plans. In addition to these, we might mention the work of Moore (1979) who combines a technique for reasoning about actions with one for reasoning about knowledge (see below). The interaction between action and knowledge has not been discussed in this book (and, indeed, has not yet been adequately explored in AI). Yet, this interaction is quite fundamental because actions typically change the state of knowledge of the actor, and because knowledge about the world is necessary in order to perform actions.

Hendrix (1975a; 1979, pp. 76ff) discusses the use of semantic networks for representing processes. Grosz (1977) and Robinson (1978) use structures similar to procedural nets [Sacerdoti (1977)] to help interpret natural language statements occurring in a dialogue with a user who is participating in a process. Schank and Abelson (1977) propose structures for representing processes and plans for use in natural language understanding applications. Schmidt, Sridharan, and Goodson (1978) propose techniques for recognizing plans and goals of actors from their actions. All of these efforts are contributing to our ability to formalize—and thus ultimately to build systems that can reason about—plans, actions, and processes.

10.3.2. REPRESENTING PROPOSITIONAL ATTITUDES

Certain verbs, such as *know, believe, want,* and *fear,* can be used to express a relation between an *agent* and a *proposition,* as illustrated by the following examples:

> Sam knows that *Pete is a lawyer.*
> Sam doesn't believe that *John is a doctor.*
> Pete wants it to rain. (Or, Pete wants that *it be raining.*)
> John fears that Sam believes that *the morning star is not Venus.*

The italicized portions of these sentences are propositions, and the relations *know*, *believe*, etc., refer to *attitudes* of agents toward these propositions. Thus, *know*, *believe*, etc., are called *propositional attitudes*. A logical formalism for expressing propositional attitudes must have a way of expressing the appropriate relations between agents and attitudes.

It is well known that there are several difficulties in developing such a logical formalism. One difficulty is the problem of *referential transparency*. From the statements *John believes Santa Claus brought him presents at Christmas* and *John's father is Santa Claus*, we would not want to be able to deduce the statement *John believes John's father brought him presents at Christmas*. These problems have been discussed by logicians for several years, and various solutions have been proposed [see, for example, the essays in Linsky (1971)].

Moore (1977, 1979) discusses the problems of formalizing propositional attitudes for AI applications. He points out several difficulties with straightforward approaches and shows how a *modal logic* with a *possible worlds semantics* can be used to overcome these difficulties for the attitude *know*. He then proceeds to show how this approach can be embedded in first order logic so that the usual sorts of AI theorem-proving systems can be used to reason about knowledge. (As we mentioned earlier, Moore also links his logic of knowledge with a logic of actions.)

Several other approaches have also been suggested. McCarthy (1979) proposes that *concepts* of domain entities be added to the domain of discourse and shows how a first-order formulation involving these concepts avoids some of the standard difficulties. Creary (1979) extends this notion. Elschlager (1979) considers the problem of consistency of knowledge statements in formulations that treat concepts as domain entities.

Although formalizations for propositional attitudes have largely been the concern of logicians, the problem is fundamental to future advances in AI. Natural language communication between humans seems to depend on the ability of the participants to make inferences about each others' beliefs, and we should expect that natural language understanding systems will require similar abilities. Also, when two or more AI systems cooperate to solve problems, they will need to be able to reason about each others' goals, knowledge, and beliefs. Cohen (1978) discusses how a system can plan to affect the state of knowledge of another system by *speech acts*. Much more work along these lines needs to be done.

10.3.3. META-KNOWLEDGE

A good solution to the problem of reasoning about the knowledge of others ought also to confer the ability to reason about one's own knowledge. We would like to be able to build systems that know or can deduce whether or not they know facts and rules about certain subjects without having to scan their large knowledge bases searching for these items. We would also like systems to have knowledge about when and how to use other knowledge. As mentioned in the bibliographic remarks section of chapter 6, various researchers have suggested that systems containing meta-rules be used to control production systems.

Collins (1978) has suggested that meta-knowledge would be useful in deducing object knowledge. For example: Since I would know it if Henry Kissinger were three meters tall, and since I don't know that he is, he isn't. Meta-level reasoning is also an easy way to solve many problems. Bundy et al. (1979) and Weyhrauch (1980) illustrate this principle applied to solving equations.

Two elegant arrangements of systems and metasystems are LCF [Cohn (1979)] and FOL [Weyhrauch (1979)]. Weyhrauch stresses the ability of FOL to refer to itself while avoiding problems of circularity. Self-reference has been a haunting but illusive theme in Artificial Intelligence research. For an interesting book about problems of self-reference in logic, music, and art, see Hofstadter (1979).

The matters that we have briefly discussed in this prospectus are now the subjects of intense AI research activity. Empirical explorations and new research results can be expected to challenge and expand the AI paradigms and formalisms that have proved useful for organizing past results. In this book, we have used certain organizing ideas—such as generalized production systems, the language of the predicate calculus, and heuristic search—to make our story just a bit simpler and more memorable. We cannot now tell whether new results will fold in easily to the existing story or whether they will require the invention of new themes or a completely new plot. That is how science and technology progress. Whatever the new results, we do know, however, that their description will be as important as their invention in order that we (and machines) will be able to understand them.

426

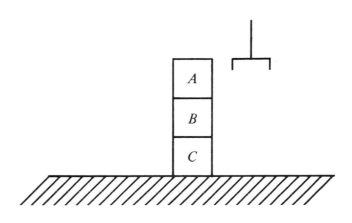

BIBLIOGRAPHY

MNEMONICS FOR SYMPOSIA, PROCEEDINGS, AND SPECIAL COLLECTIONS

COLLECTED WORKS

AHT

    Elithorn, A., and Jones, D. (Eds.) 1973. *Artificial And Human Thinking*. San Francisco: Jossey-Bass.

AIHP

    Findler, N. V., and Meltzer, B. (Eds.) 1971. *Artificial Intelligence and Heuristic Programming*. New York: American Elsevier.

AI-MIT

    Winston, P. H., and Brown, R. H. (Eds.) 1979. *Artificial Intelligence: An MIT Perspective* (2 vols.). Cambridge, MA: MIT Press.

AN

    Findler, N. V. (Ed.) 1979. *Associative Networks—The Representation and Use of Knowledge in Computers*. New York: Academic Press.

CT

    Feigenbaum, E., and Feldman, J. (Eds.) 1963. *Computers and Thought*. New York: McGraw-Hill.

CVS

    Hanson, A. R., and Riseman, E. M. (Eds.) 1978. *Computer Vision Systems*. New York: Academic Press.

KBS

    Davis, R., and Lenat, D. 1980. *Knowledge-Based Systems in Artificial Intelligence*. New York: McGraw-Hill. In press.

MI1

Collins, N. L., and Michie, D. (Eds.) 1967. *Machine Intelligence 1*. Edinburgh: Edinburgh University Press.

MI2

Dale, E., and Michie, D. (Eds.) 1968. *Machine Intelligence 2*. Edinburgh: Edinburgh University Press.

MI3

Michie, D. (Ed.) 1968. *Machine Intelligence 3*. Edinburgh: Edinburgh University Press.

MI4

Meltzer, B., and Michie, D. (Eds.) 1969. *Machine Intelligence 4*. Edinburgh: Edinburgh University Press.

MI5

Meltzer, B., and Michie, D. (Eds.) 1970. *Machine Intelligence 5*. Edinburgh: Edinburgh University Press.

MI6

Meltzer, B., and Michie, D. (Eds.) 1971. *Machine Intelligence 6*. Edinburgh: Edinburgh University Press.

MI7

Meltzer, B., and Michie, D. (Eds.) 1972. *Machine Intelligence 7*. Edinburgh: Edinburgh University Press.

MI8

Elcock E., and Michie, D. (Eds.) 1977. *Machine Intelligence 8: Machine Representations of Knowledge*. Chichester: Ellis Horwood.

MI9

Hayes, J. E., Michie, D., and Mikulich, L. I. (Eds.) 1979. *Machine Intelligence 9: Machine Expertise and the Human Interface*. Chichester: Ellis Horwood.

PCV

Winston, P. H. (Ed.) 1975. *The Psychology of Computer Vision*. New York: McGraw-Hill.

PDIS

Waterman, D., and Hayes-Roth, F. (Eds.) 1978. *Pattern-Directed Inference Systems*. New York: Academic Press.

RDST

Wegner, P. (Ed.) 1979. *Research Directions in Software Technology*. Cambridge, MA: MIT Press.

RM

Simon, H. A., and Siklóssy, L. (Eds.) 1972. *Representation and Meaning: Experiments with Information Processing Systems*. Englewood Cliffs, NJ: Prentice-Hall.

RU

Bobrow, D. G., and Collins, A. (Eds.) 1975. *Representation and Understanding*. New York: Academic Press.

SIP

Minsky, M. (Ed.) 1968. *Semantic Information Processing*. Cambridge, MA: MIT Press.

TANPS

Banerji, R., and Mesarovic, M. D. (Eds.) 1970. *Theoretical Approaches to Non-Numerical Problem Solving*. Berlin: Springer-Verlag.

PROCEEDINGS

IJCAI-1

Walker, D. E., and Norton, L. M. (Eds.) 1969. *International Joint Conference on Artificial Intelligence.* Washington, D.C.; May.

IJCAI-2

1971. *Advance Papers, Second International Joint Conference on Artificial Intelligence.* London: The British Computer Society; September. (Xerographic or microfilm copies available from Xerox University Microfilms, 300 North Zeeb Rd., Ann Arbor, MI, 48106; or from University Microfilms Ltd., St. John's Rd., Tylers Green, Penn., Buckinghamshire HP10 8HR, England.)

IJCAI-3

1973. *Advance Papers, Third International Joint Conference on Artificial Intelligence.* Stanford, CA; August. (Copies available from Artificial Intelligence Center, SRI International, Inc., Menlo Park, CA, 94025.)

IJCAI-4

1975. *Advance Papers of the Fourth International Joint Conference on Artificial Intelligence* (2 vols.). Tbilisi, Georgia, USSR; September. (Copies available from IJCAI-4, MIT AI Laboratory, 545 Technology Sq., Cambridge, MA, 02139.)

IJCAI-5

1977. *Proceedings of the 5th International Joint Conference on Artificial Intelligence* (2 vols.). Massachusetts Institute of Technology, Cambridge, MA; August. (Copies available from IJCAI-77, Dept. of Computer Science, Carnegie-Mellon University, Pittsburgh, PA, 15213.)

IJCAI-6

1979. *Proceedings of the Sixth International Joint Conference on Artificial Intelligence* (2 vols.). Tokyo; August. (Copies available from IJCAI-79, Computer Science Dept., Stanford University, Stanford, CA 94305.)

PASC

   1974. *Proceedings of the AISB Summer Conference.* (Copies available from Dept. of Artificial Intelligence, University of Edinburgh, Hope Park Sq., Edinburgh, EH8 9NW, Scotland.)

PCAI

   1978. *Proceedings of the AISB/GI Conference on Artificial Intelligence.* Hamburg; July. (Copies available from Dept. of Artificial Intelligence, University of Edinburgh, Hope Park Sq., Edinburgh, EH8 9NW, Scotland.)

SCAISB-76

   1976. *Conference Proceedings, Summer Conference on Artificial Intelligence and Simulation of Behavior.* Department of Artificial Intelligence, University of Edinburgh; July. (Copies available from Dept. of Artificial Intelligence, University of Edinburgh, Hope Park Sq., Edinburgh, EH8 9NW, Scotland.)

TINLAP-1

   Nash-Webber, B., and Schank, R. (Eds.) 1975. *Proceedings of Theoretical Issues in Natural Language Processing.* Cambridge, MA; June.

TINLAP-2

   Waltz, D. (Ed.) 1978. *Proceedings of TINLAP-2: Theoretical Issues in Natural Language Processing 2.* University of Illinois; July. (Copies available from the Association for Computing Machinery, P.O. Box 12105, Church Street Station, New York, NY, 10249.)

WAD

   Joyner, W. H., Jr. (Ed.) 1979. *Proceedings of the Fourth Workshop on Automated Deduction.* Austin, Texas; February.

433

REFERENCES

Abraham, R. G. 1977. Programmable automation of batch assembly operations. *The Industrial Robot*, 4(3), 119-131. (International Fluidics Services, Ltd.)

Agin, G. J. 1977. Vision systems for inspection and for manipulator control. *Proc. 1977 Joint Automatic Control Conf.*, vol. 1, pp. 132-138. San Francisco, CA; June. New York: IEEE.

Aho, A. V., Hopcroft, J. E., and Ullman, J. D. 1974. *The Design and Analysis of Computer Algorithms*. Reading, MA: Addison-Wesley.

Allen, J. 1978. *Anatomy of LISP*. New York: McGraw-Hill.

Allen, J., and Luckham, D. 1970. An interactive theorem proving program. In *MI5*, pp. 321-336.

Amarel, S. 1967. An approach to heuristic problem-solving and theorem proving in the propositional calculus. In J. Hart and S. Takasu (Eds.), *Systems and Computer Science*. Toronto: University of Toronto Press.

Amarel, S. 1968. On representations of problems of reasoning about actions. In *MI3*, pp. 131-171.

Ambler, A. P., et al. 1975. A versatile system for computer-controlled assembly. *Artificial Intelligence*, 6(2), 129-156.

Anderson, J., and Bower, G. 1973. *Human Associative Memory*. Washington, D.C.: Winston.

Athans, M., et al. 1974. *Systems, Networks and Computation: Multivariable Methods*. New York: McGraw-Hill.

Ball, W. 1931. *Mathematical Recreations and Essays* (10th ed.). London: Macmillan & Co.

Ballantyne, A. M., and Bledsoe, W. W. 1977. Automatic proofs of theorems in analysis using non-standard techniques. *JACM*, 24(3), 353-374.

Banerji, R., and Mesarovic, M. D. (Eds.) 1970. *Theoretical Approaches to Non-Numerical Problem Solving.* Berlin: Springer-Verlag.

Barr, A., and Feigenbaum, E. A. 1980. *Handbook of Artificial Intelligence.* Stanford, CA: Stanford University Computer Science Dept.

Barrow, H., and Tenenbaum, J. M. 1976. *MSYS: A System for Reasoning about Scenes,* Tech. Note 121, Artificial Intelligence Center, Stanford Research Institute, Menlo Park, CA; March.

Barstow, D. 1979. *Knowledge-Based Program Construction.* New York: North-Holland.

Baudet, G. M. 1978. On the branching factor of the alpha-beta pruning algorithm. *Artificial Intelligence,* 10(2), 173-199.

Bellman, R., and Dreyfus, S. 1962. *Applied Dynamic Programming.* Princeton, NJ: Princeton University Press.

Berliner, H. J. 1978. A chronology of computer chess and its literature. *Artificial Intelligence,* 10(2), 201-214.

Berliner, H. J. 1979. The B* tree search algorithm: A best-first proof procedure. *Artificial Intelligence,* 12(1), 23-40.

Bernstein, M. I. 1976. *Interactive Systems Research: Final Report to the Director, Advanced Research Projects Agency.* Rep. No. TM-5243/006/00, System Development Corporation, Santa Monica, CA.

Bibel, W., and Schreiber, J. 1975. Proof search in a Gentzen-like system of first-order logic. In E. Gelenbe and D. Potier (Eds.), *International Computing Symposium 1975.* Amsterdam: North-Holland.

Biermann, A. W. 1976. Approaches to automatic programming. *Advances in Computers* (vol. 15). New York: Academic Press.

Binford, T. O., et al. 1978. *Exploratory Study of Computer Integrated Assembly Systems,* Memo AIM-285.4, Fifth Report, Stanford Artificial Intelligence Laboratory, Stanford University, September.

Black, F. 1964. *A Deductive Question-Answering System.* Doctoral dissertation, Harvard, June. (Reprinted in *SIP,* pp. 354-402.)

Bledsoe, W. W. 1971. Splitting and reduction heuristics in automatic theorem proving. *Artificial Intelligence*, 2(1), 55-77.

Bledsoe, W. W. 1977. Non-resolution theorem proving. *Artificial Intelligence*, 9(1), 1-35.

Bledsoe, W.W., and Bruell, P. 1974. A man-machine theorem-proving system. *Artificial Intelligence*, 5(1), 51-72.

Bledsoe, W. W., Bruell, P., and Shostak, R. 1978. *A Prover for General Inequalities*. Rep. No. ATP-40, The University of Texas at Austin, Departments of Mathematics and Computer Sciences.

Bledsoe, W. W., and Tyson, M. 1978. *The UT Interactive Theorem Prover*. Memo ATP-17a, The University of Texas at Austin, Math. Dept., June.

Bobrow, D., and Raphael, B. 1974. New programming languages for Artificial Intelligence research. *ACM Computing Surveys*, vol. 6, pp. 153-174.

Bobrow, D. G., and Collins, A. (Eds.) 1975. *Representation and Understanding*. New York: Academic Press.

Bobrow, D. G., et al. 1977. GUS, A frame-driven dialog system. *Artificial Intelligence*, 8(2), 155-173.

Bobrow, D. G., and Winograd, T. 1977a. An overview of KRL, a knowledge representation language. *Cognitive Science*, 1(1), 3-46.

Bobrow, D. G., and Winograd, T. 1977b. Experience with KRL-0: one cycle of a knowledge representation language. In *IJCAI-5*, pp. 213-222.

Bobrow, D. G., and Winograd, T. 1979. KRL: another perspective. *Cognitive Science*, 3(1), 29-42.

Boden, M. A. 1977. *Artificial Intelligence and Natural Man*. New York: Basic Books.

Boyer, R. S. 1971. *Locking: A Restriction of Resolution*. Doctoral dissertation, University of Texas at Austin, August.

436

Boyer, R. S., and Moore, J S. 1979. *A Computational Logic.* New York: Academic Press.

Brown, J. S. 1977. Uses of Artificial Intelligence and advanced computer technology in education. In R. J. Seidel and M. Rubin (Eds.), *Computers and Communications: Implications for Education.* New York: Academic Press.

Buchanan, B. G., and Feigenbaum, E. A. 1978. Dendral and Meta-Dendral: their applications dimension. *Artificial Intelligence,* 11(1,2), 5-24.

Buchanan, B. G. and Mitchell, T. M. 1978. Model-directed learning of production rules. In *PDIS,* pp. 297-312.

Bundy, A. (Ed.) 1978. *Artificial Intelligence: An Introductory Course.* New York: North Holland.

Bundy, A., and Stone, M. 1975. A note on McDermott's symbol-mapping problem. *SIGART Newsletter,* no. 53, pp. 9-10.

Bundy, A., et al. 1979. Solving mechanics problems using meta-level inference. In *IJCAI-6,* pp. 1017-1027.

Cassinis, R. 1979. Sensing system in supersigma robot. *9th International Symposium on Industrial Robots,* Washington, D.C., September. Dearborn, MI: Society of Manufacturing Engineers. Pp. 437-448.

Chang, C. L. 1979. Resolution plans in theorem proving. In *IJCAI-6,* pp. 143-148.

Chang, C. L., and Lee, R. C. T. 1973. *Symbolic Logic and Mechanical Theorem Proving.* New York: Academic Press.

Chang, C. L., and Slagle, J. R. 1971. An admissible and optimal algorithm for searching AND/OR graphs. *Artificial Intelligence,* 2(2), 117-128.

Chang, C. L., and Slagle, J. R. 1979. Using rewriting rules for connection graphs to prove theorems. *Artificial Intelligence,* 12(2).

Charniak, E., Riesbeck, C., and McDermott, D. 1979. *Artificial Intelligence Programming.* Hillsdale, NJ: Lawrence Erlbaum Associates.

437

Codd, E. F. 1970. A relational model of data for large shared data banks. *CACM*, 13(6), June.

Cohen, P. R. 1978. *On Knowing What to Say: Planning Speech Acts.* Tech. Rep. No. 118, University of Toronto, Dept. of Computer Science. (Doctoral dissertation.)

Cohen, H. 1979. What is an image? In *IJCAI-6*, pp. 1028-1057.

Cohn, A. 1979. High level proof in LCF. In *WAD*, pp. 73-80.

Collins, A. 1978. Fragments of a theory of human plausible reasoning. In *TINLAP-2*, pp. 194-201.

Collins, N. L., and Michie, D. (Eds.) 1967. *Machine Intelligence 1.* Edinburgh: Edinburgh University Press.

Constable, R. 1979. A discussion of program verification. In *RDST*, pp. 393-403.

Corkill, D. D. 1979. Hierarchical planning in a distributed environment. In *IJCAI-6*, pp. 168-175.

Cox, P. T. 1977. *Deduction Plans: A Graphical Proof Procedure for the First-Order Predicate Calculus.* Rep. CS-77-28, University of Waterloo, Faculty of Mathematics Research, Waterloo, Ontario, Canada.

Crane, H. D. 1978. *Beyond the Seventh Synapse: The Neural Marketplace of the Mind.* Research Memorandum, SRI International, Menlo Park, CA; December.

Creary, L. G. 1979. Propositional attitudes: Fregean representation and simulative reasoning. In *IJCAI-6*, pp. 176-181.

Dale, E., and Michie, D. (Eds.) 1968. *Machine Intelligence 2.* Edinburgh: Edinburgh University Press.

Date, C. J. 1977. *An Introduction to Database Systems*, (2nd ed.). Reading, MA: Addison-Wesley.

Davis, R. 1976. *Applications of Meta Level Knowledge to the Construction, Maintenance and Use of Large Knowledge Bases.* Doctoral dissertation, Stanford University, Stanford Artificial Intelligence Laboraratory, Memo 283. (Reprinted in *KBS*.)

Davis, R. 1977. Meta-level knowledge: overview and applications. In *IJCAI-5*, pp. 920-927.

Davis, R., and King, J. 1977. An overview of production systems. In *MI8*, pp. 300-332.

Davis, R., and Lenat, D. 1980. *Knowledge-Based Systems in Artificial Intelligence*. New York: McGraw-Hill. In press.

Davis, M., and Putnam, H. 1960. A computing procedure for quantification theory. *JACM*, 7(3), 201-215.

Dawson, C., and Siklóssy, L. 1977. The role of preprocessing in problem solving systems. In *IJCAI-5*, pp. 465-471.

de Kleer, J., et al. 1979. Explicit control of reasoning. In *AI-MIT*, vol. 1, pp. 93-116.

Deliyani, A., and Kowalski, R. 1979. Logic and semantic networks. *CACM*, 22(3), 184-192.

Derksen, J. A., Rulifson, J. F., and Waldinger, R. J. 1972. The QA4 language applied to robot planning. *Proc. Fall Joint Computer Conf.*, vol. 41, Part 2, pp. 1181-1192.

Dietterich, T. G. and Michalski, R. S. 1979. Learning and generalization of characteristic descriptions: evaluation criteria and comparative review of selected methods. In *IJCAI-6*, pp. 223-231.

Dijkstra, E. W. 1959. A note on two problems in connection with graphs. *Numerische Mathematik*, vol. 1, pp. 269-271.

Doran, J. 1967. An approach to automatic problem-solving. In *MI1*, pp. 105-123.

Doran, J., and Michie, D. 1966. Experiments with the graph traverser program. *Proceedings of the Royal Society of London*, vol. 294 (series A), pp. 235-259.

Doyle, J. 1979. A truth maintenance system. *Artificial Intelligence*, 12(3).

Duda, R. O., and Hart, P. E. 1973. *Pattern Recognition and Scene Analysis*. New York: John Wiley and Sons.

Duda, R. O., Hart, P. E., and Nilsson, N. J. 1976. Subjective Bayesian methods for rule-based inference systems. *Proc. 1976 Nat. Computer Conf. (AFIPS Conf. Proc.)*, vol. 45, pp. 1075-1082.

Duda, R. O., et al. 1978a. Semantic network representations in rule-based inference systems. In *PDIS*, pp. 203-221.

Duda, R. O., et al. 1978b. *Development of the Prospector Consultation System for Mineral Exploration*. Final Report to the Office of Resource Analysis, U.S. Geological Survey, Reston, VA (Contract No. 14-08-0001-15985) and to the Mineral Resource Alternatives Program, The National Science Foundation, Washington, D.C. (Grant No. AER77-04499). Artificial Intelligence Center, SRI International, Menlo Park, CA; October.

Duda, R. O., et al. 1979. *A Computer-Based Consultant for Mineral Exploration*. Final Report, Grant AER 77-04499, SRI International, Menlo Park, CA; September.

Dudeney, H. 1958. *The Canterbury Puzzles*. New York: Dover Publications. (Originally published in 1907.)

Dudeney, H. 1967. *536 Puzzles and Curious Problems*, edited by M. Gardner. New York: Charles Scribner's Sons. (A collection from two of Dudeney's books: *Modern Puzzles*, 1926, and *Puzzles and Curious Problems*, 1931.)

Edwards, D., and Hart, T. 1963. *The Alpha-Beta Heuristic* (rev.). MIT AI Memo no. 30, Oct. 28. (Originally published as the Tree Prune (TP) Algorithm, Dec. 4, 1961.)

Ehrig, H., and Rosen, B. K. 1977. *Commutativity of Independent Transformations of Complex Objects*. IBM Research Division Report RC 6251 (No. 26882), October.

Ehrig, H., and Rosen, B. K. 1980. The mathematics of record handling. *SIAM Journal of Computing.* To appear.

Elcock E., and Michie, D. (Eds.) 1977. *Machine Intelligence 8: Machine Representations of Knowledge.* Chichester: Ellis Horwood.

Elithorn, A., and Jones, D. (Eds.) 1973. *Artificial And Human Thinking.* San Francisco: Jossey-Bass.

Elschlager, R. 1979. Consistency of theories of ideas. In *IJCAI-6*, pp. 241-243.

Ernst, G. W. 1969. Sufficient conditions for the success of GPS. *JACM*, 16(4), 517-533.

Ernst, G. W., and Newell, A. 1969. *GPS: A Case Study in Generality and Problem Solving.* New York: Academic Press.

Evans, T. G. 1968. A program for the solution of a class of geometric-analogy intelligence-test questions. In *SIP*, pp. 271-353.

Fahlman, S. E. 1974. A planning system for robot construction tasks. *Artificial Intelligence*, 5(1), 1-49.

Fahlman, S. 1975. Symbol-mapping and frames. *SIGART Newsletter*, no. 53, pp. 7-8.

Fahlman, S. E. 1979. Representing and using real-world knowledge. In *AI-MIT*, vol. 1, pp. 453-470.

Feigenbaum, E. A. 1977. The art of Artificial Intelligence: I. Themes and case studies of knowledge engineering. In *IJCAI-5*, pp. 1014-1029.

Feigenbaum, E., Buchanan, B., and Lederberg, J. 1971. Generality and problem solving: a case study using the DENDRAL program. In *MI6*.

Feigenbaum, E., and Feldman, J. (Eds.) 1963. *Computers and Thought.* New York: McGraw-Hill.

Feldman, J. A., and Sproull, R. F. 1977. Decision theory and Artificial Intelligence II: the hungry monkey. *Cognitive Science*, 1(2), 158-192.

Fikes, R. E. 1975. Deductive retrieval mechanisms for state description models. In *IJCAI-4*, pp. 99-106.

Fikes, R. E., and Nilsson, N. J. 1971. STRIPS: a new approach to the application of theorem proving to problem solving. *Artificial Intelligence*, 2(3/4), 189-208.

Fikes, R. E., Hart, P. E., and Nilsson, N. J. 1972a. New directions in robot problem solving. In *MI7*, pp. 405-430.

Fikes, R. E., Hart, P. E., and Nilsson, N. J. 1972b. Learning and executing generalized robot plans. *Artificial Intelligence*, 3(4), 251-288.

Fikes, R. E., and Hendrix, G. G. 1977. A network-based knowledge representation and its natural deduction system. In *IJCAI-5*, pp. 235-246.

Findler, N. V. (Ed.) 1979. *Associative Networks—The Representation and Use of Knowledge in Computers*. New York: Academic Press.

Findler, N. V., and Meltzer, B. (Eds.) 1971. *Artificial Intelligence and Heuristic Programming*. New York: American Elsevier.

Floyd, R. W. 1967. Assigning meanings to programs. *Proc. of a Symposium in Applied Mathematics*, vol. 19, pp. 19-32. (American Mathematical Society, Providence, RI.)

Frege, G. 1879. Begriffsschrift, a formula language modelled upon that of arithmetic, for pure thought. In J. van Heijenoort (Ed.), *From Frege to Gödel: A Source Book In Mathematical Logic, 1879-1931*. Cambridge, MA: Harvard Univ. Press, 1967. Pp. 1-82.

Friedland, P. 1979. *Knowledge-based Experiment Design in Molecular Genetics.* Doctoral dissertation, Stanford University, Computer Science Dept. Report CS-79-760.

Friedman, D. P. 1974. *The Little LISPer*. Science Research Associates, Inc.

Gallaire, H., and Minker, J. (Eds.) 1978. *Logic and Databases*. New York: Plenum Press.

Galler, B., and Perlis, A. 1970. *A View of Programming Languages.* Reading, MA: Addison-Wesley.

Gardner, M. 1959. *The Scientific American Book of Mathematical Puzzles and Diversions.* New York: Simon and Schuster.

Gardner, M. 1961. *The Second Scientific American Book of Mathematical Puzzles and Diversions.* New York: Simon and Schuster.

Gardner, M. 1964, 1965a,b,c. Mathematical games. *Scientific American,* 210(2), 122-130, February 1964; 212(3), 112-117, March 1965; 212(6), 120-124, June 1965; 213(3), 222-236, September 1965.

Gaschnig, J. 1979. *Performance Measurement and Analysis of Certain Search Algorithms.* Report CMU-CS-79-124, Carnegie-Mellon University, Dept. of Computer Science, May.

Gelernter, H. 1959. Realization of a geometry theorem-proving machine. *Proc. Intern. Conf. Inform Proc.,* UNESCO House, Paris, pp. 273-282. (Reprinted in *CT*, pp. 134-152.)

Gelernter, H. L., et al. 1977. Empirical explorations of SYNCHEM. *Science,* 197(4308), 1041-1049.

Gelperin, D. 1977. On the optimality of A*. *Artificial Intelligence,* 8(1), 69-76.

Genesereth, M. R. 1978. *Automated Consultation for Complex Computer Systems.* Doctoral dissertation, Harvard University, September.

Genesereth, M. R. 1979. The role of plans in automated consultation. In *IJCAI-6*, pp. 311-319.

Goldstein, I. P., and Roberts, R. B. 1979. Using frames in scheduling. In *AI-MIT*, vol. 1, pp. 251-284.

Goldstine, H. H., and von Neumann, J. 1947. Planning and coding of problems for an electronic computing instrument, Part 2 (vols. 1-3). Reprinted in A. H. Taub (Ed.), *John von Neumann, Collected Works* (vol. 5). London: Pergamon, 1963. Pp. 80-235.

Golomb, S., and Baumert, L. 1965. Backtrack programming. *JACM*, 12(4), 516-524.

Green, C. 1969a. Application of theorem proving to problem solving. In *IJCAI-1*, pp. 219-239.

Green, C. 1969b. Theorem-proving by resolution as a basis for question-answering systems. In *MI4*, pp. 183-205.

Green, C. 1976. The design of the PSI program synthesis system. *Proceedings of Second International Conference on Software Engineering*, San Francisco, CA, pp. 4-18.

Green C. C., and Barstow, D. 1978. On program synthesis knowledge. *Artificial Intelligence*, 10(3), 241-279.

Grosz, B. J. 1977. *The Representation and Use of Focus in Dialogue Understanding*. Tech. Note 151, SRI International Artificial Intelligence Center, SRI International, Menlo Park, CA; July.

Grosz, B. J. 1979. Utterance and objective: issues in natural language processing. In *IJCAI-6*, pp. 1067-1076.

Guard, J., et al. 1969. Semi-automated mathematics. *JACM*, 16(1), 49-62.

Hall, P. A. V. 1973. Equivalence between AND/OR graphs and context-free grammars. *CACM*, vol. 16, pp. 444-445.

Hammer, M., and Ruth, G. 1979. Automating the software development process. In *RDST*, pp. 767-790.

Hanson, A. R., and Riseman, E. M. (Eds.) 1978. *Computer Vision Systems*. New York: Academic Press.

Harris, L. R. 1974. The heuristic search under conditions of error. *Artificial Intelligence*, 5(3), 217-234.

Hart, P. E., Nilsson, N. J., and Raphael, B. 1968. A formal basis for the heuristic determination of minimum cost paths. *IEEE Trans. Syst. Science and Cybernetics*, SSC-4(2), 100-107.

Hart, P. E., Nilsson, N. J., and Raphael, B. 1972. Correction to "A formal basis for the heuristic determination of minimum cost paths." *SIGART Newsletter*, no. 37, December, pp. 28-29.

Hayes, J. E., Michie, D., and Mikulich, L. I. (Eds.) 1979. *Machine Intelligence 9: Machine Expertise and the Human Interface.* Chichester: Ellis Horwood.

Hayes, P. J. 1973a. The frame problem and related problems in Artificial Intelligence. In *AHT*, pp. 45-49.

Hayes, P. J. 1973b. Computation and deduction. *Proc. 2nd. Symposium on Mathematical Foundations of Computer Science*, Czechoslovakian Academy of Sciences, pp. 105-118.

Hayes, P. J. 1977. In defence of logic. In *IJCAI-5*, pp. 559-565.

Hayes, P. J. 1978a. *The Naive Physics Manifesto* (working papers), Institute of Semantic and Cognitive Studies, Geneva; May.

Hayes, P. J. 1978b. *Naive Physics 1: Ontology for Liquids* (working papers), Institute of Semantic and Cognitive Studies, Geneva; August.

Hayes, P. J. 1979. The logic of frames. In *The Frame Reader*. Berlin: De Gruyter. In press.

Hayes-Roth, F., and Waterman, D. 1977. Proceedings of the workshop on pattern-directed inference systems. *ACM SIGART Newsletter*, no. 63, June, pp. 1-83. (Some of the papers of the workshop that do not appear in *PDIS* are printed here.)

Held, M., and Karp, R. M. 1970. The traveling-salesman problem and minimum spanning trees. *Operations Research*, vol. 18, pp. 1138-1162.

Held, M., and Karp, R. 1971. The traveling salesman problem and minimum spanning trees—Part II. *Mathematical Prog.*, vol. 1, pp. 6-25.

Hendrix, G. G. 1973. Modeling simultaneous actions and continuous processes. *Artificial Intelligence*, 4(3,4), 145-180.

Hendrix, G. G. 1975a. *Partitioned Networks for the Mathematical Modeling of Natural Language Semantics.* Tech. Rep. NL-28, Dept. of Computer Science, University of Texas at Austin.

Hendrix, G. G. 1975b. Expanding the utility of semantic networks through partitioning. In *IJCAI-4*, pp. 115-121.

Hendrix, G. G. 1979. Encoding knowledge in partitioned networks. In *AN*, pp. 51-92.

Hewitt, C. 1972. *Description and Theoretical Analysis (Using Schemata) of PLANNER: A Language for Proving Theorems and Manipulating Models in a Robot.* Doctoral dissertation (June, 1971), MIT, AI Lab Rep. AI-TR-258.

Hewitt, C. 1975. How to use what you know. In *IJCAI-4*, pp. 189-198.

Hewitt, C. 1977. Viewing control structures as patterns of passing messages. *Artificial Intelligence*, 8(3), 323-364.

Hewitt, C., and Baker, H. 1977. Laws for communicating parallel processes. In B. Gilchrist (Ed.), *Information Processing 77, IFIP*. Amsterdam: North-Holland. Pp. 987-992.

Hillier, F. S., and Lieberman, G. J. 1974. *Introduction to Operations Research* (2nd ed.). San Francisco: Holden Day.

Hinxman, A. I. 1976. Problem reduction and the two-dimensional trim-loss problem. In *SCAISB-76*, pp. 158-165.

Hofstadter, D. R. 1979. *Gödel, Escher, Bach: An Eternal Golden Braid.* New York: Basic Books.

Hopcroft, J. E., and Ullman, J. D. 1969. *Formal Languages and Their Relation to Automata.* Reading, MA: Addison-Wesley.

Horowitz, E., and Sahni, S. 1978. *Fundamentals of Computer Algorithms.* Potomac, MD: Computer Science Press.

Hunt, E. B. 1975. *Artificial Intelligence.* New York: Academic Press.

Jackson, P. C., Jr., 1974. *Introduction to Artificial Intelligence.* New York: Petrocelli Books.

Joyner, W. H., Jr. (Ed.) 1979. *Proceedings of the Fourth Workshop on Automated Deduction*, Austin, Texas; February.

Kanade, T. 1977. Model representations and control structures in image understanding. In *IJCAI-5*, pp. 1074-1082.

Kanal, L. N. 1979. Problem-solving models and search strategies for pattern recognition. *IEEE Trans. of Pattern Analysis and Machine Intelligence*, PAM1-1(2), 193-201.

Klahr, P. 1978. Planning techniques for rule selection in deductive question-answering. In *PDIS*, pp. 223-239.

Klatt, D. H. 1977. Review of the ARPA speech understanding project. *Journal Acoust. Soc. Amer.*, 62(6), 1345-1366.

Kling, R. E. 1971. A paradigm for reasoning by analogy. *Artificial Intelligence*, vol. 2, pp. 147-178.

Knuth, D. E., and Moore, R. W. 1975. An analysis of alpha-beta pruning. *Artificial Intelligence*, 6(4), 293-326.

Kornfeld, W. A. 1979. ETHER—a parallel problem solving system. In *IJCAI-6*, pp. 490-492.

Kowalski, R. 1970. Search strategies for theorem-proving. In *MI5*, pp. 181-201.

Kowalski, R. 1972. AND/OR Graphs, theorem-proving graphs, and bidirectional search. In *MI7*, pp. 167-94.

Kowalski, R. 1974a. Predicate logic as a programming language. *Information Processing 74*. Amsterdam: North-Holland. Pp. 569-574.

Kowalski, R. 1974b. *Logic for Problem Solving*. Memo no. 75, Dept. of Computational Logic, University of Edinburgh, Edinburgh.

Kowalski, R. 1975. A proof procedure using connection graphs. *JACM*, vol. 22, pp. 572-595.

Kowalski, R. 1979a. Algorithm = logic + control. *CACM*, 22(7), 424-436.

Kowalski, R. 1979b. *Logic for Problem Solving*. New York: North-Holland.

Kowalski, R., and Hayes P. 1969. Semantic trees in automatic theorem proving. In *MI4*, pp. 87-101.

Kowalski, R., and Kuehner, D. 1971. Linear resolution with selection function. *Artificial Intelligence*, 2(3/4), 227-260.

Kuehner, D. G. 1971. A note on the relation between resolution and Maslov's inverse method. In *MI6*, pp. 73-90.

Kuipers, B. 1978. Modeling spatial knowledge. *Cognitive Science*, 2(2), 129-153.

Kuipers, B. 1979. On representing commonsense knowledge. In *AN*, pp. 393-408.

Latombe, J. C. 1977. Artificial intelligence in computer aided design. In J. J. Allen (Ed.), *CAD Systems*. Amsterdam: North-Holland.

Lauriere, J. L. 1978. A language and a program for stating and solving combinatorial problems. *Artificial Intelligence*, 10(1), 29-127.

Lehnert, W., and Wilks, Y. 1979. A critical perspective on KRL. *Cognitive Science*, 3(1), 1-28.

Lenat, D. B. 1976. *AM: An Artificial Intelligence Approach to Discovery in Mathematics as Heuristic Search.* Rep. STAN-CS-76-570, Stanford University, Computer Science Dept.; July. (Reprinted in *KBS*.)

Lesser, V. R. and Corkill, D. D. 1979. The application of Artificial Intelligence techniques to cooperative distributed processing. In *IJCAI-6*, pp. 537-540.

Lesser, V. R., and Erman, L. D. 1979. *An Experiment in Distributed Interpretation.* University of Southern California Information Sciences Institute Report No. ISI/RR-79-76, May. (Also, Carnegie-Mellon University Computer Science Dept. Technical Report CMU-CS-79-120, May.)

Levy, D. 1976. *Chess and Computers.* Woodland Hills, CA: Computer Science Press.

Levi, G., and Sirovich, F. 1976. Generalized AND/OR graphs. *Artificial Intelligence*, 7(3), 243-259.

Lin, S. 1965. Computer solutions of the traveling salesman problem. *Bell System Tech. Journal*, vol. XLIV, no. 10, December 1965.

Lindsay, P. H., and Norman, D. A. 1972. *Human Information Processing: An Introduction to Psychology.* New York: Academic Press.

Lindstrom, G. 1979. *Alpha-Beta Pruning on Evolving Game Trees.* Tech. Rep. UUCS 79-101, University of Utah, Dept. of Computer Science.

Linsky, L. (Ed.) 1971. *Reference and Modality.* London: Oxford University Press.

London, R. L. 1979. Program verification. In *RDST*, pp. 302-315.

Loveland, D. W. 1978. *Automated Theorem Proving: A Logical Basis.* New York: North Holland.

Loveland, D. W., and Stickel, M. E. 1976. A hole in goal trees: some guidance from resolution theory. *IEEE Trans. on Computers*, C-25(4), 335-341.

Lowerre, B. T. 1976. *The HARPY Speech Recognition System.* Doctoral dissertation, Carnegie-Mellon University; Tech. Rep., Computer Science Dept., Carnegie-Mellon University.

Luckham, D. C. 1978. A study in the application of theorem proving. In *PCAI*, pp. 176-188.

Luckham, D. C., and Nilsson, N. J. 1971. Extracting information from resolution proof trees. *Artificial Intelligence*, 2(1), 27-54.

McCarthy, J. 1958. Programs with common sense. *Mechanisation of Thought Processes, Proc. Symp. Nat. Phys. Lab.*, vol. I, pp. 77-84. London: Her Majesty's Stationary Office. (Reprinted in *SIP*, pp. 403-410.)

McCarthy, J. 1962. Towards a mathematical science of computation. *Information Processing, Proceedings of IFIP Congress 1962*, pp. 21-28. Amsterdam: North-Holland.

McCarthy, J. 1963. *Situations, Actions and Causal Laws.* Stanford University Artificial Intelligence Project Memo no. 2. (Reprinted in *SIP*, pp. 410-418.)

McCarthy, J. 1977. Epistemological problems of Artificial Intelligence. In *IJCAI-5*, pp. 1038-1044.

McCarthy, J. 1979. First order theories of individual concepts and propositions. In *MI9*.

McCarthy, J., et al. 1969. A computer with hands, eyes, and ears. *Proc. of the American Federation of Information Processing Societies*, vol. 33, pp. 329-338. Washington, D.C.: Thompson Book Co.

McCarthy, J., and Hayes, P. J. 1969. Some philosophical problems from the standpoint of Artificial Intelligence. In *MI4*, pp. 463-502.

McCharen, J. D., Overbeek, R. A., and Wos, L. A. 1976. Problems and experiments for and with automated theorem-proving programs. *IEEE Trans. on Computers*, C-25(8), 773-782.

McCorduck, P. 1979. *Machines Who Think.* San Francisco: W. H. Freeman.

McDermott, D. V. 1975a. Symbol-mapping: a technical problem in PLANNER-like systems. *SIGART Newsletter*, no. 51, April, pp. 4-5.

McDermott, D. V. 1975b. A packet-based approach to the symbol-mapping problem. *SIGART Newsletter*, no. 53, August, pp. 6-7.

McDermott, D. V. 1975c. *Very Large PLANNER-Type Data Bases.* MIT Artificial Intelligence Laboratory Memo. 339, MIT; September.

McDermott, D. V., and Doyle, J. 1980. Non-monotonic logic I. *Artificial Intelligence*, forthcoming.

McDermott, D. V., and Sussman, G. J. 1972. *The CONNIVER Reference Manual*, MIT AI Lab. Memo 259, May. (Rev., July 1973.)

McDermott, J. 1979. Learning to use analogies. In *IJCAI-6*, pp. 568-576.

Mackworth, A. K. 1977. Consistency in networks of relations. *Artificial Intelligence*, 8(1), 99-118.

Manna, Z., and Waldinger, R. (Eds.) 1977. *Studies in Automatic Programming Logic.* New York: North-Holland.

Manna, Z., and Waldinger, R. 1979. A deductive approach to program synthesis. In *IJCAI-6*, pp. 542-551.

Markov, A. 1954. *A Theory of Algorithms.* National Academy of Sciences, USSR.

Marr, D. 1976. Early processing of visual information. *Phil. Trans. Royal Society* (Series B), vol. 275, pp. 483-524.

Marr, D. 1977. Artificial intelligence—a personal view. *Artificial Intelligence*, 9(1), 37-48.

Martelli, A. 1977. On the complexity of admissible search algorithms. *Artificial Intelligence*, 8(1), 1-13.

Martelli, A., and Montanari, U. 1973. Additive AND/OR graphs. In *IJCAI-3*, pp. 1-11.

Martelli, A., and Montanari, U. 1975. From dynamic programming to search algorithms with functional costs. In *IJCAI-4*, pp. 345-350.

Martelli, A., and Montanari, U. 1978. Optimizing decision trees through heuristically guided search. *CACM*, 21(12), 1025-1039.

Martin, W. A. 1978. *Descriptions and the Specialization of Concepts.* Rep. MIT/LCS/TM-101, MIT Lab. for Computer Science, MIT.

Martin, W. A., and Fateman, R. J. 1971. The MACSYMA system. *Proc. ACM 2d Symposium on Symbolic and Algebraic Manipulation*, Los Angeles, CA, pp. 23-25.

Maslov, S. J. 1971. Proof-search strategies for methods of the resolution type. In *MI6*, pp. 77-90.

Medress, M. F., et al. 1977. Speech understanding systems: Report of a steering committee. *Artificial Intelligence*, 9(3), 307-316.

Meltzer, B., and Michie, D. (Eds.) 1969. *Machine Intelligence 4.* Edinburgh: Edinburgh University Press.

Meltzer, B., and Michie, D. (Eds.) 1970. *Machine Intelligence 5.* Edinburgh: Edinburgh University Press.

Meltzer, B., and Michie, D. (Eds.) 1971. *Machine Intelligence 6.* Edinburgh: Edinburgh University Press.

Meltzer, B., and Michie, D. (Eds.) 1972. *Machine Intelligence 7.* Edinburgh: Edinburgh University Press.

Mendelson, E. 1964. *Introduction to Mathematical Logic.* Princeton, NJ: D. Van Nostrand.

Michie, D. (Ed.) 1968. *Machine Intelligence 3.* Edinburgh: Edinburgh University Press.

Michie, D. 1974. *On Machine Intelligence.* New York: John Wiley and Sons.

Michie, D., and Ross, R. 1970. Experiments with the adaptive graph traverser. In *MI5*, pp. 301-318.

Michie, D., and Sibert, E. E. 1974. Some binary derivation systems. *JACM*, 21(2), 175-190.

Minker, J., Fishman, D. H., and McSkimin, J. R. 1973. The Q* algorithm— a search strategy for a deductive question-answering system. *Artificial Intelligence*, 4(3,4), 225-244.

Minker, J., and Zanon, G. 1979. *Lust resolution: Resolution with Arbitrary Selection Function*, Res. Rep. TR-736, Univ. of Maryland, Computer Science Center, College Park, MD.

Minker, J., et al. 1974. MRPPS: an interactive refutation proof procedure system for question answering. *J. Computers and Information Sciences*, vol. 3, June, pp. 105-122.

Minsky, M. (Ed.) 1968. *Semantic Information Processing.* Cambridge, MA: The MIT Press.

Minsky, M. 1975. A Framework for Representing Knowledge. In *PUV*, pp. 211-277.

Mitchell, T. M. 1979. An analysis of generalization as a search problem. In *IJCAI-6*, pp. 577-582.

Montanari, U. 1970. Heuristically guided search and chromosome matching. *Artificial Intelligence*, 1(4), 227-245.

Montanari, U. 1974. Networks of constraints: fundamental properties and applications to picture processing. *Information Science*, vol. 7, pp. 95-132.

Moore, E. F. 1959. The shortest path through a maze. *Proceedings of an International Symposium on the Theory of Switching, Part II.* Cambridge: Harvard University Press. Pp. 285-292.

Moore, J., and Newell, A. 1973. How can MERLIN understand? In L. Gregg (Ed.), *Knowledge and Cognition.* Hillsdale, NJ: Lawrence Erlbaum Assoc.

Moore, R. C. 1975a. *Reasoning from Incomplete Knowledge in a Procedural Deduction System.* Tech. Rep. AI-TR-347, MIT Artificial Intelligence Lab, Massachusetts Institute of Technology, Cambridge, MA.

Moore, R. C. 1975b. A serial scheme for the inheritance of properties. *SIGART Newsletter*, No. 53, pp. 8-9.

Moore, R. C. 1977. Reasoning about knowledge and action. In *IJCAI-5*, pp. 223-227.

Moore, R. C. 1979. *Reasoning About Knowledge and Action.* Tech. Note 191, SRI International, Artificial Intelligence Center, Menlo Park, CA.

Moses, J. 1967. *Symbolic Integration.* MAC-TR-47, Project MAC, Massachusetts Institute of Technology, Cambridge, MA.

Moses, J. 1971. Symbolic integration: the stormy decade. *CACM*, 14(8), 548-560.

Mylopoulos, J., et al. 1975. TORUS—a natural language understanding system for data management. In *IJCAI-4*, pp. 414-421.

Nash-Webber, B., and Schank, R. (Eds.) 1975. *Proceedings of Theoretical Issues in Natural Language Processing.* Cambridge, MA; June.

Naur, P. 1966. Proofs of algorithms by general snapshots. *BIT*, 6(4), 310-316.

Nevins, A. J. 1974. A human-oriented logic for automatic theorem proving. *JACM*, vol. 21, pp. 606-621.

Nevins, J. L., and Whitney, D. E. 1977. Research on advanced assembly automation. *Computer* (IEEE Computer Society), 10(12), 24-38.

Newborn, M., 1975. *Computer Chess.* New York: Academic Press.

Newborn, M. 1977. The efficiency of the alpha-beta search on trees with branch-dependent terminal node scores. *Artificial Intelligence*, 8(2), 137-153.

Newell, A. 1973. Production systems: models of control structures. In W.G. Chase, (Ed.), *Visual Information Processing.* New York: Academic Press. Chapter 10, pp. 463-526.

Newell, A., Shaw, J., and Simon, H. 1957. Empirical explorations of the logic theory machine. *Proc. West. Joint Computer Conf.*, vol. 15, pp. 218-239. (Reprinted in *CT*, pp. 109-133.)

Newell, A., Shaw, J. C., and Simon, H. A. 1958. Chess-playing programs and the problem of complexity. *IBM Jour. R&D*, vol. 2, pp. 320-355. (Reprinted in *CT*, pp. 109-133.)

Newell, A., Shaw, J. C., and Simon, H. A. 1960. Report on a general problem-solving program for a computer. *Information Processing: Proc. of the Int. Conf. on Information Processing*, UNESCO, Paris, pp. 256-264.

Newell, A., and Simon, H. A. 1963. GPS, a program that simulates human thought. In *CT*, pp. 279-293.

Newell, A., and Simon, H. A. 1972. *Human Problem Solving.* Englewood Cliffs, NJ: Prentice-Hall.

Newell, A., et al. 1973. *Speech Understanding Systems: Final Report of a Study Group*. New York: American Elsevier.

Nilsson, N. J. 1965. *Learning Machines: Foundations of Trainable Pattern-Classifying Systems*. New York: McGraw-Hill.

Nilsson, N. J. 1969. Searching problem-solving and game-playing trees for minimal cost solutions. In A. J. H. Morrell (Ed.), *Information Processing 68* (vol. 2). Amsterdam: North-Holland. Pp. 1556-1562.

Nilsson, N. J. 1971. *Problem-solving Methods in Artificial Intelligence*. New York: McGraw-Hill.

Nilsson, N. J. 1973. *Hierarchical Robot Planning and Execution System*. SRI AI Center Technical Note 76, SRI International, Inc., Menlo Park, CA, April.

Nilsson, N. J. 1974. Artificial Intelligence. In J. L. Rosenfeld (Ed.), *Technological and Scientific Applications; Applications in the Social Sciences and the Humanities, Information Processing, 74: Proc. of IFIP Congress 74*, vol. 4, pp. 778-801. New York: American Elsevier.

Nilsson, N. J. 1979. A production system for automatic deduction. In *MI9*.

Nitzan, D. 1979. Flexible automation program at SRI. *Proc. 1979 Joint Automatic Control Conference*. New York: IEEE.

Norman, D. A., and Rumelhart, D. E. (Eds.) 1975. *Explorations in Cognition*. San Francisco: W. H. Freeman.

Okhotsimski, D. E., et al. 1979. Integrated walking robot development. In *MI9*.

Paterson, M. S., and Wegman, M. N. 1976. *Linear Unification*. IBM Research Report 5304, IBM.

Pitrat, J. 1977. A chess combination program which uses plans. *Artificial Intelligence*, 8(3), 275-321.

Pohl, I. 1970. First results on the effect of error in heuristic search. In *MI5*, pp. 219-236.

455

Pohl, I. 1971. Bi-directional search. In *MI6*, pp. 127-140.

Pohl, I. 1973. The avoidance of (relative) catastrophe, heuristic competence, genuine dynamic weighting and computational issues in heuristic problem solving. In *IJCAI-3*, pp. 12-17.

Pohl, I. 1977. Practical and theoretical considerations in heuristic search algorithms. In *MI8*, pp. 55-72.

Pople, H. E., Jr. 1977. The formation of composite hypotheses in diagnostic problem solving: an exercise in synthetic reasoning. In *IJCAI-5*, pp. 1030-1037.

Pospesel, H. 1976. *Introduction to Logic: Predicate Logic*. Englewood Cliffs, NJ: Prentice-Hall.

Post, E. 1943. Formal reductions of the general combinatorial problem. *American Jour. Math.*, vol. 65, pp. 197-268.

Pratt, V. R. 1977. *The Competence/Performance Dichotomy in Programming*. Memo 400, January, MIT Artificial Intelligence Laboratory, MIT.

Prawitz, D. 1960. An improved proof procedure. *Theoria*, vol. 26, pp. 102-139.

Quillian, M. R. 1968. Semantic memory. In *SIP*, pp. 216-270.

Raphael, B. 1968. SIR: semantic information retrieval. In *SIP*, pp. 33-134.

Raphael, B. 1971. The frame problem in problem-solving systems. In *AIHP*, pp. 159-169.

Raphael, B. 1976. *The Thinking Computer: Mind Inside Matter*. San Francisco: W. H. Freeman.

Raphael, B., et al. 1971. *Research and Applications—Artificial Intelligence, Stanford Research Institute Final Report on Project 8973*. Advanced Research Projects Agency, Contract NASW-2164; December.

Raulefs, P., et al. 1978. A short survey on the state of the art in matching and unification problems. *AISB Quarterly*, no. 32, December, pp. 17-21.

Reddy, D. R., et al. 1977. *Speech Understanding Systems: A Summary of Results of the Five-Year Research Effort.* Dept. of Computer Science, Carnegie-Mellon University, Pittsburgh, PA.

Reiter, R. 1971. Two results on ordering for resolution with merging and linear format. *JACM*, vol. 18, October, pp. 630-646.

Reiter, R. 1976. A semantically guided deductive system for automatic theorem proving. *IEEE Trans. on Computers*, C-25(4), 328-334.

Reiter, R. 1978. On reasoning by default. In *TINLAP-2*, pp. 210-218.

Rich, C., and Shrobe, H. E. 1979. Design of a programmer's apprentice. In *AI-MIT*, vol. 1, pp. 137-173.

Rieger, C., and London, P. 1977. Subgoal protection and unravelling during plan synthesis. In *IJCAI-5*, pp. 487-493.

Robbin, J. 1969. *Mathematical Logic: A First Course.* New York: W. A. Benjamin.

Roberts, R. B., and Goldstein, I. P. 1977. *The FRL Primer.* Memo 408, MIT Artificial Intelligence Laboratory, MIT.

Robinson, A. E. 1978. *Investigating the Process of Natural Language Communication: A Status Report.* SRI International Artificial Intelligence Center Tech. Note 165. SRI International, Menlo Park, CA; July.

Robinson, J. A. 1965. A machine-oriented logic based on the resolution principle. *JACM*, 12(1), 23-41.

Robinson, J. A. 1979. *Logic: Form and Function.* New York: North-Holland.

Rosen, C. A., and Nitzan, D. 1977. Use of sensors in programmable automation. *Computer* (IEEE Computer Society Magazine), December, pp. 12-23.

Rosen, B. K. 1973. Tree-manipulating systems and Church-Rosser theorems. *JACM*, vol. 20, pp. 160-187.

Roussel, P. 1975. *Prolog: Manual de reference et d'utilisation.* Groupe d'Intelligence Artificielle, Marseille-Luminy; September.

Rubin, S. 1978. *The ARGOS Image Understanding System.* Doctoral dissertation, Dept. of Computer Science, Carnegie-Mellon University, November. (Also in *Proc ARPA Image Understanding Workshop*, Carnegie-Mellon, Nov. 1978, pp. 159-162.)

Rulifson, J. F., Derksen, J. A., and Waldinger, R. J. 1972. *QA4: A Procedural Calculus for Intuitive Reasoning.* Stanford Research Institute Artificial Intelligence Center Tech. Note 73, Stanford Research Institute, Inc., November.

Rumelhart, D. E., and Norman, D. A. 1975. The active structural network. In D. A. Norman and D. E. Rumelhart (Eds.), *Explorations in Cognition.* San Francisco: W. H. Freeman.

Rustin, R. (Ed.) 1973. *Natural Language Processing.* New York: Algorithmics Press.

Rychener, M. D. 1976. *Production Systems as a Programming Language for Artificial Intelligence Applications.* Doctoral dissertation, Dept. of Computer Science, Carnegie-Mellon University.

Sacerdoti, E. D. 1974. Planning in a hierarchy of abstraction spaces. *Artificial Intelligence*, 5(2), 115-135.

Sacerdoti, E. D. 1975. The non-linear nature of plans. In *IJCAI-4*, pp. 206-214.

Sacerdoti, E. D. 1977. *A Structure for Plans and Behavior.* New York: Elsevier.

Sacerdoti, E. D., et al. 1976. QLISP—A language for the interactive development of complex systems. *Proceedings of AFIPS National Computer Conference*, pp. 349-356.

Samuel, A. L. 1959. Some studies in machine learning using the game of checkers. *IBM Jour. R & D*, vol. 3, pp. 211-229. (Reprinted in *CT*, pp. 71-105.)

Samuel, A. L. 1967. Some studies in machine learning using the game of checkers II—recent progress. *IBM Jour. R & D*, 11(6), 601-617.

Schank, R. C., and Abelson, R. P. 1977. *Scripts, Plans, Goals and Understanding.* Hillsdale, NJ: Lawrence Erlbaum Assoc.

Schmidt, C. F., Sridharan, N. S., and Goodson, J. L. 1978. The plan recognition problem: an intersection of psychology and Artificial Intelligence. *Artificial Intelligence*, 11(1,2), pp. 45-83.

Schubert, L. K. 1976. Extending the expressive power of semantic networks. *Artificial Intelligence*, 7(2), pp. 163-198.

Schubert, L. K., Goebel, R. G., and Cercone, N. J. 1979. The structure and organization of a semantic net for comprehension and inference. In *AN*, pp. 121-175.

Shannon, C. E. 1950. Programming a computer for playing chess. *Philosophical Magazine* (Series 7), vol. 41, pp. 256-275.

Shapiro, S. 1979a. The SNePS Semantic Network Processing System. In *AN*, pp. 179-203.

Shapiro, S. 1979b. *Techniques of Artificial Intelligence.* New York: D. Van Nostrand.

Shirai, Y. 1978. Recognition of real-world objects using edge cue. In *CVS*, pp. 353-362.

Shortliffe, E. H. 1976. *Computer-Based Medical Consultations: MYCIN.* New York: American Elsevier.

Siklóssy, L., and Dreussi, J. 1973. An efficient robot planner which generates its own procedures. In *IJCAI-3*, pp. 423-430.

Sickel, S. 1976. A search technique for clause interconnectivity graphs. *IEEE Trans. on Computers*, C-25(8), 823-835.

Simmons, R. F. 1973. Semantic networks: their computation and use for understanding English sentences. In R. Schank and K. Colby (Eds.), *Computer Models of Thought and Language.* San Francisco: W. H. Freeman. Pp. 63-113.

Simon, H. A. 1963. Experiments with a heuristic compiler. *JACM,* 10(4), 493-506.

Simon, H. A. 1969. *The Sciences of the Artificial.* Cambridge, MA: The MIT Press.

Simon, H. A. 1972a. On reasoning about actions. In *RM*, pp. 414-430.

Simon, H. A. 1972b. The heuristic compiler. In *RM*, pp. 9-43.

Simon, H. 1977. Artificial Intelligence systems that understand. In *IJCAI-5*, pp. 1059-1073.

Simon, H. A., and Kadane, J. B. 1975. Optimal problem-solving search: all-or-none solutions. *Artificial Intelligence*, vol. 6, 235-247.

Slagle, J. R. 1963. A heuristic program that solves symbolic integration problems in freshman calculus. In *CT*, pp. 191-203. (Also in *JACM*, 1963, vol. 10, 507-520.)

Slagle, J. R. 1970. Heuristic search programs. In *TANPS*, pp. 246-273.

Slagle, J. R. 1971. *Artificial Intelligence: The Heuristic Programming Approach.* New York: McGraw-Hill.

Slagle, J. R., and Dixon, J. K. 1969. Experiments with some programs that search game trees. *JACM*, 16(2), 189-207.

Smith, R. G. 1978. *A Framework for Problem Solving in a Distributed Environment.* Doctoral dissertation, Stanford University, Computer Science Dept., Report STAN-CS-78-700; December.

Smith, R. G. 1979. A framework for distributed problem solving. In *IJCAI-6*, pp. 836-841.

Smullyan, R. M. 1978. *What Is The Name of This Book: The Riddle of Dracula and Other Logical Puzzles.* Englewood Cliffs, NJ: Prentice-Hall.

Soloway, E. M. 1978. *"Learning = Interpretation + Generalization": A Case Study in Knowledge-Directed Learning.* Doctoral dissertation, University of Massachusetts at Amherst, Computer and Information Science Dept., Technical Report 78-13; July.

Sridharan, N. S. 1978. *AIMDS User Manual—Version 2.* Rutgers University Computer Science Tech. Report CBM-TR-89, Rutgers, June.

Srinivasan, C. V. 1977. *The Meta Description System: A System to Generate Intelligent Information Systems. Part I: The Model Space.* Rutgers University Computer Science Tech. Report SOSAP-TR-20A, Rutgers.

Stallman, R. M., and Sussman, G. J. 1977. Forward reasoning and dependency-directed backtracking in a system for computer-aided circuit analysis. *Artificial Intelligence*, 9(2), 135-196. (Reprinted in *AI-MIT*, vol. 1, pp. 31-91.)

Stefik, M. 1979. An examination of a frame-structured representation system. In *IJCAI-6*, pp. 845-852.

Stockman, G. 1977. *A Problem-Reduction Approach to the Linguistic Analysis of Waveforms.* Doctoral dissertation, University of Maryland, College Park, MD.; Computer Science Technical Report TR-538.

Sussman, G. J. 1975. *A Computer Model of Skill Acquisition.* New York: American Elsevier.

Sussman, G. J. 1977. Electrical design: a problem for artificial intelligence research. In *IJCAI-5*, pp. 894-900.

Sussman, G. J., and Stallman, R. M. 1975. Heuristic techniques in computer aided circuit analysis. *IEEE Trans. on Circuits and Systems*, CAS-22(11), November.

Sussman, G., Winograd, T., and Charniak, E. 1971. *Micro-Planner Reference Manual*, MIT AI Memo 203a, MIT, 1970.

Takeyasu, K. et al. 1977. An approach to the integrated intelligent robot with multiple sensory feedback: construction and control functions. *Proceedings 7th Intern. Symp. on Industrial Robots*, Tokyo, Japan Industrial Robot Assoc., pp. 523-530.

461

Tate, A. 1976. *Project Planning Using a Hierarchic Non-Linear Planner.* Research Report no. 25, Department of Artificial Intelligence, University of Edinburgh.

Tate, A. 1977. Generating project networks. In *IJCAI-5*, pp. 888-893.

Turing, A. M. 1950. Checking a large routine. *Report of a Conference on high speed automatic calculating machines*, University of Toronto, Canada, June 1949, Cambridge University Mathematical Laboratory, pp. 66-69.

Tyson, M., and Bledsoe, W. W. 1979. Conflicting bindings and generalized substitutions. In *WAD*, pp. 14-18.

Ulrich, J. W. and Moll, R. 1977. Program synthesis by analogy. In *Proceedings of the Symposium on Artificial Intelligence and Programming Languages* (ACM); *SIGPLAN Notices*, 12(8); and *SIGART Newsletter*, no. 64, pp. 22-28.

vanderBrug, G. J. 1976. Problem representations and formal properties of heuristic search. *Information Sciences*, vol. II, pp. 279-307.

vanderBrug, G., and Minker, J. 1975. State-space, problem-reduction, and theorem proving—some relationships. *Comm. ACM*, 18(2), 107-115.

van Emden, M. H. 1977. Programming with resolution logic. In *MI8*, pp. 266-299.

van Vaalen, J. 1975. An extension of unification to substitutions with an application to automatic theorem proving. In *IJCAI-4*, pp. 77-82.

Vere, S. A. 1978. Inductive learning of relational productions. In *PDIS*, pp. 281-295.

Wagner, H. 1975. *Principles of Operations Research* (2nd ed.). Englewood Cliffs, NJ: Prentice-Hall.

Waldinger, R. J. 1977. Achieving several goals simultaneously. In *MI8*, pp. 94-136.

Waldinger, R. J., and Lee, R. C. T. 1969. PROW: A step toward automatic program writing. In *IJCAI-1*, pp. 241-252.

Waldinger, R. J., and Levitt, K. N. 1974. Reasoning about programs. *Artificial Intelligence*, 5(3), 235—316. (Reprinted in Z. Manna and R. J. Waldinger (Eds.), *Studies in Automatic Programming Logic*. New York: North-Holland, 1977.)

Walker, D. E., and Norton, L. M. (Eds.) 1969. *International Joint Conference on Artificial Intelligence*. Washington, D.C.; May.

Walker, D. E. (Ed.). 1978. *Understanding Spoken Language*. New York: North Holland.

Waltz, D. 1975. Understanding line drawings of scenes with shadows. In *PCV*, pp. 19-91.

Waltz, D. (Ed.) 1977. Natural language interfaces. *SIGART Newsletter* no. 61, February, pp. 16-64.

Waltz, D. (Ed.) 1978. *TINLAP-2*, University of Illinois, July.

Warren, D. H. D. 1974. *WARPLAN: A System for Generating Plans*. Memo 76, Dept. of Computational Logic, University of Edinburgh School of Artificial Intelligence, June.

Warren, D. H. D. 1977. *Logic Programming and Compiler Writing*. Res. Rep. No. 44, Dept. of Artificial Intelligence, University of Edinburgh.

Warren, D. H. D., and Pereira, L. M. 1977. PROLOG—The language and its implementation compared with LISP. *Proceedings of the Symposium on Artificial Intelligence and Programming Languages* (ACM); *SIGPLAN Notices*, 12(8); and *SIGART Newsletter*, no. 64, pp. 109-115.

Waterman, D., and Hayes-Roth, F. (Eds.) 1978. *Pattern-Directed Inference Systems*. New York: Academic Press.

Wegner, P. (Ed.) 1979. *Research Directions in Software Technology* Cambridge, MA: The MIT Press.

Weiss, S. M., Kulikowski, C. A., Amarel, S., and Safir, A. 1978. A model-based method for computer-aided medical decision-making. *Artificial Intelligence*, 11(1,2), 145-172.

Weissman, C. 1967. *LISP 1.5 Primer*. Belmont, CA: Dickenson Publishing Co.

Weyhrauch, R. 1980. Prolegomena to a theory of mechanized formal reasoning. *Artificial Intelligence*, forthcoming.

Wickelgren, W. A. 1974. *How to Solve Problems*. San Francisco: W. H. Freeman.

Wiederhold, G. 1977. *Database Design*. New York: McGraw-Hill.

Wilkins, D. 1974. A non-clausal theorem proving system. In *PASC*.

Wilkins, D. 1979. Using plans in chess. In *IJCAI-6*, pp. 960-967.

Will, P., and Grossman, D. 1975. An experimental system for computer controlled mechanical assembly. *IEEE Trans. on Computers*, C-24(9), 879-888.

Winker, S. 1979. Generation and verification of finite models and counterexamples using an automated theorem prover answering two open questions. In *WAD*, pp. 7-13.

Winker, S. and Wos, L. 1978. Automated generation of models and counterexamples and its application to open questions in ternary boolean algebra. *Proc. Eighth Int. Symposium on Multiple-Valued Logic* (IEEE), Rosemont, Illinois.

Winograd, T. 1972. *Understanding Natural Language*. New York: Academic Press.

Winograd, T. 1975. Frame representations and the declarative/procedural controversy. In *RU*, pp. 185-210.

Winograd, T. 1980a. *Language as a Cognitive Process*. Reading, MA: Addison-Wesley, forthcoming.

Winograd, T. 1980b. What does it mean to understand language? *Cognitive Science*, 4. To appear.

Winston, P. H. 1972. The MIT robot. In *MI7*, pp. 431-463.

Winston, P. H. (Ed.) 1975. *The Psychology of Computer Vision.* New York: McGraw-Hill.

Winston, P. H. 1975. Learning structural descriptions from examples. In *PCV*, pp. 157-209.

Winston, P. H. 1977. *Artificial Intelligence.* Reading, MA: Addison-Wesley.

Winston, P. H. 1979. *Learning by Understanding Analogies.* Memo 520, MIT Artificial Intelligence Laboratory, April. (Rev., June.)

Winston, P. H., and Brown, R. H. (Eds.) 1979. *Artificial Intelligence: an MIT Perspective* (2 vols.). Cambridge, MA: MIT Press.

Wipke, W. T., Ouchi, G. I., and Krishnan, S. 1978. Simulation and evaluation of chemical synthesis—SECS: an application of artificial intelligence techniques. *Artificial Intelligence,* 11(1,2), 173-193.

Wong, H. K. T., and Mylopoulos, J. 1977. Two views of data semantics: a survey of data models in artificial intelligence and database management. *Information,* 15(3), 344-383.

Woods, W. 1975. What's in a link: foundations for semantic networks. In *RU*, pp. 35-82.

Woods, W., et al. 1976. *Speech Understanding Systems: Final Technical Progress Report.* (5 vols.), BBN No. 3438. Cambridge, MA: Bolt, Beranek and Newman.

Zadeh, L. 1979. A theory of approximate reasoning. In *MI-9.*

Zisman, M. D. 1978. Use of production systems for modeling asynchronous, concurrent processes. In *PDIS*, pp. 53-68.

AUTHOR INDEX

SUBJECT INDEX

A*:
  admissibility of, 76-79
  definition of, 76
  optimality of, 79-81
  properties of, 76-84
  references for, 95
Abstract individuals, 389-391
ABSTRIPS, 350-354, 357
Actions, reasoning about, 307-315, 424
Actor formalism, 419
Add list, of STRIPS rules, 278
Adders, in DCOMP, 336
Admissibility, of search algorithms, 76
Advice, added to delineations, 406-408
AI languages, 261
  references for, 267, 270, 417, 418
Alpha-beta procedure, for games, 121-126
  efficiency of, 125-126
  references for, 127
Alphabetic variant, 141
AM, 422
Amending plans, 342-349
Analogies, 317-318, 421
Ancestor node, in graphs, (see Graph notation)
Ancestry-filtered form strategy, in resolution, 171
AND/OR form:
  for fact expressions, 196-199
  for goal expressions, 213-215
AND/OR graphs and trees:
  definition of, 40-41, 99-100
  references for, 49, 127
  for representing fact expressions, 197-199
  for representing goal expressions, 213-215
  for robot problem solving, 333
AND nodes, in AND/OR graphs, 40, 99-100
Answer extraction, in resolution, 175
  Skolem functions in, 184
  references for, 189

Answer statements:
  in resolution, 176
  in rule-based systems, 212
Antecedent, of an implication, 135
AO*:
  definition of, 104-105
  references for, 127
Applications of AI, 2-9, 11-15
Atomic formulas, in predicate calculus, 132
Attachment, procedural, 173-174, 232, 234, 400-401
Automatic programming, 5-6
  by DCOMP, 348-349
  references for, 14, 269
  by resolution, 191
  by RSTRIPS, 331-333
  by rule-based systems, 241-253
  by STRIPS, 305-307
Automation, industrial, 13-14

B-rules:
  definition of, 34
  for robot problems, 287-292
  for rule-based deduction systems, 214-215
Backed-up values, in game trees, 116
Backtracking control strategies:
  algorithms for, 55-57, 59
  definition of, 24-25
  examples of, 25-26, 57-58, 60-61
  references for, 50, 94
Backward production systems, 32-34
  for robot problem solving, 287-296
  for theorem proving, 212
Bag, 229
Base set, of clauses, 163
Beliefs, reasoning about, 424-425
Beta-structures, 412
Bidirectional production systems, 32-34
Bidirectional search, 88-90
Blackboard systems (see Production systems)
Blocks world, 152-155, 275